CHRISTOPHER ISHERWOOD

CHRISTOPHER ISHERWOOD

His Era, His Gang, and the
Legacy of the Truly Strong Man

DAVID GARRETT IZZO

UNIVERSITY OF SOUTH CAROLINA PRESS

UNIVERSITY OF SOUTH CAROLINA *BICENTENNIAL*

© 2001 University of South Carolina

Published in Columbia, South Carolina, by the
University of South Carolina Press

Manufactured in the United States of America

05 04 03 02 01   5 4 3 2 1

Library of Congress Cataloging-in-Publication Data

Izzo, David Garrett.
    Christopher Isherwood : his era, his gang, and the legacy of the truly
strong man / David Garrett Izzo.
        p. cm.
    Includes bibliographical references and index.
    ISBN 1-57003-403-6 (alk. paper)
    1. Isherwood, Christopher, 1904– 2. Isherwood, Christopher, 1904—
Friends and associates. 3. Isherwood, Christopher, 1904– —Influence.
4. Authors, English—20th century—Biography. 5. Sensitivity (Personality
trait) I. Title.
PR6017.S5 Z745 2001
823'.912—dc21   2001000749

Permission to quote from "The Wishing Tree" is granted by Vedanta Press.

Permission to quote "The Recessional from Cambridge" is granted by Enitharmon Press.

Photos are provided courtesy of the Vedanta Society of Southern California.

to Carol Ann Corrody
the Manageress
and Martin Blank
the Truly Strong Man

We teach best what we need to learn most.

Robert Forster

CONTENTS

ILLUSTRATIONS

ACKNOWLEDGMENTS

I would like to thank the staff at the University of South Carolina Press: Barry Blose for his faith in this project and for urging me to make it as good as it could be; the readers, who liked it and offered constructive suggestions for improvement; Olga Marino, who kept me in order; Dan Turner for sensitive editing.

I also extend my thanks to the Vedanta Society of Southern California for inspiring both Isherwood and the author; a special thanks to Bob Adjemian of the Vedanta Press for his gracious permission to quote the story "The Wishing Tree" at length, which is in *The Wishing Tree: Christopher Isherwood on Mystical Religion,* and to Jnana for the photos from the Society's archives.

Thanks go as well to the Enitharmon Press for permission to quote in full Isherwood's poem "The Recessional from Cambridge," from *The Mortmere Stories,* edited by Katherine Bucknell.

Last, I would like to express a particular appreciation to Don Bachardy. And colleagues, friends, family: Edward Mendelson for his enduring support; Tom Bechtle, of Locust Hill Press; Richard and Jan Londraville; Doug Wixson; Chris Wheatley; Chris Freeman,and Jim Berg for including me in their essay collection *The Isherwood Century* and inspiring this author's companion volume, *W. H. Auden: A Legacy* (forthcoming); the novelist Richard Stern and his wife, the poet Alane Rollings, and Richard's friend, the gay poet and activist Edgar Bowers; the novelist and gay spiritualist Toby Johnson; Eric S. Rabkin; Adrienne Hacker-Daniels; Lincoln Konkle; Nancy Bunge; Bob Combs; the Chapel Hill gang: John Duguid, who was Auden's student, Peter Bileckjyi, Gene Thornton, Michael and Laura Brader-Araje, Bill Loesser and Linda Saarrema; in New York: Paul, Rosemary, and P. J. Izzo; Bill, Yong, Mary Ann, Lauren, and Billy Corrody, Lo and David Corrody, Mark, Lucille, and Dan Fink; my students past and present.

INTRODUCTION

> Any given event in any part of the universe has as its determining condi-
> tions all previous and contemporary events in all parts of the universe.
>
> Aldous Huxley

Many of the British writers between the wars (1919–1939) indicted the failed liberalism that led to World War I. They also believed that the punitive Treaty of
Versailles that ended the first war would lead to a second. The 1920s emphasized the
residual shock of the war with a cynical nihilism that is represented by T. S. Eliot's
The Waste Land in 1922 and the novels of Aldous Huxley, particularly *Point
Counterpoint* in 1928. Huxley's novel summed up the 1920s by portraying the seemingly pointless frivolity of the middle and upper classes that actually masked pervasive despair. Eliot and Huxley were adults during the war and fully understood the
events that caused it, the horror of the war itself, and the debilitating consequences
that followed it. The writers who succeeded Eliot and Huxley in the 1930s were only
some ten to fifteen years younger than their artistic predecessors. This new generation of writers, exemplified by Christopher Isherwood, W. H. (Wystan Hugh)
Auden, and Stephen Spender, was distanced from the causes of the war but became
the inheritors of the war's effects. Rather than being cynical nihilists like the 1920s
writers, they became cynical idealists who rejected their predecessors and wished to
create a socialist world inspired by the experiment of the Soviet Union.

Identified as the Auden Generation (most notably by Samuel Hynes in his
book of the same name), Isherwood, Auden, and Spender were aided and abetted by Edward Upward, Cecil Day Lewis, Rex Warner, William Plomer, John
Lehmann, Geoffrey Grigson, Louis MacNeice, and Michael Roberts, among others. Although the 1930s has been identified with Auden, one could say that
Isherwood, as the oldest of the main trio, influenced Auden, and Auden influenced
the rest. Isherwood contributed to a redefining of the male hero (and antihero) by
moving him toward his more contemporary configuration: the sensitive man.
Isherwood's generation witnessed a precipitous end to prewar traditions. This
new world was confronted by an unknown future that would be either a socialist utopia, a fascist tragedy, or both. From that era's uncertain perspective to our
own era's uncertain perspective, the antihero's changing face has been a progress
of different masks. His development can be roughly traced from the 1920s to the
present (see Table 1).

The antihero's evolutionary process began after World War I when writers
such as Huxley blamed the war's causes on the "old men" in high places. These
writers also recognized the paranoia of the middle and upper classes who feared
that the Bolsheviks would take over Britain and redistribute their bourgeois

TABLE 1

Decade	Hero vs. antihero type	Exemplar (book, film, icon)
1920s	bitter, cynical war hero	*The Waste Land, Point Counterpoint*
1930s	Truly Strong Man who copes, vs.	*Grapes of Wrath*, Tom Joad
	Truly Weak Man, vainglorious	T. E. Lawrence
1940s	victorious war hero vs.	*The Best Years of Our Lives*, Eisenhower
	the jaded, cynical, and numbed	*The Age of Anxiety*
1950s	nuclear family man (in the Gray Flannel Suit) vs.	Eisenhower (again!?)
	Marlon Brando, James Dean	*The Wild One, Rebel Without a Cause*
1960s	sincerely liberated (reacting to repressed, complacent 1950s) vs.	*Island* (Aldous Huxley)
	pseudo liberated, very confused (reacting to repressed, complacent 1950s)	*The Graduate*
1970s	narcissist in polyester, EST-man, vs.	Warren Beatty, *Shampoo*, *Saturday Night Fever*
	Jack Nicholson	*Five Easy Pieces*
1980s	corporate raider vs.	*Wall Street*
	New Ager	Shirley MacLaine
1990s	sensitive man vs.	*The Bridges of Madison County*
	control freak	*Sleeping with the Enemy*

world in a socialist mold. In the 1920s the bitter war heroes, such as the martyred poet Wilfred Owen, and the disengaged cynics depicted by Huxley and Eliot, became magnets for the youthful intelligentsia who would become fervently engaged activists in the next decade. In the 1930s Isherwood developed the "mythified" dichotomy of the Truly Strong and Truly Weak Man. Although the Strong Man and Weak Man could be distinct individual personas, more often the Strong Man and Weak Man represented conflicting aspects within the same person. Isherwood's generation developed this mythos by emphasizing the conflicts of divided minds that anticipated the future of literary characterization ushered in by Auden's *Age of Anxiety* after World War II. Isherwood was the chief proponent of the theme of conflicted personality, for who could have sounded more divided than the Christopher William Bradshaw Isherwood once described by Auden as "a cross between a cavalry major and a rather prim landlady."[1]

Isherwood's writing during the ten years before *Lions and Shadows* was published in 1938 implicitly portrayed the Truly Strong and Truly Weak Man theme. The autobiographical *Lions and Shadows*, however, explicitly traces, according to its subtitle, "an education in the Twenties" shared by many in Isherwood's generation, who endured the guilt of not having been in the war. Consequently, they were unable to prove themselves as had the noble dead war heroes, including Isherwood's father. These martyred fathers, husbands, brothers, uncles, sons, cousins, and friends were eulogized endlessly and represented a constant source to Isherwood and his peers of a latent, or not-so-latent, sense of guilt by comparison. This contrast engendered profound psychological insecurity that was magnified by widowed, possessive mothers who were intent on dominating their sons. As Cambridge undergraduates from 1925 to 1928, Isherwood and Edward Upward agonized over these insecurities and transformed them into their Mortmere fantasies. These short stories were outrageous yet deadpan satires of the middle and upper classes of which they were members. Mortmere signified an us-against-them mentality. To Isherwood and Upward, "Them," or "The Others," meant the "poshocracy" who had caused the war in order to protect and preserve the British traditions and class divisions that had given them disproportionate advantages. Upward, who became a communist in the 1930s, was the perfect accomplice to Isherwood, who said of his intellectual counterpart: "His natural hatred of all established authority impressed me and I felt that it [would be] a weakness in myself not to share it."[2] They categorized this antagonism as one requiring Tests that would prove they were just as capable as the noble dead had been. For example, Isherwood purchased an unneeded motorcycle in order to emulate T. E. Lawrence. The goal of these Tests was to cross a metaphorical "Northwest Passage" within the mind. Similar pseudo-heroic posturings in the 1920s were soon to be trivialized by the harsher realities of the next decade: the depression, fascism, propaganda emerging to its full power, Stalinism, and the travesty of the Spanish Civil War. For Isherwood's generation, this world of the 1930s was one of pervasive paranoia, with shadowy deals and betrayals thought to be standard operating procedure. By the time *Lions and Shadows* was published in 1938, Isherwood realized quite clearly that the unconscious, symptomatic acts associated with school life in the 1920s now had a more consciously recognizable context in the 1930s. The Test was now understood to have been a symptom caused by the much more profound thematic dichotomy of the Truly Weak and the Truly Strong Man.

The Truly Weak Man, exemplified by T. E. Lawrence, suffered from a compulsion to prove himself by seeking, confronting, and passing Tests of rebellious derring-do. It did not matter whether the Tests were actual or imagined. Conversely, the Truly Strong Man was "pure-in-heart," to invoke Auden's phrase co-opted from the psychologist Homer Lane. In *Lions and Shadows* Isherwood defines the Truly Strong Man in the terms "spoken of by the homicidal paranoiac whose statement is quoted by [the German psychologist] Bleuler: 'the signs of the truly strong are repose and good-will. . . . the strong individuals are those who without any fuss do their duty. These have neither the time nor the occasion to throw themselves into a pose and try to be something great.'" Isherwood adds, "In other words, the Test exists only for the Truly Weak Man: no matter whether he passes it or whether he fails, he cannot alter his essential nature."[3] The Truly Weak Man can pass individual Tests, but he can never truly be satisfied because the underlying subconscious needs that are motivating the Tests are not really being assuaged.

The Truly Weak Man must try to decipher the psychological compulsions that push him to prove himself so that he can aspire to overcome them and become Truly Strong instead. In the interim his bifurcated self struggles to reconcile these conflicting urges, resulting in a duality of a private face and a public face. There is a confusion of his public and private spheres, inner and outer personas, real and fantasy worlds. Isherwood symbolizes this ambivalent division of inner and outer in *Mr. Norris Changes Trains,* published in 1935. Arthur Norris is a suave but amoral arms dealer, smuggler, liar, and cheat operating in a nefarious Berlin where he first befriends, then later betrays, the pseudo-Isherwood character called William Bradshaw. When Bradshaw first visits Arthur's Berlin apartment, he finds two front doors side by side. One bears a nameplate *Arthur Norris. Private* and the other door's nameplate reads *Arthur Norris. Import and Export.* Upon entering, Bradshaw is surprised to find that "the Private side of the entrance hall was divided from the Export side only by a thick hanging curtain."[4] Consequently, no real distinction existed, only an ambiguous blurring of inner and outer, public and private, Truly Weak and Truly Strong.

The dissemination of the Truly Weak and Truly Strong mythos occurred when, in the 1920s, Isherwood befriended Auden, who was three years younger, and Spender, who was younger by five, and they incorporated his (and Upward's) themes into their work. Auden, in 1930, and Spender, in 1933, achieved celebrity ahead of Isherwood, but with Auden as a medium, Isherwood's themes of the Truly Weak and Truly Strong Man, us against them, and the divided mind became the staging area for those who gave homage to Auden as the de facto leader of his generation. Britain's Angry Young Men of the 1930s emulated Isherwood by emulating Auden. This like-minded group signified their mutual admiration through artistic imitation and by dedicating their poems, plays, and prose to each other. These works developed and amplified the Mortmere themes originated by Isherwood and Upward.

As the decade progressed the satiric tone that was highlighted in the writings of the early 1930s gave way to more alarmist poetry, prose, and essays that served as warnings about the advance of fascism. The principal theme of these warnings was the conflict of the Truly Weak and Truly Strong Man who battles with public and private personas. This duality was summarized succinctly by Auden in 1932 with his dedication of *The Orators* to Stephen Spender:

> Private faces in public places
> Are wiser and nicer
> Than public faces in private places.[5]

If one feels comfortable enough to wear his private face in public, showing his true Self without resorting to masks and posturing, then one is pure-in-heart and Truly Strong. Since revealing one's private self is easier said than done, the Auden Generation knew this was a path to seek, rather than a destination assured. The hero's worthiness comes from the search, and the sincere search is the goal in itself. When the tumultuous 1930s ended with the start of World War II, the Angry Young Men bitterly realized that they had not changed the world for the better, but that the world had defeated them. In the struggle just to save the world, they knew that they could only hope to change themselves individually. During the war the need for single-minded heroes outweighed the reality of the divided personality that the Auden Generation had nurtured. Consequently, the conflicted antihero would temporarily step aside. He would reassert himself permanently after the war when the conflict of public and private, inner and outer, weak and strong became not just an intellectual's dilemma, but the generalized modus operandi for the post-war era. Hereafter, the antihero represented Everyman, whose thoughts and actions were symptoms of his (or her) quest for a reconciliation of a bifurcated self into one Self, pure-in-heart and Truly Strong.

In 1939, Auden and Isherwood's quests led them to New York, where Auden stayed and embraced Christian existentialism. Isherwood, shaken by the failures of the 1930s, said at the time that "it was the lack of values which was making me feel so insecure."[6] Isherwood headed west to Southern California to see two more expatriates, Aldous Huxley and Gerald Heard (lay scientist, spiritual philosopher, raconteur, and the basis for the character Augustus Parr in Isherwood's *Down There on a Visit*). Huxley and Heard were absorbing the wisdom of Vedanta, principally the teachings of the Upanishads and the Bhagavad-Gita. Their teacher was Swami Prabhavananda, the subject of Isherwood's last book, *My Guru and His Disciple*, published in 1980. In this autobiography Isherwood describes an extraordinary thirty-seven-year friendship with Prabhavananda and also traces his own spiritual development. By many accounts Isherwood, during this long discipleship, did become pure-in-heart and Truly Strong. By the 1960s he was a role model and champion for the gay community as well as a mentor to younger writers. For Isherwood in 1939, however, this could not have seemed more impossible:

So I despaired and did nothing, blaming New York for my jitters. [It was not caused by New York] but by an emptiness inside myself, of which I was not fully aware. I was empty because I had lost my political faith—I couldn't repeat the left-wing slogans which I had been repeating throughout the last few years. It wasn't that I had lost *all* belief in what the slogans stood for, but I was no longer whole-hearted. My leftism was confused by an increasingly aggressive awareness of myself as a homosexual and by a newly made discovery that I was a pacifist. Both these individualistic minority-attitudes kept bringing me into conflict with leftist major-ity-ideology.

I called myself a pacifist because Heinz, the German boy I had lived with for five years during the nineteen-thirties, was about to be conscripted into the Nazi army and I found it unthinkable that I should ever help to cause his death, how-ever indirectly.

What I now needed to learn were positive pacifist values, a pacifist way of life, a Yes to fortify my No.[7]

The Yes took form when Huxley and Heard introduced Isherwood to the Swami:

I first met the Hindu monk called Swami Prabhavananda in 1939. . . . Throughout that period [until the Swami's death in 1976] as his often backsliding disciple but always devoted friend, I observed him lovingly but critically. Thus I quickly became convinced that he was neither a charlatan nor a lunatic, and then, more slowly, became more aware of a Presence within him, which was altogether other than his usually charming, sometimes cantankerous, sometimes absurd Bengali self. It was a Presence to which Gerald Heard, fastidiously avoiding the word "God," would refer to as "This Thing."[8]

Over the years, "This Thing" imbued Isherwood with a joy that eventually allowed him to say he began each day with a sense of inexplicable happiness. To say eventually is key since there was much backsliding. From 1939 to 1945 Isherwood wrote no fiction and devoted himself to the study of Vedanta and in helping the Swami with new translations of Vedic texts. His lapses, however, convinced him he would not last as a full-fledged monk. Instead he pledged to be a lay follower. This meant he could slip out the back door when temptation overcame him. In 1945 Isherwood tried fiction again with the short novel *Prater Violet.* Influenced deeply by his spiritual study, particularly of the Bhagavad-Gita, *Prater Violet* is a Vedantic novel about an aspiring Truly Strong Man.

To trace the development of the Truly Strong Man one must trace the path of Isherwood's literary evolution and his influence on the Auden Generation. Part 1, Frantic: The Tearing Down, 1904–1939, will examine the bitter Isherwood who rebelled against everything traditional in the aftermath of World War I. The Truly Weak Man was the symptomatic result of his anger. Part 2, Vedantic: The Building Up, 1939–1986, will examine the Isherwood who found something to believe in as a Vedantist. These beliefs gave him hope that there was meaning in a world that had seemed meaningless. This sense of hope inspired a new direction in his writing that incorporated his spiritual beliefs. Part 2 will benefit from Isherwood's own words as he recorded them in his diaries of 1939 to 1960. In these diaries, first published in 1996, Isherwood copiously details his conversion to Vedanta in a way that must be taken into account in order to reconsider the work of his American years. Yet his quest for a life of the spirit did not begin in America, but was made more conscious to him there. Unconsciously, his quest began long before. A lesson of the Bhagavad-Gita is that all events lead one to his or her destiny in ways not always clear when they happen. Another lesson is that the pure-in-heart Truly Strong Man inspires others who will follow his example. Isherwood's first Vedantic novel, *Prater Violet,* is a parable about an aspiring Truly Strong Man, and he continued to write parables to instruct his readers. This study also hopes to teach by example. The exemplar is Christopher Isherwood. His lesson is how one may overcome psychological adversity and become a Truly Strong Man.

ABBREVIATIONS

CHRISTOPHER ISHERWOOD

AC   *All the Conspirators.* New York: New Directions, 1958.

F6   *The Ascent of F6.* Isherwood and W. H. Auden. New York: Random House, 1937.

CK   *Christopher and His Kind.* New York: Farrar, Straus, Giroux, 1976.

CC   *The Condor and the Cows.* New York: Random House, 1949.

D   *Diaries: Volume One, 1939–1960.* ed. Katherine Bucknell. New York: Harper-Collins, 1997.

DS   *The Dog beneath the Skin.* Isherwood and W. H. Auden. London: Faber and Faber, 1935.

DV   *Down There on a Visit.* New York: Simon and Schuster, 1962.

E   *Exhumations.* New York. Simon and Schuster, 1966.

GB   *Goodbye to Berlin.* New York: New Directions, 1947.

KF   *Kathleen and Frank.* New York: Simon and Schuster, 1971.

JW   *Journey to a War.* Isherwood and W. H. Auden. New York: Random House, 1939.

LS   *Lions and Shadows.* London: Hogarth Press, 1938.

M   *The Memorial.* London: Hogarth Press, 1932.

MR   *A Meeting by the River.* New York: Simon and Schuster, 1967.

N   *Mr. Norris Changes Trains.* New York: New Directions, 1947.

GD   *My Guru and His Disciple.* New York: Farrar, Straus, Giroux, 1980.

PV   *Prater Violet.* New York: Random House, 1945.

SM   *A Single Man.* New York: Simon and Schuster, 1964.

BG   *The Song of God: Bhagavad-Gita.* Trans. with Swami Prabhavananda. Hollywood: Marcel Rodd, 1944.

W   *The World in the Evening.* New York: Random House, 1954.

W. H. AUDEN

CP   *Collected Poems.* ed. Edward Mendelson. New York: Random House, 1976.

DD   *The Dance of Death.* New York: Random House, 1934.

O   *The Orators.* London: Faber and Faber, 1932.

STEPHEN SPENDER

SP   *Poems.* New York: Random House, 1934.

WW   *World within World.* London: Hamish Hamilton, 1951.

PART 1

FRANTIC: THE TEARING DOWN, 1904–1939

1 SEEDS OF BITTERNESS
Themes in Gestation: Nature vs. Nurture

It was part of the romantic mythology in which Stephen delighted to cloak his contemporaries, to present himself as a learner at the feet of Auden, the great prophet, but to suggest that behind both of them stood an even greater Socratic prophet, cool in the centre of the stormy drama of remote Berlin: Christopher Isherwood.

John Lehmann[1]

Who is that funny-looking man so squat with a top-heavy head . . .
A brilliant young novelist?
You don't say!

W. H. Auden
written for Isherwood in 1937[2]

Spender and Auden always acknowledged their respect for Isherwood as a writer and as an influence. They also considered him the rebellious leader of their iconoclastic trio. Isherwood rebelled against British tradition and the Auden Generation joined him in their efforts to rescue the seat of the British Empire, about which Auden asked in 1932: "What do you think about England, this country of ours where nobody is well?"[3]

Born on 26 August 1904 Christopher Isherwood became a literary elder brother and symbolic godfather not only to Auden and Spender but also to those of the Auden Generation who, in emulating Auden, were emulating Isherwood. Their sensitive antiheroes began to represent more realistic dichotomies of the modern conflicted individual who struggles to exist in a hostile world and who attempts to reconcile this outer threat with the inner, bifurcated self that this external world engenders.

Did Isherwood invent the sensitive man? Of course not. Life and literature develop incrementally from antecedent influences. Thomas Hardy, George Moore, E. M. Forster, Aldous Huxley, among others, were Isherwood's antecedents for the novel. For literature in general, Eliot's *The Waste Land* was the apocalyptic vision that opened the eyes of Isherwood's generation. Isherwood's important role was not invention, but definition. He defined the modern hero/antihero in specific terms such as the Truly Weak and Truly Strong Man, the Northwest Passage, and the Test. Isherwood did so by trial and error. He placed his test subject, himself, in the rapid-changing post-World War I environment and recorded his reactions, at first without self-consciousness, then with a limited degree of self-consciousness, and finally with conscious purpose. Never has a writer so aptly described through fictionalized autobiography and factual autobiography

the nature of his individual development in the changing world. Moreover, his particular case was recognized by the Auden Generation to be the universal one. Auden may
have been in the driver's seat, but Isherwood gave directions.

• • • • • •

The world Christopher Isherwood was born into was one of a class-stratified,
people-in-their-places traditionalism that was about to give way from the weight
of its own pretensions. The upper classes were habituated to generations of
authoritarianism begun in an agrarian culture neatly divided into a few landowners, and everyone else. This arrangement was cut and dried, and certainly not to
the benefit of the majority. The basic stability of the farm economy, with its
small-town, church-centered culture, endured until the arrival of the industrial
revolution, which brought with it the new middle class. These were the makers
and merchants who were derogatorily referred to as being "in trade" by the aristocratic upper classes. The makers and merchants were literally in the middle of
the land-owners and the landless peasant farmers. They were judged by the lords
as "commoners." However, over time these commoners often had more money
than the land-owning lords who looked down on them. Eventually this emerging middle class asserted their own political rights and the House of Commons
was created as a response to the House of Lords. The middle class brought with
them the ideas that would formulate British liberalism.

The middle class also brought with them the industrialized city-state, which
oversaw the slow demise of an agrarian culture when the peasant farmers fled to the
cities. This exodus further weakened the power of the landowners who now lorded
over unworked fields that no longer produced the income to which they were accustomed. Meanwhile the depersonalized, Dickensian city-state stratified its constituents into random alienated herds, and the poor city workers were now as bad or
worse off than when they had been poor farm workers. Instead of being lorded over
by landed nobles, they were lorded over by capitalists. This is a rudimentary
overview of the world Isherwood, Auden, and Spender were born into, one whose
class conflicts (aristocratic upper class vs. in trade upper class vs. the put-upon working class) would culminate in the world-shattering travesty of World War I.

Christopher Isherwood's case in this overall scenario is instructive for understanding how the larger conflicts affected the individual. Isherwood's father, Frank,
was of an aristocratic heritage, while his mother, Kathleen, was from a family in
lucrative trade. In marrying Frank, Kathleen increased her status in the social world
even though Frank was relatively poor compared to her family. Frank's lack of
money was not because his family did not have any money, but because, according
to the British custom of primogeniture, Frank, being the second son, did not
inherit any money. Tradition dictated that Frank's father, John Isherwood, would
leave his entire estate to the eldest son, Henry, who in deference to this preordained
status assumed a lordly attitude toward his two younger brothers. In Isherwood's
biography of his parents, *Kathleen and Frank,* he explains this tradition:

Henry, as the eldest son, would in due course inherit the Marple estates and money from his father. . . . the rest of the children were thus left to make their own way in life, with little or no assistance. This was the customary arrangement and it had the advantage of keeping property in one piece. No doubt most younger brothers and sisters recognized the good sense of it in theory, but it inevitably created a psychological barrier between them and the heir. This didn't worry Henry, however. He took his privileged position for granted and already behaved with the grandeur of the head of a family. John Isherwood, who lazily hated disputes, abetted him in his attitude by agreeing to whatever he demanded (*KF* 121).

Frank Isherwood was left to fend for himself. He became a career soldier as did many second sons of the upper classes. Kathleen's father did not believe a mere soldier was worthy of his only child and delayed giving his blessing for as long as possible. Kathleen's stubbornness finally forced him to relent. This was a trait that her son would know well.[4] Her father also understood that Kathleen, at thirty-five, was ancient in late Victorian terms.

Frank Isherwood was a soldier by default, saying in a letter to Kathleen before their marriage, "I'm afraid, you know, I'm not really built for a warrior." He also wrote that the humdrum military life did not satisfy "the things which lie on my 'soul side'" (*KF* 95). Frank's "soul side" was far more sensitive and cultured than the average warrior's, and he had aptitudes for art and culture that he could not afford while Henry could afford art and culture for which he had scant aptitude. Frank painted, played music, acted in amateur theatricals, and read avidly. He would later encourage Christopher to enjoy artistic pursuits as well. Frank Isherwood was a reluctant aristocrat who saw no need to act a part for which he lacked material means. Considering that his family name alone had not earned any respect from Kathleen's father, one can see Frank's modesty as having been to some degree a question of necessary humility. According to biographer Brian Finney, Christopher Isherwood took after his father in this regard. "Until the publication of *Kathleen and Frank* in 1971 [Isherwood] appears to have consistently underplayed his aristocratic connections on his father's side." Even in the 1960s, "Isherwood was clearly still embarrassed . . . by the snobbery associated with his upbringing."[5] As Isherwood would make clear later, this snobbery was ingrained in his mother and she, without success, attempted to transfer it to her son. Why should he have an attitude about his name without the money to back it up? Certainly Isherwood's lack of aristocratic pretentiousness was supported when as a young adult he received a small allowance from his uncle, Henry, in return for entertaining the older man with descriptions of Christopher's homosexual adventures. Going to his uncle with hat in hand could only further remind Isherwood of his tenuous position and the class-conscious tradition that had put him in it. After the First World War, Isherwood would develop a hatred for the traditional past, blaming it for his father's death in the war. He would also rebel against the expectations others placed on him. In particular, he could not abide the expectations imposed on him by his mother. Isherwood would later say, "For Kathleen the Past was happier, one might almost say by definition. She was intensely obstinate in maintaining this attitude. Like every devotee of the Past she could always find reasons why the present was inferior to it. Frank's death became her final unanswerable argument" (*KF*, 10–11).

One must examine Isherwood's prewar childhood to understand how his later rage was a reaction to a previous happiness altered permanently by the war, his father's death, and his mother's reaction to Frank's death. Isherwood's particular reactions exemplified the disillusioned responses of the Auden Generation as a whole.

A Nurturing of Fantasy

"Christopher was an imaginative, precocious child"—this is how Isherwood describes himself in *Kathleen and Frank* (317). Since the 1930s he had written of himself in the third person in both fiction and autobiography—categories that for him were barely distinct. When, as a precocious child, Isherwood lived at Marple Hall, which was built in the late fifteenth century, it seemed to him a cavernous and mysterious playhouse featuring interconnected attics that "were related in Christopher's imagination to one of his great early myth books—*The Roly-Poly Pudding*, by Beatrix Potter" (*KF*, 307).

Kathleen and Frank contributed to Christopher's "mythifying" by indulging him in games and fantasies. The mythmaking that began in his childhood continued for the rest of Isherwood's life. Katherine Bucknell, the editor of Isherwood's diaries, says in her introduction, "At its most autobiographical, Isherwood's history writing . . . tipped over from history into mythology."[7] Later his highbrow literary peers would also make myths by engaging in what Samuel Hynes calls in *The Auden Generation* "parable-art."[6]

Turning history into myth started early for Isherwood as Kathleen and her son began their own journal in 1910, *The History of my Friends*. It was "a tiny book," according to Isherwood, "in Kathleen's script and presumably written at Christopher's dictation. But did Christopher literally dictate it? It reads like an attempt at collaboration between a child and an adult, in which each is trying to mimic the tone of the other" (*KF*, 348). That Kathleen enjoyed the collaborative effort is so noted in her journal, where she also writes of her husband's contributions to their son's imagination: "Frank amused Christopher drawing him little figures representing Anne Boleyn. . ." (*KF*, 348). As Kathleen reported repeatedly in her diaries, she and Frank seemed to enjoy being part of these fantasies just as much as their son did. Isherwood records Kathleen writing that "his father started teaching him French words and continued his instruction by publishing a paper called 'The Toy-Drawer Times' every morning, illustrated!" (*KF*, 349). Frank would keep up this paper for over four years until Christopher went away to school in 1914. In addition to "The Toy Drawer Times," another aspect of the morning regimen included Frank's son watching his father exercise. Isherwood recalled that Frank was "naked except for his undershorts. Christopher can remember taking a pleasure which was definitely erotic in the sight of his father's muscles tensing and bulging within his well-knit body, and in the virile smell of his sweat" (*KF,* 349–50).

While one does not wish to overestimate this remark about his father's "well-knit body," which is told by Isherwood the historian at age sixty-seven looking back matter-of-factly at his youth, one cannot forget that Isherwood the author chose very carefully what he wished his readers to know. Putting aside any conjecture about what it meant to Isherwood's future sexual orientation, one can read this episode of childhood eroticism in terms of how it encouraged Isherwood to admire his father as both mentor and myth. Isherwood also recalls that "As a teacher, Frank was fairly patient. But sometimes he would fly into rages with Christopher and shake him. Christopher may have been frightened a little, but this too is a sensual memory for him: his surrender to the exciting strength of the big angry man" (*KF,* 350). Isherwood wants readers to know that his father took an active role in his son's upbringing in addition to exerting a subliminal influence on his son's psyche; in this way, Isherwood sets the stage for the profound psychological trauma he experiences when Frank does not return from World War I. When he describes his response to the loss of his father, readers feel it sharply, even though he understates the impact on himself while clearly delineating the pain and loss felt by his mother. What is important in Isherwood's recounting of his childhood prior to the war is that both parents strongly encouraged his youthful imagination to create stories and myths that would become a compulsion for Isherwood the adult.

In 1915, when Isherwood's father, the reluctant soldier, went missing literally, so did Isherwood's mother figuratively. In one blow the two benefactors of his imaginative faculty left him to create secondary worlds on his own. All children do so, but during and after World War I, many were imagining other worlds not just for self-entertainment, but to escape autistically from either the tragedy of a personal loss or to mask the pervasive general gloom of collective loss. After the war Freudian psychoanalysis began to emerge as a major ideology. The influence of psychoanalysis meant that everyone was talking about imaginative escapism as having something to do with sex. (In Isherwood's case this sense of escapism was commingled with the erotic component of Frank's exercise regimen.) Certainly, psychoanalysis allowed adults to look back at themselves as children and speculate on possible motivations for the imaginative games they played and the stories they told. For Isherwood's generation the idea that the child was the father of the man was taken very seriously, especially by the child without a father because of the war. For this child, escapism was often a psychological necessity.

SECONDARY WORLDS

Imaginative mythmaking in children is more pronounced in a context when there is a greater need to escape everyday reality. Isherwood's great friend and kindred spirit, W. H. Auden, at age sixty-three, looked back at his childhood to explain a thought process that pertained not only to himself as an artist, but to any artist:

> Between the ages of six and twelve I spent a great many of my waking hours in the fabrication of a private secondary *sacred* world the elements of which were (a) a limestone landscape, and (b) an industry—lead mining. It is no doubt psychologically significant that my sacred world was autistic, that is to say, I had no wish to share it with others.
>
> From this activity, I learned certain principles which I was later to find applied to all artistic fabrication. Firstly, whatever elements it may include, the initial impulse to create a secondary world is a feeling of awe surrounded by encounters in the primary world, with sacred beings or events. Though every work of art is a secondary world, such a world cannot be constructed *ex nihilo* but is a selection and recombination of the contents of the primary world. I was free to select this and reject that, on one condition, that both were real objects in the primary world, physical impossibilities and magic means were forbidden. At this point I realized it was my moral duty to sacrifice aesthetic preference to reality or truth. When I began writing poetry, I found that the same obligation was binding. A poet must never make a statement simply because it sounds exciting; he must also believe it to be true. This does not mean that one can only appreciate a poet whose beliefs coincide with his own. It does mean that one must be convinced that the poet really believes what he says, however odd that belief may seem to oneself.[8]

Auden asserts that an artistic secondary world will have no meaning if it is created from a realm that a reader cannot recognize as a possible truth. The need for a secondary world as a form of autistic escapism is a fact of human nature that children discover early. Fantasy as escapism is normal—on a temporary basis. Everyone, child or adult, wishes for temporary escapes from the everyday world. The more troublesome that everyday world is, the longer one spends in a secondary world, and the more complex the secondary world becomes. A majority of people to some degree straddle both worlds, sometimes blurring the primary and secondary worlds into each other; it is the degree that one becomes absorbed in a secondary world, not the nature of the secondary world, that determines the fine lines between neuroses, psychoses, and insanity. Severe autistics withdraw permanently into a secondary world; for them, there is no blurring of primary and secondary worlds because the autistic's primary world is only understood by himself and, therefore, cannot be accessed and understood by the many. For relatively normal children of any generation, fantasy escapes into secondary worlds are standard, and these escapes are elementary training for the subsequent coping mechanisms that children will need when they become adults. Human beings sometimes require themselves to be somewhere else physically or metaphysically. Very often that somewhere else is self-constructed within the inner world of the mind and not otherwise present in the outer world of the body. For the most part the average person keeps this secondary world to himself. Conversely, the artist is a person who usually chooses to make his secondary world available for public consumption.

The artist is prolonging his childhood with the sanction of others who give their approval to him because he is willing to share his creations with them. The artist gets to play his game of art and continue his childlike fantasizing, which is what all adults really wish to do in various vicarious ways. Non-artists can vicariously fantasize through the artist's art. Non-artists love the artist because they can participate in his secondary world secondarily. The adult who is a childlike artist is viewed by his audience as a benefactor. The artist is a metaphorical child playing at a game and by extension his audience gets to play the game too. For the artist and the audience, this play in a secondary world is a means to forget one's responsibilities in the primary world. According to Auden,

> The writing of art is gratuitous, i.e, play. . . . Natural man hates nature, and the only act which can really satisfy him is the *acte gratuite*. His ego resents every desire of his natural self for food, sex, pleasure, logical coherence, because desires are given, not chosen, and his ego seeks constantly to assert its autonomy by doing something of which the requiredness is not given, that is to say, something which is completely arbitrary, a pure act of choice. . . . In addition to wanting to feel free, man wants to feel important. . . . The rules of a game give it importance by making it difficult to play.[9]

THE DISRUPTION OF ISHERWOOD'S SECONDARY WORLD

As a child, Isherwood was encouraged to play games and feel important. From 1904 to 1914 he was protected, nurtured, and as imaginative as his parents allowed him to be, which was a great deal. Since his brother, Richard, did not arrive until 1911, Christopher Isherwood enjoyed himself in a playful and exclusive womb-extending cocoon, a metaphorical safe haven emulating the warmth and security of gestation. His imagination was fostered in creating his own and his father's "newspapers." Consequently, he began his inclination to give reports of his life, whether in diaries, actual autobiography, or autobiographical fiction. Things were to change. His play-filled paradise was to face a disruption first and then become totally shattered.

In 1914 Isherwood was sent away to St. Edmund's preparatory school. To be sent away to school was quite normal for a boy of his social class. A year later, before he had even remotely gotten over what he would later consider to have been his ostracism, he suffered a second and more permanent personal cataclysm: the death of his father. He was forced to understand that Frank was never going to draw or write "The Toy-Drawer Times" again. Worse, he would have to endure his father's death while spending most of his time at St. Edmund's, where, in his mind, the upper-class British traditions that killed his father were perpetuated.

THE BRITISH PUBLIC SCHOOL: TRAINING "THE LIBERAL FASCIST" FOR EMPIRE BUILDING

A dominant theme that emerges from the recollections of the Auden Generation is the pervasive hatred of their experiences in preparatory and public schools. They did not recall so much that they were being prepared for life by receiving a classical education at the schools, but that they were being prepared for their lives as the class-conscious protectors and saviors of the British Empire. Although empire-saving as an end may not seem so deleterious, it was the means to this end that the future intellectuals and artists reacted against so strongly. They considered the public school to be anti-intellectual, anti-working class, anti-egalitarian, and concerned only with the preservation of the monied classes at the expense of everyone else. As Auden said of these schools in a 1934 essay, "The mass production of gentlemen is their *raison d'etre,* and one can hardly suggest that they should adopt principles which would destroy them. The fact remains that the public school boy's attitude to the working-class and to the not-quite-quite has altered very little since the [the first World] war. . . . their lives and needs remain as remote to him as those of another species. [This is] true of the staff as well. . . . a master was sacked for taking part in left-wing politics outside the school . . . which seems to me a shameful thing."[10]

It was indeed a shame. Any hint of nonconformity by students was, for the most part, stunted by the great majority of the teachers. The masters discouraged progressive ideas that students may have learned from their parents. More precisely, while Isherwood and Auden were encouraged by their parents in artistic endeavors that encouraged independent thinking, the school's masters wanted dependent thinking instead. Auden recalled, "a master once caught me writing poetry in prep. . . . He said, 'you shouldn't waste your sweetness on the desert air like this Auden'; today I cannot think of him without wishing him evil."[11] This remark was first written in 1934, but Auden's anger lasted into his old age, since he would repeat the comment decades later.

The underlying intent of the prep and public schools was to maintain the old order within the school and inculcate it in the students. While the Auden Generation protested against the perpetuation of traditions that they saw as anachronistic failures, they were in the minority. The great majority of their fellow students had no objections concerning how they were being trained in such schools. They would have approved of the preservation of their status as class-conscious "gentlemen." The Auden Generation were the "aesthetes" who were in opposition to the "hearties."

The hearties were the anti-intellectual athletes and players of games both physical and psychological. Their games were often played among themselves, but were more often directed against the aesthetes and the lower grades. The hearties were expected by the school to demand obedient conformity from members of the lower grades and were given the power to use or abuse corporal punishment in order to get it. Conformity meant adherence to a school's rules of conduct. In themselves these rules were not unreasonable; however, students were encouraged on their "honor" to tell on each other when rules were violated. Auden remembers this honor system as ultimately dishonorable:

> I feel compelled to say that I believe no more potent engine for turning [students] into neurotic innocents, for perpetuating those very faults of character which it was intended to cure, was ever devised. Everyone knows that the only emotion that is fully developed in a boy of fourteen is the emotion of loyalty and honour. By appealing to it, you can do almost anything you choose, you can suppress the expression of all those emotions, particularly the sexual, which are still undeveloped; like a modern dictator you can defeat almost any opposition from other parts of the psyche, but if you do, if you deny these other emotions their expression and development . . . they will not only never grow up, but they will go backward . . . like all things that are shut up.
>
> [This] meant that [at school] the whole of our moral life was based on fear, not to mention the temptation it offered to the natural informer, and fear is not a healthy basis. It makes one furtive and dishonest, unadventurous. The best reason I have for opposing fascism is that at school I lived in a fascist state.[12]

Auden and his fellow aesthetes reiterated time and again that they lived in a state of peer-induced fear. The by-product of fear is paranoia. Isherwood would later say, "Paranoia is a kind of heightened awareness which makes one see how extraordinary ordinary life is—or can seem, if one wishes. What else but this were Edward and I cultivating at Cambridge, when we invented Mortmere?"[13] Paranoia became a dominant strain in the literature of the 1930s. While the writers of the mid-to-late 1930s responded to the actual fascism in Europe, the Auden Generation's writings of the early 1930s were initially responses to the home grown fascism of the public schools. In 1938 when Isherwood published *Lions and Shadows,* he subtitled it "an education in the twenties." The fear and paranoia detailed in this autobiography were derived from his public school life but were also readily understandable to a readership feeling its own fear and paranoia about Hitler and Mussolini. Isherwood's message to readers was that they would be able to relate the contemporary fascism of the 1930s to the de facto fascism of the public schools in the 1920s.

AESTHETES AND HEARTIES: HIGHBROWS AND LOWBROWS

The distinction of aesthetes and hearties in the public schools can be extended to a more comprehensive dichotomy of the distinction between highbrows and lowbrows in pre–World War II British culture at large. Aesthetes equate to highbrows and hearties to lowbrows. In the British public schools, the lowbrow hearties who constituted the majority regarded highbrow aesthetes with suspicion. This was also the case in the larger world, where there existed that amorphous entity identified as the lowbrow Public by the nineteenth-century Christian existential polemicist, Søren Kierkegaard.[14] Defining Kierkegaard's construct of the Public enhances an understanding of the Auden Generation's writings of the 1930s. Kierkegaard believed the anonymous Public was the bastard child of the industrial revolution, universal education, and mass media. This Public can be influenced by the media but cannot be held accountable for any resulting behaviors that these media appeals might provoke. The Public is composed of individuals who can be manipulated in general but need not be responsible for anything in particular because they are not identifiable as specific human beings. Media can influence an anonymous Public to take sides on an issue, yet these unidentifiable individuals can remove themselves from the consequences of their choices by fading into their anonymity as a so-called silent majority. In effect, by reading and hearing the news in private, one can be moved to love or hate another person or group without the personal scrutiny or judgment that might involve the conscience. Anonymity permits irresponsibility. The anonymous Public becomes the proverbial "They" that authority figures can invoke to praise conformists and chastise nonconformists. This concept of a Kierkegaardian Public is crucial in understanding the rise of propaganda in the 1930s. How did this Public and its anonymity come about?

     In the agrarian, small-town culture before the industrial revolution, anonymity was less prevalent, and thus the concept of an impersonal Public was not as applicable. The anonymous Public emerged from the depersonalized, industrialized city-state, in which mass production necessitated a strict regimentation among workers. This regimentation required a universal, basic education that allowed workers to function in their roles as cogs in the mechanized city. These workers would then consume the goods they were exposed to by advertising and perpetuate their own existences in a slavish cycle. Universally, if minimally, educated, this easily influenced Public consumes media and not necessarily with great discernment. As Auden said in 1937, "Our age is highly educated / There is no lie our children cannot read."[15] It was one thing for the mass producers to influence the Public to become mass consumers through advertising, but it became something quite nefarious when tyrants like Hitler and Mussolini used the media to influence the Public to be mass followers through propaganda.

     The differences between the lowbrow Public and the highbrows are often associated with money. Those with more income may have access to a better education and more culture than those with less. However, the factor that ultimately determines who becomes a highbrow is not strictly based on money, or social status, or snobbery, or even innate intellectual capacity. What makes highbrows distinct from lowbrows is their intellectual ability combined with a desire for more than just utilitarian knowledge. The lowbrow passively observes, while the highbrow actively observes and gains insight from these observations. Auden said that a highbrow is "Someone who is not passive to his experience but who tries to organise, explain, and alter it, someone, in fact, who tries to influence history: a man struggling in the water is, for the time being, a highbrow. The decisive factor is the conflict between the person and his environment."[16]

When a person chooses to be a highbrow in order to overcome his environment, this choice can also entail a challenge to the authority ruling that environment. Throughout history, highbrows in general and artists in particular have been considered threats to authority, a tendency observed by Auden, who wrote,"Why should the authorities feel that a highbrow artist is important enough to be worth destroying? It can only be because so long as artists exist, making what they please, even if it is not very good, even if very few people appreciate it, they remind the management of something the management does not like to be reminded of, namely that the managed people are people with faces, not anonymous numbers."[17] Highbrows are nonconformists. Lowbrows are conformists. Thus, a natural antipathy exists between the two groups. Emerging totalitarian regimes have typically targeted intellectuals as potential enemies because intellectuals tend to question the propaganda that lowbrows often accept at face value. Management cannot afford for highbrows to blow the whistle on them by alerting the lowbrows to the way those in power manipulate them. It is easier for tyrants to suppress or eliminate highbrows, rather than to face the potential resistance of questioning lowbrows. The first in Britain to recognize the rise of fascism in Europe in the 1930s as a destructive force were the highbrows, those former aesthetes who had already experienced a form of fascism in the public schools.

The public school would be Christopher Isherwood's first adventure away from his safe cocoon. At St. Edmund's school he would begin his rebellion against established authority and he would also meet W. H. Auden.

STRANDED, THEN ABANDONED

Isherwood's accounts of his school days can be found in both his official and fictional autobiographies. From his first book in 1928 to his last in 1980, Isherwood reacted to the same themes that first tortured him as an adolescent: public school, his father's disappearance, his mother's grief. It could be said that his writings were evolving chapters in a single long work about how Christopher Isherwood suffered from, then overcame, his adolescence.

In *Kathleen and Frank*, Isherwood writes that just before his departure to St. Edmund's his mother took him to London and entertained him royally. They went to Madame Tussaud's Wax Museum, the Natural History Museum, Westminster

Abbey, the Zoo, and the Aerodrome. Then Isherwood writes: "Christopher's last requests had now all been granted. On May 1 he could no longer put off remembering he was a condemned man"(*KF,* 394–95). And off he went to St. Edmund's, his first time away from home. Social custom required that a child of Isherwood's class be sent off to school. A class-conscious Kathleen could not do otherwise. Nonetheless, she parted with her son very reluctantly, as she notes in her 1914 diary:

> May 1. Poor C—till we were actually sitting in the train I do not think he realized, but it was a trying moment—the other boys all knowing each other and he a stranger and alone for the first time. . . . he just managed to keep back the tears. It was a truly dreadful moment to me, seeing him go off so small and inexperienced into the unknown.
>
> May 2. Wondering all day what my dear C is doing.
>
> May 3. Wondered *much* how Christopher was getting on.
>
> May 4. Could hardly sleep, so anxious to get C's Sunday letter! (*KF,* 395)

Isherwood was not to learn of his mother's concern for him until fifty-three years later. By then he had softened his attitude towards her, since, having matured, he was more able to accept that his mother had only done what society had conditioned her to do. At the time, however, Isherwood only understood that he had been sent away from his womb-cocoon paradise into an environment that was, by design, cold and threatening. Auden, among others, would attest that in winter the cold threatened literally, and he had a horror of the cold and cold baths to the end of his life. The schools "made men" of these children by having them endure a harshness that was meant to prepare them for protecting the Empire. Copious memoirs by hundreds of former students describe their public school experiences in terms that today might suggest child abuse. Yet, at the time, public school was considered mandatory by otherwise intelligent parents. A nurtured, protected child was suddenly unprotected. Class expectations can be a difficult dilemma for parents and children alike. For sensitive, highbrow children such as Kathleen's Christopher, who had little in common with the hearties who were in the majority, peer pressure could be difficult indeed. Isherwood recalls his first impression of St. Edmund's. There were "lists of names on notice boards, name-tags on clothes, names read out at roll call—names which make you less, not more, of an individual, which remind you hourly that you are now the household darling no longer, just one among many: Bradshaw-Isherwood, C. W. This feeling of lost importance is at the bottom of so-called homesickness; it isn't home you cry for but your home-self" (*KF,* 397).

Written in 1967 Isherwood's reference to his "home-self" reflects an older Isherwood interpreting his past from a Vedantic perspective. The centered, stable "Self" of Vedanta's unified consciousness that had been growing within him as a nurtured child was knocked off-center at St. Edmund's. Isherwood would spend the rest of his life trying to find his balance again. Isherwood then describes himself at school: "This weird little creature had a voice and a precocious way of expressing himself which could be marvelously irritating. Once when [a teacher] had asked him a question and he answered, 'I haven't the remotest idea,' she . . . slapped his face. He was a tireless chatterer, a physical coward who lacked team spirit, a bright scholar who soon became bored and lazy, a terrible showoff. [He hated sports;] it was chiefly the seriousness of organized athletics which daunted him" (*KF*, 398–99).

The imaginative precocity that had been a virtue in his parents' nurturing home was now, at St. Edmund's, seen by the masters as a vice that signified independent non-conformity that needed to be quashed. As for sports, which Auden also hated, the hearties lived for them fanatically as if they were war games.

On 4 August 1914 Frank was sent to the front. The reluctant soldier wrote to his wife regularly until his last letter dated 6 May 1915.

His silence is recorded in Kathleen's diary:

> May 12. A sad long day of no news and horrible anxiety.
> May 13. No news.
> May 14. . . . to War Office. I thought possibly I might hear of the wounded.
> The suspense is awful.

The entries of 15 May to 20 May detail strenuous efforts to get information.

> May 21. No news of Frank.
> May 22. No news. It seems an everlasting silence. (*KF*, 462–65)

The silence was permanent. Frank was missing and no real confirmation of his death was ever made. For the duration of the war, another three years, Kathleen could not put away the possibility that Frank was still alive, perhaps a prisoner, or even shell-shocked with amnesia. The inability to confirm Frank's death would haunt Kathleen. Isherwood, stranded at St. Edmund's, could no longer even look forward to temporary relief when visiting his home during vacations. His home was now a war widow's home, with his mother dressed in black and displaying the taciturn demeanor expected of her—in 1932 Isherwood would record this scene in his novel, *The Memorial.* In *Kathleen and Frank,* he describes his mother's response to the loss of her husband: "Her earlier fears and scruples, her vulnerability and even her grief were modified by a saving toughness: the toughness of an organism that has decided to survive" (*KF*, 485–86). Kathleen survived by withdrawing emotionally. Isherwood gives this retrospective account as a compassionate and understanding adult. However, Isherwood the eleven-year-old child could only have known that, from a psychological standpoint, he had been stranded then abandoned in just over a year. Katherine Bucknell writes in her Introduction to Isherwood's *Diaries* that "Don Bachardy recalled in 1994, that over the many years of nights which they spent sleeping very close beside one another, Isherwood would sometimes cry out in his sleep, a yelping animal cry, not human. At these moments, Bachardy sensed that, in his sleep, Isherwood was in a place of horror, and he would wake Isherwood, who would always express his relief. But Isherwood never could say where he had been; he could never precisely articulate the dream, nor it seems, could he rid himself of it."[18] One can speculate that the seeds of disruption leading to the nightmares began when Isherwood was eleven.[19] At the time there was little for him to do but react with fear, anger, and rebellion.

US AGAINST THE WORLD

In the afterword to *Kathleen and Frank,* Isherwood describes the aftermath of his psychological abandonment and defines the terms of the rebellion that his isolation engendered in him. He returned to St. Edmund's in the fall of 1915 wearing the black crape band which would mark him as an "Orphan of a Dead Hero" (*KF,* 501). At first it gave him a status that was a slight reward for the conditions of his abandonment. The other boys intuitively "had the psychology of primitive tribesmen and could recognize a numen when they saw one" (*KF,* 501). Nonetheless, they could only deal with the armband as a symbol, being too young to understand the profound meaning of Isherwood's grief in order to truly commiserate with him. Even the other boys who wore the armband did not speak of it to each other according to Isherwood, since any overt communication of grief would not conform to the British stiff-upper-lip tradition. The illusory vanity derived from the "numen" of the arm-band faded quickly. "Christopher soon found that being a Sacred Orphan had grave disadvantages—that it was indeed a kind of curse which was going to be upon him for the rest of his life" (*KF,* 502). Isherwood learned that this curse came with a duty to honor the memory of his "Hero-Father" and to act exactly as The Others demanded of him. The Others included "the disembodied voices from pulpits, newspapers, books. It was easy for these impressive adults to make a suggestible little boy feel guilty. Yet he soon started to react to his guilt . . . with a rage against The Others which possessed him to the marrow of his bones, he rejected their Hero-Father, you deny the authority of the Flag, the Old School Tie, the Unknown soldier, The Land That Bore You and the God of Battles" (*KF,* 502).

Isherwood came to realize that by denying the fabricated Hero-Father of The Others, he was denying his real father. To prevent this, Frank would have to become the old Frank, "the Frank who had told him stories and drawn drawings for him and taught him the magic of make-believe. He wasn't going to surrender Frank to The Others. . . . He would create a father-figure of his own, the antiheroic hero" (*KF,* 503). Frank became the leading player of a game created in his son's mind. Frank was now the sensitive artist who pretends to be a soldier and fools everyone (except Christopher). By doing so Frank "demonstrates the absurdity of the military mystique and its solemn cult of War and Death" (*KF,* 503).

Isherwood then lends great import to his own interpretation of one of Frank's last letters to Kathleen, seeing it "as a statement of his last wishes and a speech for [his son's] defense. His father wrote: 'I don't think it matters very much what Christopher learns as long as he remains himself and keeps his individuality and develops on his own lines. . . . The whole point of sending him to school was . . . to make him like other boys . . . [but] I for one would much rather have him as he is.' Christopher interpreted this freely as 'Don't follow in my footsteps! Be all the things I never was. Do all the things I never did and would have liked to do—including the things I was afraid of doing, if you can guess what they were! Be anything except the son The Others tell you you ought to be. I should be ashamed of that kind of son. I want an Anti-Son'" (*KF*, 505). In Isherwood's retrospective interpretation, Frank sanctioned his son's future rebellion. Frank and Christopher were to be the Anti-Heroic father and Anti-Son versus the Heroic-father and The Others. A significant problem was that one of The Others was Kathleen. As the "Holy Widow" her peers expected her to be, she sustained the memory of the Hero-Father and supported The Others in placing demands on her son in the Hero-Father's name. Since The Others were constituted from the proverbial "They" of the anonymous unidentifiable Public, the focal point for Isherwood's rage and rebellion became his identifiable mother. He was to run away from her literally and figuratively by staying away from home as much as possible and by deliberately not matching the expectations she had for him.

Isherwood later mythologized this crucial period of his life by giving it a schema and nomenclature. This period of his pubescent adolescence would have been difficult under ideal circumstances let alone during severe psychological trauma. In the next decade psychoanalysis became prevalent and every thought and action had, for an angry Isherwood, a hidden meaning waiting to be discovered by him and "mythified" accordingly.

Later, Isherwood's predilection for referring to himself in the third person allowed him to observe the past as a witness who could objectify his thoughts and actions with detachment. His artistic stance was, *I* didn't do it! *He* did it! According to his biographer, Brian Finney, Isherwood's penchant for mythmaking helps him to impose order on an otherwise chaotic existence: "Obviously his mythopoeic faculty has helped Isherwood understand and live at peace with himself. But just as he has found himself unable to write novels based on his own experience until he has sufficiently distanced himself from it, so his mythic constructs are invariably later interpretations and explanations of the raw material of his life that is all too anarchic at the time. The need for orderly explanation . . . helps him to accept his rearranged past, to see it in a much wider context . . . but the raw material for these myths is a great deal more unruly than they suggest."[20]

Confusion ruled Isherwood's mental state after his father's death. Before Isherwood experienced "the need for orderly explanation" through writing, he somewhat exorcized his need for order through compulsive-obsessive tidiness. Yet his need to escape from The Others would be implemented in the manner he had first learned in his early childhood. He would create secondary worlds.

For Isherwood the only good thing that happened at St. Edmund's was that in his final year there, 1918, he met Auden who was in his first year. Their mutual dislike of the school would bond them permanently, even though after Isherwood left St. Edmund's, it would be seven years before they would meet again. During his last three years at St. Edmund's, Isherwood's bitterness festered silently. In his final two years at the school, he played the role that Kathleen and The Others expected of him. Now fourteen, he was to enter Repton in 1919 and his anger would begin to form a voice. There, he would find an ally who would not only listen, but understand.

Repton: The Anti-Others

Even though the actual fighting ended in 1919, World War I was far from over. During the war the blanket requirement of blatant patriotism was demanded and vocal opponents were the enemy of the people. Now the previously silent minority, the Anti-Others, would begin to assert themselves and find a more receptive audience. The prewar traditions were ready to be challenged. The working-class who bore the brunt of the war's sacrifice were not so inclined to fall back into their old roles and were more impatient with the monied classes. Workers chafed at being expected to accept the prewar conditions that had been predicated on the old system of noblesse oblige. They were not so willing to wait for favors and began demanding them even in the face of violent opposition. The emotional toll of the war had affected more than just workers, and the hope was that the new world of psychoanalysis would heal the individual mind and, by extension, the collective mind. Moreover, the communist revolution in the U.S.S.R. offered an alternative to capitalism's class divisions, and workers were joined by artists and intellectuals in their admiration of the new Russia.

Consequently, Isherwood would now have company; yet, as a minority, the Anti-Others would sometimes have to operate subversively. This was particularly true for students who had to live at schools still dominated by prewar masters, prewar money, and hearties. After his tenure at St. Edmund's preparatory school, Isherwood was not enthused to try his new public school, Repton: "I had arrived at my public school thoroughly sick of masters and mistresses, having been emotionally messed about by them at my preparatory school, where the war years had given full licence to every sort of dishonest cant about loyalty, selfishness, patriotism, playing the game and dishonouring the dead. Now I wanted to be left alone."[21]

Isherwood wanted to be left alone by the masters and the hearties who represented The Others. This did not mean he wanted to be left completely alone. Adolescents need approval from some quarter, and this Anti-Other insurgent highbrow would seek a fellow rebel. Insurgency is clannish and secretive by nature. The British public school was also clannish, with the hearties jockeying for position. Aesthetes were more suspect than ever. There were consequences for those who did not conform. Fear and paranoia had a real basis that often included physical pain and humiliation. The highbrows like Isherwood had to pretend not to be highbrows and seem to participate normally in the world of the hearties that they actually hated. Since the mind does not like a vacuum, if one refuses to acknowledge the prevailing world, another world has to take its place. This is when the highbrow, reacting to his environment and driven by psychological necessity, creates a secondary world.

Of this necessity, Auden would later say, "The identification of fantasy is an attempt to avoid one's own suffering; the identification of art is the sharing in the suffering of another."[22] Isherwood would cultivate escapist fantasy to avoid his own suffering. He later became a writer to share his art with others and obtain their approval. He did so in order to counter his feelings of rejection that had motivated him to create art in the first place. To reject the tradition of Kathleen's world and the people in it meant to accept those who were also rejected by that world. Concerning this desire to bond with fellow highbrow rebels, Stephen Spender said: "My revolt against the attitude of my family led me to rebel altogether against morality, work and discipline. Secretly I was fascinated by the worthless outcasts, the depraved, the lazy, the lost, and wanted to give them that love which they were denied by respectable people."[23]

At Repton Isherwood met his lifelong Anti-Other friend Edward Upward. Upward was in his third year when Isherwood arrived and was firmly devoted to rebelliousness. According to Katherine Bucknell, "Upward's grandfather was a congregationalist with radical Calvinist sympathies, and his father, a doctor effectively an atheist. Upward's mother trained briefly as a nurse, tried acting, and traveled abroad. Evidently Upward identified with the radical values of his paternal forbears, but from childhood he hated his mother's social snobbery, and his impulse to rebel was perhaps born out and certainly intensified by his wish to defy her."[24]

This desire for rebellion would attract Isherwood. He and Upward also had similar ideas in creating fantasies about The Others. At St. Edmund's Isherwood identified the enemy by pretending to be one of them through judicious infiltration—a spy in their midst. Consorting with the enemy increased his disdain and hatred for them that was fomenting into a clear picture of who they were, what they represented, and how they could be overcome. This picture, in gestation through eight years at St. Edmund's and Repton, would be put into an imaginary framework that peaked at Cambridge. Though this initial framework did not as yet define the dichotomy of the Truly Weak and Truly Strong Man in those terms, Isherwood and Upward dealt with the concept subliminally in the escapist parable-fantasies of their secret city of the imagination, Mortmere.

2 ACTS OF REBELLION I
Themes Subliminal: Cries for Approval

To prepare a face to meet the faces that you meet.

T. S. Eliot
"The Love Song of Alfred J. Prufrock," 1917[1]

He thought of the millions who had been and were still being slaughtered.
. . . he thought of their pain, all the countless separate pains of them; pain
incommunicable, individual, beyond the reach of sympathy . . . pain without sense or object, bringing with it no hope and no redemption, futile,
unnecessary, stupid. In one supreme apocalyptic moment he saw, he felt
the universe in all its horror.

Aldous Huxley
"Farcical History of Richard Greenow," 1920[2]

I have frequently been accused, by reviewers in public and by unprofes-
sional readers in private correspondence, both of vulgarity and wickedness—on the grounds, so far as I have been able to discover, that I reported
my investigations into certain phenomena in plain English and in a novel.
The fact that many people should be shocked by what he writes practically
imposes it as a duty upon the writer to go on shocking them. For those
who are shocked by truth are not only stupid, but morally reprehensible as
well; the stupid should be educated, the wicked punished and reformed.

Huxley, *Vulgarity in Literature,* 1930[3]

In "Prufrock," Eliot confers upon modern humanity the duality of having an inner
and outer self and suggests that the outer self requires a mask to hide the inner self
from The Others. Huxley, the caustic satirist, emphasizes, as does Eliot, bitter
despair and declares that he is obligated to do so if it is the truth.

In the 1920s the lowbrow majority passively went about their business and
the emotional residue that they felt from the war years was addressed only on a
subliminal level. Conversely, the sensitive, activist highbrows with their more
acute reactions to the war were determined that attention should be paid to the
causes behind the war so that it would never happen again. A large share of the
blame for the war went to the moneyed classes and the depersonalized industrial
metropolis. The artists and intellectuals could not ignore this—and they did not.
They also knew that the harshly punitive Versailles Treaty, which the victorious
capitalist infrastructure had imposed on the vanquished capitalist infrastructure,
was a bitter pill that would someday have to be swallowed by both sides—as it
would be in the 1930s, when the residual tensions of the First World War

exploded into World War II. Since the intellectuals were bemoaning the complex city-state that had produced an anonymous public unknown to each other and susceptible to media manipulation, the bywords for change among the high-brows of the 1920s were decentralization, simplicity, and reality. Highbrows are a vocal minority, and a minority of any kind always has underdog status. To Isherwood, Upward, Auden, and Spender, highbrows were to be counted as Anti-Others with whom they could sympathize and, more importantly, empathize. The quartet's own rebelliousness now had a viable context. They had literary heroes to emulate, such as T. S. Eliot for poetry and Aldous Huxley for the novel. Eliot's *The Waste Land* and Huxley's four novels of the 1920s, culminating in *Point, Counterpoint,* attacked the status quo and made Eliot and Huxley interna-tional sensations. Each said what the highbrow minority wanted to hear, and each also provided an outlet for the many who shared their bitterness but hereto-fore had not been able to articulate it. This is the role the artist plays in society; as Auden said, through fantasy, the artist attempts to avoid his own suffering and through his art shares his suffering with others. Auden also argued that, for a poet, "The reaction one hopes for from a poem is that the reader will say, 'Of course I've always known that, but I've never realized it before.'"[4] For the Auden Generation, parable-art should prompt readers to understand their latent feel-ings. For parable-artists, polemic didacticism—i.e., propaganda—is insincere and less effective for telling the truth; conversely, they also realized that lies suited propaganda well. This sensitivity to truth was a reaction to the heavy-handed propagandized cant of their public school years.

Since art-as-literature shares emotions with others in order to gain their approval, the telling is as important as or more important than the creating. Of this, Huxley said, "The people who have understood most have been endowed with the gift of telling what they understood. I doubt there have been many mute and inglo-rious Miltons."[5] Auden agreed, saying, "The first half of art is perceiving. The artist is the person who stands outside and looks, stands even outside himself and looks at his daydreams. The second half of art is telling. If you asked any artist why he works . . . he would say, 'to make money and amuse my friends.'"[6]

Although Isherwood and Upward did not make any money from the fan-tasies they created, they certainly intended to amuse themselves and confirm their solidarity as Anti-Others. They were a clan of two forming a secret society with codes and a nomenclature that they had created to assert their surreptitious autonomy amid suffocating authority. When the clan of two later added allies, particularly Auden, the expanded clan would maintain this internalized gang mentality of exclusive secret knowledge that was understood by them, but obscure to The Others.

The tribe or group or gang mindset was cultivated in the 1920s in response to the idea that society needed to decentralize and let people get to know each other again.[7] The details of this mentality are chronicled in Isherwood's *Lions and*

Shadows, which he subtitled "An Education in the Twenties." The education he details had little to do with formal schooling but elucidated the emotional state of his generation, which suffered the guilt of not having been in the war and falling short by comparison with those who had. At least this was their estimation of how they were regarded by The Others. *Lions and Shadows* is Isherwood's first official autobiography after four novels and the three plays written with Auden. However, all of his novels prior to *Lions and Shadows* are unofficial autobiography disguised as fiction. They are parables depicting the themes that he and Upward had formulated at both the conscious and unconscious levels, particularly that of the Truly Weak and Truly Strong Man. By the time of *Lions and Shadows,* Isherwood understood what he had not been quite so sure of before and wanted to take credit, along with Upward, for defining the psychology that was so prevalent among the highbrows of their generation. Since this psychology forms the basis of the Truly Strong and Truly Weak Man theme, *Lions and Shadows* deserves full attention, for it is here that Isherwood's unconscious themes became consciously delineated for posterity.

OUT OF THE SHADOWS

In 1958 Isherwood wrote an introduction to the first American edition of his initial novel *All the Conspirators.* This novel was originally published in 1928 and dedicated to Edward Upward, as it was again thirty years later. Isherwood notes in the 1958 introduction that his obscure style of 1928 sometimes did not even make sense to himself: "see what you can make of, for example, the first three and a half pages of the last chapter! I now detect a great deal of repressed aggression in this kind of obscurity. Young writers are apt to employ it as a secret language which is intelligible only to members of their group. Outsiders are thereby challenged to admit that they don't understand it or are dared to pretend they do—to be unmasked in any case, sooner or later, as squares." Isherwood was clearly stating that one method of rebellion by the Anti-Others against The Others was to write in a "secret language." He then defines his past role in the context of 1928: "The Angry Young Man of my generation was angry with the Family and its official representatives; he called them hypocrites, he challenged the truth of what they taught. He declared that a Freudian revolution had taken place of which they were trying to remain unaware. He accused them of reactionary dullness, snobbery, complacency, apathy. While they mouthed their platitudes, he exclaimed, we were all drifting toward mental disease, sex crime, alcoholism, suicide."[8] One can only conjecture if, in invoking the image of sex crime, Isherwood is referring to his homosexuality, which in Britain in 1928 and long after was a criminal offense and, therefore, marked another form of Isherwood's rebellion.

In *Lions and Shadows,* Isherwood looks back and interprets the neuroses he did not fully understand in the 1920s. This was a pattern and obsession for him, to go back and reexamine his past in order to better understand his present. In

1938, after a decade of portraying characters and their symptoms, Isherwood, perhaps in response to the obscurantism that he and Auden were sometimes accused of, decided he would share the "secret language" with a wider audience. Now thirty-four, with some success as a writer to fortify his ego's insecurities, Isherwood was still angry, but slightly less rebellious and combative. With fascism ever more threatening after the travesty of the Spanish Civil War, and another, wider war seemingly inevitable, Isherwood and the other members of his gang finally had their attention averted away from themselves. They had to face the reality that the fascist oppression of the old school with the hearties and their paddles was now being manifested by "gangs" of fascist armies with their guns and bombs. In Germany, it was as if the hearties had achieved the final end of their training and turned into a herd-intoxicated mass mob fueled by nationalist propaganda. Compared to the threat of fascism, the tacit school conflicts and generational warfare of the 1920s did not become less important, but less palpably immediate to Isherwood and his associates. *Lions and Shadows* is an autobiographical parable comparing the 1920s to the 1930s. In Germany the former schoolchildren of the 1920s became the Hitler Youth of the 1930s. England of the 1920s had its own fascist in Sir Oswald Mosley, and his British Youth were brainwashed in the public schools. The threat of a Mosley was not to be taken lightly; the highbrows such as Huxley, and later Isherwood, were sounding an alarm against Mosely's home-grown fascism. Huxley's *Brave New World,* published in 1932, and Storm Jameson's *In the Second Year,* published in 1936, both provided futuristic depictions of Britain as a fascist state, even though they were written by two members of the 1920s old guard. The new guard of the 1930s also made use of literary art to critique the rise of fascism in works such as Isherwood and Auden's plays, *The Dog beneath the Skin* (1935), *The Ascent of F6* (1937), and *On the Frontier* (1938). Rex Warner's novel *The Professor* (1938), which was a retelling of Jameson's *In the Second Year* that was as brilliant as her original had been, served to counter the influence of fascist thought. These works were anti-fascist parables. For a didactic critique of fascists-in-training, one can turn to *Lions and Shadows.*

AFTER A LONG EXILE, FINALLY, A COMRADE

In *Lions and Shadows,* which covers an entire decade, the chilly anti-relationship between Isherwood and his mother is indicated by the scant references to her. He never refers to her as mother or Kathleen, but as "female relative." For a thirty-four-year-old Isherwood, this seems to be rather obtuse, stubborn, and petulant. Even later, in his extensive diaries, where Isherwood gives full proper names to virtually everyone he knew, Kathleen remains merely "M." until her death in 1960. It was not until he was ready to write *Kathleen and Frank* that Isherwood, prompted by the humanity so evident in his parents' letters and diaries, gave his mother back her identity. Nonetheless, since *Lions and Shadows* concerns Isherwood's mind during the post-war 1920s, it excludes Kathleen as a possibility for emotional sanctuary. He would have to find it in someone else.

At Repton in 1921 Isherwood met Edward Upward, on whom Allen Chalmers is based in both *All the Conspirators* and *Lions and Shadows;* the parallels are so exacting that one is justified in conflating what Isherwood writes about Chalmers with what he remembers about Upward. He now had a counterpart with whom he could express his feelings about life in general and The Others in particular. Upward would be a catalyst for Isherwood to formulate the themes that permanently dominated his writing thereafter. Upward would also be a life-long sounding board for these writings. Isherwood would say of Upward in 1958, "After half a lifetime, Edward Upward is still the friend he has always been; still the judge before whom all my work must stand trial and from whose verdict, much as I sometimes hate to admit it, there is no appeal."[9] Isherwood sent all of his writing to Upward for guidance. By doing so he wished to hear from the one voice who had been there from the beginning of his writing career. Upward gave support to Isherwood's quest for thematic continuity.

As described in *Lions and Shadows* this mutually supportive gang of two fashioned a secondary world of fantasy to avoid their suffering at the hands of The Others: "We had to stick together we told each other. We were venturing like spies, into an enemy stronghold. They, our adversaries, would employ other tactics down there; they would be sly, polite, reassuring; they would invite us to tea. We should have to be on our guard. 'They'll do everything they can to separate us,' I said darkly, for I had adopted Chalmers phraseology and ideas . . . and now talked exactly like him: 'every possible bribe will be offered'" (*LS,* 23). Isherwood furthers the analogy of their friendship as a kind of conspiracy: "Chalmers glanced at me with a faint mysterious smile and I had the feeling, as so often, that we were conspirators" (*LS,* 27).

By deriving their own "phraseology" and perpetuating it within a clannish insulation, Isherwood and Upward signified that they were indeed "conspirators" in a highbrow minority of two. As so many clans before them had done, going back to the primeval tribe, they asserted their autonomy in the archetypical pattern begun long before with their progenitors' earliest attempts at making language. Isherwood and Upward's own language-making was a normal, reactionary human activity. Despite whatever precocious cleverness with which they credited themselves at the time, the differences were merely in the nuances, but not in the goal, which was to make them feel unique rather than ubiquitous. Through their secret communication, Isherwood and Upward made themselves a unique, non-conforming us against a conformed them. By doing so they fostered a gang mentality that required strict adherence to their shared views, which were bolstered by their disparagement of propaganda engendered by The Others.

For example, in visiting Paris on a school trip, the clan of two visited a build-ing called *Les Invalides*. Isherwood records the visit in *Lions and Shadows:* "I was very impressed by the coloured lighting, but I wasn't going to show it. Chalmers had denounced the building in advance—a shrine to war! And of course, one couldn't admit that a shrine to war was anything but vulgar and ugly" (28). Nor would Isherwood wish to refute his ally and risk rejection by him.

As a clan of two each became the paramount influence on the other. Since Upward was older and wiser by a year, he was usually the initiator of new ideas that helped to make these two highbrow conspirators distinct from The Others. After Upward discovered Baudelaire, he told Isherwood: "It's the very greatest. . . . I shall never forget the first time I . . . you see he exposes once and for all, the tremendous sham . . . the thing we never realized at school. . . ." To which Isherwood responded: "His . . . excitement set me on fire. . . . I had to buy my first copy of Baudelaire before the book stores closed. Without it, that night, I should not have slept a wink" (*LS,* 30).

Baudelaire's secret life of the mind—certainly not included in Repton's cur-riculum—encouraged Isherwood and Upward to live in their own secret world and this was another sign of their clandestine independence. More mild rebellion was exhibited in Isherwood's school work such as a paper on "Chivalry in English Literature." Isherwood refers to it with self-mocking bemusedness. "The keynote of the paper was anti-industrialism and hurrah for the bold decorative Middle Ages before the machines, when Life (I quoted) was 'colour and warmth and light.'" (In 1933 Auden would write an article on "How to Be Masters of the Machine," which also attacked the industrial city-state.[10]) Isherwood next "proposed a motion before the debating society that 'in the opinion of this house, patriotism is an obstacle to civilization'" (*LS,* 43). Upward agreed and for Isherwood to have said so out loud right after the war was certainly a stroke of defiant Independence, which, while he undoubtedly meant it in and of itself, was said more to please the clan by asserting their private autonomy in a public manner.

Between them, Upward said, there was mainly agreement, especially about art: "What mattered more than anything else to us . . . was art—not just our art but also the art of those . . . we admired. We educated each other . . . of our lat-est discoveries. We read aloud to each other. I remember our reading alternate chapters of George Moore's *Esther Waters.*[11] Our most startling discovery was Shakespeare, whose fame we had assumed to be one of the many frauds our elders had tried to impose on us. Christopher was disgusted at what he regarded as 'insincerity' on my part, but after reading *Hamlet* he too was converted. . . . What above all made us friends at Repton and at Cambridge was our enthusiasm for literature and our ambition to be writers."[12]

This collaborative study of art and the mutual ambition to write intensified their relationship. Isherwood would later say: "Art, rightly practiced, is a way of religion."[13] Later, as a Vedantist, art became a form of devotion to God. According to Katherine Bucknell, "The friendship between them generated the sheer excitement more usually associated with erotic love, and they channelled all their energy into art."[14] By invoking the idea of erotic love, Bucknell implies that the "sheer excitement" they felt was actually what the mystics call the Vision of Eros. This vision is the intense love of one person that is pseudo-erotically charged, but, in Isherwood and Upward's case, minus the actual sex. For mystics this is a state that can be a prelude to the Vision of Agape, which is the love for all existence as transcendentally integrated. Isherwood and Upward had a transcendent friendship that Isherwood would thereafter struggle to emulate through various partners, but would not find again until meeting the Swami, and later, Don Bachardy.

With all of their agreement artistically and philosophically, one difference, however, on the more mundane plane, was the issue of tidiness. Isherwood was compulsively tidy; Upward was not. To Isherwood this vice of Upward was actually a virtue: "His untidiness made his two rooms seem homely and inhabited. I recognized this, with admiration and occasional irritation: my own tidiness was hopelessly ingrained—in my sitting-room, even the matchbox has its proper position; a position which Chalmers never failed to disturb" (LS, 50). He then describes through Chalmers some other examples of Upward's lackadaisical messiness, which also sound like a description of the equally untidy W. H. Auden; perhaps opposites do attract. Isherwood further refers self-mockingly— but quite seriously—to his compulsive-obsessiveness that he manifested through his neatness and also in his hypochondria.

Compulsive obsessiveness is a symptomatic response to a sometimes conscious, but more often, unconscious feeling that something is psychically awry. Every effort must be made to put things in order or to find a vicarious substitute for that which is missing in the psyche. Highbrows and artists, perhaps due to their increased ability to actively perceive rather than passively observe, feel their neuroses and psychoses more acutely, whether they are reacting to an actual knowledge and understanding of their causes or just the symptoms of the causes. Identification of the compulsive-obsessive symptoms will not necessarily end them. Even identifying the underlying cause of the obsession may not stop the compulsion. Often the only hope is that once one understands that he is a compulsive-obsessive, one might redirect the compulsion away from deleterious manifestations, such as rabid tidiness, into a more productive outlet—like art. In the psychoanalysis-influenced 1920s, the idea of analyzing underlying motivations was not only prevalent, but was almost a parlor game among the highbrows. See, for example, Huxley's novels of that decade. Art, depending on one's degree of participation, was seen as either a therapeutically cathartic expiation or just another debilitating denial of reality.

In the late 1920s, Auden, inspired by the theories of psychologist Homer Lane, would say all illnesses—mental or physical—are symptoms of psychoses: a cold is not caused by a virus, but by an underlying guilt. Auden later modified his belief that physical illnesses were purely psychosomatic, but at the time, this explanation—which he employed to analyze his friends in the detached manner of a clinician—could not have done anything but aggravate Isherwood's hypochondria. Auden's father was a physician as was Upward's, so Auden lent an air of authority to his speculations, which made them even more disconcerting to Isherwood. In writing of the compulsive-obsessive artist, Auden equates an artist's tendencies concerning external order or tidiness with the degree to which the artist feels an internal disorder: "It is interesting to speculate on the relation between the strictness and musicality of a poet's form and his own anxiety. It may well be . . . that the more he is conscious of an inner disorder and dread, the more value he will place on tidiness in the work as a defense, as if he hoped that through his control of the means of expressing his emotions, the emotions themselves, which he cannot master directly, might be brought to order."[15] Auden also suggested that, "Both in life and in art the human task is to create a necessary order out of an arbitrary chaos. A necessary order implies that the process of its creation is not itself arbitrary; one is not free to create any order one chooses. The order realized, must, in fact, have been already latent in the chaos, so that successful creation is a process of discovery. As long as this remains latent and unconscious, conscious life must appear arbitrary; one grows up in the degree to which this unconscious order becomes conscious and its potentialities developed, to the degree that one's life ceases to be arbitrary, to the degree that one becomes conscious of and true to one's fate. An artist is someone who is able to express human development in a public medium."[16]

Aldous Huxley agreed. The agreement between Huxley and Auden on a number of matters is evident in their work as essayists.[17] For instance, in his essay, "Art," Huxley gives a similar explanation of how an artist uses artistic form to combat inner psychological disorder: "To use a phrase originally used by Clive Bell, the artist gives order to the world in terms of: 'significant form.' What he does is try and perceive forms inherent in nature and to find a symbolic equivalence for these forms which he then imposes upon the world in order to produce the order which he feels so supremely important. The artist seeks to impose this order of beauty and significant form upon both the external reality and internal reality within himself. He wants always to see himself in relation to the world and to create symbolically a harmony in which both fit."[18] The more disharmony one feels, the greater the need to achieve harmony to displace the anxiety that the disharmony fosters. The passages by Auden and Huxley, besides dealing with the psychological aspects of the artist's inner and outer life, intimate that this duality also has a metaphysical basis. After Isherwood first tried art as a means to find

internal order, he then became a Vedantist. The metaphysical basis of seminal
Vedantism evolved into what Huxley called the Perennial Philosophy.

In the 1920s, however, the prospect of a spiritual life, according to which the
teenage Isherwood might, as Huxley said, "see himself in relation to the world
and to create symbolically a harmony in which both fit," was as remote as his
enlisting in the army. Prior to his conversion to Vedanta all he had known of religion was the traditional Christianity of The Others who had bleated "Onward
Christian Soldiers" during the war and were in his eyes guilty of the warmonger-
ing that had killed his father. Nonetheless, compulsive obsessions are substitutes
in the external world for a void in the inner world. Isherwood was dealing with
a latent spiritual need by turning it inside out. He overwhelmed himself with
external fixations so as not to accept that, in his perception, his father and mother
had exiled him from the cocoon paradise that he was now trying to replace with
tidiness, clanship, and the secondary world of "us" against "them." Isherwood
began his fantasy formulation by playing at a secret language. This was a game in
Auden's terms that Isherwood chose to play so that he might achieve some degree
of autonomy that would distract him from the actual source of his problems—a
lack of self-esteem caused by his self-perceived parental abandonment. The symptoms were cries for approval from someone who would later be considered by
Isherwood himself to have been Truly Weak.

THE WATCHER IN SPANISH

Isherwood's compulsive obsessions, fantasies, and game-playing were assertions of
autonomy that Isherwood pursued to counter his feeling of being otherwise powerless and out of control. Each, in its way, was a secondary world within which he
could pose as the master who could make his existence feel less arbitrary by being
more controlling. The escapism of fantasy is a conceit that elevates one's self-esteem
by giving one the illusion of being able to create the world in his own image, not the
other way around. Fantasy is also an attempt, as Auden said, "to create a necessary
order out of an arbitrary chaos." To seek order is immediately followed by the
attempt to maintain it; consequently, while seeking order through fantasy and a
secret language, Isherwood and Upward sought to guard this order from the temptations or "bribes" of the enemy by setting up an imagined doppelganger who symbolized the clan's conscience: "'The Watcher in Spanish' was the latest of our
conceits. . . . He appeared to us in moments when our behavior was particularly
insincere; one might be telling a boastful story, or pretending an interest in heraldry,
or flattering the wife of a don—and there, suddenly, he would be standing, visible
only to ourselves. . . . His mere presence was a sufficient reminder and warning.
Mutely, he reminded us that the 'two sides' continued to exist, that our enemies
remained implacable. . . . he warned us never to betray ourselves by word or deed.
He was our familiar, our imaginary mascot, our guardian spirit" (*LS,* 53–54).

For Isherwood and Upward the Watcher in Spanish served as an alter ego who reminded each of the other. The silent Watcher affirmed their Anti-Other status against The Others, with whom any contact was a dangerous, disloyal flirtation. Isherwood was to be especially careful: "Chalmers was particularly alarmed by what he regarded as my dangerous weakness for the society of the 'poshocracy'—a word he had coined to designate the highest of our social circles" (*LS,* 54–55). This circle would have welcomed Isherwood's name and status, and he was certainly tempted. "Their civilized, flattering laughter went to my head. The truth was, in my heart, I really enjoyed society" (*LS,* 57). When Isherwood tried to get Upward to soften his resistance toward the Poshocracy so that they could enjoy the enemy's society together, they had their "first serious quarrel" (*LS,* 58). Upward tested the loyalty of a guilty Isherwood, who passed by forsaking society and remaining loyal to the clan of two. This was the first Test in the context of the Truly Strong and Truly Weak Man mythos. Upward did not have Isherwood's status and could have resented what may have seemed to him Isherwood's *noblesse oblige* in wanting to introduce him to the higher social circle. He may have also feared losing Isherwood to this circle.

Having passed the Test, Isherwood thereafter rejected any but the most minimal contact with the Poshocracy and solidified his relationship with Upward:

> We were the other's ideal audience; nothing, not the slightest innuendo or the subtlest shade of meaning, was lost between us. A joke which, if I had been speaking five minutes to a stranger, would have taken five minutes to lead up to and elaborate and explain, could be conveyed to Chalmers by the faintest hint. In fact, there existed between us that semi-telepathic relationship. . . . Our conversation would have been hardly intelligible to anyone who had happened to overhear it; it was a rigmarole of private slang, deliberate misquotations, bad puns, bits of parody and preparatory school smut:
>
> "Ashmeade's giving a political tea-party to six puss-dragons from the union."
> "Let's go in and *j'en apelle it.*"
> "No good. They'd only namby us off. It'd just be quisb."
> "What are Ashmeade's politics?"
> "He's a lava-Tory." (*LS,* 65–66)

This secret code—for example, Upward said "quisb" meant "squirm-making"[19]—was a game that compensated for the rejection they felt from their mothers and the society their mothers represented. Isherwood and Upward defended themselves, in turn, by rejecting The Others in what amounted to a face-saving preemptive strike: You are not rejecting us; we are rejecting you and everything about you! This included rejecting The Others' language, which Isherwood and Upward refuted by creating their own language. Their new proprietary language renamed things and constructs in the mythopoeic manner of the archetypal Adam who gained dominion over his new and intimidating world by naming what was in it. Metaphorically, each new person—a new Isherwood or new Upward—is a new Adam, one who discovers the world for the first time, over and over again. Isherwood and Upward, as new Adams who were also in a new and intimidating world represented by Repton and Cambridge, would assert their opposition to the primary world by replacing it with a secondary world created from their secret language.

SEXTRACT FROM A FIRKIN OGRESS

Upward would say of this secondary world, "We went in for a good deal of pastiche. I remember parts of one of mine which was a parody of a piece by Joyce called *Extract from a Work in Progress* (the work subsequently published as *Finnegan's Wake*) and my title was *Sextract from a Firkin Ogress.*" [20] Upward is describing the kind of letters he and Isherwood wrote to each other during vacations—or "vacs." The terms "pastiche" and "parody" signify a conscious understanding that they were reinventing in their own language what they had understood of the language in the literature they had previously read. All people using language are in fact engaged in parody and pastiche in the sense that language is always a reaction to what has come before its creation.

Through language the ego conceptualizes the duality that seems to exist in both the internal and external worlds. (Mistakenly, one must add, from the mystic's standpoint, as to the mystic, there is no duality.) An individual's relation to another or many others is, "I am I; you are not *I*." Language creates this sense of duality and then it is language that attempts to overcome the duality. Language is not about what we know, but it is the analogous means that attempts to convey how we feel about what we know. Language represents all of humanity's knowledge, moving from our tribal roots to the present in a perpetual continuum. Words signify little until one relates them to his own contextual catalog of stored information and correlates them into a coherent message. A present context is constituted from a previous context. The one and the many react to the past. One imitates what he has learned from others before one can speak on his own; one must pastiche and parody what already exists before one can develop a more distinct voice—distinct, but never completely unique, since the voice that emerges is still reacting to and extrapolating from antecedent influences.

Language is a system of symbolic analogies. Auden said he could not "look at anything without looking for its symbolic relation to something else." [21] As a symbol system, language is prone to manipulation by subjective egos that want to use the symbols as the means to personal ends. Since words are analogous to reality but can never duplicate reality, they imperfectly substitute for immediate experience, a point articulated by Auden: "most of the power of words comes from their not being like what they stand for." [22] Words are dependent on interpretation by individuals who experience the world from a unique, subjective viewpoint. Of the subjective nature of individual perspective, Auden concluded: "Even when two persons share the same mother-tongue, neither speaks it in exactly the same way: What the speaker says in light of his experience, the listener has to interpret in light of his, and these are not the same. Every dialog is a feat of translation."[23] This feat is even more prodigious when the dialogue of the two becomes the dialogue of the many between the mass media and the mass as represented by the public.

Lowbrows take words at face value, whether these words are true or not. For highbrows, words have both literal and figurative meanings that are dependent on a speaker's intent. It is from intent that the power of language derives. For highbrow writers, words constitute a complex and challenging game. Isherwood and Upward viewed words as the map to escape from the world of The Others, since reinventing words gave them a world into which they could escape. The sense of escape into a secondary world creates a duality that signifies the distinctions between outer world and inner world, public and private, past and future, Truly Weak and Truly Strong. Isherwood and Upward's approach in creating a secondary world was to create a kind of reductio ad absurdum image of the real world. They depicted English tradition as a framework for the ridiculous. That they took the trouble to create a secondary world as a reaction to the primary world proves rather than disproves that the effect of the primary world on Isherwood and Upward was quite serious. In Isherwood's frantic stage, language heightened his sense of duality and separateness, even when he was trying to find himself; in his Vedantic stage, he believed that language bridged over his sense of duality and separateness as he actually began to find himself. At Cambridge, however, Isherwood was still frantic as he fantasized his escape routes.

THE DEAD MOTHER: PRELUDES

In her introduction to *The Mortmere Stories* Katherine Bucknell writes: "This book contains the fragmentary remains of an elaborate imaginative game played by Christopher Isherwood and Edward Upward when they were undergraduates at Cambridge in the 1920s. The stories and poems associated with the invented village of Mortmere are the product of a high-spirited, playful, and obsessively private adolescent friendship that lingered self-consciously in the nursery even as Isherwood and Upward aspired to launch themselves as serious literary artists."[24] For Isherwood particularly, his lingering "self-consciously in the nursery" through the Mortmere fantasies was a continuation of the womb-cocoon of his pre-St. Edmund's childhood and the happy mornings of Frank's "Toy-Drawer Times." Those father-son chronicles were reflections of prewar English tradition. Mortmere was the rejection of that tradition by pastiching the prewar style, but, as Bucknell notes, "mocking it ruthlessly, deflating and exaggerating by turns, joking hilariously, discovering sinister and vivid significance in ordinary events."[25]

In 1966 Upward recalled "that Christopher and I never regarded our Mortmere writing as anything more than an imaginative game. Neither of us saw it as the kind of writing we most wanted to do."[26] For the clan of two their game was also an assertion of autonomy and a cry for approval. The game was symptomatic of their refusal to conform to the conventional requirements of school, family, or country. The game was also something to do for two highbrows as distractions from their profound boredom with the old masters teaching the old stuff in the old way. Later Isherwood acknowledged that the Mortmere game was a prelude to his serious writings, which he knew not to take too seriously. Writing to Upward in 1949 he said, "I never cease to be grateful to you for having helped me to acquire the play instinct early, with Mortmere, the glee, the insane Mortmere-anarchic elements in all experience, however ghastly."[27] Mortmere encouraged him to see that the dramatic contrast of the real and the absurd can coincide in everyday life and be duplicated in fiction.

In the 1920s this concept was acted on by Isherwood and Upward intuitively. By 1949, however, Isherwood was well-versed in the Vedantic concept concerning the "reconciliation of opposites" such as love/hate, peace/war, order/anarchy, sensible/absurd, reason/passion, inner/outer, public/private, and Weak/Strong. In Vedic cosmology these conflicting forces are inevitable and ultimately desirable. The energy created by the ensuing metaphysical fission is what fuels the progress of man's collective consciousness. Consequently, when Isherwood refers to the play instinct, this term refers to the play of opposites that exists within the illusion of Maya. For Vedantists, Maya is what man perceives when his ego deludes him into thinking he is separated from the world rather than integrated with the world. Man, in his ego-motivated delusion mistakenly observes what appears to be the aforementioned duality of "I am I; you are not I." According to Vedantist philosophy, there is no duality so that "all experience, however ghastly" it seems on the surface to a finite individual mind, is actually all of a tapestry to the infinite world mind. In 1949, as Isherwood looked back on the 1920s, this Vedantist conception of the world made perfect sense to Isherwood; in the the 1920s, however, very little made sense, and the ghastly was merely ghastly, without any allusion to it being the flip side of a more benevolent cosmic reality. Nonetheless, just because Isherwood at Cambridge could not fathom that the underlying motivations for creating Mortmere were much more than a game, the unconscious motivations existed just the same. They were in fact cries for approval through acts of rebellion that signified a wish to preserve the sanctuary and unity of his prewar childhood.

As preludes to the Mortmere stories, Isherwood and Upward elaborated on their secret language and established parameters for their clan-of-two opposition: "Our jokes were usually connected in some way with the college, the Poshocracy and the dons. The dons were, for us, utterly remote and unreal figures like bogies in a child's book; we were careful to avoid contact with them [in order] to maintain more completely our vision of the two sides, 'the combine' directed expressly against ourselves. . . . in addition . . .we had invented an ideal, imaginary don, the representative of all his kind, to be our special enemy and butt. We named him Laily (which means 'loathly')—a word taken from a ballad [that mentions a 'laily worm']" (*LS*, 166).

Laily, or the Worm, soon became as important as the Watcher in Spanish. Isherwood and Upward "referred to him in terms of disgust that were almost affectionate" (*LS*, 66). Laily was that person who would now be identified as the pseudo-intellectual buffoon who, while lost in the library, still wanted to "be accepted by the Poshocracy [and was] careful to pretend an enthusiasm for athletics and team spirit" (*LS*, 66–67). Since Isherwood's and Upward's mothers would have liked their sons to become dons, no doubt this added to their antipathy. Laily was a version of the Isherwood who had wanted Upward to get chummier with the Poshocracy, which had precipitated their "first serious quarrel." Laily served as both a mocking of The Others and as a self-parody with which Isherwood mocked himself. One must be wary of Laily, who could easily succumb to the fascistic peer pressure demanded of the old school honor code in order to ingratiate himself with the Poshocracy and would snitch on the Anti-Others without remorse.

Isherwood and Upward's game took over all aspects of their Cambridge existence; they saw spies and enemy agents everywhere: "we alone, of all the undergraduates in Cambridge, had seen through their tremendous and imposing bluff" (*LS*, 67). Imaginary Others have to live somewhere, so Upward first created the "Other Town" and then renamed it "The Rats' Hostel." Isherwood said their creation "became gradually defined in [their] minds as a name for a certain atmosphere, a genre: the special brand of medieval surrealism [they] had made [their] own" (*LS*, 69–70). Isherwood then provides a poem that Upward wrote at the height of their Rats' Hostel phase:

> It is an old word how the door
> has closed on other mimes before,
> And time countercheck's man's jest,
> And how the blague of splendid state
> Is hushed beyond the wormhouse gate . . .
>
> (*LS* 71)

Obscure by design in case the poem should fall into the hands of the enemy, the term "wormhouse gate" refers to Laily and the entrance to the Rats' Hostel. The obscurity was their own joke that made the secret game worthwhile. Auden later adapted obscurantism into his earliest work, which also tacitly depicted the old school wars. This made his early art attractive by its mystery. There was certainly obscurity in Auden's early work to the general readership, but not to the gang of Isherwood and Upward.

During the Rats' Hostel period Isherwood said that he "had been writing away at a novel— *the* novel, I might almost call it; for it was much less of a work of art than a symptom—of a certain stage of public development in a member of a certain class, living in a certain country and subjected to a certain system of education." The themes of their game were

> now to be taken seriously in a very typical specimen of the "cradle-to-coming-of-age" narrative. . . . we young writers of the middle twenties were all suffering, more or less subconsciously, from a feeling of shame that we hadn't been old enough to take part in the European war. The shame, I have said, was subconscious: in my case, at any rate, it was suppressed by the strictest possible censorship. . . . Like most of my generation, I was obsessed by a complex of terrors and longings connected with the idea "War." War, in this purely neurotic sense, meant The Test. The test of your courage, of your maturity, of your sexual prowess: "Are you really a man?" Subconsciously . . . I longed to be subjected to this test; but I also dreaded failure. . . . I was so certain that I should fail—that, consciously, I denied my longing to be tested altogether. I denied my all-consuming morbid interest in the idea of "war." I pretended indifference. The War, I said, was obscene . . . a bore. (*LS*, 74–76)

Since there was no war, Isherwood would devise a reasonable substitute, suggesting that "'war,' which could never under any circumstances be allowed to appear in its own shape, needed a symbol—a symbol round which I could build up my daydreams about 'The Test.' Gradually, in the most utter secrecy, I began to evolve a cult of the public-school system" (*LS*, 77). What evolved was the pseudo-war of a clan of one versus snobbism, hypocrisy, and the hearties. Isherwood understood that while the de facto fascism of the public school was superficially a source of humor, it was also, subliminally, a nefarious danger: "It is so very easy, in the mature calm of a library, to sneer at all this homosexual romanticism [that is, the structures of power in an all-boys school]. But the rulers of Fascist states do not sneer—they profoundly understand and make use of just these phantasies and longings. I wonder how, at this period, I should have reacted to the preaching of an English Fascist leader clever enough to serve up his 'message' in a suitably disguised and palatable form? He would have converted me inside half an hour—provided always that Chalmers hadn't been there to interfere" (*LS*, 78–79).

Isherwood follows this passage with a juxtaposed symptomatic manifestation of his unconscious state: "My 'war' complex now brought me to a sensational decision: I would buy a motorcycle. . . . The Poshocracy was much intrigued: Isherwood becomes a hearty. . . . here was a quaint new pose. . . . 'The Test' had now transformed itself into a visible metal contraption." (*LS*, 83). This

Test failed as the motorcycle scared Isherwood more than encouraged him, causing him to feel ashamed because it made him "quisb" (or squirm). Putting the
motorcycle behind him Isherwood began to keep a diary, starting a new obsession that he pursued to the end of his life. The diary was much safer and certainly
more therapeutic. He could write about the Test instead of riding a motorcycle
that might kill him.

With the diary Isherwood picked up a new compulsive obsession, in addition to his tidiness and hypochondria. Isherwood's new persona was "Isherwood
the Artist . . . an austere ascetic, cut off from the outside world, in voluntary exile,
a recluse. He stood apart from and above 'The Test'—because the Test was something for the common herd, it applied only to the world of everyday life.
Isherwood refused the Test—not out of weakness, not out of cowardice, but
because he was subjected . . . to a 'Test' of his own: the self-imposed Test of his
integrity as a writer" (*LS,* 97–98). Isherwood realized that Isherwood the artist
was something he could do in private as compared to Isherwood the motorcyclist
who had ridden the motorcycle in front of that common herd known as the public.
Instead of acknowledging any failure on his part with regard to the motorcycle
experiment, Isherwood claimed the failure was actually a success, since it taught him
that a visible Test was for the weak. The real Test for the isolated highbrow artist
was another matter entirely. Isherwood's psychology of opposition was now
beginning to form a scheme.

Since Isherwood and Upward were to be artists overseeing a secret city of the
imagination, this meant that merely thinking about such a world would not suit
their new vocation. In order to adopt this new artist-as-writer guise, they would
have to put their thoughts on paper; consequently, to identify this new phase, a
new name was needed to succeed Other Town and Rats' Hostel. This would be
Mortmere.

THE DEAD MOTHER: ACTUALITY

The Mortmere stories are quite conventional in stylistic presentation, but their content depicts absurd chaos. The stories are told with understated British reserve as a
contrast to the bizarre nonsense they depict. Isherwood and Upward were imitating
late-nineteenth-century and early-twentieth-century prewar popular stories. These
included the adventures of Conan Doyle's highbrow detective, Sherlock Holmes,
and his loyal friend, Dr. Watson, and also the anti-adventures of E. W. Hornung's
gentleman burglar, Raffles, the amateur "cracksman" and his partying pal, Bunny
Manders. (Incidentally, Hornung was Conan Doyle's brother-in-law and intended
Raffles and Manders as a parody of Holmes and Watson.) Years later, Isherwood
explained his admiration for Holmes: "Since I was ten years old, the adventures of
Sherlock Holmes have been my favourite escape-reading; I have turned to them in
times of sadness, boredom, and ill-health and never found myself disappointed.

Holmes is truly one of the great comic characters in our literature; but it is doubt-
ful if Doyle himself would have agreed with this statement or even have taken it as
a compliment. . . . His comic quality seems to me this: he is a classic caricature of
the Amateur Detective, in whose person the whole art of detection is made ridiculous." According to Isherwood, Holmes is "ridiculous" in the sense that his ego-dri-
ven detecting genius makes all detectives seem amateurs even though he is
supposedly the actual amateur. One can see that such a character would appeal to
Isherwood in particular and to highbrow loners in general, as Holmes has for over a
hundred years. For Isherwood, Holmes "has the sanction of his own peculiar kind
of madness. Like Captain Ahab, he is possessed by the insanity of the chase. Holmes'
Moby Dick is Dr. Moriarty."[28] Isherwood's Moby Dick was his traumatic memory
of the war, which he was attempting to exorcize with a Mortmere world that
ridicules British tradition, just as Holmes and Raffles ridiculed Scotland Yard.

Like Holmes and Watson, Raffles and Manders—Isherwood and Upward
were an equally inseparable duo who saw these fictional figures as counterparts.
Holmes and Raffles were loners by necessity acting upon their own singular
moral code, which had little to do with the common herd. Holmes sneered at
Scotland Yard and the authority the Yard represented (or misrepresented).
George Orwell, another rebel of the 1930s, said that Hornung had a "tendency
to take the side of the criminal" and that "Raffles is presented to us . . . not as an
honest man who has gone astray, but as a public-school man who has gone
astray."[29] Isherwood's sense of connection to Holmes is further evidenced by the
fact that, in *Lions and Shadows,* the only school-master Isherwood and Upward
admire is called Mr. Holmes.

By parodying earlier styles and genres, Isherwood and Upward were mocking British traditions and the public schools that perpetuated them. The school
masters are depicted as self-imagined Knights Templar who are safeguarding
Britain by speaking in platitudes that ignore post-war changes. The masters
would say the same old cant with oblivious straight faces that made them appear
as buffoons. The Mortmere stories satirically paralleled the outworn tradition of
the schools and the masters by also being told in a straight-faced manner; yet, the
absurdities described threw stuffy British propriety out the window. Isherwood
and Upward told the stories with narrators named Hynd and Starn (puns on
hind and stern) to signify that they were asses.

Isherwood and Upward drew maps and compiled long lists of characters, plots,
and potential titles. Many stories were begun but few finished, as the game was more
in the devising than in the final execution. A number of titles are reminiscent of the
Holmes and Raffles stories: "The Horror in the Tower," "The Adventures of Fooby
Bevan," "The Javanese Sapphires," "The Garage in Drover's Hollow," "The
Convocation," "Letter to the Tutor of Corpus After a Year's Historical Study," and
"The Recessional from Cambridge." Mortmere characters included Donald

Gunball, who is an "unashamed vulgarian, a drunkard and a grotesque liar. Gunball's world was the world of delirium tremens: he saw wonders and horrors all about him, his everyday life was lived amidst two-headed monsters, ghouls, downpours of human blood, and eclipses of the sun—and everything he accepted with the most absolute and placid calm. Next is Reverend Casmir Welken, rector of Mortmere "who had been guilty of moral offences with a choirboy and had later suffered pangs of conscience, persuading himself that his dead wife was appearing to him in the form of a succubus" (*LS*, 102). Dr. Mears "was the Mortmere physician. He was the author of a book called *Awards and Miseres of Astronomy* [an echo of Baudelaire]. He had divided mankind into two main groups—'Dragoons' and 'Dorys': Dragoons were subdivided into 'Puss-dragoons,' 'Cogs-dragoons and 'Imperials'; Dorys into 'Itchers,' 'Repellers' and 'Consumers'—and each of these three subdivisions could be further classed as 'Pouters,' 'Poupees,' 'Buttocks' or 'Throstles.' (I leave it to the recognition of all these types to the reader's imagination and personal taste)" (*LS*, 111). The Watcher in Spanish, Laily, The Others, and Anti-Others had grown from their original formative oral sketches and were now extended, extrapolated, and aggrandized into pseudo-legends:

> "It is strange," said Starn, as they left the ruinous and deserted mansion, "but tonight I feel moved, as never before, to acquaint you with a passage in my life, upon which for many years I have scarcely dared even to meditate."
>
> "Pray do so, then, by all means," replied Hynd. "The time is propitious—and we have far to go."
>
> "I must first then require your indulgence while I speak of my University days," Starn began, "for it is to that time period that my story relates."[30]

Indeed, Mortmere relates to the "University days" and for Isherwood to the long-seething rebellion he had begun at St. Edmund's.

Isherwood and Upward wrote an "Introductory Dialogue" concerning how Mortmere came to be: "at Cambridge we were anxious for an expression of the mental atmosphere which had surrounded us for the past eighteen months. Baudelaire. Death worship. . . . Our social fears swept us from one extreme to the other. The dons were our bogies or dummies. The college cliques were groups of plush tom-cats or combines to be fought with daggers. . . . there was another element than the pure story. A self-consciousness . . . [our] cult of the sinister . . . . All the characters are insane. . . . And there had always, therefore, to be the sane or semi-sane outside observer of the action. The observer must be a cypher. . . . Hynd and Starn were cyphers . . . [as was] the Watcher in Spanish. A presence representing our combined personalities. We regarded ourselves as rebels, self-appointed pariahs. The Laily-Worm was the symbol of the Public-School social-team spirit. . . . We were uncertain whether to make him a sycophant who consorted with the social majority to further his private academic ambitions, or the complete figure of the ludicrous, because unathletic team-enthusiast. We soon found the self-seeking scholarship-hunter a better victim than the scrum-dope." [31]

As regards the "mythifying" process of Mortmere, Isherwood and Upward sometimes implied a quasi-mysticism meant to further elevate story into legend. Side by side, however, with the faux-mystical eloquence are decidedly non-mystical descriptions: "That evening the snow began to fall. I retired early to bed and sat watching the flakes as they drove past my window and into the night. It occurred to me that they resembled the crowding spermatozoa on their midnight journey towards the House of Life."[32] There are also "cult of the sinister" passages that betray more of a paranoid, Holmesian manner:

> I had, of course, been careful to isolate the sauce from the rest of the food on my plate. I now began tentatively to explore its contents with the prong of my fork. In a few moments I had disinterred five small white tablets from the general mess. These I contrived to convey, unseen, to the interior of my cigarette case. . . .
>
> The shock of discovery led my thoughts, by an obvious association of ideas, to the chamber in the tower. An unbearable curiosity mastered my fears. I resolved to pay it a second visit. . . . I set out for the spiral staircase. On this occasion, how-ever, I had armed myself with an automatic pistol. . . .[33]

There are criticisms of the Poshocracy with broad caricatures: "Andrew Henry deVere Isaac John Arlington [Andy] Shanks was the living personification of medi-ocrity. . . . he was remarkable for only two things—his wealth and his stupidity."[34]

Isherwood and Upward also criticize themselves—or at least record the way they perceived that The Others would criticize them:

> "Yes," continued Sir Murgatroyd [speaking to Mr. Starn]. "There's something the matter with the boy. . . . my son is—well, practically insane."
>
> "Insane?" I echoed in horror.
>
> "It amounts to the same thing," replied Sir Murgatroyd, testily, "The boy is utterly unnatural—a monstrosity. He is, in a word, insensible to the pleasures proper to his age."
>
> "I presume," I began, "that his—that physically—?"
>
> "Fooby is perfectly equipped for his mortal lot," said Sir Murgatroyd. "If he were not, it would be a different matter. But this indifference—this lack of enthu-siasm—is extremely painful to me—"

In this passage Isherwood refers to the son's (or his own) "lack of enthusiasm" for the Poshocratic world the boy's father represents. This critique of father-son relations and Poshocracy continues:

> All at once I was struck by the bitter irony of the situation—that such a father should have begotten such a son. "Surely," I said to myself, "this is the method by

which our sins are punished, even while we are still alive." It was a solemn and affecting thought and I was touched with pity for the old man. I tried to console him.

"Surely, sir," I said, "it is early to judge your son's tastes. Perhaps a little more experience will ripen his judgment."

Sir Murgatroyd, comprehending the implied suggestion, informs Starn that he has been "questioning many Cambridge men of late" and has heard something of Starn's career: "You are, I believe, tolerably vicious." He then bribes Starn to take his son to London and "to provide him, by every means within your power, with the experience which, we are both agreed, would be so invaluable." Debauchery ensues, but not in full detail as "the remainder of this fable was burnt by the common hang-man."[35] The point of the story is to show that Poshocracy will go to any lengths to quash non-conformity.

Isherwood did not mind poking fun at his own personal foibles. Starn and Hynd are driving in the country when they get a punctured tire and stop at a garage where the workers, in anticipation of a visit from their boss, are frantically putting all in order:

> Starn inquires, "And he insists on Tidiness?"
>
> "Oh yes sir, 'e's nuts on it. 'E take on something frightful if anything isn't just so."
>
> "He's got a temper has he?"
>
> "An 'orful temper, sir. I've never seen nor heard anything like it."[36]

Clearly this passage shows that Isherwood was not above parodying his own compulsive obsession with tidiness.

In "Christmas in the Country," some straightforward vulgarity satirizes the sophisticated drawing-room genre: "And now I watched him as he escorted Miss Belmare into the refreshment-room. For a moment, her voice was audible above the sounds of the dance. 'I hope I'm not old-fashioned,' she was saying, 'but I've no sort of use for these bloody lesbians. I believe in girls being able to give a man a bloody good clean straight fuck, and no nonsense. I hope you're with me there, even if you do wear collars fit for a eunuch.'" And when she hears a bad joke, she says, "if you can't think of anything funnier than that, you'd better save your wind for farts."[37]

At Cambridge Mortmere was a preoccupation for Isherwood and Upward and continued to be afterwards as well. Their secret city became the substitute reality for a Cambridge reality that neither could tolerate. For Isherwood Mortmere's reality overtook the Cambridge reality when he decided to get "sent down" or thrown out of school so that he could pursue writing as a career instead of staying at Cambridge to become a don. His method for expulsion was to "Camp" his final exams by providing Mortmere-ish answers. (Isherwood would later define High and Low Camp in *The World in the Evening* [1954].) This was the ultimate rebellious joke that only Isherwood's youthful and misguided ego-centricism could have imagined was really a stroke of independence. If this was a Test, it was another symptom of a Truly Weak cry for approval that masked his inability to communicate with his mother and tell her that he did not want to become a don but a writer instead.

If this was the case, there were easier ways to leave Cambridge. The Mortmere fantasy was an extension of Isherwood's "Toy-Drawer-Times" child-hood, and the preservation of that womb-cocoon took psychological precedence over any conventional method of rebelling against his mother, Cambridge, and the British tradition. Katherine Bucknell adds, "In Mortmere he let his imagina-tion run wild, overcoming even the smallest restraints of reason and decorum within the apparently secure parameters of a nursery game." Bucknell thought that "Upwards' example enabled him to do this. At Repton, Isherwood had admired 'Chalmers' for his great commitment to rebellion, his more thorough going defiance of school authority."[38]

In *Lions and Shadows* Isherwood explains that he was motivated to leave Cambridge early because Upward, a year ahead of him, would be leaving: "And, next autumn, Chalmers would be gone. That was the blackest part of the whole prospect. I simply couldn't imagine how I should be able to bear Cambridge without him. Suppose I stayed on and did, somehow, get a degree: what would become of me? I should have to be a schoolmaster. But, I didn't want to be a schoolmaster—I wanted, at last, to escape from that world. . . . How I longed to be independent . . . and I had to wait another whole year. . . . Chalmers and I were walking round the college. . . . I said: 'You know, there's a perfectly simple way out of this. I shall have to get myself sent down.' Chalmers was delighted" (*LS*, 125–26). After his exam Isherwood was asked by his tutor to explain himself:

> The tutor spoke his language: I had shown ingratitude to the college and to those who had taught me, I had betrayed my responsibilities. . . . I sat silent. What was there to say? My act now seemed more than ever unreal to me: failing the tri-pos had merely been an extension of dream-action on the plane of reality. How was I to tell the tutor that we had often plotted to blow him sky-high with a bomb? How could I talk to this perfect stranger about Mortmere and Hynd and Starn. . . . He was asking me whether the trouble had been money. Oh no sir. Had it anything to do with a woman. No sir. Nothing. Was it—any other kind of trouble? [Isherwood's dash would seem to indicate that the tutor was implying homosexual trouble.] I felt very apologetic. I should hardly have blamed him if he had given me a good smack-ing. (*LS*, 134–35)

Saved from a formal expulsion, Isherwood was asked to leave Cambridge. His rebellious cry for approval had accomplished that much of an end, although by *Lions and Shadows* even he seemed to realize that his means of exiting was rather silly, and he had, indeed, deserved a "good smacking." In 1925 he was free from the university, but he was hardly free from the psychic need that had motivated the creation and imaginative exploration of Mortmere, even to the point of Mortmere insinuating its way into his exam. Camping the exam was Isherwood's Test for himself and another cry for approval intended to maintain his esteem with Upward. Since, by his own definition, all Tests that seek attention are symptomatic of insecurity, Isherwood had been Truly Weak. Had he been capable of calm self-appraisal, he might have chosen to withdraw from Cambridge quietly, but he was immaturely frantic and could not fathom what he was truly afraid of. He would say years later concerning another emotional predicament, "What I am really trying to run away from is myself."[39] He began running away from Kathleen and Frank after St. Edmund's and his father's death. He ran towards fantasy, which was an extension of the pre-St. Edmund's womb-cocoon. The fantasies of Mortmere began at Cambridge but did not end there; they followed Isherwood into the workaday world. Under the pressures of the everyday world, Mortmere succumbed to Isherwood's changing reality and underwent significant transformations.

THE RECESSIONAL FROM CAMBRIDGE

Upon departing from Cambridge, Isherwood wrote a long, defiant, and unapologetic Mortmere poem concerning his exit:

> Midnight. It is the hour so long deferred
> But yet before we leave, tutor, a word.
>
> . . . we take our leave and go
> Into the darkness from those pleasant snuggeries,
>
> Warm dens well fit for academic buggeries
> And social antics. You will never know
> Why, when the clouds massed, ochreous and bloody,
> We left you, quietly sitting, tutor, in your study.
>
> Therefore, we leave you, snug in Cambridge town
> With your cigar, your glass of old dry sherry,
> Your smirking and pum-busted-secretary,
> Curtly dictating with closed eyes and frown:
> Dear Starn, the Master has removed your name
> From the college books. Personally I will not blame. . .
>
> Outcast, subject to disapproving glances,
> We pack our suitcases and pay our bills,
> Casually scatter tips and arsenic pills

And leave, two idiots who have missed their chances.
Yes, tutor, two young men must go alone
Into the night, because Beauty ailed them to the bone.

And yet, not quite alone. A certain few
Chosen companions, a jolly troup
Come with us, such as would gladly stoop
To eat dog's excrement like Irish stew,
To savor cat's urine like caviare,
Rather than blaspheme the beauty which they are.[40]

Isherwood follows these lines with a long litany of the Mortmere locales and characters who were the "chosen companions, the jolly troup" that would accompany himself and Upward into the world. The secondary world of Mortmere was dominating the primary world of Isherwood's perceptions and in one form or another Mortmere would do so for the rest of his life. Isherwood would make his way in a new world where The Others still lurked, but where they were not so clearly defined as they had been at school. Gray areas would intrude into Mortmere's unrelenting black and white frontiers.

When he left Cambridge in 1925, Isherwood was twenty-one years old and had money saved from his school allowance. He had no real expenses since he had gone home to live with the "female relative." To mark the occasion of his entry into the non-school world, Isherwood bought a second-hand car: "Unlike my motor-bicycle, the Renault had no connection whatever with 'The Test.' She represented, indeed a mood of complete irresponsibility. I could hardly have found a more absurd way of spending my money" (LS, 136). One could say it was a Test of a different sort, another cry for attention and autonomy by doing something entirely gratuitous. He certainly got attention, by chauffeuring all who asked, until he tired of it.

One of these offered rides, however, introduced him to the Mangeot family, the basis for the Cheurets in Lions and Shadows: Andre, a concert violinist, his wife, Olive (Rose in Lions and Shadows), and two young boys, Sylvain and Fowke (Edouard and Jean in Lions and Shadows). Isherwood let himself be adopted by them and co-opted their lives by becoming Mangeot's secretary, turning a part-time situation into a full-time excuse to be in their company: "This is how real human people live, I thought as my eyes wandered over the comfortable untidiness of the large room. . . . This was another world" (LS, 139). It was another secondary world for Isherwood. After having admired Upward's messiness, which Isherwood saw as a sign of independence compared to his own fussiness, untidiness had become a virtue. "I could hardly believe in my astounding good luck. That I should be allowed to come to this house every day; to have a part . . . in the life of the Cheuret family seemed too wonderful to be true" (LS, 141). Isherwood found a surrogate family to give him approval. He also had a job, which allowed him to rationalize his having left Cambridge. In fact, his job paid a pittance, and he was really living off the allowance that his mother—the unnamed one—was still giving him. Another benefit to Isherwood in knowing the violinist was that "Cheuret's career was a salutary object-lesson to 'Isherwood-the artist'"(*LS,* 147). By associating with an artist, Isherwood could feel like one himself, like an aspiring writer. Consequently, his ego received some much needed encouragement, since he was accepted into a new womb-cocoon by a bohemian family of Anti-Others, he was encouraged in his ambition to be a writer, and he was able to be an older brother figure to twelve-year-old Sylvain. Sylvain drew animal cartoons and Isherwood matched them with nonsense poems, which together they made into a storybook. Not only had Isherwood reinserted himself into a new womb-cocoon, he was duplicating a fantasy component of the original. The storybook with Sylvain was called, *People One Ought to Know,* a title that recalls *The History of My Friends,* a storybook Isherwood created when he was a child. *People One Ought to Know* was not published in book form until 1982. An introduction by Sylvain's nephew, Andrew Mangeot, explains the original's creation:

> Christopher worked in the mews house at Cresswell Place for about a year and quickly became one of the family. He fell in love with all its members and they, in turn, looked upon him as the elder brother and son he longed to be. It was, in a sense, from the former role that *People One Ought to Know* grew, [and] tracing [it] to the completed project is really a glimpse into the impulsiveness of childhood. Sylvain began by humanizing a couple of delightful comic animal sketches. . . . Pleased with the drawings but dissatisfied with [his own] poetry, Sylvain decided Christopher might be able to do better. . . . Every mad couplet still preserves the happiness and enjoyment of that youthful idyllic interlude, the empathy with drawings that were entirely lacking in self-consciousness and therefore so perfectly right; and most of all, the deep love for the temporary home and family where, by sheer chance, he found himself.[41]

When Andrew Mangeot refers to the "impulsiveness of childhood," one can include a twenty-one- year-old Isherwood who knew little of the world and had spent much of his time at school fantasizing. He continued to do so with Sylvain. Isherwood said of this period: "I had fallen in love with the entire family. My attitude towards them became violently possessive. . . . I wanted, in some vague daydream manner, to help and protect them against the outside world that seemed to menace their gaiety and their curious quality of innocence: and I wanted also, contradictorily, to be taken under their wing, to be acknowledged by them as elder brother and son" (*LS,* 153). Isherwood wanted to be "Christopher the hero-savior" and protect his new family against The Others. He continued in his compulsive-obsessive way to see his new life with the Mangeots as a continuation of his us against them mentality.

He now felt part of a real "clan." In this setting, the clan of two now became the clan of five, and the residue of Mortmere was evident in the Christopher-Sylvain storybook collaboration. The storybook features Sylvain's drawing of a crocodile with a top hat, long coat, and small carpetbag initialed H.S.Z. The drawing is accompanied by the following lines from Isherwood:

> Here Mr. Z——, a crocodile,
> Boards the boat train for Carlisle.
> Living is cheap there, that's the reason
> So many are visiting it this season.
> The careless shopmen leave large chops
> Hanging outside butchers' shops,
> And if you're clever, you can lunch,
> Without paying, off a bunch
> Of liver sausages, or maybe
> A stupid nursemaid's left a baby
> Unprotected in its pram—
> (Babies are nice with ham)—
> Hence the sleek and Jolly Smile
> On the face of this crocodile.[42]

Much of the doggerel verse in their collaboration has a dash of adolescent macabre that must have delighted Isherwood as much as it did Sylvain. This paternal and fraternal role was a new and welcome one for Isherwood, who had the opportunity to do something for others rather than The Others doing things to him. In 1925 it may have been his father whom Isherwood was emulating while he enjoyed his relationship with Sylvain. With Upward, who was a year older, Isherwood had been the slightly younger brother waiting for his elder to lead by example. With Sylvain, Isherwood was to reverse roles. He was no longer just a follower; he now had the opportunity to be the teacher, nurturer, and protector, a role that intimated the possibilities—however latent and as yet unconscious—of the Truly Strong Man.

Conversely, the influence of Mortmere was still very apparent, finding its way into the verses he wrote for Sylvain and serving as the subject of new stories. "The Javanese Sapphires" was written for Sylvain. In it, a giant python swallows the sapphires. This story recalls the Holmes adventures of "The Blue Carbuncle" and "The Six Napoleons." When Starn talks with the owner of the sapphires, an old-school chum, his former classmate remembers the glory days on "the inside of a [rugby] scrum," and Starn responds, "I should have expected you to remember that *our* school life was not devoted to Rugby Football."[43] There is a plot to steal the sapphires that includes the mention of spies and guns and a mocking parrot who repeats the platitudes of The Others. This story forecasts the plots, replete with spies, guns, platitudes, and references to psychology, that were to become staples of the early Auden and his imitators of the 1930s.

Another Mortmere story of this period is "Prefatory Epistle to my Godson on the Study of History." The pseudo-godson is Sylvain. In 1972, Auden published, *Epistle to a Godson,* a volume of poems dedicated to Stephen Spender's son Philip (the title is Auden's homage to Isherwood's story). In "Prefatory Epistle," Starn proclaims that "man is the sole and supreme irrelevance. He is without method, without order, without proportion. His childish passions, enthusiasms, beliefs are unsightly protuberances in the surface of the Universal Curve." Starn adds, "how perfect would be the evolutions of nature in a world unpeopled." Starn also warns his godson to be skeptical of the New Testament saying in a footnote: "I refer to this exploded forgery with all due reference to Professor Pillard, who has, by the Historical Method, clearly proved that it is the work of Mr. Aldous Huxley."[44] Huxley in the 1920s was a marked man by The Others who considered him the most cynical of the post-war cynics.

Isherwood's time in the Mangeot household saw Mortmere take a slightly different turn as prompted by his big-brotherly response to the Mangeot children. The stories were parables cautioning the bohemian Mangeots about the nefarious world of The Others. As such, these stories were a prelude to the "parable-art" that would become a standard for him in the 1930s.

In 1927 the culmination of Mortmere for Isherwood was his last and most ambitious story in this setting and the ultimate us-against-them parable, called "The World War." The war in question, however, is not any real war but the old school wars of St. Edmund's, Repton, and Cambridge, now aggrandized into a saga of mythic conflict with heavy satire and sarcasm. In "The World War" there are lines, ideas, and themes that would be reiterated over the next thirteen years by Isherwood, Auden, and their generation: enemies, known and unknown; spies, secret agents, traitors; borders and frontiers (actual and of the mind); a fascist-like leader before the term had the meaning it would soon have; battles with tanks, an air raid with a commander in "yachting-cap and white ducks," poison gas; memorials with wry inscriptions, and, of course, grieving mothers spouting patriotism. Following are some examples from "The World War" that are tone-setters for future works by Isherwood and his peers during the first half of the 1930s when noir satire preceded the bleaker work of the latter half of the decade:

A principal objective: "possession of Miss Forster's Academy for Young Ladies."

An unusual tank: "This remarkable engine of offence contained two arm-chairs, a sofa, a dumb-waiter, a gramophone and a library of the best hundred authors."

A remarkable coincidence in the infirmary: "I felt myself sensibly embarrassed. 'Am I right,' I asked, 'in supposing that all these brave young fellows are suffering from exactly the same complaint—wound, I should have said?'" (The wound is not identified, but one can surmise on one's own. This "wound" would be echoed in 1932 with Auden's "Letter to a Wound" from *The Orators.*)

A quest for a missing friend: "Starving and disguised, I had wandered deep into the heart of the enemy's territory; worn out, yet never weary of my search for my young comrade."

A supreme generalissimo who says: "It is my intention to wage this campaign

to the last drop of *your* blood. There will be no retreat, no capitulation, no surrender. There will be no prisoners or wounded. There will be no relaxation of any
kind."[45] For Isherwood there was, indeed, "no relaxation of any kind." His Anti-
Other stance was solidified and enhanced by knowing the bohemian Anti-Other
Mangeots. More importantly, his knowing the Mangeots heightened the contrast
of their world, which he visited as much as possible, and the world of his
estranged "female relative" where he still lived. His mother represented The
Others and The Others symbolized to Isherwood all of the psychodrama that had
produced Mortmere in the first place and culminated in "The World War." The
elements of this story would carry over into Isherwood's writings of the late
1920s through the 1930s: the us-against-them theme, hatred of the old school,
anti-Poshocracy, and a sense of anti-tradition through parody of the past and of
the present, which included the mocking of Isherwood's own generation and the
self-mocking of Isherwood himself.

From 1914 to 1925, except for vacations, Isherwood had been away from
Kathleen and Frank's womb-cocoon for as long as he had been in it before going
off to St. Edmund's. At school he had been in another cocoon as a form of jail
that was the opposite extreme from the safe "home-self" world that had seemingly ostracized him. For twenty-one years there had been very little middle
ground between these extremes. This polarization can be seen from the contrast
of the secondary worlds Isherwood indulged in: from 1904 to 1914 there was
"The Toy-Drawer-Times," whereas from 1914 to 1925 there was Mortmere.

At Cambridge Isherwood had made sporadic attempts to write realistic
fiction. He abandoned them as unsatisfactory, and they may well have been so,
since he did not have enough real-life experience to call upon as a resource. This
was changing. Isherwood would have new settings for a realistic novel, one which
would take the comic-strip warfare of Mortmere and depict those broad themes
in terms of the more subtle psychological warfare he associated with his mother
and The Others. The paranoid duality of Mortmere, with its traditional style but
bizarre content, had served Isherwood well as a source of broad cartoon entertainment. This duality allowed Isherwood and Upward to give voice to their one-
sided anger aimed at the monolithic, impersonal old school. Now there were
actual people to deal with, which meant undertones and unvoiced inferences that
needed a more realistic technique. Life could no longer be clearly divided into
the blacks and whites of Mortmere. If Isherwood was to become an artist, he now
had to fill in the gray areas. Much of this gray area was compounded by
Isherwood's having told his mother that he was homosexual. Isherwood was
attempting to shock his mother; however, she apparently accepted this news far
better than her son predicted. He was able to bring home his companions to stay
over, and she continued to give him his allowance.

A Transition to Reality

In *Lions and Shadows,* Isherwood describes how he gave up any hope of the Mortmere stories actually being publishable after he met the Mangeots. He realized that absurd plots and characters cannot truly exist side by side with what he called "ordinary people" (*LS,* 165). His new life with the Mangeots required that his writing try another direction. Even though Upward was no longer the exclusive influence on Isherwood's life, he was still an important one, and it would be Upward who inspired a new technique of writing for Isherwood.

Isherwood went to visit Upward in Cornwall, where Upward had the position of live-in tutor. Isherwood listened raptly to Upward's "new theories about novel-writing in general: 'I saw it all suddenly while I was reading *Howard's End.* . . . [E. M.] Forster's the only one who understands what the modern novel ought to be . . . our frightful mistake was that we believed in tragedy: the point is, tragedy's quite impossible nowadays. . . . We ought to aim at being essentially comic writers. . . . The whole of Forster's technique is based on the tea-table: instead of trying to screw all his scenes up to the highest possible pitch, he tones them down until they sound like mother's-meeting gossip. . . . In fact, there's actually *less* emphasis laid on the big scenes than on the unimportant ones: that's what's so utterly terrific. It's the completely new kind of accentuation—like a person talking a different language'" (*LS,* 173–74). Isherwood and Upward were already attuned to making up a different language. Nonetheless, this "new kind of accentuation" was not exactly new, but a return to a style that was actually quite old.

After World War I, the highbrows who sought to change the conditions that had led to the war drew on the following bywords: decentralization, simplicity, reality. Lowbrows were content to forget the war and retreat into the secondary worlds of the cinema and escapist fiction that emphasized style over substance. Among the highbrows, however, there was a call for substance over style. In the 1920s Aldous Huxley wrote copiously on the need for simplicity and reality in literature (and life) with essays such as, "The Subject Matter of Poetry," and "Tragedy and the Whole Truth."[46] He made two assertions: (1) everything and anything between the mundane and the magnificent could and should be suitable subject matter for literature if the artist writes about it as sincere truth and (2) the artist's striving for reality in art was not new but a mode that was as old as classical antiquity: Writing in 1923, Huxley asserted,

> [Writers today] are at liberty to do what Homer did—to write freely about the immediately moving facts of everyday life. Where Homer wrote of horses and tamers of horses [we] write of trains, automobiles, and the various species of . . . bohunks who control the horse-power. Much too much stress has been laid on the newness of the new poetry; its newness is simply a return from the jeweled exquisiteness of the eighteen-nineties to the facts and feelings of ordinary life. There is

nothing intrinsically novel or surprising in the introduction into poetry of machinery and industrialism, of labour unrest and modern psychology: these things
belong to us, they affect us daily as enjoying and suffering beings; they are part of
our lives, just as the kings, the warriors, the horses and chariots, the picturesque
mythology were part of Homer's life. . . . The critics who would have us believe
that there is something essentially unpoetical about a bohunk (whatever a bohunk
may be) and something essentially poetical about Sir Lancelot of the Lake are, of
course, simply negligible.[47]

Writing in 1933, Auden agreed. "[The poet writes about] birth, death, the
Beatific vision, the abysses of hatred and fear. . . . Yes, all of these, but not these only.
Everything that we remember no matter how trivial: the mark on the wall, the joke
at luncheon, word games . . . are equally the subject of poetry. We shall do poetry a
great disservice if we confine it only to the major experiences of life."[48] Auden would
also argue that "a moment in which the characters are emotionally relaxed may be
just as significant as one in which they are emotionally stirred."[49] This idea reflects
the "tea-tabling" technique that Upward admired in Forster. To "tea-table" was to
reveal important and even emotional information without necessarily doing so in a
traditionally histrionic tragic scene. Jane Austen had mastered tea-tabling a century
earlier, particularly in *Emma*. Isherwood himself alludes to tea-tabling in a
Mortmere story when a character says: "You know, I think the trouble with all you
literary johnnies is that you're always looking for mysteries in the most ordinary
everyday things."[50]

With respect to the "ordinary, everyday things," Huxley writes that the commonplace and the tragic can be combined:

> What are the values of Wholly-Truthful art? Wholly-Truthful art overflows the
> limits of tragedy and shows us, if only by hints and implications, what happened
> before the tragic story began, what will happen after it is over, what is happening
> simultaneously elsewhere (and "elsewhere" includes all those parts of the minds and
> bodies of the protagonists not immediately engaged in the tragic struggle). Tragedy
> is an isolated eddy on the surface of a vast river that flows majestically, irresistibly,
> around, beneath, and to either side of it. Wholly-Truthful art contrives to imply the
> existence of the entire river as well as the eddy. . . . Consequently, Wholly-Truthful
> art produces in us an effect quite different from that produced by tragedy. Our
> mood when we have read a Wholly-Truthful book is never one of heroic exultation;
> it is one of resignation, of acceptance. (Acceptance can also be heroic.) The cathar-
> sis of tragedy is violent and apocalyptic; but the milder catharsis of Wholly-Truthful
> literature is more lasting. There is no reason why the two kinds of literature should
> not exist simultaneously. . . . The human spirit has need of both.[51]

Isherwood was not yet thinking in quite these terms, but his recognition of
Forster's technique shows that he understood that there was a difference between

Mortmere and a novel. Now that Forster was the new icon for emulation, Isherwood made tea-tabling a matter of life and fiction: "In my journal, I raged against myself, as the fawning spaniel, the born parasite, the masochistic self-confessor, the public lavatory that anyone might flush. But I'd astonish them yet. . . . the change would begin . . . into the new life. . . . I was Christopher Isherwood no longer, but a satanically proud, icy, impenetrable demon; an all-knowing, all-pardoning saviour of mankind; a martyr-evangelist of the tea-table, from whom the most atrocious drawing-room tortures could wring no more than a polite proffer of the buttered scones" (*LS*, 196–97).

Isherwood would now be a detached observer of human behavior. He would later incorporate his observations into tea-table renditions which would understatedly reveal the hidden tragedies concealed by polite teatime banter. Isherwood's initial attempt at realism was a novel titled *Seascape with Figures*. Upward, his sounding board, was not impressed. Isherwood decided to put it aside and undertake further philosophical mulling.

In this mulling phase Isherwood planned an "immense novel; nothing less ambitious than a survey of the post-war generation." In technique, he said, "The treatment must be nearly pure *Objective*. The epic myth. In a sense, there must be no actual 'development.' Like gossip. Very slow-moving maddeningly deliberate genre-packed scenes" (*LS*, 206). Auden would later say that the literary artist was "a mixture of spy and gossip."[52] Isherwood said of his planned novel that the "title was to be *The North-West Passage*. . . . it was a private key to a certain group of responses; all needless to say, related to the idea of 'The Test.' More rationally, it symbolized, in my mind, the career of the neurotic hero, the Truly Weak Man—antithesis of 'the truly strong man' spoken of by the homicidal paranoiac whose statement is quoted by Bleuler: 'The feeling of impotence brings forth the strong words, the bold sounds to battle are emitted by the trumpet called persecution insanity. The signs of the truly strong are repose and good will. . . . the strong individuals are those who without any fuss do their duty. These have neither the time nor the occasion to throw themselves into a pose and try to be something great.'"

Isherwood then suggests that, for the Truly Strong Man, "it is not necessary for him to try and prove to himself that he is not afraid. . . . The Test exists only for the Truly Weak Man: no matter whether he passes it or whether he fails, he cannot alter his essential nature. The Truly Strong Man travels straight across the broad America of normal life, taking always the direct reasonable route. But 'America' is just what the truly weak man, the neurotic hero, dreads. And so, with immense daring, and with an infinitely greater expenditure of nervous energy, he prefers to attempt the huge northern circuit, the laborious, terrible north-west passage, avoiding life; and his end, if he does not turn back, is to be lost for ever in the blizzard and the ice" (*LS*, 206–208).

While this description shows Isherwood's comprehension of his own neurosis, understanding a neurosis does not mean overcoming it; in Isherwood's case he was far from changing himself, but knew enough about his inner psychology to depict it in the characters of his own work. The excitement of the theme, however, overwhelmed the practical details of actually writing the novel, as Isherwood finally conceded, "I was trying to pack a small suitcase with the contents of three cabin trunks: my little comedy of bohemian life was so overloaded with symbolism [that the] interplay of *motifs* (to use a very favourite word of mine just then) would have been merely a series of descriptions of effects" (*LS*, 208).

Isherwood abandoned it, but *The North-West Passage* is one of the most important novels never written. Isherwood's conceptualization established the theme of the Truly Weak and Truly Strong Man. Of even greater importance is the theme that, within each individual, the poles of Truly Weak and Truly Strong are inevitably in conflict. They are opposing aspects within one person that are attempting to find balance and create intense friction in the effort. This duality is like the Vedantic reconciliation of opposites that fuels the progress of the universe. In 1926 Isherwood knew nothing of this metaphysical concept, but was subconsciously acting on the idea. Vedantists believe universal truths exist whether one recognizes them at a particular time or not. For some, what was once intuited subliminally will be more tangibly elucidated over time. This was the case for Isherwood. When he came to America in 1939, he was attracted to Vedanta because it explained and gave a nomenclature to ideas and themes he had only partially understood before.

Isherwood summarizes the plot and characterizations of *The North-West Passage* to demonstrate that his theme was practicable even if the actual writing of it was not quite as assured. After having described a certain amount of almost neo-mystical histrionics, Isherwood arrives at the key component with respect to the direction of his future writing: "Roger Garland becomes increasingly fascinated by the personality of Tommy. Indeed, he comes to feel that Tommy and he are united by some mysterious bond: there is even a physical resemblance between them. (*What I was actually trying to suggest was that Tommy and Roger were two halves or aspects of the same person.* Tommy is an embodiment of Roger's dream of himself as an epic character: in fact both Roger and Tommy are the Truly Weak Man—but, while Tommy will one day be lost trying to force the North-West Passage, Roger will never even dare to attempt it)" (*LS*, 211). After a number of Roger's machinations, and an argument with a woman, Katherine (Could this represent Kathleen?), "Tommy has rushed out of the house, jumped on to his appallingly powerful motor-bicycle and ridden away at full speed." Roger, who is jealous of Tommy's daring, assures Katherine that Tommy would never really hurt himself but also declares that "their whole cult of Tommy has been a fake. He is a nice boy; [but] there is nothing in the least wild or dangerous about him; he is perfectly tame . . . [and she] needn't worry." Ironically, Tommy's dead body is eventually carried back with a broken neck from a crash.

Katherine blames Roger for having encouraged Tommy in the foolhardiness Roger enjoyed vicariously. Then Roger, representing Isherwood's perspective, says, "And, thinking the whole affair over in the course of the months that follow, Roger comes to the conclusion that this is perfectly true. 'After all,' he reflects, not without a certain furtive conceit, 'it is people like myself who are dangerous. We are the real destroyers'" (*LS*, 212–13). The life within the mind generates the Truly Weak symptoms of neuroses and psychoses. Sometimes bystanders like Roger can influence others to their destruction.

The idea of "halving" that is explored in *The North-West Passage* became a standard in Isherwood's diaries and fiction:

> In May 1939, Isherwood writes of film director Berthold Viertel (who becomes the basis of the character Bergmann in *Prater Violet*) that "all of his arguments were, so plainly, between the two halves of himself." (*D*, 41)
>
> In March 1956, Isherwood records the following entry: "During the hashish episode, it should become clear that Dante and Denny [in the novel *Down There on a Visit*] are two halves of the same person. They are said to resemble each other." (*D*, 592)
>
> His entry for October 1958 shows further evidence of his concern with the doubling motif: "As for Don (Bachardy)—he's a complete family, and I wouldn't exchange this relationship for any other kind; unless—yes—the perfect twin brother.." (*D*, 781)

For Isherwood and his generation, duality became a principle that drove their art.

In *The North-West Passage*, the persistent conflict of us against them still dominated, but had also evolved into us against us, I against you, and, ultimately, I against I. Isherwood's years away at school had clearly demarcated the frontier between The Others and Anti-Others. Having been asked to leave Cambridge because of his Truly Weak trashing of his exams, he was forced to live like a spy with the enemy—his mother—while pursuing his own identity with the Mangeots. Furtively, he recorded the daily doings of both worlds, concluding that neither was so clearly black and white as the unreal world he created in the Mortmere stories. He recognized that the human animal, starting with himself, had coping guises for different aspects of existence, which required, as Eliot had said in "Prufrock," that one "prepare a face to meet the faces that you meet." Isherwood began to recognize the value of socially realistic fiction. He realized that his art should imitate life; human beings are psychological puzzles and should be depicted as such in novels. Characters should have their underlying duality revealed in the contexts of their normal, everyday, tea-table lives, as they chat superficially while spitting the occasional venom that reveals all.

3 ACTS OF REBELLION II
Themes Enunciated: The Guru and His Disciples

It is curious that before I knew Isherwood and before I had a read a word by him, I had been so convinced by his legend. . . . Auden seemed to us the highest peak within the range of our humble vision from Oxford; for Auden there was another peak, namely Isherwood . . . he was the Critic in whom Auden had absolute trust. If Isherwood disliked a poem, Auden would destroy it without demur. After I saw Isherwood . . . he simplified all the problems which entangled me, merely by describing his own life and his own attitudes.[1]

Perhaps my greatest debt to Christopher is the confidence he gave me in my work. He was more than a young rebel passing through a phase of revolt against conventional morality and orthodox religion. He also recognized that nearly everyone wanted something out of life which he or she had been taught to conceal. He was on the side of the forces which make a work of art, even more than he was interested in art itself and on the side of the struggle towards self-realization. He simply believed in his friends and their work.[2]

Stephen Spender, 1951

Yet how beautiful your books are,
So observant, so witty, so profound
And how nice you are really,
So affectionate, so understanding, so helpful, such wonderful company
A brilliant young novelist?
My greatest friend?
Si, Signor.[3]

W. H. Auden, 1937

Auden's and Spender's fond recollections acknowledge Isherwood's friendship and influence. Isherwood's personal world view was also enhanced, since a teacher learns from his students. Before meeting the Mangeots, Auden, and Spender, Isherwood's range of friends and acquaintances largely began and ended with Upward. According to Spender, when he and Isherwood first met, "he told me how, when he was at Cambridge, he and Chalmers [Upward] had isolated themselves completely, remaining almost entirely in one or other of their rooms, writing the stories about a fantasy world called Mortmere."[4] Even Spender played the game by using the name of Chalmers instead of Upward.

After leaving Cambridge Isherwood's world expanded. Mortmere would not be enough if he was to consider himself seriously as Isherwood the artist. As Spender said, Isherwood "was on the side of the forces which make a work of art." If so, he would need to understand and harness these forces, if not to take control of himself, then to take control over his art. As seen in Isherwood's *The North-West Passage* he had thought out the concepts of the Test and the Truly Weak and Truly Strong Man. At this stage a Truly Strong Man was no more than an ideal as role models seemed scarce. There were many examples of the Truly Weak Man, starting with Isherwood himself. Since Isherwood considered psychology important to his artistic development, 1927 was a propitious time for him to reacquaint himself with Oxford's leading amateur psychologist, Wystan Hugh Auden, who is called Hugh Weston in *Lions and Shadows*.

Isherwood recalls that their psychoanalytic discussions of life and art helped him to define the scheme of the Truly Weak and Truly Strong Man. In 1976 Isherwood describes his life-long interest in psychology by explaining the main theme of his autobiographical *Christopher and His Kind*: "It is a description of the inner drives and external forces which took me away from England. I'm always conscious of the psychosomatic aspect of life. I mean, in other words, that there is part of one's will over which one has no conscious control."[5] In 1927 he was not quite so rational on the subject.

DODO MINOR

> At my preparatory school, during the last two years of the War, there had been a boy named Hugh Weston . . . nicknamed "Dodo Minor" because of the solemn and somewhat birdlike appearance of his bespectacled elder brother. . . . His father was a doctor: Weston had discovered, very early in life, the key to the bookcase which contained anatomical manuals with coloured German plates. To several of us . . . he confided the first naughty stupendous breath-taking hints about the facts of sex. . . . With his hinted forbidden knowledge and stock of mispronounced scientific words, portentously uttered, he enjoyed among us, his semi-savage credulous school fellows the status of a kind of witch-doctor. . . . Just before Christmas, 1925, a mutual acquaintance brought him to tea. I found him very little changed. (*LS*, 181–82)

Auden gave Isherwood the opportunity for dialogue on art interpreted through psychological theory. This interested Isherwood enormously in relation to himself and his writing. When Auden casually told Isherwood that he had switched from his childhood interest of lead-mining to poetry, Isherwood just as casually asked to see some of his poetry and "a big envelope full of manuscript arrived, a few days later, by post. . . . I was touched and flattered to discover, bit by bit, that he [Auden] admired me; looked up to me, indeed, as sort of literary elder brother. My own vanity and inexperience propelled me into this role easily enough" (*LS,*

189–90). Each spurred the other's imagination. Isherwood said later: "We were always making things up, having fantasy conversations to describe the future to each other, telling stories, discussing everything you can imagine, giving imitations of people, making up parodies of different writers—the way people talk when they know each other very well."[6] Isherwood notes that when Auden's tastes moved away from Thomas Hardy and Edward Thomas to T. S. Eliot and *The Waste Land,* their conversations now required Eliot-like allusions for what they called *The Waste Land* Game: "quotations and misquotations were allowed, together with bits of foreign languages, proper names and private jokes" (*LS,* 190). The duo played with a private nomenclature that suited their mutual artistic interests. Isherwood was looking for a new way of writing that was to be more objective. Auden believed that a writer's detachment should be like the empirical eye of the scientist. To make his point Isherwood writes that Auden did not use so much artistic terms but "substituted oddments of scientific, medical and psycho-analytical jargon: his magpie brain was a hoard of curious and suggestive phrases from Jung, Rivers, Kretschmer and Freud. He peppered his work liberally with such terms as 'eutectic,' 'sigmoid curve,' 'Arch-Monad,' 'ligature,' 'gastropod'; seeking therefore to produce what he himself described as a clinical effect. To be 'clinically minded' was, he said, the first duty of a poet. Love wasn't exciting or even romantic or even disgusting; it was funny. . . . Poetry must be classic, clinical and austere" (*LS,* 191).

In addition to campaigning for clinical austerity, Auden also declared his "feelings about heroic Norse literature—his own personal variety of 'War-fixation.'" Isherwood began to read Icelandic sagas and he reached a startling conclusion: "These warriors, with their feuds, their practical jokes, their dark threats conveyed in puns and riddles and deliberate understatements: they seemed so familiar—where had I met them before? Yes, I recognized them now: they were the boys at our preparatory school. Weston was pleased with the idea: we discussed it a good deal, wondering which of our school fellows best corresponded to the saga characters. In time, the school-saga world became for us a kind of Mortmere—a Mortmere founded upon our preparatory-school lives, just as the original Mortmere had been founded upon my life with Chalmers at Cambridge" (*LS,* 192–93). For Isherwood, Upward, and Auden, the profound influence of their pubescent and adolescent prep and public school years continued to haunt their conceptions of real life. The crossing of the saga with the old school was an imaginative leap, but one that was a continuation of the imaginative leaping that their progenitors had begun long before in the primeval tribe. "Mythifying" is a necessary component of human development. Myths explain the inexplicable: thunder, lightning, rainbows, human existence. The myths of the tribe became rituals so that the tribe developed and retained a singular identity that enabled it to cohere and grow into the city, state, and nation. In the past, it was the *teller,* the poet or bard as historian, who acquired a higher status in the tribe's hierarchy because of his gift for "mythifying." Auden believed that primitive man developed language as a reactionary process:

> If an Australian aborigine sits down on a pin he says, "ow." Dogs with bones growl at the approach of other dogs. English, Russian, Brazilian, all mothers "coo" to their babies. Sailors at any port, pulling together on a hawser: watch them and listen—heaving, they grunt together "Ee-ah." This is the first language.
>
> We generally think of language being words used to point to things, to say something is *this* or *that,* but the earliest use of language was not this: it was used to express the feelings of the speaker; feelings about something happening to him (the prick of the pin), or attitudes towards other things in the world (the other hungry dog; the darling baby), or, again, as a help to doing something with others of his own kind (pulling the boat in).
>
> Life is one whole thing made up of smaller whole things. The largest thing . . . the universe . . . the smallest . . . the negative electrons of the atom which run round its central positive nucleus, already a group. So too for us, nucleus and cell, cell and organ, organ and the human individual, individual and family, nation and world, always groups. . . . The whole cannot exist without the part, nor the part without the whole.[7]

There is no real distinction between the particular or the universal, and language is the recording secretary of this perpetual continuum. The non-duality of the particular within the universal and the construct of a "perpetual continuum" are basic tenets of mysticism. In Vedantic terms, Isherwood and Auden in the 1920s were reacting intuitively to subconscious truths that they would later place in a philosophical context.

Isherwood and Auden were recognizing the perpetual continuum in connecting the ancient Icelandic sagas to the contemporary old school saga. As contemporary *tellers,* they would "mythify" particular aspects of the old school by identifying those aspects within the school context that would be universally recognizable in any context. As Isherwood said, the school boys were the same as the saga warriors.

With this realization that the Icelandic sagas had just been ancient realities that were turned into myths, Isherwood understood that myths were just previous realities extrapolated and aggrandized. He would no longer need to write about the mentality of the old school in the more rarified metaphors of Mortmere; now he could attempt to depict them directly: "I actually tried the experiment of writing a school story in what was a kind of hybrid language composed of saga phraseology and schoolboy slang. And soon after this, Weston produced a short verse play in which the two worlds are so confused that it is almost impossible to say whether the characters are epic heroes or members of a school O.T.C. [Officer Training Corps]" (*LS,* 193). The story was "Gems of Belgian Architecture." Auden's play was an earlier version of what became *Paid on Both Sides.* Both were written in the obscurantist secret code of their exclusive gang. The Isherwood-Auden gang continued where the Isherwood-Upward gang left off.

There was no need to pretend that the old school was something else, as

Isherwood and Upward had done with Mortmere. The "feuds" and "dark threats" of the sagas were understood to be no different than the feuds and dark threats of their experiences at school. Isherwood's writing would now be a direct reaction to his miserable school life. Mortmere's extended metaphor had been broad fantasy to "avoid suffering." Now, somewhat distanced from the prison of school itself, Isherwood deals more realistically with his memories of it in "Gems of Belgian Architecture." Though written in 1927, this story was not published until 1965 in *Exhumations*. In "Gems" Isherwood writes down the first conscious intimations of the Test and of the Truly Weak and Truly Strong Man.

Jewels of Isherwood's Infrastructure

This story is based on St. Edmund's during World War I and reiterates an atmosphere shrouded with the cult of the dead, the patriotic cant and rant, and the pressure to conform. The "Gems" of the title are picture-cards from cigarette packs that the boys obtain by "cadging" them from soldiers stationed near the school. Compiling a completed set is a game that achieves status and alleviates boredom. Clans are formed and feud accordingly with a precise penal code. One punishment for perceived transgressions is to be "gorse-bushed." Isherwood details this penalty in his introduction to "Gems."

> To be thrown into the midst of one of these prickly bushes was painful, needless to say, even dangerous; but the real misery of the punishment was that it expressed complete rejection, expulsion from our society. In my story, because of its saga overtones, the gorse-bushing of Dwight has to be an act of revenge; but it was usually inflicted as a punishment for the sin of sins, which we called "side."
>
> For new bugs [freshmen], side could be almost any behavior which attracted attention to you and suggested therefore that you were forgetting your utter insignificance within the social system. . . . It was not mere presumption, it was an arrogance amounting to impiety. Toward the end of my first term [when Isherwood was twelve years old] a senior . . . was found guilty of side. The other seniors dragged him out of the house . . . chased him all over the grounds. I shall never forget [his] face. . . . he was just a hunted animal, blind with panic, and we were all enemies. He was caught and gorse-bushed at last. He dragged himself out of the bush . . . hardly able to see what he was doing for tears . . . humiliated as he probably never would be, never could be again, in his life. No one spoke to him. We moved aside as he passed. He was an outcast.[8]

At the old school, pain and humiliation were tangible threats. Fear and paranoia were daily realities as well, and one effect of fear is to feel anger at being out of control. If so, then Isherwood's anger at being in such a place could only be directed at the place itself and the person who had sent him there—his mother.

In 1965, when "Gems of Belgian Architecture" was first published, Isherwood believed he needed to explain its obscurantism:

An interval of at least five years is supposed to separate the two halves of the story, but you will probably not become aware of it until you have read on for a couple of paragraphs. In those days I loved to mystify my reader. Indeed, it is quite possible that you may end up baffled . . . so I had better explain that the plot revolves around Sladen. Sladen yielded to the threats of Dog major's spy and swapped number nine of Gems after he had promised it to Dwight. Later ashamed of his cowardice, he stole the entire set of Gems from Griffin's locker and hid them. . . . Maybe he had intended to give them to Dwight after the theft had been forgotten, but was afraid to do so. There are hints that Dwight was Sladens's particular hero at the school; this would explain Sladen's rather flirtatious behavior toward Dwight in the final episode [five years later] and his drunken attempt to create a big theatrical scene, a confrontation of the present and the past, by producing the Gems in the presence of Dwight and his ex-enemy, Griffin. Anyhow, the gems have disappeared from their hiding place, so the scene falls flat.[9]

In letting five years pass from prep school to college, Isherwood "planned to show a group . . . who have evolved historically . . . from the tenth to the twentieth century."[10] The sagas of the past are not so different from the neo-sagas of the present. Isherwood believed the idea for the story better than its execution, but there are important elements in it that indicate a transition from Mortmere to the novels that would be forthcoming.

Retained from Mortmere and in the saga manner are nicknames: Dog Major, Dog Minor (based on Auden), Sale, Footer. There is also a codified nomenclature: "Dog Major's Firm" means his clan, which is in opposition to other "firms." Each firm enlists agents and "spies in all the walks." Highlighted is a vicious competition for the card collecting that seems pointless except to the young psyches desperate for approval. Isherwood's point about pointless competition is that it is Truly Weak. There are leaders and followers with peer pressure to exact loyalty. Implicit and explicit warfare climax with a "gorse-bushing" in the first half of the story. Dwight is gorse-bushed by Dog-major and Griffin's firm, after which he takes a target rifle and shoots at Griffin, barely missing him.

The second half is about the transition from the "tenth to the twentieth century." This transition is in the guise of a superficial sophistication, reminiscent of Eliot's notion of a public face and private face in "Prufrock," rather than in real maturity. One sees how childhood events influence the future. Dwight has become quite chummy with Griffin and the public gorse-bushing of five years before is no longer an issue. This would seem to indicate that the mutual murderous attacks were some kind of tribal bonding.

Sladen, who acted surreptitiously in attempting to help Dwight, but in doing so, precipitated the gorse-bushing, suffers guilt over Dwight's humiliation. This affects Sladen much more than it seems to have affected Dwight, at least with respect to Dwight's public face. There is a great deal in both halves of "Gems" about saving or losing face. Even Dwight, while making amends with Griffin, seems to do so more because they had been leaders and, to that extent, peers, rather than out of any underlying sense of acting Truly Strong. By contrast, he is condescending to Sladen, who is not on a social par with Griffin and therefore unacceptable.

In "Gems," the Mortmere warfare has been extended to us against them and us against us. The distinctions between the students are clear in the first half. There is Dog Major's and Griffin's firm against Dwight's firm. The turnabout in the second half, where former enemies seem to be friends, at least superficially, is more ambiguous, more like the fuzzy edges of real life. This is a reflection of Isherwood's experiences away from Cambridge. At Cambridge he and Upward were the clan of two versus everyone. This is comparable to the first half of "Gems." After Cambridge, Isherwood lived at home, consorting with the enemy. Away from home, he began to know more people socially, and the previously clear divisions of school life were no longer clear. Consequently, in the second half of "Gems," just as in the second half of Isherwood's real life, the divisions are not clear either.

The text itself emphasizes this division through language. The first half contains schoolboy slang: "Griffin let it be published that any junior caught swapping with Dwight would get lammed. Dwight said that nobody need be windy about that, because if Griffin started any lamming he'd get lammed himself; and anyway Griffin was such a flabster" (*E*, 178).

In the second half the boys are eighteen and striving to act like the "gentlemen" they had been trained to be at their prep and public schools; they sound like they have just come from their exclusive Poshocrat club:

> "My God, Ross, do you see that? If that isn't the bloody limit."
>
> ". . . Do you know, I'll bet you anything you like, Legge deliberately worked it so that everybody shall see him talking to a Blue. It's just the sort of idiotic preschoolish thing he'd do. He probably went straight up to Horniman and simply tacked himself on."
>
> "Why shouldn't he, the poor boy, if it amuses him?"
>
> ". . . It's in the most filthily bad taste, that's all." (*E*, 190–91)

Isherwood made the following remarks about the dialogue he invented for another story, also written in 1927: "I had a superstitious faith in the power of exact reporting. Scraps of overheard slang and dialogue, especially the dialogue of strangers, were jotted down and treasured by me; I used them like spells which could bring an entire scene back to life."[11] By using "scraps" of dialogue to inspire scenes, Isherwood was enacting the tea-table technique. Casual conversation implies psychological clues. This is Wholly-Truthful art, as opposed to tragic scenes in which characters unload with histrionic speeches that tell all. In real life, tragic scenes are memorable but rare. The Wholly-Truthful tea-table is where stories are really told— or not told. Since people use language as a medium for the ego to interact with other egos, language is often more about concealing than revealing. In their efforts to combine the saga with the old school, Isherwood and Auden had two concerns regarding their interpretation of psychology in relation to art: (1) the mythological aspects of the saga reflect the past and show how that past inevitably becomes the antecedent influences that dominate the present, and (2) psyches in the present are conflicted with an inner duality that is attempting to resist the influence of the past consciously while succumbing to that influence subconsciously. The two halves of "Gems" convey how the past influences the present. Like Dwight and Griffin, some can overcome the past, or at least appear to do so; however, some cannot defeat the past, a fact evident in Sladen's continuing guilt, since he is denied redemption in the present because the cards are not where he had hidden them five years before. The Truly Weak are motivated by the past, trying by present actions to overcome some unconscious shortcoming engendered by past events.

PAID IN RECIPROCATION

The theme of the past haunting the present also dominates the "short verse play," in which "the two worlds [saga and school] are so confused that it is almost impossible to say whether the characters are epic heroes or members of the school O.T.C." In 1927 and 1928 when Auden wrote the first version of the play that would later become *Paid on Both Sides,* he was depicting the old school as a police state. The early version was not published until 1977 in *The English Auden.* Edward Mendelson said in his introduction to this version that it had been "printed from a typescript that Auden had given to Isherwood."[12] Isherwood gave it to Mendelson after Auden's death in 1973. The early version is half the length of the later play as eventually published by T. S. Eliot in the *Criterion* of January 1930. Later that year, the play was reprinted in Auden's first published book, *Poems.* This was also through the auspices of Eliot, who was poetry editor for the publishers Faber and Faber.

In *Early Auden,* Mendelson's chapter, "Family Ghosts," considers *Paid on Both Sides* to be the result of themes and ideas that had gestated in Auden's poems of the previous two years—poems that Isherwood had read and arbitrated upon in his role of literary mentor. Of these poems, Mendelson notes that Auden had imitated "Eliot's driest and most satiric manner," and that "most of the poems Auden wrote during his first years at Oxford describe variations on a single theme: life is a constant state of isolation and stagnated desire."[13] Much of this isolation was brought about by the alienating effects of the depersonalized industrial city-state. Even more of the isolation was brought about by the old school where the highbrow, unathletic Auden remembered that he had felt isolated from the general run of the hearties. Auden's early poems feature an impersonal witness as a cypher in the manner of the Watcher in Spanish, or a Hynd or Starn. Auden's cypher is the unidentified stranger, wandering through town and country, belonging to neither. Of these poems, Mendelson points out that "The Watershed" is aptly titled since it marks the beginning of Auden's maturity as a poet:

> Added to Auden's familiar landscape, and—as the second part of "The
> Watershed" shows— barred from entering it, is a new figure, distant, obscure,
> observant. . . . everything about this observer seems forbiddingly ambiguous. Who
> and where is he? His estranged condition . . . is the true Auden country.
>> Stranger, turn back again, frustrate and vexed:
>> This land, cut off, will not communicate,[14]

What was the cause of this estrangement?

Auden as a child had also been raised in a nurturing womb-cocoon by progressive parents who encouraged his intellectual independence. And like
Isherwood, he was sent away to school to find that there's no place like home.
Auden, at least, did not have to cope with the death of his father and the grief of
a war widow. However, Auden's father served in the war and was away from home
for nearly all of four years. Still, anyone who remembers his school days as a "fascist state" has not discounted the negative influence of having been there. In
Lions and Shadows, Isherwood recalls that when he and Auden met again in
1925, "we began to chatter and gossip: the preparatory school atmosphere
reasserted itself. We revived the old jokes . . . we remembered how Spem [a mas-
ter] used to pinch our arms for not knowing the irregular verbs. . . . Weston was
brilliant at doing one of Pa's sermons: how he wiped his glasses, how he coughed,
how he clicked his fingers when somebody in chapel fell asleep. ('Sn Edmund's
Day . . . Sn Edmund's Day . . . Whur does it *mean?* Whur did it mean to *them,
then, theah?* Whur does it mean to *ers, heah, nerw?*') We laughed so much." (*LS,*
183–84). Auden's imitation would be used to great effect in Isherwood's *The
Memorial* and Auden's *The Orators,* both published in 1932.

Though this Auden rendition is repeated by Isherwood as a source of humor,
it contained in it the crux of their generation's dilemma: they were constantly
reminded of the past ("Whur did it mean to *them, then, theah?*") and constantly
asked to compare themselves to it ("Whur ders it mean to *ers, heah, nerw?*").
They were not allowed to belong to the past they preferred—the womb-cocoon;
instead, they were expected to honor the traditional past that compared them to
The Others. The self-identity for both Auden and Isherwood was as cyphers who
were passive witnesses. In this state of limbo, the neutral cypher is his own ghost,
neither Truly Weak nor Truly Strong. Even to be Truly Weak would have been
preferred to a state of non-being. A cry for approval would have at least indicated
some reaction to existence. For the highbrow a reaction signifies a desire for a
change in his environment. Conversely, a passive cypher is a mute eunuch inca-
pable of empowerment and the possibility of giving or receiving love.

The battle between the past and the present sets up the divisive demilitarized
zone of the Auden-Isherwood "frontier," a theme that would become a pivotal concept in the 1930s. Mendelson writes, "The war that peace occasionally interrupts is
a civil war between the broken fragments of a whole. Its forces are mutually opposed

efforts toward wholeness made by different halves of a divided city or a divided self.
This civil war, as Auden wrote to Isherwood in a verse letter in April 1929, was 'our
study and our interest.'"

> Although your medium is that other Christopher,
> The most prodigious of literary forms [the novel],
> to both this is our study and our interest:
> The fortunes and manoeuvres of this civil war,
> Man's opposite strivings for entropic peace,
> Retreat to lost homes or advance to new.[15]

According to Mendelson, "Auden wrote in his 1929 journal, 'The Tyranny of the
Dead one cannot react against.' *Paid on Both Sides* is a study in that tyranny.'"[16] For
Auden, with Isherwood's encouragement, the early and later versions were part of
their "study" and "interest" in the predicament of their generation.

Mendelson believes the play "is an autobiographical study also. [Auden, in]
annotating a friend's copy of the play in the 1940's, called it 'A parable of English
Middle Class (professional) family life 1907–1929.'"[17] 1907 represents Auden's
year of birth and 1929 is the play's date of completion. "Parable" is the key word
and presents another byword for the 1930s. The play is narrated by a cypher-witness
and is autobiographical only to those who recognize that it is a secret code about the
old school. Nothing in it is about Auden's life as it is represented in biographical
files; instead, everything in it seems to contribute to a psychological profile of
Auden (and Isherwood). Mendelson notes: *"Paid on Both Sides* is subtitled 'A
Charade,' and a charade implies a solution. However opaque the manner of the
play, its story is simple. It is a tragedy of revenge. Two mill-owning families have
been feuding for generations. The son of one family, John Nower, and the daughter of the other, Anne Shaw, fall in love. A truce is declared on the occasion of
their engagement. But on their wedding day one of the Shaws, urged on by his
mother, murders Nower, avenging the Shaw brother whom Nower had earlier
killed. . . . The play . . . fluctuates from schoolboy slang to alliterative Old
English pastiche; all murders are reported in the rhythms of Old English verse."[18]

The use of the old style for the murders may have signified the pastiche
aspect of the play, particularly in the early version, which is a Mortmere-like
satire in a bare-bones depiction that is stripped to the psychological essentials of
the Isherwood-Auden schema: us against them, saving face, *faux* allegiance,
unreasonable peer pressure, and stultifying alienation. The early version "emphasizes only the matter of the inherited past and what might be called the social
genetics of 'habit.'"[19] The ideas and habits of the middle class and the old school
are emphasized by Auden's careful descriptions of the characters' costumes and
props: dinner jackets, trench coats, homburgs, sportsman's guns, field glasses.
The play's "announcer" is in the "uniform of a cinema commissionaire, [and has]

a megaphone." The members of the chorus are deliberately depicted as hearties in "rugger [rugby] things. The leader wears a scrum cap."[20] In the early version, there are also more extensive stage directions that signify satirical intentions: *Someone does a cartwheel across the stage.*[21] The prop list and directions are largely left out of the later version, which increases the latter's obscurantism for the reader or viewer; without them, the particulars of Britain and the old school give way to a more ambiguous and starkly serious universal portrayal of human nature. Although the subtitle, "A Charade," implies a solution, there is not one, except in the sense that, through recognition of the events depicted, one might learn how to avoid their cyclical repetition. In terms of the Isherwood schema one avoids being Truly Weak by not continuing the killing cycle, choosing instead to be Truly Strong by starting a new cycle of peace. Much of the Truly Weak and Truly Strong theme in the play—early or late versions—is not explicit, but subliminal. Later the theme would be more pronounced for the Isherwood-Auden plays in collaboration. The farce aspects of *Paid on Both Sides* would be featured in *The Dog beneath the Skin* (1935). The tragic aspects would reappear in 1936 for *The Ascent of F6,* in which the antihero Michael Ransom (based on T. E. Lawrence) would exemplify the choices of the Truly Weak and Truly Strong Man. By then Auden had Isherwood's theme clearly in focus because his friend was the co-author. In fact, by 1934 Auden would define the theme in a book review of a T. E. Lawrence biography. The importance of the Isherwood-Auden reunion is that, through "Gems of Belgian Architecture" and *Paid on Both Sides,* one sees that their discussions of the old school influenced their own work and that of the Auden Generation in the next decade. It was almost 1928, the year of Isherwood's debut in what Auden had called "the most prodigious of literary forms," the novel.

ALL THE CONSPIRATORS

From the time he left Cambridge in 1925, Isherwood the artist had been letting go of Mortmere and developing a new form of writing. His themes, augmented by his discussions with Auden, revolved around the North-West Passage, the Test, and the Truly Weak and Truly Strong Man. Isherwood's technique was to use the "jewels" in his journals as they had been recorded by him as a cypher-witness. He was a silent gossip who listened for material at the tea-table conversations by which he pretended to be bored. Isherwood, having already given up on that massive epic based on *The Northwest Passage,* settled on a slice of recent life—his own. *All the Conspirators* features two of Isherwood's internal conflicts: (1) the Mangeots' bohemian lifestyle opposed to living at home with the "female relative's" traditional lifestyle; (2) Isherwood the artist opposed to Isherwood-the-aristocrat. This second conflict included his preference for knowing Anti-Others, such as Upward and Auden, instead of knowing any of The Others—or conspirators—that the "female relative" would have liked him to know. The Others are no longer the arch cartoon buffoons of Mortmere but composites of real people who live the duality of "public faces in private places." As Isherwood said of Tommy and Roger in the never completed *North-West Passage*, certain characters would represent "two aspects or halves of the same person." For Isherwood and Auden the duality of public and private as learned at the old school was a psychological conflict "metaphorized" into armed conflict.

Isherwood said that his own conflicts and compulsive hypochondria[22] were "a manifestation of [his] tireless sense of guilt" over being "sent down" from Cambridge (*LS*, 217): "It was now a year and a half since I had left Cambridge; but had I ever completely escaped? No, I had not" (*LS*, 216). He could not escape because the real prison was in his mind, which he had learned from his psychology sessions with Auden. Isherwood referred to the "analyst-patient relationship" between Auden and himself as being "permanent and profound" (*LS*, 217). Psychological introspection was an important prelude to his writing *All the Conspirators*.

The novel opens with Philip Lindsay (based on Isherwood as the would-be artist) who has just quit his dull office job in the city. He visits the Scilly Isles with his friend, the rebellious Allen Chalmers, a medical student and also an amateur artist. Philip has run off to avoid telling his mother that he has given up a job that was gotten for him by a family friend. While on the trip, Allen the rebel has a drunken episode that disturbs Philip's Poshocratic sensibility. This sensibility is one Lindsay would have been loathe to admit. Philip then returns to London and his mother, who, by enlisting more of The Others, wrenches every bit of guilt out of Philip so that he returns to the office job, thoroughly defeated, depressed, and bitter.

When Victor Page, an old Poshocratic schoolmate of Philip, meets Philip's sister Joan, mother Lindsay manipulates an inevitable engagement. Victor, in sympathy with Philip's need to get out of his office job, uses his Poshocratic connections to get his future brother-in-law a post in Kenya. Joan and Allen, knowing Philip cannot handle this much independence, discourage him. Philip does not yield. This is a Test to throw in his mother's face, but the night before his departure, he becomes ill and cannot go.

During his convalescence Philip is treated as a child again by his mother; his illness also gives him an excuse for not going back to the office. Philip, while recovering, sells three paintings and wins a local poetry prize. With something to brag about, Mrs. Lindsay relents in her pressure that Philip conform. At the novel's end, Philip even has the gall to tell Allen that, compared to himself, Allen does not have the nerve to try new things, or, in effect, new Tests. Philip says this to Chalmers while Philip is still living at home under his mother's doting.

All the Conspirators is a major rewrite of *Seascape with Figures*. In *Lions and Shadows* Isherwood explains how his novel evolved:

Towards the end of July, I finished my revised version of *Seascape with Figures*. I had improved it, I hoped. Certainly, it was livelier: what Chalmers had called "stage directions" ("he said, " "she answered," " he smiled," "they both laughed,") had been cut down to a minimum—indeed, it was now very nearly impossible to guess which of the characters was supposed to be speaking: and there were several "thought-stream" passages in the fashionable neo-Joyce manner which yielded nothing in obscurity to the work of the master himself. The murder was cut—"tea-tabled" down to an indecisive, undignified scuffle; and the ending was an apotheosis of the Tea-Table, a decrescendo of anti-climaxes. My two chief characters, the medical student and the dilettante artist, now resembled Chalmers and Philip more strongly than ever. [By Philip, he meant Hector Wintle, another Cambridge classmate, but Philip was also, if not more so, Isherwood.]

Rewriting the *Seascape* had taught me a great deal; I had begun to discover my limitations, to know what I could do and what I couldn't. I was strongest on dialogue, weakest on abstractions and generalizations: I must never try to address the reader—whenever I do so, I utter platitudes or tied myself up in knots; I must stick to the particular and the special instance. My characterization was flashy but thin; I was a cartoonist, not a painter in oils. Love scenes I had better avoid—until I learned something about them.

I thought of the novel (as I hoped to learn it) essentially in terms of technique, conjuring, or chess. The novelist, I said to myself, is playing a game with his reader; he must continually amaze and deceive him, with tricks, with traps, with extraordinary gambits, with sham climaxes, with false directions. I imagined a novel as a contraption— like a motor bicycle, whose action depends upon the exactly co-ordinated working of all its interrelated parts; or like a conjurer's table, fitted with mirrors . . . and trapdoors. I saw it as something compact, and by the laws of its own nature, fairly short. In fact, my models were not novels at all, but detective stories, and the plays of Ibsen and Tchekhov. (*LS,* 258– 59)

Looking back from 1938 to 1928, Isherwood knew that at age twenty-three he had relied on tricks to compensate for a lack of the perspective and depth that only comes with experience. In 1928, Isherwood the artist wrote his novel—as he had written everything else before it—as a Test; it was very apt that he would have "imagined a novel as a contraption—like a motor-bicycle" since his purchase of one had been another Test and another device he had not quite mastered before giving up on it. Fortunately, he stuck to writing. In a 1972 interview, the sixty-eight–year-old Isherwood gave advice that could have been useful to the young Isherwood in 1928: "I've had a good deal of experience talking to kids who write . . . as a guest professor. What I always point out to them is . . . that so often they're really bluffing. I say over and over . . . 'Why are you telling me this?' A writer must always be able to answer that question. Why are we being told this? What is the point of it? No story is ever told without a point . . . everybody knows that if you're telling a story you're

capping it, you're capping something that somebody else has said, or you're illuminating some point such as You can't trust women, or You can't trust Eskimos, and
this you illustrate by your story."

Isherwood was tacitly reiterating that language is less about what one knows,
but more about how one feels about what one knows. As for his students, he said,
"I find again and again that they don't know *why* they're writing the damn thing! It's
all, just sort of, they thought it might be cute. I think the great danger is that thing
of being an entertainer who gets up on stage and is amusing from moment to
moment." This sounds like the younger Isherwood who was "playing a game with
his reader . . . with tricks." In the 1972 interview Isherwood reached this conclusion:
"Of course there *are* writers who are brilliant entertainers but who aren't there merely
to amuse the audience. Their whole performance has an overall intention."[23]

As Isherwood admitted in the introduction to the 1957 reissue of *All the
Conspirators,* he himself was not sure of his "overall intention" in 1928: "See what
you can make of, for example, the first three and a half pages of the last chapter.
. . . Perhaps you will be able to enjoy this book simply as a period piece—smiling at its naive attempts at a James Joyce thought-stream, its aping of the mannerisms of Stephen Dedalus, its quaint echoes of Virginia Woolf, its jerky
flashback narration crudely imitated from E. M. Forster."[24]

Isherwood's comments in 1938, 1957, and 1972 all apply to his first novel; it
is awkward, decidedly unsubtle, cryptic in spots, heavy-handed in others.
Nonetheless, whatever the flaws, the novel's value is a primer for Isherwood's
thoughts about the old school, the possessive mother and dominated son, the Test,
the North-West Passage, and the Truly Weak and Strong Man. In his first novel, the
Truly Strong Man is present only by his emphatic absence in comparison to the
Truly Weak caricatures that Isherwood depicts. As with many a first novel, the
author could not resist the opportunity for therapeutic confession and expiation.

Towards the end of the novel, after the various psychological conflicts are laid
bare, Philip, the Truly Weak Son, has a stream-of-consciousness dream about the
old school:

> For the first day or two, the new boys hung about the passages, keeping
> together. . . . A baize notice board in the passage. . . . Any boy found ragging or
> fooling in the lavatories will be severely dealt with. . . . Garvel got lammed for
> using a senior's bat. . . . They talked and quarrelled among themselves. . . . Let's
> rebel. . . . We're going to chuck you out into that gorse-bush. . . . Please sir, I want
> to go home. . . .
>
> MY DARLING MOTHER,
>
> I am quite certain that I shall always loathe and detest this place. Do please
> come and take me away as soon as you possibly can. I *hate it.* (*AC,* 213–14)

Isherwood (in the guise of Philip) writes the letter he had not written to Kathleen
years before.

The portion of the novel that precedes this sequence is designed to lead up to it. The symptomatic effects of the old school on Philip come first, then the reader is shown that the school was the cause. The past at the old school has predicted the present and the residual bitterness and vulnerability engendered by that past cannot be shaken off. The conflict of past against present is symbolized near the novel's end in a confrontation between Victor, the past-invoking Poshocrat, and Allen, the present-future rebel. Philip, on the eve of the Kenya Test that he had hoped to thrust in his mother's face, has vanished melodramatically. He leaves a cryptic note that panics his family because its deliberate ambiguousness hints at suicide. Victor visits Allen, demanding he produce Philip or say where he is. Allen, proving he does not know where Philip is, asks for an apology. Victor refuses and threatens Allen "not to show yourself at Bellingham Gardens anymore, you might find it unpleasant." This exchange follows:

> Victor turned as if to go.
> "Just one minute," said Allen.
> Victor staggered; took a large pace back. The lamp shivered and its flame gave a flutter. Allen half smiled. Down they went, rolling . . . gasping in each other's faces. Locked. At the second tap on the door, they broke loose.
> "Come in."

The landlady enters bringing cocoa. Victor rushes out and Allen thinks: "He'd probably have killed me. . . . Mrs. Rose saved my life" (*AC*, 227–28).

Philip's best friend, Chalmers, gets to smack the Poshocratic past in the face. For Allen, however, defending his often contrary friend requires a great deal of patience as Chalmers refers to him as "Philip, Blessed Saint and Martyr." Allen knows that sometimes he has to "bear a great deal" in order to be Philip's friend (*AC*, 48). Earlier in the novel, when Philip and Allen are ready to return home to London from their trip to Scilly, Allen asks Philip what his mother will think of his quitting the office. Philip answers: "I really neither know nor care." Allen sees through this false face: "You do know, and you'll probably be made to care a great deal" (*AC*, 52). Philip, guilty "Saint and Martyr" that he is, will care enormously.

Upon his return, Philip's first meeting with his mother denotes the mother-son theme for the rest of Isherwood's career:

> Philip climbed wearily the thirty steps to his bedroom. On the landing he came face to face with his mother. She had been waiting for him there. The meeting had no drama, for both had passed the climax of anticipation. For some moments neither spoke. Then Philip said:
> "Hullo." They regarded each other blankly.
> Mrs. Lindsay, once pretty, was now small, pale, grey-haired. She powdered her nose without skill, leaving visible grains and streaks of rawness. The lines of her

face suggested pathos, boredom and nervous irritability. She screwed them now into an expression intended to be scornful, actually merely ugly.

"So you've come back?"

He nodded. Suddenly, he felt physically tired all over. It was as if they had already been talking for hours. He regarded her stupidly, intently, confused by irrelevant memories, associations, suggested by the stair-carpet, the lithographs and the little rugs. A queer atrophy of the will. There seemed to be nothing to say. He thought: "I'm being hypnotized."

Watching her son's face, she flung out emotionally:

"No wonder you were afraid to tell us what you'd done."

Philip said nothing.

"And now"—the sound of her own plaintive voice was giving her confidence— "what's your next scheme? What do you imagine is going to happen to you? Have you thought of that? Who do you think is going to help you next?"

Philip roused himself with cowardice and distaste to answer her.

"I'm going to help myself."

Again she made the scornful grimace.

"Oh! And since when have you done that?"

"It's time I started."

"It is, certainly."

Mrs. Lindsay is applying the guilt with a heavy brush, yet backs off ever so slightly so as not to alienate her son completely. She asks:

"So what do you mean to do?"

"You know quite well. I want to have a chance at painting and writing."

"Painting and writing!" She shied like a pony at the words. "How are you to live?"

"I suppose I can sell my work."

"You've been doing a lot while you were away, of course?"

"Of course," he lied.

Her question, as in older, earlier quarrels, had seemed telepathic.

His mother then asks him why he left his job: "Because I loathed the office. I told you so over and over again." This response does not matter to her. She does not even believe this could be the sole reason:

"There isn't—anything else is there. I'm your mother, Philip. I think I have a right to know."

Her voice though harsh, had a certain eagerness. Would she have preferred that to this? The definite to the indefinite? At least, then, the situation would have been plainer. The suggestion, in Philip's present mood, could not even make him smile.   Nevertheless, she saw at once, her mistake. Already perplexed and over-wrought, she had been near to tears. She easily shed them now.

"You don't know how much you've hurt me."

He stood before her; bored, shamed, wishing only to get away. Presently, she recovered herself a little:

"How are you going to explain all this to people?" (*AC,* 65–68)

By "people," Mrs. Lindsay means of course The Others. For Mrs. Lindsay the keeping up of appearances supersedes any real needs Philip has.

Later Mrs. Lindsay resorts to an old standby that Philip cannot really refute: "Your father always hoped that you would make a position for yourself in the world" (*AC,* 79). Of remarks like these, Isherwood the cypher-narrator writes: "Thus were the tactics of their domestic guerilla warfare reduced to a routine" (*AC,* 127).

All of the elements of Isherwood's thematics are contained in this sequence: the son needs to test himself and establish his own identity apart from his mother, his dead father, and the past. The mother resists, wanting the son to cling to her and preserve the past as represented by the husband she has lost. She worries about what The Others will think, which further alienates the son against her and The Others. The mother will not accept responsibility that she might be at fault so she casts about for blame elsewhere. Elsewhere points toward the cryptic "that," which is given without further explanation but seems to have to do with her son's sexuality. In 1928 Isherwood is not defining orientation or gender. Isherwood's allusion, however oblique, is still another rebellious cry for approval. This allusion will be tacitly reiterated later when Mrs. Lindsay and Joan discuss Allen. Mrs. Lindsay considers Allen a bad "influence over anybody so weak-minded as Philip" (*AC,* 103). Joan defends Allen. Her mother thinks Victor's opinion of Philip will be lowered if Victor thinks that Philip may have a gay friend or that Philip may be gay himself. For mother Lindsay, nothing should interfere with Joan's engagement and the income this represents.

In his study of Isherwood, Claude Summers suggests that Victor himself has repressed homosexual urges, which are betrayed in his awkward courting of Joan.[25] This possibility might explain Victor's antipathy towards Allen, who may or may not be homosexual. In 1928, Isherwood could not overtly express the theme of homosexuality. Indeed, it would not be until 1954 and *The World in the Evening* that Isherwood would depict homosexual characters explicitly.

At the end of *All the Conspirators* Philip is living at home. He is encouraged by the "success" of his art, which he has indirectly achieved by his narcissistic displays of hypochondria that have kept him home and out of the office. Thus fortified, he boldly—and with the most absurd irony worthy of Mortmere—tells Chalmers, the friend who had defended him, "You see, Allen, what I really dislike about your attitude is that it gets you nowhere. You refuse to venture, that's what it is. You're timid. Oh, I grant you one's got to have the nerve. . ." (*AC,* 255). Philip says this to Allen while being catered to by his once-hated mother in his once-hated home.

In *All the Conspirators* Isherwood's life becomes his art. In an Isherwood letter of 9 September 1926 he expresses his frustration over living at home: "By the time you return I shall have gone mad . . . everything here is vile. . . ."[26] In the novel, Philip says, "Allen, it's intolerable. I thought I could stand a good deal, but to-day—everything's been absolutely vile. . ." (*AC*, 133).

Isherwood's themes also found their way into the very brief poems that Auden titled "Shorts," written from 1928 to 1930: the Truly Weak protagonist in one goes to a bar, starts a quarrel or a war, hunts or mountain climbs which is his public mask because

No one guesses you are weak.[27]

Meanwhile, the real hero stays in the bar rather than create Tests because he is Truly Strong and does not need to prove anything. In *The Ascent of F6* (1936), Isherwood and Auden would also use mountain-climbing imagery as a Test, as Michael Ransom attempts to climb to the peak of F6.

Another "Short" describes a mother who berates her son when he is well but supports him when he is ill. Is this Mrs. Lindsay and/or Kathleen?

Conversely, a little of Auden can be found in *All the Conspirators,* a connection illustrated in Isherwood's line, "A gas-works rose sombrely amidst pavilions and changing-sheds" (*AC*, 63–64). This line is reminiscent of references in Auden's early poems to the urban landscape of industry and machines such as "mill-shed hammering" (1928)[28] and "ramshackle engine" (1927).[29] Auden's favorite walk at Oxford was around the nearby gas-works and sometimes Isherwood was his companion. Isherwood and Auden's influence on the path of contemporary literature would expand as Isherwood talked to Auden, and Auden talked to Cecil Day Lewis, who talked to his best friend, Rex Warner, and so on. Within this sphere of influence both Isherwood and Auden would soon be talking to the third member of their literary triumvirate, Stephen Spender.

A PERIOD OF TRANSITION

Stephen Spender was at Oxford in 1927 with Auden, Day Lewis, Warner, and Louis MacNeice. That year, *Oxford Poetry, 1927* appeared with a preface written jointly by Auden and Day Lewis that was considered the declaration of independence of the coming 1930s poets from their predecessors. The preface acknowledges the era's new world of psychoanalysis and its impact on the poet:

> A tripartite problem remains, and may be stated thus: (a) The psychological conflict between self as subject and self as object, which is patent in the self-consciousness and emotional stultification resultant from the attempt to synchronize within the mind the synthesis and the analysis of experience. Such appears to be the prime development of this century, our experiment in "the emergent evolution of mind." Emotion is no longer necessarily to be analysed by "recollection in tranquility": it

is to be prehended emotionally and intellectually at once. And this is of most importance to the poet: for it his mind that must bear the brunt of the conflict and may be the first to realize the new harmony which would imply the success of this synchronization.[30]

The duality of subject and object, private and public, inner and outer, would be the key to the poet's new world, one which gives homage to Freud in science and Eliot in verse. By stating that emotion "be prehended . . . intellectually at once," Auden and Day Lewis were declaring that the poet should be an active participant, recorder, transcriber, and interpreter of existing circumstances. The poet as activist was a crucial aspect of the Auden Generation and this aspect is exemplified by a well-known quote from the Auden–Day Lewis introduction: "All genuine poetry is in a sense the formation of private spheres out of public chaos."[31]

This process is also one of Self-realization. One determines to what degree one is Truly Weak, even while trying to be Truly Strong. One cannot become strong without understanding why he has been weak; one cannot know the heights without having climbed to them from the depths. The highbrow learns about himself from the energy needed for the climb. If one sees always from the peak, there is no basis for comparison. Of this need for comparison, Aldous Huxley observes:

> The soul *cannot* always feel what it feels sometimes; mortal breath *cannot* express the passion then inspired; and the perfect height *cannot* be lived on, only visited. The clauses remain conditional—always. If they were fulfilled, man would lose all the qualities which we admire as distinctively human. Virtue is possible only in an unethical universe and in beings whose minds are so made that they cannot always remain at their highest pitch. Consistently rewarded, virtue would cease to be virtue; and if the soul did not have its weary spells of feeling the flesh and the flesh of feeling the chain, there would be no such things as heroism and endurance. Man might be happier . . . but less interesting and, at bottom, ignobler.[32]

Huxley's contrast implies that a Vedantic reconciliation of opposites creates the energy that leads to the metaphysical understanding of one's transcendent Self as opposed to one's limited self. In Vedanta cosmology the universal Self is symbolized by the capital "S" that signifies a metaphysically ego-less unity as compared to the lower-case "s" that signifies a physically separated, ego-full disunity.

Literature unifies separated individuals by presenting the poet's "private spheres" for recognition by the Kierkegaardian Public that endures the "public chaos." Literature also represents the artist intimating his "private chaos" for "public spheres." The anonymous individuals making up the amorphous Kierkegaardian Public desperately desire to know that there are like souls existing within an otherwise impenetrable and alienated mass. Art connects the particular to the universal and the one to the many. Art does so by reaching one person at a time, reminding each individual that there is some underlying transcendent identification between individual minds and that this identification reflects the perpetual continuum of a world mind. For the passive lowbrow majority who just observe, this is a subconscious process. The activist highbrow as philosopher-poet or poet-philosopher observes and perceives. Then he explains these perceptions to the rest of us.

Isherwood at this point did not yet have a philosopher's calm, largely because he was still living at home with the "female relative." It was time to move out. Isherwood's friend, Roger East, had married in January 1927, and Isherwood took over East's bachelor flat: "Bill Scott, a friend of the Cheurets, helped me move in; Jean and Edouard were in and out all day long, sorting and arranging my books on the plank shelves which I had fitted up at one end of the room. Madame Cheuret chose the material for my curtains and the cover for my divan bed. . . . I had always plenty of company and, there was my landlady, Mrs. Partridge, perpetually ready for a chat" (*LS,* 219–20). Mrs. Partridge would be the first of the landladies who would end up in his fiction. "Mrs. Rose," the cocoa-bearer who interrupted the fight between Chalmers and Victor Page, was likely based on Mrs. Partridge.

Isherwood was proud of his first bachelor flat, yet he said that "the room only came into being" when he was receiving visitors: "Left alone in it . . . I couldn't sit still . . . touching the curtains, aligning the table with the bed, altering the position of a book, like a small shopkeeper who waits for customers. . . . Every object, big or small . . . had its place in the pathologically tidy scheme of my existence. Mine was the rigid tidiness of the celibate: that pathetically neat room, as I now picture it, seems to cry out for the disorderly human traces of cohabitation—the hairbrush discovered among your papers in the drawer, the unfamiliar queer-feeling garments in the dark cupboard, the too small slipper you vainly try to pull on when half awake, the wrong tooth-brush in your glass . . . and in the tea-cup the strange lustrous single hair. But the room, as long as I occupied it, remained virgin, unravished. . . . Only Polly East, that merciless perceiver, noticed that anything was lacking: 'What's Bisherwood [Polly's playful name for him] done to this room?' she asked. 'It's quite different from when you had it Roger. He's made it all sort of respectable—like a public park'" (*LS,* 222–23).

Isherwood implies that everything has to do with sex, and he finally gives his symptomatic compulsive-obsessive tidiness a rationale that he had previously alleviated at Cambridge through the fantasy release of Mortmere:[33] Isherwood needed a lover. In 1938, he did not specify which gender he preferred. He would later redress this omission in his 1976 autobiography *Christopher and His Kind,* which picks up where *Lions and Shadows* leaves off. By 1976, in the new era of gay liberation that he had helped initiate, Isherwood thought it was time to tell the truth he had left out almost forty years before. Isherwood begins *Christopher And His Kind* by saying, "There is a book called *Lions and Shadows,* published in 1938, which describes Christopher Isherwood's life between the ages of seventeen and twenty-four. The author conceals important facts about himself" (*CK*, 1). *The* most important fact that he left out of *Lions and Shadows* was that he was homosexual, although one with very little practical experience. In this regard he confirms that prior to his Berlin years, he was, for the most part, like his first bachelor room, "virgin [and] unravished":

> At school, Christopher had fallen in love with many boys and had been yearningly romantic about them. At college he had managed to get into bed with one. This was due entirely to the initiative of his partner, who, when Christopher became scared and started to raise objections, locked the door, and sat firmly on Christopher's lap. I am still grateful to him. I hope he is alive and may happen to read these lines.
>
> Other experiences followed, all of them enjoyable but none entirely satisfying. This was because Christopher was suffering from an inhibition, then not unusual among upper-class homosexuals; he couldn't relax sexually with a member of his own class or nation. (*CK*, 3)

Consequently, this inhibition became Isherwood's real motivation for going to Berlin a year later; however, in 1927, all he knew was that there was a need that was not being filled. Isherwood-the-lover was not yet an image that he could fill his ego with; Isherwood the artist would have to suffice. The latter image cemented his friendship with Auden. Through Auden, he would meet another aspiring artist who would look up to him since Isherwood had already published a novel.

A DERANGED SHELLEY

From the vantage point of his bachelor flat, Isherwood could see that, because he had not finished his Cambridge degree, few occupations were available to him except tutoring, which he considered temporary until his writing paid his way. He was still getting his allowance from "M." Isherwood sometimes felt cut off from the mainstream that his public face ostensibly detested, but his private self had a secret yearning to be accepted into: "But beneath all my note-taking, my would-be scientific detachment, my hatred, my disgust, there was the old sense of exclusion, the familiar grudging envy. For, however I might sneer, these people *were* evidently enjoying themselves in their own mysterious fashion, and why was it so mysterious to me? Weren't they of my own blood, my own caste? Why couldn't I—the would-be novelist, the professional observer—understand them?" While Isherwood notes that, "Chalmers," "Weston," and "Madame Cheuret" would all have disparaged the upper classes as well, "are we really glad? Does anybody ever feel sincerely pleased at the prospect of remaining in permanent opposition, a social misfit for the rest of his life. I wanted—however I might try to persuade myself, in moments of arrogance, to the contrary—to find some place, no matter how humble in the scheme of society. Until I do that, my writing will never be any good; no amount of talent or technique will redeem it: it will remain a greenhouse product; something, at best, for the connoisseur or the clique" (*LS*, 249).

All the Conspirators was the obscure and limited "greenhouse product"; nonetheless, it proved that the very young Isherwood was certainly a novelist. His second novel *The Memorial* in 1932, would be less obscure, less limited. In it Isherwood would still rebel against The Others, but he would also have more sympathy for them as victims of their society and culture. This slight shift indicates a maturing Isherwood—an increased sense of maturity, however, that did not yet extend to his relation with Kathleen. Stephen Spender had similar sentiments about the upper class, feeling that he was a member of it, but not really one of them. Isherwood, Auden and Spender would later become more accepting of their own class, which they had rejected when they were young, iconoclastic rebels. From their middle years on they would remain distinct individuals, but each was more able to move back and forth from their roles as philosopher-poets to their roles as celebrities among the crowd they once had eschewed. Spender certainly did not turn down his knighthood. And Isherwood, though spending most of the 1930s running around Europe and then fleeing to America, would later own a British-made Sunbeam automobile.[34]

In 1929 Isherwood met Spender, the basis for Stephen Savage in *Lions and Shadows*, through Auden, who had shown Isherwood the "typescript of an undergraduate he had got to know at [Oxford]. 'He's mad,' said Weston [of Spender] by way of preface. As for Spender's short story, Auden said, 'I think it's very good indeed.'" Isherwood agreed:

> The story . . . described a young man's visit to the home of some male and female cousins. The young man is almost incredibly shy, gauche, tactless and generally neurotic; and his social shortcomings are exaggerated by contrast with the elegance, beauty and grace of his hosts. They appear to him as beings from another world; and his hopeless adoration of them fills him with self-hatred and despair. The cousins, on their side, are amused by the young man, they make fun of him, lightly, without malice; exposed to their unconsciously cruel mockery, he suffers tortures of humiliation—culminating in an extraordinary scene, in which, being unable to understand the simple mechanism of a folding card-table, he breaks down altogether and bursts into tears. (*LS*, 279–80)

Isherwood admired the story because the protagonist is recognizable as an angst-driven victim of The Others. The neurotic cousin could have been Isherwood. "Having finished it," Isherwood said, "I agreed with Weston: indeed the story was not quite like anything else I had ever read. You really cared about the problems of the blundering, tormented young man. The hero was so absorbingly interested in himself, in his own sensations and in everybody who came into contact with him that you couldn't help sharing his interest. In fact, the experience was so vivid as to be quite painful. You blushed for him, you squirmed at his every faux-pas; you wanted, simultaneously, to kick and protect and shake him" (*LS*, 280). "The Cousins" would later appear in Spender's 1935 short story collection *The Burning Cactus*.

Spender's story is autobiographical. Spender was writing about his inner world and he was, if not quite "mad" as Auden had said, a tall and gangly exposed nerve-end: "He burst upon us, blushing, sniggering loudly, contriving to trip over the edge of the carpet—an immensely tall, shambling boy of nineteen. . . . he shared his experiences, like a banquet with his friends" (LS, 281). "He was the slave of his friends" because Spender was very needy of emotional reciprocation and hoped for more than he could possibly receive. Isherwood said that his "kindness was so touching that it sometimes made me feel quite irritable . . . I couldn't hope to compete with it" (LS, 282). Eventually, the pressure of his trying to match Spender's cloying nature eventually led to their having a very brief falling out during the Berlin years.

Spender wanted to meet Isherwood, whom Auden had described as a great sage and the novelist. Auden, the amateur psychologist, liked to arrange things. He was an exponent of Oxford's group theories and was trying to arrange a group of his own. Isherwood and Spender would later remember Auden's arranging with indulgence.[35]

In his 1951 autobiography, World within World, Spender explains the positive influence of Isherwood on an awkward nineteen-year-old who felt stifled at Oxford: "He simplified all the problems which entangled me, merely by describing his own life and his own attitudes towards these things. . . . Isherwood had a peculiarity of being attractively disgusted and amiably bitter . . . with a kind of inexpressible pain which yet had something smiling about it." Isherwood was long accustomed to wearing the role of wise martyr as a cloak to hide his inner anxiety and to protect his sensitive vulnerability. Highbrow sensitivity can sometimes be a curse when the highbrow struggles with his environment, but for an artist, sensitivity can also be a blessing. It is from sensitivity that an artist's work derives. Spender explains the influence that Isherwood had on him: "We walked around . . . and it was as though Christopher were making circles around my world. . . . Isherwood hated the dons for being divided between their academicism and the provincial gossip which is the social life of Oxford and Cambridge: he hated undergraduates for their snobbishness and exclusiveness. The whole system to him was one which denied affection: and was based largely on fear of sex. His hatred extended beyond Oxford. It was for English middle-class life. He spoke of Germany as a country where all obstructions and complexities of life were cut through." Isherwood had not been to Berlin yet; this view of Germany was reported to him by Auden, who was the first of the trio to go. What Isherwood really meant by "the complexities of life were cut through" was that sexual attitudes were freer in Berlin. Spender is quite clear about how much Isherwood influenced the direction of his life:

> When he talked, his words had an effect on me like the end of *Alice in Wonderland*. All the players in my game seemed suddenly to turn into a pack of cards. I was determined now to leave Oxford, to write and to live. A few months

later, when I went to Hamburg, the opening words of a journal which I kept at the time were:

1929. July 22nd, Hamburg.

Now I shall begin to live.

Resolution for the long vac. To do absolutely none of the work set for me by my Oxford tutor. Now I am away from England, I shall begin my own work, and whether I stay at Oxford or not, from now on I shall continue to do that and no work but that.

My own work is poetry and novels. I have no character or will power outside my work. In the life of action, I do everything that my friends tell me to do, and have no opinions of my own. This is shameful, I know, but it is so. Therefore I must develop that side of me which is independent of other people. I must live and mature in my writing.

My aim is to achieve maturity of soul. . . . After my work, all I live for is my friends.[36]

Five years later Spender would say, "My poetry is rather irrelevantly and dangerously linked to my self-respect."[37]

In 1929 Spender was quite abashed and honored to have Auden and Isherwood as friends, and just as insecure about keeping them as friends. Spender would purchase a handpress and print the first "volume" of Auden's poems, many of which ended up in the Faber and Faber first edition. When the Faber edition was published in 1930, Auden was immediately recognized as a force. Many who would be influenced by Auden, including Cecil Day Lewis as the first to emulate Auden, were also being influenced by Isherwood.

HELLO TO BERLIN

In *Lions and Shadows,* Isherwood describes his sentiments about attending medical school: "At the beginning of October, 1928, I began my career as a medical student — not without the darkest misgivings" (*LS,* 285). The misgivings were justified. Isherwood does not give any explicit explanation as to why he even considered going to medical school in the first place. Perhaps he went because his friend Hector Wintle was there, or else he thought that since *All the Conspirators* had made him neither famous nor rich, he should have a back-up career. Or perhaps he was trying to please the "female relative." Whatever the reason, the result was a disaster; he quickly realized he was not cut out to be a doctor: "This was Cambridge again, but worse. Worse, because this time, I was honestly trying, seriously doing my best. I couldn't flatter myself with conceited lies about my Art: my Art was a flop, a declared failure on the open market. And I coudn't hide myself in Mortmere: Mortmere had failed us, dissolved into thin air. . . .The whole thing had been a day-dream from the start. . . . Was I, indeed, a total misfit, a hundred per cent incompetent? I couldn't, I daren't face such thoughts." (*LS,* 288)

Isherwood lasted just a year in medical school and the only benefit was that he began his second novel there. This was another escape mechanism as Mortmere and *All the Conspirators* had been. He said that "the novel was to be called . . . *The Memorial*. It was to be about war: not the war itself, but the effect of the idea of 'war' on my generation. It was to give expression to my own 'war' complex. . . . Like Tolstoy, I would tell the story of a family. . ." (*LS*, 296). At this point Auden returned from his first visit to Berlin and was "full of stories from Berlin, that astonishingly vicious yet fundamentally so respectable city, where even the night-life has a cosy domestic quality and where the films were the most interesting in Europe." The night life meant bars with "boys"—something Isherwood could not say in *Lions and Shadows,* but would later make up for in *Christopher and His Kind.* In addition to the discovery of Berlin itself, Auden had met John Layard (upon whom Barnard is based in *Lions and Shadows*), a disciple of the psychologist Homer Lane. Of Layard, Isherwood said, "In Weston, he had found an intelligent listener who became, overnight, an enthusiastic disciple" (*LS*, 299). Isherwood continues that, according to Layard's interpretation of Lane, "Every disease, Lane had taught, is itself a cure—if we know how to take it, There is only one sin: disobedience to the inner law of our own nature. The results of this disobedience show themselves in crime or disease; but the disobedience is never, in the first place, our own fault—it is the fault of those who teach us, as children, to control God (our desires) instead of giving him room to grow. . . . Conventional education . . . inverts the whole natural system in childhood, turning the child into a spurious adult. So that later, when the child grows up physically into a man, he is bound to try to regain his childhood—by means which, to the outside world, appear ever more and more unreasonable. . . . Diseases are therefore only warning symptoms of the sickness of the soul" (*LS*, 299–300).

Lane's references to childhood sounded wonderful; and for two homosexuals who felt constrained in Britain, Lane, plus Berlin, sounded even better. Isherwood writes that Auden's "whole vocabulary . . . was renovated . . . he was reproving me for harbouring a 'death-Wish. . . . 'You've got to drop all that . . . You must be pure in heart.'" Isherwood then defines the term as per Auden: "The pure-in-heart man became our new ideal. He was essentially free and easy, generous with his money and his belongings, without worries or inhibitions. . . . He was a wonderful listener, but he never 'sympathized' with your troubles; and the only advice he ever gave was in the form of parables—stories about other people which you could apply to your own problems. . . . He was entirely without fear" (*LS*, 303–04). The pure-in-heart man is Truly Strong. A pure-in-heart man would later be exemplified in Swami Prabhavananda, proving to Isherwood that the Truly Strong Man could actually exist as a priest, seer, teacher, and mystic.

The pure-in-heart man who is "essentially free and generous" became the role model of the 1930s, as the Auden gang would freely and generously support each other's art, help each other get published, and generally act upon altruistic inclinations. Auden in the late 1930s married—on paper only—Thomas Mann's daughter Erika so she could flee Germany and stay in Britain. The influence of the Lane-Auden-Isherwood connection was profound for the coming decade because (1) the persona of the Truly Strong Man now had an enhanced status, having been given the official sanction by a great authority—Lane, and because (2) the concept of parable-art, which both Isherwood and Auden had already enacted, was now also sanctioned. Private spheres could become parables to explain public chaos. These two themes became integral aspects of the Isherwood-Auden schema, and would be widely imitated in the 1930s and after.

As for Isherwood there could only be one place for him to find redemption from his medical school fiasco and his feeling of being a misfit. This was Berlin: "You want to commit the unforgivable sin, to shock Mummy and Daddy and Nanny, to smash the nursery clock, to be a really naughty little boy. . . . If you stick to your safe London nursery-life, you never *will* grow up. You'll die a time-shrivelled Peter Pan. At present, you're exactly seven years old. . . . I told my family [who were] patient but bewildered as ever, [and they] agreed sadly" (*LS*, 307). By family, Isherwood really meant "Mummy" who was still without a name. By "unforgivable sin," the Isherwood of 1938 was not being specific.

In 1976 he would rectify this lack of specificity in *Christopher and His Kind*. He goes back in time to this section in *Lions and Shadows* and gives the real low-down: "[Layard] had introduced Wystan to Lane's revolutionary teachings, thus inspiring him to use them as a frame of reference for his poems. . . . 'Publish each healer . . . It is time for the destruction of error . . . prohibit sharply the rehearsed response . . . Harrow the house of the dead . . . The game is up for you and the others . . . Love . . . needs death . . . death of the old gang [the past of The Others] . . . New styles of architecture, a change of heart.'" Then Isherwood puts matters on a more viscerally personal level by reiterating the Lane philosophy, particularly about freeing one's inner desires: "Life-shaking words! When Christopher heard them . . . they justified a change in his own life which he had been longing but not quite daring to make. Now he burned to put them into practice, to unchain his desires and hurl reason and sanity into prison. However, when *Lions and Shadows* suggests that Christopher's chief motive for going to Berlin was that he wanted to meet Layard, it is avoiding the truth . . . that wasn't why he was in such a hurry . . . it was Berlin itself he was hungry to meet; the Berlin Wystan had promised him. To Christopher, Berlin meant Boys" (*CK*, 2).

Isherwood made his decision and told everyone except Auden whom he would surprise in Berlin. This was commitment by declaration with no turning back. It was March 1929. The decade of the Auden Generation was nine months away. The first shot from this generation, however, came during 1929, and was fired—not by Auden, Isherwood, or Spender—but by the emulative Cecil Day Lewis.

TRANSITIONAL POEM

In his 1960 autobiography Day Lewis said of Auden's verse, which he had read when they were classmates at Oxford: "The vigor of the language, the exciting novelty of the images and ideas embodied in these early poems, and the delighted sense they gave me of a poetry which, so to say, knew its own mind—all this proved so infectious that my own verse became for a time pastiche-Auden."[38] In October 1929, the Hogarth Press published *Transitional Poem,* a title entirely apt not only for Day Lewis, but for his generation to announce its coming and declare that the passive, cynical nihilism of Eliot and Huxley's 1920s would give way to an active, yet still cynical iconoclasm for the 1930s. Day Lewis, whose first two books of verse, *Beechen Vigil* (1925) and *Country Comets* (1927), were pastorally Georgian and influenced by the light verse of Humbert Wolfe, kept his traditional pre-Auden technique in *Transitional Poem,* but loaded it with post-Auden influences, many of which were those of Isherwood and Auden in philosophical collaboration.

Transitional Poem is about the psychology of the transitions in a maturing human mind. This single mind, by extension, represents the corresponding maturity of the collective Oxfordian group mind or the world mind of Vedanta. Day Lewis did not know Vedanta directly, but was interpreting it indirectly from the influence of W. B. Yeats, who was also an influence on Auden. The Yeats connection is noted by Samuel Hynes in commenting on *Transitional Poem:* "More fundamental to the structure are oppositions: mind/body, ideal/real, infinite/finite, love/fear, eternity/time. Day Lewis's use of these terms echoes Yeats very closely, indeed the whole sequence is heavy with Yeatsian borrowings, and it is not surprising that Day Lewis used Yeats's word for such oppositions: 'antinomies.'"[39] Yeats based much of his own cosmology on Vedic cosmology and augmented it with Neo-Celtic nuances. In 1938, Yeats would render a translation of the Upanishads. The antinomies in *Transitional Poem* that echo Yeats are based on the Vedantic reconciliation of opposites, which create the energy that allows the world mind to progress, although in a time frame of eons, not single lifetimes. (In Vedanta, each single lifetime is integral to, and co-existent with, all past, present, and future lifetimes.) Day Lewis takes a particular mind, or "private sphere," and in his four transitions of that mind aims to demonstrate how the single mind merges into the universal mind in order to overcome "public chaos." At the end of the poem the transitions are defined in endnotes that emulate Eliot's notes for *The Waste Land:* "The central theme of this poem is the single mind. The poem is divided into four parts, which essentially represent four phases of personal experience in the pursuit of single-mindedness: it will be seen that a transition is intended from one part to the next such as implies a certain spiritual progress and a consequent shifting of aspect." Day Lewis then categorizes the four aspects: "(1) metaphysical, (2) ethical, (3) psychological, (4) an attempt to relate the poetic impulse with the experience as a whole."[40] This postscript explanation seems to literary critic Elton Edward Smith to be "a little bit of intellectual swank imported after the poems were written." To Smith the poem itself is not quite up to these distinct definitions, although one can see that there is some process of psychological maturation.[41] With respect to the psychological progress in the poem, another possible influence was American poet Conrad Aiken, Eliot's Harvard class-mate and friend, who had been living in England for years. Aiken's long poems of the previous twelve years and his autobiographical novel *Blue Voyage* (1927) were studies in psychological and metaphysical exploration, with Freud as the center of Aiken's hurricanes.[42]

Transitional Poem is a young man's poem, full of imitative energy. Even though it would be eclipsed a year later by Auden's arrival, it is still a worthy poem. Its value was recognized on publication, which was concurrent with the stock market crash of 1929, a catastrophic event that represented the symbolic arrival of the 1930s. This poem, with its Isherwood-Auden schema that Day Lewis had emulated from Auden directly, introduced themes for the coming decade: the divided mind, the mind's metaphysical progress, the rejection of tradition for new ways of thinking that could cope with new types of crises, and the poet as an activist who is pure in heart and Truly Strong. Hynes has more than capably detailed how Day Lewis incorporated these themes and their derivation from the Auden-Isherwood influence. The psychological transitions in the poem are, as Hynes said, "a conventional young man's statement of the transition from adolescence to manhood."[43] The young man is both one man and Everyman, or at least every poet. As Everyman, he attempts the North-West passage of the Truly Weak who attempts to learn how to become Truly Strong.

The allusions to Auden are both explicit and tacit. Explicitly, Day Lewis refers to the "tow-haired Poet"[44] and uses an Auden epigram to open part 4,[45] in which Day Lewis makes a closing statement about finding a new world: "There are going to be some changes made to-day."[46] Day Lewis refers to the "Hawk-faced man,"[47] Rex Warner, a mutual friend whom Auden calls by name in *Paid on Both Sides*.[48] He also refers to the "rag and bone man," Yeats.[49] Tacitly, Day Lewis evokes the Auden who, influenced by Lane, said life's lessons should be taught as parables. The following phrases highlight examples of Day Lewis emulating what he had read in Auden's poems. *Day Lewis:* "I became lord of / Light's interplay—stoker of an old parable."[50] He also echos Auden's aloof cypher-witness who is on the outside looking in. *Auden:* "As the hawk sees it or the helmeted airman."[51] Day Lewis: "As arrogant as the hawk as he mounts the morning."[52] Then there is Auden on the conflicting duality in man's nature. *Auden:* "While the divided face has no grace."[53] Day Lewis: "The mind against its own forked speculation."[54] Then the Auden (plus Isherwood) who tries to break from the past: *Auden:* "But their ancestral curse,"[55] *Day Lewis:* "the ancestral curse."[56] Finally, the Auden influence is again explicitly credited:

> Last the tow-haired poet, never done
> With cutting and planing some new gnomic prop

> To jack his all too stable universe up:—
> Conduct's Old Dobbin, thought's chameleon.
> Single mind copes with split intelligence,
> Breeding a piebald strain of truth and nonsense,[57]

With the last line, Day Lewis tempers the previous praise, as if to say he knows enough to separate the wheat from the chaff.[58] Nonetheless, *Transitional Poem* would not have been an early clarion for the 1930s without the influence of Auden and Isherwood. Ultimately, the message of *Transitional Poem* is that the Truly Weak Everyman can heal his divided mind by rejecting the past to move forward as a single-minded Truly Strong Man who is carefree, generous, and an active iconoclast. Day Lewis became one of the artistic leaders of the next decade. He was the first in the 1930s to take his cues from Auden and Isherwood.

In *Transitional Poem,* there is a line that refers to "vain motions."[59] In the endnotes, Day Lewis explains that the phrase comes from "Henry James, *The Ambassadors:* 'Whether or no he had a grand idea of the lucid, he held that nothing ever was in fact—for anyone else—he explained. One went through the vain motions, but it was mostly a waste of life.'"[60] The vain motions are for the Truly Weak. James was an icon for the Auden Generation. Spender particularly helped revive his reputation in the 1930s. James had an impact on the trio's own writing for that decade and beyond.

CABARET

For Isherwood, Berlin in March 1929 was a rebellious revelation. This was an escape from England. Now he would take on the combined persona of Isherwood the artist and Isherwood the daring expatriate wanderer. Both roles were guises for his real purpose. In his mid-twenties and fairly repressed sexually, he would be Isherwood-the-pseudo-satyr: "He wanted to go back into the world of his adolescent sexuality and reexperience it, without the inhibitions which had spoiled his pleasure. . . . At school, the boys Christopher had desired had been as scared as himself. But now the innocent lust which had fired all that ass-grabbing, arm-twisting, sparring and wrestling half naked in the changing room could come out stark naked into the open without shame and be gratified in full" (*CK,* 31). This blunt evaluation of why he went to Berlin was written nearly fifty years later when Isherwood was justifiably asserting his gay liberation and speaking as a leader of the movement. His re-evaluations of the past are fascinating, as he looks back at his real motivations in previous contexts.

The earlier Isherwood was a cypher-witness hiding strong emotions behind a seeming objectivity. The later Isherwood realized that the younger Isherwood was running away from himself by writing this way. In *Christopher and His Kind* he is clear about his earlier omissions. There is a section in which he compares what he actually wrote in his Berlin stories with what he really felt at the time. In retrospect he interprets why he had hidden his true feelings. In addition, in

Christopher and His Kind Isherwood rediscovers his mother's name, calling her Kathleen throughout. After forty years of the "female relative" or "M," this says more about his psychic reconciliation with her than any written explanation would have. Isherwood began calling her by name in *Kathleen and Frank,* but, since she was the co-subject of a biography, he had no choice; in *Christopher and His Kind,* he did have one. At the end of *Kathleen and Frank,* he said that, although it is ostensibly about his parents, it was really about himself. Psychologically it was, since it represented a confessional of his own unfair recalcitrance toward his mother, which was as much or greater than the stubbornness he attributed to her. In reality she seemed more tolerant than he was. This is not to discount his very real feelings, and subjective perception is more real to an individual than any reality observed of him by third persons. Isherwood's use of the third person when he was writing about himself was an overstated guise of objectivity to mask the subjective pain that he was concealing. This could explain his later need for telling the truth about what he had already written, such as his re-evaluation of the Berlin stories.

When Isherwood first arrived in Berlin, he was very much the outsider looking in. He did not yet know German and in order to meet boys he communicated through interpreters. This must have added to even rudimentary exchanges elements of surreal sexual tension and suspense. He was looking through a window as a spy; he was seeing, but not necessarily hearing or understanding. This may have been tense, but it was also exciting. Isherwood the artist was reminded how crucial the use of language is. As Isherwood's German vocabulary slowly increased, so did his audacity: "Christopher's relations with many of the boys soon became easy and intimate. Perhaps they recognized and were drawn to the boyishness in him. He felt a marvelous freedom in their company. He who had hinted and stammered in English, could now ask straight out in German for what he wanted. His limited knowledge of the language forced him to be blunt and he wasn't embarrassed to utter foreign sex words, since they had no associations with his life in England" (*CK,* 31).

In English, words had denotative meanings, but also connotative meanings that were consciously or unconsciously symbolic of thought processes within a pattern. In English a single word became a reference for many other words and associations. Using German words provided a distancing from the linked references that the synonymous words had in English. The new German words took on the aspect of mere sounds without the usual amount of corresponding emotional baggage that the words would have had in the more associative English. Isherwood later said that "he had learned German simply and solely to talk to his sex partners. For him, the entire German language . . . was irradiated with sex. For him, the difference between a table and *ein tisch* was that a table was the dining table in his mother's house and *ein tisch* was *ein tisch* in the Cosy Corner" (*CK,* 21). Isherwood's new secret language was derived from visceral responses to his libido.

The first boy that Isherwood made sounds toward was Bubi ("baby"). Isherwood imbued him with a romantic aura that fit the Lane version of the Truly Strong Man: "In addition to being able to play the German Boy and the blond, Bubi had a role which he created for himself; he was the Wanderer, the Lost Boy, homeless, penniless, dreamily passive yet tough, careless of danger, indifferent to hardship, roaming the earth. Bubi's vulnerability, combined with his tough independence, was powerfully attractive and at the same time teasing. You longed to protect him, but he didn't need you. Or did he? You longed to help him but he didn't need help. Or would he? Wystan wasn't at all impressed by Bubi's performance as the Wanderer. Yet, largely to please Christopher, he wrote a beautiful poem about Bubi, 'This Loved One'" (*CK*, 5).

Just a few pages later, Isherwood, like Auden, became less infatuated with Bubi's performance. Auden's poem is indicative of his friendship with Isherwood and the mutual influence one had on the other. This influence includes the still developing Isherwood-Auden schema that the poem reflects. Auden begins, "Before this loved one"[61] were many other lovers of the moment who at those particular moments were each the special one. Before these lovers there were only the ancestry and history of England that haunts like ghosts to influence the present and create the vulnerability that requires the crossing of frontiers (Berlin) to overcome. If read without a context, pretext, or subtext, this poem can be obscure to the non-initiated or non-members of the gang. The ghosts of the past, of families and history, hinder the search for love in the present and future. Solace can be found only at the frontier, or no-man's land. For the pioneer, Berlin had no past or tradition. The penetration into the frontier becomes the quest of an aspiring Truly Strong Man who recognizes the ways in which he is Truly Weak and strives to overcome his weaknesses. "This Loved One" is a romantic representation of Auden and Isherwood's "mythified" view of their world.

AUDEN: POEMS

In October 1929 *Transitional Poem* was published and Day Lewis introduced Auden's innovative ideas in a traditional manner. This partially prepared a similar audience for the arrival of Auden's non-traditional *Poems* in May 1930. Auden's poems reject the past in terms of their content, but Auden also rejects traditional poetic technique by inventing a new diction. This is what set him apart from his poetic predecessors, including Day Lewis. Auden's famous obscurity in these poems becomes less obscure in light of the Isherwood-Auden schema. The poems also benefit enormously from Edward Mendelson's study, *Early Auden*. Auden's poems are written in the secret code of a game directed at the intimates and nonsquares who were part of their gang. Before they were published, the poems had been written, as Auden said, "to amuse my friends," and were read by Isherwood and then a selected few Anti-Others, such as Day Lewis and Spender. The poems have a purpose: to be coded passwords into the Isherwood-Auden cosmology. According to Mendelson, the "poems were taken as fragments of an activist allegory whose key, although hidden, really did exist. Auden's readers while agreeing on this view were divided into two camps: those who complained that the key was a private myth or private joke reserved for a coterie of cronies and insiders, and those who felt *they* were the insiders, by virtue of membership in Auden's generation, and proceeded to fill the gaps in his broken pattern with their own political and psychological enthusiasms."[62]

These political enthusiasms included socialism and Marxism, and for the misinterpreters, fascism. The psychological and metaphysical enthusiasms centered on Freud, Jung, Yeats's version of Vedanta, and Gerald Heard, who was Auden's friend and influenced him with his theories of an "evolving consciousness." Heard postulated in numerous books that history is a sequence of "inevitable phases of a single evolutionary process—evolution being carried on now in the mind as it was once carried on in the body."[63] Heard's theme of an evolving consciousness can be found in Auden's poems. The quester in these poems is a cypher-witness seeking the North-West Passage by crossing borders and exploring frontiers that are symbols of his divided mind. He is conflicted within himself because he is separated from his real need, which is, Mendelson observes, "submergence in the undifferentiated sea"[64] of the world mind's collective consciousness. In Vedanta the ocean is the metaphorical symbol for an undifferentiated consciousness into which individual drops of water representing separated egos merge, signifying mystical transcendence into one ocean of cosmic unity. Auden said previously that "Life is one whole thing made up of smaller whole things . . . always groups. . . . The whole cannot exist without the part, nor the part without the whole." Much of Auden's thought in 1929 was influenced by Heard's theories, which, though Auden thought them new, were actually quite old. Heard would learn when he came to America with Aldous Huxley in 1937 that his theories had been explained by Vedantic cosmology 2,500 years before.

Consequently, in 1930, Auden's early poems, as influenced by Heard, correlated to Vedanta, even though at the time neither Auden nor Heard realized it. Mendelson says of Auden that "the question he asked in his first poems was not What should I do now? but Of what whole can I be part?"[65] Auden was looking for some kind of psychic integration for himself in particular, for his highbrow group in general, and everyone universally. For the most part, however, his supporters and imitators asked just the first part of the question, "What should I do now?" They interpreted Auden's poems with their martial images as a call to action. This was a call he had not actually intended; yet, he did not mind being thought of as responsible for it. When Isherwood and Auden went to America in 1939, Isherwood followed Heard to California to learn about "this thing," which Heard realized was the basis of his previous theories. "This thing" was Vedanta. Auden stayed in New York and never accepted Isherwood and Heard's Vedanta philosophy, even though Auden had been heading in the same direction. Auden stopped short of rejecting Christianity, as Isherwood and Heard had done; instead he returned to the high Anglicanism of his childhood but did so while writing about his own unique brand of mysticism that was derived from a quasi-Kierkegaardian existentialism and Christian mysticism. At bottom there is little difference between Vedanta and Auden's hybrid mysticism. Each reflects the Perennial Philosophy espoused by Huxley, which means that they are both derived from the original Vedas, the basis of all the world's spiritual systems. In part 2, which will detail Isherwood's conversion, the Perennial Philosophy will be explicated. At this point, one can say that in 1930 both Isherwood and Auden where unconsciously seeking what they would later find and were on the path that would ultimately take them there.

In 1930, however, their conscious paths were still uncertain. Auden's poems were more like random darts thrown at a large but not entirely charted map. For Auden and Isherwood there were still many areas that were labeled "waiting to be explored." This map was filled in to some extent by preexisting ideas and the language that represented these ideas. Auden and Isherwood understood that language can teach or deceive depending on how it is used or misused. Consequently, Auden's early poems are minimalist in the use of language, forsaking standard syntax to strip them down to words as symbols with the barest embellishment. Language always represents the past because it can only exist as a reactionary medium to what has come before. If existing language is the chronicle of a rejected past, then conventional language needs to be rejected and remade also.

Auden repeats a point made by Kierkegaard: "Life is learned backwards, but must be lived forwards."[66] In 1930 Isherwood and Auden might have interpreted this aphorism to mean that, even though one learns from the past, one must abandon it in order to move forward. Later, they would interpret to mean that life is a perpetual continuum; what *was* is integral to what *is* and to what *will be*. The past is integral to the present and future, and all three are undifferentiated in the mystical sense; they are only falsely observed as separate entities by the ego's misinterpretation. For Isherwood and Auden the latter interpretation would come later. In 1930 the former interpretation was the only one that seemed relevant: the past was rejected, and the future is now.

Auden and Isherwood's imaginative border is the metaphor that draws the line between past and future; the frontier beyond the border is the no man's land or the Northwest Passage that one needs to cross in order to escape from the past and move forward. Over time, Mendelson notes, "the idea of the border slowly generated its antithesis: the idea of an undifferentiated unity beyond the border."[67] This unity can also be seen as a mystical unity where there are no borders at all.

In the 1930s few readers of Auden's *Poems* saw them as metaphysical. What many readers embraced from them was that the future was right now and for themselves to make. These poems were written before the stock market crash but not published until eight months after it when the effects were taking hold; the poems seemed to be abstract warnings that had anticipated the crisis and were now metaphorically referring to it. Featuring the old school symbolism of "spies," "secret agents," "firms," "leaders," "borders," and "frontiers," the poems were interpreted as parables for class animosities, political animosities, and international animosities. The world had become a scary place, a place where paranoia was justified. The fascist paranoia of the old school had graduated to the world at large and Auden's poems, which present the old school "mythified" into saga, reflect this world. Auden's critical acclaim made him a leader by default. He had intended his poems for a small circle of friends; that circle grew to encompass the entire decade.

In Auden's *Poems* the play *Paid on Both Sides* is reprinted, having been in the *Criterion* two months earlier. The poems follow the play in the volume. Because the play's imagery of feuding, war, and the cursed past is somewhat less obscure than similar imagery in the poems, the play provides readers with a frame of reference for interpreting the poems. Mendelson's *Early Auden* supplies the best source for a complete interpretation of the poetry. For the purposes of this study, one can focus on those poems that are pertinent to the Isherwood-Auden thematic schema.

The original volume is dedicated to Christopher Isherwood. The dedication consists of four lines, in which the speaker honors the man who stands up vertically in public, but truly values the man who is at peace when he is horizontal. This epigram is about the split between the public man (vertical) and the private man (horizontal). The private man can only achieve inner peace through the releases provided by sex, dreams, and death. The "vertical man" is the conscious man as he exists in society; his public face can be honored, but it is only from his private face that he can truly be known and valued.

In his early poems Auden began a lifelong quest to achieve a metaphysical balance in an otherwise divided mind. Within the mind the degree of conflict between public and private, inner and outer, love and fear, is determined by how much one needs to escape from his public face through daytime fantasy or nighttime dreams. The degree of corresponding withdrawal one makes from everyday existence is in proportion to the pain one feels while living in that existence. While one's public face may appear convivial and adjusted, this face may only be the mask of one role—the gregarious glad-hander—which is a disguise for a frustrated, maladjusted private face. Behind this public face is a secret persona, such as Isherwood the artist. Fantasy and dreams are the psychological means by which the private face relieves the internal pressures caused by the wearing of a public mask. The wearer of the mask is always reminded by the proverbial Watcher in Spanish that this mask is insincere and a denial of private truth. This sense of masking one's genuine identity takes on personal significance for Isherwood and

Auden, who hid their homosexuality, which was not only subject to moral cen-
sure by The Others but also subject to a criminal penalty that could incur jail
time. If one does not listen to his inner self, then he becomes "a *cypher* with codified
conduct and a vacant vessel for a heart" (italics added).[68]

The codified conduct is the conformist behavior of The Others. As a cypher,
one can appear to publicly conform to this code while privately yearning to fulfill
a sublimated inner role, such as Isherwood the artist. The public face may be
admired, but it hides a private emptiness, a theme exemplified in a poem about
a rich Other who appears to be suave and accomplished as he steps in and out of
limousines while deftly wearing his cape. He would seem to be a figure to be
envied by the poor, but, in fact, he is only acting. In truth, he is not a heroic
figure; instead, he is "poised between shocking falls on *razor-edge*"[69] and his apparent sense of clever balance is an act. Long before Auden invoked the razor-edge
metaphor, this image was used in the Upanishads. This poem could have been
interpreted by socialists and communists as representing the false face of capitalism. They would have also liked this phrase from another poem that puts "proletariat against police."[70] This figure who is wearing a mask recalls Robinson's
"Richard Cory" as well as Isherwood's alienated cypher-witness. This figure needs
the release of fantasy and dreams to console his hatred for the public role he dis-
dains. If there is no solace from fantasy or dreams, the only other consolation that
could substitute for or complement inner fantasy would come from meeting a
sympathetic friend or lover. This is not easy. Finding a commiserating friend is
difficult, seeking a lover who helps more than hurts is even harder and that often
is still "of no use."[71] There is "no use" because the subjective "I" and "you" do not
speak the same language. Written in January, 1929, this phrase, "no use," reflects
the Berlin aftermath of the boy bars and the nightly mating ritual. The poem that
contains it also dramatizes the impenetrable isolation between individuals separated from each other and from the collective consciousness of undifferentiated
unity. This poem explores the problem of miscommunication. Language, foreign
or otherwise, is a barrier. Language is a "feat of translation" as Auden would later
call it between "another I" and "another you," in which the ego, in collaboration
with the mouth's duplicity, often obfuscates both truth and unity. Still, even
while understanding that there is a divide between the "two," the future hope will
be that the "two" can learn to communicate with each other and then this "two"
will teach another "two" and form the small group. The Re-education of individual and then collective consciousness starts with "twos and twos" who form a
group and change can spread from group to group until all of society has learned
to live as one.

The "two" can become one through love, if the psychological barriers of the
past can be overcome. The selfish ego is symptomatic of the Truly Weak Man.
Abnegation of the selfish ego is how one becomes selfless and Truly Strong. "Too
Dear, Too Vague" suggests that an ambitious love is a barrier to true love for it is

ego-generated. Ambition by its nature separates and causes the anxiety that leads to "The tightening jaw."[72] An ego-bound ambitious love cannot succeed because the ego divides the mind and sets up barriers to protect itself from its own vulnerable sensitivity. To shed the ego while still remaining sensitive requires one to forsake the fear of failure and allow love to overcome the obstacles that the ego sets up in self-defense. Auden's version of the Layard-Lane ideal states that it is the inhibition caused by the ego that is the underlying cause of fear. To be free of the inhibition caused by the ego is to be free of fear. In 1929 and 1930 Isherwood and Auden sometimes blurred Layard-Lane to confuse love and promiscuity. Auden's poems acknowledge this confusion but still express hope that sex might lead to love. Yet it is so hard to make a commitment to another while one also fears rejection. One always invades, but never explores, "For this is hate and this is fear."[73] For Auden, to invade is sex alone; to explore is to seek love if one can overcome fear. The ego fears rejection more than it needs love and will set up Watchers in Spanish who guard against the weakness of giving in to love. Auden calls these watchers "Sentries against inner and outer."[74] What is their plan? Will they bring war or peace? Can they be bribed by the ego, which will attempt to look noble but instead gives in to the lies made by a duplicitous mouth, which, controlled by the ego, will pursue strategies of betrayal.

These sentries, posted by the ego's fear, prevent a raid on the emotions that might be love, but the sentries also lock out the enduring peace that could come if true love were let in. Betrayal of the private sphere that wants love will come from one's own ego-generated defense mechanisms. The mouth collaborates with the ego and speaks through a public mask of insincerity. The ego tells the deceitful mouth to lie in order to conform to the codified conduct of The Others, but the person behind the ego then suffers for denying the true voice of his inner self. The Weak succumb to the code and lie; the Strong do not.

Human nature reflexively juxtaposes one's self to other selves to determine where one stands in relation to his public and private faces. In the poem "1929" Auden thinks of a master he once hated who has died of cancer, and a friend who has attempted to explain his own failings. One always compares one's self to other selves, some of whom are worth emulating. As an example Auden notes the "Absence of fear in Gerhart Meyer . . . *the truly strong man.*"[75] In "1929" Auden explicitly states that there are Weak and Strong, which he now realizes is to be expected and recognized without making judgments about persons in either camp. This does not mean one should ignore or be fooled by the faults of the Weak; yet, one can still be wary of human nature in general but still love people in particular. The Truly Strong Man does not judge the Truly Weak Man, but tries to help him. The Weak can learn from the example of the Strong. This is a precept of the Bhagavad-Gita. The friend who failed could have been Isherwood at medical school, or Layard who had attempted suicide, or both.

Auden also implies in "1929" that a new race might be needed to develop the traits of the Truly Strong for the future. Foreigners go to new countries and will intermarry to create a new race, and then there will also be a new language so that the soul can "Be weaned at last to independent delight."[76] The allusion to Berlin is evident along with the need to create a new language to replace the old language that represents the past.

Auden's *Poems* aroused his generation, who saw in them a sense of sociopolitical activism instead of the psychological and metaphysical activism he had intended. His peers made him famous, even if many of them had no clear idea— or else created their own idea—of what he was talking about. Auden accepted their approval and was even swayed over to their political activism during the mid-1930s. Still, the early poems were not sociopolitical battle cries, but psychometaphysical parables about the evolution of consciousness. With Isherwood's influence Auden incorporated into his metaphysical questing the concepts of the Test, the Northwest Passage, and the Truly Weak and Truly Strong Man.

THE DISCIPLES

Starting with Isherwood, then Auden, then Spender, the angry young men of the 1930s lined up behind the themes that Auden's impact put in front of them. What Eliot had done for the 1920s, Auden did for the 1930s; he became the standard and others would react to him. Auden was recognized as the new voice of poetry, and poems from Auden country were looked for in the work of others by publishers who wanted to be in step. Friends of Auden, such as his Oxford classmates, would soon benefit from the reflection of his aura of influence, including Day Lewis, Spender, MacNeice, Warner and anyone else who featured Audenesque ideas and allusions in their work. The depression and events in the U.S.S.R., Italy, and Germany demanded a response from the British literati. A new kind of poet and a new style of poetry were expected to give the answers to these vexing political questions. The short story and the novel also developed new voices to join with the poets. Isherwood, however, was largely missing this clamor since he chose to stay in Berlin, mainly to continue meeting boys and to avoid his mother.

Isherwood was energized himself by the tumultuous world of a Berlin inexorably headed for Hitler's rise. Auden and Spender visited Berlin and admired Isherwood's spartan life. Isherwood had now added a second mask to the mask of Isherwood the artist. This was Isherwood the martyr who chose an ascetic life in Berlin rather than live in the comfort of his homeland where he could not bear the hypocrisy of The Others.

In 1929 and 1930 Isherwood worked on his second novel, *The Memorial.* This book, however, would not be published until 1932 when Spender importuned John Lehmann of the Hogarth Press to convince Leonard and Virginia Woolf to publish it. In 1932 this novel of a post-World War I "education in the twenties" was reviewed favorably but did not propel Isherwood into the middle of the new scene because its topic had been superseded by current events of the 1930s. However, even if *The Memorial* was not about the currently new England, but of the recently old England, this old England was influenced by Isherwood's view of the new Berlin. His long stay there had distanced him from Britain and allowed him to consider his former home with more emotional detachment. The freedom of Berlin and his ability to meet male lovers was an emotional release. Consequently, the blind hostility towards home was somewhat ameliorated by a little more compassion. Isherwood was not completely forgiving or forgetting, but he was more willing to see The Others as being conditioned by forces beyond their control.

The Memorial includes the Lane-Layard ideas that had been incorporated into the Isherwood-Auden dialogue on the Truly Weak and Truly Strong Man. Isherwood began his second novel in England but rewrote it in Berlin. Although it was not published until 1932, *The Memorial* will be considered here as a product of Isherwood's experience from 1929 to 1930. The writing in *The Memorial* is far more assured than the writing in *All the Conspirators*, and *The Memorial* reiterates more skillfully the same themes of the first novel: hatred of the war, rejection of the traditions that led to the war, the widowed mother exerting the influence of guilt on a bound, Truly Weak son, and the undertones of homosexual liaisons. Augmenting these themes are characters with greater depth who are adapted from Isherwood's life. Mary Scriven and Margaret Lanwin are both derived from Olive Mangeot. Other characters refer to John Layard, Upward, Isherwood's paternal grandfather, and a T. E. Lawrence-like Truly Weak Man who is defined with a more explicit depiction of the Test. The novel has four sections taking place in this order: 1928, 1920, 1925, and 1929.[77]

1928: Isherwood introduces the Vernon family, titularly headed by "Squire" John who, like Isherwood's paternal grandfather, is in a semiinvalid, semisenile dotage. His daughter, Mary Scriven, has never lived down her elopement to a ne'er-do-well, who would humiliate her by having affairs before he is eventually killed in the war, leaving behind Mary and their two children, Anne and Maurice. Mary's brother Richard is also a war martyr, leaving behind his wife Lily and their son Eric, who in 1928 is a social activist. Eric is a psychological victim of his mother's enduring grief and devotion to the past. Edward Blake is Richard's childhood friend who is a war hero and a Test-driven homosexual. Blake attempts suicide at the end of this section in a verbatim replay of Auden's description to Isherwood of John Layard's suicide attempt. The fact that the expositor of Lane's ideas about the pure-in-heart man would attempt suicide was very disillusioning to Isherwood and Auden. Yet, from this episode, they learned that even heroes are fallible, a fact that makes them ultimately more human. Afterwards, the figure of the flawed antihero began to appear in their work.

1920: The characters appear in a prequel segment that focuses on the dedication of a war memorial in Squire John's village. While Isherwood caustically parodies The Others, he also makes them more sympathetically vulnerable as the seeming victims of their own world; they do not know enough to reject this hollow and controlling world. Squire John is still the center of the villagers' attention. The village includes a Mr. Ramsbottom. Though he is in trade, he is in a lucrative one. In this regard, he is somewhat suggestive of Kathleen Isherwood's father. Ramsbottom will later buy the Vernon ancestral home, as new money supplants old. The transfer is symbolic of change in the postwar world.

1925: Eric and Maurice are at Cambridge. Eric is brilliant but emotionally stuck in childhood, while Maurice is a slick heartie, talking his way out of trouble. The climax in this year occurs when Eric tells Edward Blake that he should stay away from Maurice because Blake exerts too much influence on him. This is a replay of when Victor Page visits Allen Chalmers in *All the Conspirators*. Eric is jealous of Edward's affection for Maurice, which Edward sees as a duty to his best friend's son. Eric's jealousy represents the thick undercurrent of homosexuality throughout the book.

1929: Vernon Hall, the ancestral estate, is now a run-down symbol of the past. The other characters either cling to it as such, or else reject it, or do both. Eric's generation is in transition, attempting to find its own way while being held back by emotional baggage. Eric converts to Catholicism, seemingly less for himself, but more to disavow his mother's Protestant beliefs and the past she has tried to force on him. Edward goes to Berlin to pursue boys, leaving behind Margaret Lanwin, a bohemian artist, who heretofore has accepted Edward as a platonic live-in companion.

Isherwood puts his life into his fiction. He is part Eric and Maurice; Edward is parts of Layard and Lawrence of Arabia; Richard and Ronald Charlesworth (Lily's post-war friend who would like to be more than a friend) are part Frank Isherwood; the bohemian Margaret Lanwin is based on Olive Mangeot, and Mary Scriven and her family are based on Olive Mangeot and her family. Isherwood also represents his new life in Berlin in describing an undercurrent of homosexual desire. Isherwood implies homosexuality more strongly here than in his first novel, perhaps because he had already confessed his own sexual orientation to his mother.

Just as the undertone of homosexuality persists throughout the novel's time shifts, so do the basic natures of the characters. Claude J. Summers observes: "The book's shifting time scheme . . . finally culminating in a 1929 postscript, might be expected to underline the inevitable changes wrought by time. Yet the effect is precisely opposite. The shifting time actually emphasizes the static quality of the internal lives of the characters, all of whom remain imprisoned in the past. Even those characters who most frenetically attempt to escape the past or alter the present are paralyzed by the effects of the . . . great war. Externally, much change does take place."[78] Internally, however, the characters' psyches are frozen. The themes of public against private, inner against outer, are present here along with the sense of life being a perpetual continuum of cause and effect that is both inevitable and inexorable.

Isherwood dedicates his second novel to his father. In section one, "1928," characters are introduced. The description of Mary Scriven's happily untidy and lived-in home (*M*, 12) is a description of the Mangeot home. Mary Scriven's daughter Anne thinks how everyone says, "Your mother's wonderful" (*M*, 13). Isherwood's friends thought Olive Mangeot wonderful. Mary is then set up as a counterpoint to the war widow Lily Vernon. Anne, who is more introverted than either her mother or her brother Maurice, thinks, "I'm not one of the gang" (*M*, 14). For Isherwood, the gang is still utmost, and one was either in or a square who was out. Ronald Charlesworth is a pensioned former soldier and Lily's platonic friend who cannot penetrate her grieving veil. Isherwood writes that Charlesworth, "as a young man stood a good deal of chaff from his brother officers because of his fondness for museums, art galleries, old bookshops. Now that he was retired he could . . . indulge his hobbies in comfort" (*M*, 22–23). Ronald represents Frank Isherwood as he had been, but also Frank as he never had the chance to become. As for Lily: "Since [Ronald] had known her, she had always been dressed in black" (*M*, 23): "At times, he pictured her as sort of a nun" (*M*, 25). Ronald admires her love of the past, and she says to him, "People want to destroy all this. But what have they to put in its place" (*M*, 29). Even her son Eric is not satisfactory to her. Eric is first described by Anne:

> Yes, he really is my idea of a saint, Anne thought. . . . You could have put him straight into the Bible, just as he was. . . . There was something ancient and sombre about him. And when he looked at you, you felt that he was absolutely honest and fearless and good. Perhaps they were all just a little bit afraid of Eric—yes, even Mary. They showed this when they chattered to him and made jokes in their own language, trying to pretend he was one of themselves. . . . They knew quite well that he wasn't. And really, what did any of them know about him that mattered? What had made him, for instance, at the time of the general strike, throw up his Cambridge career just when he was doing so brilliantly and was the coming man, as people said, and take to this work of his. . . . And now that he was rich, he was carrying on just the same. He must spend at least half the money from the estate [which he inherited from Squire John] on his various funds and societies and clubs. . . . He was always busy (*M*, 36–38).

Eric was busy avoiding his mother. Anne describes Eric as if he might be a Truly Strong Man; however, the Cambridge allusion suggests that Eric is Isherwood in narcissistic disguise. There are clues that Eric is not quite the imposing saint that Anne and the gang think he is, and that he is more like the figure in Auden's poem, "poised between shocking falls on razor-edge." His present public face masks his disdain for the past and the Poshocracy; his charitable works are a rebellious refutation of both. While he passively listens to some idle tea-table conversation, Eric thinks, "Do they despise me as much as I despise them? The proud enemies, smoking, laughing" (*M*, 40). Eric is consumed with guilt for having these feelings, especially towards his mother: "I'm a brute. I'm vile to her. Darling mother. Can't I help her? Must we go on like this? It seems so miserable and senseless" (*M*, 51). This is Isherwood and Kathleen Isherwood for his gang to recognize. Eric is another Philip Lindsay; Lily another Mrs. Lindsay. They are, however, given a past that explains their present.

In 1928 Edward Blake first appears in Berlin. He has been to another in a line of psychoanalysts who have not been able to help him with their "Questions about early childhood" (*M*, 56–57). Blake shoots himself but does not die: "'I've mucked it,' Edward repeated to himself" (*M*, 57). What follows is Auden's description of John Layard having also "mucked it" and then going to Auden for help. The year 1928 introduces the cast. The flashback to 1920 explains why they have become the way they are.

1920: Lily is a war widow. Her life ended with Richard's death, freezing her psyche in the past: "I shall never forget our life together. I shall never forget how happy we were. Nobody can take that away from me" (*M*, 73). Lily will resent and resist any attempt to have her move forward. Her son Eric is overwhelmed by his mother's war widow role and cannot cope either with her remoteness or the shadow of his dead father. This is demonstrated by his timidity and a debilitating stammer that is aggravated by his mother's lack of sympathy. She is ashamed of Eric because he is not the perfect son that Richard's memory deserves.

Lily is wary of Mary Scriven, Richard's sister, who is as comfortably casual as Lily is coldly reserved. Lily thinks that Mary is not suitably grieving for her brother. Lily also believes that "nobody has understood Richard but herself. That was her pride and her consolation now. He should have been sent to Oxford or Cambridge and become a don, instead of going . . . into that solicitor's office. Richard had never cared much for being a solicitor. His talents were quite wasted. . . . Nevertheless, some of the happiest hours of their married life had been spent in museums, libraries, churches. Richard developed tastes which must have been latent all the time. He began to sketch. He became good—better than herself. She was so proud of his work and showed it to everyone. . . . Darling Eric. He must fulfil what Richard would have wished. He must be a don" (*M*, 89–91). Isherwood is writing about his father and himself. Just as Richard "never cared for being a solicitor," Frank never cared for being a soldier. Next, the memorial of the title is dedicated.

The vicar reads the names of the dead in alphabetical order, which Lily resents because Richard Vernon is nearly last. Edward Blake is there, "Richard's great friend. And now Mary's friend. Lily had tried so hard . . . to like him—for everything in any way connected with Richard must be likable and nice—but she'd failed. Perhaps she'd just been jealous" (*M*, 99–100). Lily immediately feels guilty for thinking this and reminds herself of "the terrible things [Edward had] been through in the war. After his flying accident . . . she'd heard he'd been quite insane" (*M*, 100).

The Bishop speaks: "There are some here today who have looked on that scene of terrible desolation. . . . But to others, those who have not seen that land, I should like to put this question: What did the war mean to you?" (*M*, 106). Isherwood is reiterating his and Auden's recollections of the "patriotic cant" at the old school, particularly when Auden imitated an actual address they had heard. Isherwood repeats this address in *The Memorial*, just as Auden would in *The Orators*.

The majority of the action in this section takes place in the characters' minds. Mary recalls her facilely charming husband Desmond with whom she had eloped because he had not met the family's standard. Unfortunately for her, her family were right about him, for he would have affairs, sometimes deserting her and their two children. Isherwood implies that Desmond's behavior was an angry reaction to the Vernon family's rejection of him. Desmond was also killed in the war, but Mary does not become a grieving war widow like Lily. Instead, Mary thinks that her son Maurice is just like Desmond, always talking his way out of trouble: "She didn't blame him. She'd got into the habit of seldom blaming Maurice, and this, no doubt, was bad" (*M*, 108). And indeed it was bad. At the memorial dedication she reflects:

> I suppose it's hateful to think of laughing here, at this service, for a hundred and three quite decent little men who all got killed stopping Germans flying the two-headed eagle on the Conservative Club. Yes, I do feel that. No, I don't, she revolted. After all, that's only snobbery. All this cult of dead people is only snobbery. I'm afraid I believe that . . . this moment seems to me not only false but, yes, actually wicked. Living people are better than dead ones. And we've got to get on with life.
>
> The truth is, thought Mary, I want my lunch. And my corns ache dreadfully. And I despise men. (*M*, 112–13)

In Wholly-Truthful art, daily life goes on. While Mary is privately scorning the ceremony she observes Lily basking in it. The internal scene shifts to the memories of Edward Blake, who recalls when he and Richard were at school: "Then, also, had Edward been oppressed by a fatalistic sense of helplessness. Of being a tiny part of a machine. Not such a big machine. Only a school of four hundred boys. . . . How they'd all crowded together—the new youths—mutely wretched, wishing to efface themselves, unhappily trying to avoid the sarcasms of their seniors. Edward Blake had trembled, loathing it passionately, more than the others, loathing and resenting it. Hating his parents for having sent him to such a place. He'd drown himself. He'd starve to death. He'd never submit, not if they tortured him. . . . How did people endure it? Why didn't they rebel?" (*M*, 128–129). At school Edward and Richard became friends. Edward admired Richard rapturously and attributed to him the qualities of the Truly Strong Man. Bolstered by Richard's friendship,

Edward was going to take life by storm. He admitted no obstacle, no barriers. He could do anything. . . . All that he read, either of heroism or success, he
applied to himself. . . . Everywhere he saw a challenge. . . . He dared refuse no
adventure—horribly frightened as he often was. . . . He would have fought any boy
in school . . . rather than admit to being afraid. . . . He had started his school career
by hating the school; he ended by despising it. And throughout, he had no close
friend but Richard. . . . To Edward, Richard was a hero and great man. In Richard's
presence he felt genuine humility. Richard's strength and calm made him conscious
of his own weakness. He envied his friend as he envied nobody else. Richard had
no need to give proofs of his courage, to assert strength of will. He was sure of himself—therefore he did not have to fight and boast. He was brave—unnecessary for
him to climb the chapel roof or swim the river in clothes to win a shilling bet.
(*M*, 131–33)

This is a contrast of a Truly Weak and a Truly Strong Man. Isherwood implies that
Edward loved Richard—in a platonic sense only—because he was afraid to attempt
a deeper relationship, just as Isherwood had been afraid to assert his true feelings
when he was at school.

Later when Richard meets Lily, he becomes in Edward's eyes something less
than the Truly Strong Man in her company: "Poor old Richard. He'd looked rather
an ass trailing around after her." (*M*, 134). When Lily and Richard marry, "Edward,
of course, was best man. He had carried out his duties on the day in a mood of
slightly hysterical humor" (*M*, 135). At the wedding, in a role reversal, Edward supported Richard who had "comically collapsed. . . . And Edward . . . had a sense of
leadership and power over the whole party" (*M*, 135). He did not, however, have
enough power to prevent his friend from marrying and loses him for the first time.

When Mary elopes and is ostracized by her family, Edward visits Richard
and asks him to relent and see her, but Richard refuses. Edward, who had been
Weak, attempts to be Truly Strong and Richard, whom Edward had perceived as
Strong is now Weak. Neither Edward nor Lily likes each other, each seeing the
other as a rival for Richard's affection. Edward would visit Mary and be put off
by Desmond's sarcasm. He would visit Richard and just be put off by Richard's
indifference. Consequently, in order to "escape these two houses he had travelled.
China. South Africa. Brazil. Twice around the world. Had shot big game,
climbed in the Alps, been round the coast of Europe in a small sailing boat. At
any rate, he could afford to risk his life expensively. And he was happier away
from England" (*M*, 140). Edward's desire to escape confrontation by traveling
abroad is reminiscent of Isherwood's own escapist travels. Edward, after having
lost Richard to Lily, confronted Tests just as he had done at school. He was seeking the Northwest Passage as a substitute for losing Richard's friendship. The war
intervenes. After Richard is killed in battle, Edward also tries to get killed in battle.
Neither Edward nor Lily is able to recover from Richard's death.

Nor would Eric, who would have the burden of the hero-father placed on him. The Others, led by his mother and Edward, would be constant reminders of that burden. Isherwood writes of Eric (and himself): "Father had been killed while Eric was at school. This was his first year as a public school boy, and the telegram, with mother's letter following it, had seemed merely to add the darkest tinge to an already [hard] life of war rations, fagging, loneliness, discomfort, strangeness" (*M,* 149). "Fagging" was the term for the older students' abuse of the younger. Eric recalls happier times when his father would take him for walks and tell him about Sherlock Holmes. Eric then describes the patriotic cant and rant as well as the pious, yet merely obligatory condolences. Eric's vacs home are so dreaded by him because of Lily's morbidity that "even school was better than that haunted state" (*M,* 153). On future vacs, Eric, despite enormous guilt for deserting his mother, would go to Aunt Mary's for escape, as Isherwood had gone to the Mangeots.

Yet, even when Eric goes to visit his cousins Anne and Maurice, he "had violent spasms of jealousy and self-disgust in which he saw, through all their kindness, a conspiracy to conceal from him that he was merely being tolerated and pitied" (*M,* 167). Then Isherwood follows with an incident that is right out of Spender's "The Cousins." Eric's inner angst explodes in a tearful fit. Maurice, who had actually done nothing to provoke this outburst, very generously goes to Eric and, in a Truly Strong gesture, apologizes. From Maurice's brave apology, Eric "had learnt, that there was a very feminine side to Maurice's nature" (*M,* 169). In *The Ascent of F6,* Michael Ransom would also be described as having a "feminine" side. Then Eric becomes enraptured with his cousin, just as Edward Blake had been enamoured with Richard. Eric is also just as jealous of supposed interlopers on their friendship.

In book 1, "1928," Isherwood displays his cast and their various behaviors without antecedent explanation. In book 2, "1920," circumstances are depicted from which the reader surmises explanations for the characters' actions. For Isherwood, past, present, and future are a matter of cause and effect. People become what they are in the present as a reaction to the past. This reaction can be an acceptance of the past or a rejection of it, but there is always a deep connection between present and past. Whether one accepts or rejects the past by his actions in the public sphere, the psyche of the inner sphere is more static than the manifest actions would seem to indicate. Isherwood also demonstrates how elusive the idea of the Truly Weak and Truly Strong Man can be. Whether one is Weak or Strong teeters precariously on Auden's "razor-edge." In being subjectively perceived by another—for example, Edward observing Richard with Lily—one can change from Strong to Weak, depending on circumstances. Isherwood implies that one's affection for another can aggrandize the other's attributes: Edward with Richard, Eric with Maurice, Isherwood with Bubi. As Auden indicates in his poem, "This Loved One," Isherwood romanticizes his newest boyfriend, bestowing on Bubi great status, though just as quickly humanizing him again. In "1920," the reader learns about causes; in "1925," he reads about the effects.

1925: Maurice is at Cambridge getting into trouble and dodging creditors. He borrows from new dupes to pay old dupes. When this plan stalls, he tries to get cash from Edward Blake. Maurice's Cambridge tutor tells him that the next incident will be his last. Mary's inability to be stern with Maurice when he was a child has yielded his predicted irresponsibility.

Eric is still courting the dons and the Poshocracy with his public face, while he despises them privately: "Standing there, he enclosed, he enfolded them all in his hatred" (*M*, 200). Then Eric scorns them in Mortmere-ish detail and finally thinks he would like to blow them up with an "enormous charge of dynamite" (*M*, 201). He would spare only Maurice, whom he regards, despite his cousin's foibles, "like a child" (*M*, 200). His mother is still grieving. To Eric, "her listless sadness made him suddenly fierce," and he tells her, "you care more for this house than you do for human beings" (*M*, 205). In his diary, Eric writes: "Another vile scene this morning. . . . What would Father have thought. . . . Suppose Father were to come back from the grave, suppose it turned out that he'd never been killed, was a shell-shock case, unidentified in a far-away hospital—and suddenly his memory returned? This was one of Eric's nightmares. Father would come back to find that the two people he loved, who'd loved each other so much, were leading this sordid, miserable life. Eric thought: But I would shoot myself or die of shame" (*M*, 205).

Eric visits Maurice and finds Edward there with Margaret Lanwin. Eric is not pleased. Later he goes to see Edward and tells him to stay away from Maurice because he is a bad influence on him. This is a replay of Victor Page visiting Chalmers; however, in the former case, the reader is aware that Mrs. Lindsay does not like Chalmers, and she has conveyed this to Page, which is Page's motivation for interfering. When Eric goes to see Edward, his accusation seems out of the blue. Edward responds to Eric's demand by saying, "I suppose, Eric, I'm the wickedest person you've ever met?" Eric answers, "I don't think you're wicked. I think you're weak" (*M*, 222). Edward does not answer this directly but agrees not to see Maurice again. Eric leaves, "trembling, furious with himself, he knew in a moment he would burst into tears" (*M*, 224). Eric is "furious with himself" because he knows the real cause of his attack on Edward:

> Like a prisoner strapped ready for torture, Eric lay rigid, his fists clenched, in his narrow bed. Liar, he thought. Hypocrite! Liar! Cheat! He stared furiously at the dark ceiling. I was jealous. The whole thing was nothing but jealousy.
>
> I'm ten thousand times worse than Edward, Eric thought. Ten million times worse.
>
> Jealous; jealous; jealous!
>
> I'm not fit to live. (*M*, 226)

Feeling remorseful, Eric composes many drafts of an apologetic letter to Edward, but sends none. Book 3 ends. Three years later, possibly from being denied seeing Maurice and finding no viable substitute in Berlin, Edward attempts suicide.

Isherwood suggests at least the possibility of homosexual attraction in Eric's jealousy of Edward concerning Maurice and previously in Edward's jealousy of Lily concerning Richard. In both cases the attraction began at the old school, just as Isherwood's attraction to boys began at his old school.

1929: Book 4 is very short and decidedly anticlimactic, almost flat. The characters are shown to be stuck in their inner worlds while their outer circumstances affect them only superficially. For example, Maurice is still facilely charming, but now using his charm as a car salesman.

Isherwood's second novel is a replay of *All the Conspirators*, but he surpasses his first novel with more fluid and natural writing and characters who are better developed. In the former, characters' behaviors are displayed symptomatically, without any explanation of the symptoms' cause. Their behaviors are seen in the present as reactions to the past, but that past is not depicted for readers as a frame of reference. In *All the Conspirators* the reader is expected to be a detective concerning the past by interpreting the clues and symptoms of what the characters say and do in the present. However, as Isherwood himself said in his introduction to the first novel's reissue in 1957, even he found it too cryptic and obscure for readers to understand his intentions fully. Thus, in his second novel, his intentions are more wholly (and truthfully) developed by the astute use of inner monologues to help readers correlate cause and effect and to better understand the Isherwood schema, particularly the motif of the Truly Weak and Truly Strong Man.

The Memorial is autobiographical, featuring Isherwood's inner and outer life up to the time of its writing. This novel details the characters through their inner thoughts. These private thoughts are a counter to their public actions, thus showing how much in opposition one's private thoughts and public actions can be. This is the divided mind at work reflecting the new understanding of it through psychoanalysis. *The Memorial* is a statement about Isherwood's world with himself as the leading actor. By extension, he tells the universal story of his contemporaries who had gone to the old school. *The Memorial* explained the 1920s to his peers as a decade of cause and effect. They were now ready to refute that decade and become activists in the 1930s.

THE SINCEREST FORM OF FLATTERY

The Memorial was written in 1929 and 1930 but not published until 1932. It contains themes that Isherwood shared with Auden, who would become famous in 1930; however, it is helpful to see this novel as preceding Auden rather than following him. *The Memorial* also represents an Isherwood who is more sympathetic to his characters. He does not forgive The Others, but attributes to them weaknesses of human nature caused by the prevailing society. Berlin may have influenced some of this new sympathy. Isherwood wrote the first draft before he left England and then rewrote that draft entirely in Berlin. This may have allowed him a little distance to be more objective about his former home. He also observed in Berlin the insidious beginnings of the influence of Nazism. Isherwood saw firsthand the powerful effects of peer pressure and this gave him a more sympathetic understanding of the peer pressure that had dominated The Others. In Berlin he watched the slow shift in the behavior of the population towards greater fear and paranoia. He would report his findings to Auden, Spender, and John Lehmann, who visited him in Berlin and with whom he corresponded regularly. For Isherwood examples of the Truly Weak many and the Truly Strong few became part of his daily life.

Back in England, the literati still considered themselves first and foremost intellectual artists; this would change during the depression as they got caught up in the surge of popularity for socialism and for the theoretical marxism and communism thought to be exemplified by the Soviet Union. They aligned themselves intellectually with the egalitarianism of the proletariat, although few actually stood shoulder to shoulder with their ostensible role models—George Orwell was a notable exception.

The artist as activist was becoming the prevalent role for the artists of the 1930s. The artist as essayist was not new, nor was the artist as essayist who wrote on non-artistic topics. However, in the 1930s there was a proliferation of the latter. The Auden Generation wanted not only to cross borders and explore frontiers but to eradicate borders and merge the frontiers into an artistic, social, and political unity. Since their purpose was to be poets who were social activists, art and essays were to be integrated as one and the same. Essays explicated themes didactically; art "metaphorized" the same themes as parables. Elements within the art and essays were derived from the Isherwood-Auden schema: rejection of the past, Tests, exploration, the divided mind, public and private, and the Truly Weak and Truly Strong Man. Isherwood, a catalyst for the Auden Generation, was not directly participating in the revolution.

In 1930 Isherwood was still in Berlin and *The Memorial,* though completed, was not to be published for two more years. He supported himself by teaching English to those who "wanted to learn English for show-off social reasons, or to be able to read Aldous Huxley in the original" (*CK,* 21). On 6 February 1930 Isherwood wrote to Spender: "I'm very apathetic here. It's all so pleasant and I have utterly lost any sense of strangeness in being abroad. I even don't particularly care when I see England again. And when I read in my [past] diary about my life at home, it's like people on the moon" (*CK,* 36). At this time Isherwood was keeping diaries about Berlin. In these diaries there was also a detached quality since he was still a pioneer in a strange country and his German language skills, though improving, were not yet so polished that they obviated his feeling of being the outsider. These diaries would become the basis for the Berlin stories, in which Isherwood would make his famous "I am a camera" remark, implying that he was a passive observer of events. Although he may have given the impression that he passively observed, this is not to say he did not *feel.* In 1976, Isherwood looked back at the Berlin of 1930: "Here was the seething brew of his-

tory in the making—a brew which would test the truth of all the political theories . . . the Berlin brew seethed with the unemployment, malnutrition, stock-
market panic, hatred of the Versailles Treaty, and other potent ingredients. On
September 20, a new one was added; in the Reichstag elections, the Nazis . . .
became for the first time a major political party" (*CK,* 48). Isherwood noted the rise
of Nazism as did Auden and Spender when they visited Berlin. Auden would incorporate an exploration of the nature of fascism, hero worship, and the nagging
ghosts of British ancestors into his next published work, his seemingly
inscrutable long prose poem, *The Orators,* which is also his version of Mortmere.

THE ORATORS

The Orators was published in 1932 and was Auden's follow-up to the critical success
of *Poems* two years earlier. If *Poems* was thought to be obscure, much of *The Orators*
seemed impenetrable. The first edition's dust jacket text obfuscates admirably: "Of
W. H. Auden's first volume of poems the most discerning readers remarked that the
author was often very 'obscure,' but that he was unquestionably a poet, and one of
the few poets of first-rate ability who have so far appeared to voice the post-war generation, a generation which has its own problems and its profound difficulties. *The
Orators* is not a collection, but a single work with one theme and purpose, partly in
prose and partly in verse, in which the author continues his exploration of new form
and rhythm. It will not disappoint those who have been excited by the unfamiliar
metric and the violent imagination of the previous book." This is the entire description. No further word on what the "one theme" and its "purpose" might be.
Apparently, Faber and Faber's publicist was not taking any chances. Even Auden
admitted to density of *The Orators* in a preface to the 1966 reissue:

> As a rule, when I re-read something I wrote when I was younger, I can think
> myself back into the frame of mind in which I wrote it. *The Orators,* though,
> defeats me. My name seems a pseudonym for someone else, someone talented but
> near the border of sanity, who might well, in a year or two, become a Nazi.
>
> The literary influences I do remember more or less. [In *Early Auden,*
> Mendelson cites Baudelaire and D. H. Lawrence, among others.]
>
> The central theme seems to be Hero-Worship, and we all know what that can
> lead to politically. . . . my unconscious motive . . . was therapeutic, to exorcize cer-
> tain tendencies in myself by allowing them to run riot in phantasy. . . . I realize that
> it is precisely the schoolboy atmosphere and diction which act as a moral criticism
> of the rather ugly emotions and ideas they are employed to express.

Auden then suggests that by treating serious matters in a juvenile way, this "makes
it impossible to take them seriously." He notes that at the end of *The Orators* "in
one of the Odes I express all of the sentiments with which his followers hailed the
advent of Hitler, but these are rendered, I hope, innocuous by the fact that the

Fuhrer so hailed [in the Ode] is a new-born baby and the son of a friend [Rex Warner]." [79]

Auden's self-criticism may have been warranted. When *The Orators* was written there was a great deal of Mortmere in it, yet few readers knew Isherwood's name and virtually none had ever heard of Mortmere. One key to understanding *The Orators* is to see it as a new Mortmere story written with a more conscious understanding of the Isherwood-Auden schema that the Isherwood-Upward originals did not have. Edward Mendelson observes in *Early Auden* that Ode IV of *The Orators* lists characters from Mortmere as an inside joke for Isherwood's benefit. More than just names from Mortmere can be found in *The Orators;* its over-the-top outrageousness matches Isherwood's stories, as does the anger and frustration behind the satire. Subtitled "An English Study," the satire and anger are directed at the British past and the traditions that Auden and Isherwood rejected. As in Mortmere, the old school is a metaphor for Britain and the principal target of Auden's wrath. Nonetheless, even with this correlation to Mortmere, there is much in *The Orators* that remains obscure. The volume is also plagued by a sense of excessiveness, something Auden later tried to correct by cutting a great deal from the 1966 version.

The dedication of *The Orators* is to Spender:

> Private faces in public places
> Are wiser and nicer
> Than public faces in private places. [80]

On a surface level, these lines allude to Isherwood, Auden, and Spender's experiences in Berlin's gay bars. On a deeper level, it refers to the introduction of *Oxford Poetry, 1928* and the interaction of "private spheres" with "public chaos." A public face in a private place is a mask worn even during intimacy and signifies the Truly Weak Man who is not comfortable with his inner self. A private face in a public place belongs to the Truly Strong Man whose inner Self (with a Vedantic capital "S") is his only Self, which he manifests equally in public or private. Auden said the theme of *The Orators* is hero-worship. It is, but the volume does not praise hero-worship; it is a warning that those who wish to be heroes by design at whatever cost, such as Hitler, and those who need a hero to follow are Truly Weak. Auden explains the theme of the destructive power of hero-worship: "In a sense the work is my memorial to D. H. Lawrence; i.e. the theme is the failure of the romantic conception of personality. . . . The four parts . . . are stages in the development of the hero who never appears at all." Auden continues:

> Thus Part I. Introduction to influence.
> Part 2. Personally involved with hero. Crisis.
> Part 3. Intellectual reconstruction of hero's teaching. The cerebral life.
> Part 4. The effect of the hero's failure on the emotional life. [81]

The Orators is about how "no secular saviour can equal the hopes of his youthful followers."[82] Auden and Isherwood would make this point very directly in *The Ascent
of F6*. Auden was acting upon his own experiences on three counts: he was witness
to hero-worship at the old school; he observed the cult of personality as it evolved
with Hitler in Germany; his own hero Layard, for whom he had had such great
enthusiasm, as recorded in *Lions and Shadows,* later showed up at his door with a
bullet wound from a suicide attempt.

Auden's prologue, like the rest of the volume, is cryptic without a primer. Yet
it succinctly introduces the Isherwood-Auden schema, once a reader has been
primed. An unnamed stranger views the landscape and is reminded of his
"mother's figure." With "mapping pens" he traces "family names" as he charts an
expedition to some frontier. He hears subliminally: "Dear boy, be brave . . ."
which is a call that he should face his Test. "And yet this prophet" when he
returns from defending his country is greeted with "Coward, Coward," and the
"giantess," the mother figure, "cries deceiver" (*O,* 9).

The mother figure is tied to the land along with the family names that represent the past. The past must be defended and preserved. This is a Test for the
hero-son who is urged on to be brave. By succumbing to the pressure to confront
a Test, the son only proves himself to be Truly Weak and is called a coward.
Further injury is added by his own mother, who calls him a deceiver for pretending to be a hero. The prologue proclaims the Isherwood-Auden schema as
the theme. What follows is the Mortmere-ish elucidation of the theme.

Book 1 is called "The Initiates." Part 1 of book 1 is titled "Address for a Prize
Day." The address is by an ancient Other to school boys who are being prepared
for empire-saving by his cant and rant that reminds them of the war: "What does
it mean? What does it mean? Not what does it mean to them, there, then. What
does it mean to us here now? Why are we here? What are we going to do?" (*O,*
13). The address continues with warnings for the hearties to be alert for subver-
sive aesthetes (such as Isherwood, Upward, Auden, and Spender). The aesthetes
are "those who have been guilty in their life of excessive love towards themselves
or their neighbours, those guilty of defective love towards God and those guilty
of perverted love" (*O,* 14). For the ancient Other, "excessive love" in any form
that is not directed at the school and state is nonconformist and distracts one
from blind allegiance to the school and state. The lovers of themselves are
scorned because they are not joiners or game-players, preferring solitude, nature,
and the arts. In order to help them, the ancient Other exhorts the hearties to go
for a walk alone in a wood with one and subtly say: "I suppose you realise you
are fingering the levers that control eternity"(*O,* 15). The excessive lovers of their
neighbors are suffering from the fact that "They need love" (*O,* 16) and try too
hard to get it, a motif that could point to Spender's need for affirmation. The
defective lovers are compulsive-obsessives—perhaps not unlike Isherwood—who
are "often collectors" (*O,* 16). The ancient Other says they need to be kept busy:

"Hit them in the face if necessary. If they hit back you will know they are saved" (*O,* 17). The Other then describes the perverted lovers: "Last and worse, the perverted lovers. So convincing at first, so little apparent cause for anxiety. A slight proneness to influenza. . . . They've lost their nerve" (*O,* 17). Then the ancient Other depicts the hated honor system in action: "Draw up a list of rotters and slackers, of proscribed persons under headings like this. Committees for municipal improvement. . . . All these have got to die without issue" (*O,* 19). In other words, nonconformists are doomed.

"The Initiates" represents the Mortmere-ish patriotic brainwashing to which most of the hearties were susceptible. The aesthetes rejected such absurd jingoism, automatically making them appear suspect to The Others. In the second part of "The Initiates," titled, "Argument," there are three sections. In the first section, the brainwashed are ready to succumb to the cult of the leader, known only as "Him." Here, one recalls Isherwood's Mortmere tale of "The World War" as well as *Paid on Both Sides* and the poems from Auden's first volume. Of the allusions to his own poems, one might think Auden is making fun of himself and his reputed obscurity in this section. Images include: "talk of generals," "interrogation of villagers," "execution of a spy," "a tale of sexual prowess," "establishment of a torpedo base," "the mine with obsolete machinery." In the second part, the Leader's followers issue a litany of rhapsodic chants, each of which is punctuated by the name of a known public or fictional figure: "From all nervous excitement and follies of the will; from the postponed guilt and deferred pain; from the oppression of noon and from the terror in the night, O Bulldog Drummond deliver us" (*O,* 24). Sherlock Holmes and Hercules Poirot are also named. (Detective stories were Auden's favorite leisure reading.) His followers associate Him with other heroes, and mythicize Him into a saga figure. In the third section, the leader, Him, is betrayed and killed leaving behind a confused body of followers without a head. His followers use His memory as a cohering force to retain their fledgling identity. Him becomes even more mythicized combining the heroic and bizarre: "His ability to smell a wet knife at a distance of half a mile. His refusal to wear anything but silk next to his skin" (*O,* 28). The worship of Him and His past gives His followers a way to remain intact as an identifiable entity; it also prevents them, who are really school boys, from growing up.

Part 3 is a "Statement" that opens with a self-aggrandizing list of the followers' attributes that would seem to be allusions to the boys in Berlin. "One charms by thickness of wrist; one by variety of positions; one has a beautiful skin, one a fascinating smell" (*O,* 30). "One jumps out of windows for profit. . . . one makes leather instruments of torture for titled aristocrats" (*O,* 30). (In Isherwood's *Mr. Norris Changes Trains* (1935) there is a party scene of a like nature.) The list goes on for good or ill and seems to be an inventory of all possible personality types Auden can remember or imagine. Mendelson observes that the "response to the emotional vacancy left by the hero's absence is to construct a visionary orthodoxy. Like all orthodoxies it is largely an adaptation of various traditions of wisdom, many of them used in ways unimaginable to their originators."[83] The past is reconstituted to fit the needs of the present in ways that are not only unimaginable, but unrecognizable. The past perverted in this way is no longer history but propaganda. Auden parades the endless types to say that while "life is many" (O, 33), life is also an inevitable cycle of these types and their behaviors repeated over and over. For example, "The soldier shall say 'It is a fine day for hurting'" (O, 34). Auden then delves into the quasi-mystical, with what is perhaps a poke at Yeats: "Sun is on right, moon on left, powers to earth. The action of light on dark is to cause it to contract" (O, 36). What do these lines mean? Like much that precedes them, these words form a cryptic pronouncement implying some kind of eternal inevitability that governs the cycle of regenerated types. It is portentous but not to be taken too seriously, just as Auden warned that none of *The Orators* should be taken too seriously. Nonetheless, the metaphysical quality intimated by Auden was very serious to him in other contexts, if not necessarily this one.

The fourth and last part of book 1 is "Letter to a Wound." This letter is a self-satire of the kind of narcissistic martyrdom that Isherwood, Auden, and Spender recognized in themselves and their peers. The wound is not explained just as the wound was not explained in Isherwood's last Mortmere story, "The World War"; but the wound has become the speaker's preoccupation—a dangerous one, like a child's imaginary friend who has begun to supersede external reality and rationality. Auden here mocks the overweening self-introspection that his generation was prone to in their new age of psychoanalysis. Auden, by writing to the wound satirically, shows that art is an escape into a secondary world from the pain in the primary world. The irony of the satire is that the primary pain itself becomes the secondary world of the narcissistic martyr. The narcissist's private sphere personifies the wound and talks to it. By doing so he withdraws himself from public chaos and into private fantasy. Subsequently, the divided mind bifurcates the border between public and private until the private sphere *is* reality and the public sphere seems fantasy. Of the wound Auden writes: "Who'll ever guess what it is? Once I carved on a seat in the park 'We have sat here. You'd better not'" (O, 37). This hints vaguely at what only the gang knew for sure: Auden's wound had been a rectal fissure that required surgery and a prolonged healing period. Of his carving on the park bench—which symbolizes an unconscious cry for approval—he says to the wound: "Now I see that all that sort of thing is juvenile and silly, merely a reaction against insecurity and shame" (O, 37–38). This statement is not just about a wound, but it is an apologia for all reactions, physical or mental, caused by the narcissistic angst of Auden's Generation.

Book 2 is "Journal of an Airman." While book 1 was about the gang mentality of a group of followers and their focus on Him and the aftermath of Him, the airman is alone—a solitary Him in the making. He is above the din, seeing with the hawk vision of the cypher-witness who, at the right moment, will assert his identity and swoop suddenly to lead his troops. This potentiality, however, raises three questions for the airman: Who are the troops? Who are the enemy? And is there a difference? Mendelson notes, "the airman begins alone, worries over the crucial problem—'group organisation,' slowly acknowledges his reliance on an ancestor, and finally accepts the undifferentiated unity of surrender and death."[84] This summary sounds quite serious—and it is. However, this parable of serious intent is in no way serious in method. The airman's journal is about the Isherwood-Auden schema, and Auden is still combining saga, the old school, and Mortmere.

The journal seems the work of a precocious school boy fantasizing about himself as a hero while showing off his intellect. Like Mortmere, Auden's airman fantasy, however outrageous, is an escape from either pain, tedium, or both. This is not evident from a text-only reading. The seriousness behind this satiric parable requires a good deal of background knowledge of Auden (and Isherwood) in order to understand it. While this poem was still being composed, Auden remarked: "The flying symbolism is fairly obvious. The chief strands are [the airman's] uncle (Heredity-Matrilineal descent and initiations), belief in a universal conspiracy (the secret society mind), kleptomania (the worm in the root)."[85] The "dead uncle" was the black sheep of the airman's family because he was homosexual. He is based on Isherwood's Uncle Henry, still quite alive. The motif of homosexuality is implied only. The airman discovers that he and his uncle are of the same homosexual tribe and his reliance on the memory of his uncle's aggrandized image becomes an inspiration for the nephew's heroic aspirations.

The journal opens with aphorisms and charts that are quasi-philosophical and pseudo-scientific. For example: "It is a sure sign of a busybody if he talks of *laissez-faire* (*O*, 41). Auden declares that "The airman is the agent of central awareness," and as such, he must observe and analyze himself, his troops, and the enemy before he can take any action. Among the airman's observations there are staples of the Isherwood-Auden schema such as "ancestor worship," "signs of a mixed character . . . the two-faced," "enemy propaganda," and "ghost stories"(*O*, 44–46). The airman learns that the real enemy exists within his own divided mind. Later, after a dream, the airman writes, "Why the words in my dream under Uncle's picture, 'I HAVE CROSSED IT'" (*O*, 79). The dream's cryptic message is that the martyred uncle, in death, has crossed the border, braved the metaphysical frontier, and found the answers that cannot be found in life. The airman does not fully comprehend this as yet, but the dream does spur a self-realization: "My whole life has been mistaken, progressively more and more complicated, instead of finally simple. My incredible blindness, with all the facts staring me in the face, not to have realised these elementary truths" (*O*, 79). In appreciation of this realization, the airman gives credit to the dream, believing his uncle was sending him a message: "To my uncle, perpetual gratitude and love for this crowning mercy. For myself absolute humility" (*O*, 79–80). The airman's outlandish journal and his journey end. He and Auden have come to the sane understanding that salvation comes from within.

The airman's journey, though written in High Camp style, portrays the rite of passage from the mask-wearing youthful precocity and rebellion of the Truly Weak to the introspective maskless Self-knowledge of the Truly Strong. The airman began as two Lawrences: T. E. and D. H. The former is the hero who, Truly Weak, confronts Tests, and the latter is the glorifier of life worship, which emphasizes blood instead of spirit, which is also Truly Weak. By the end of his journal, the airman has merged with spirit. Auden finds salvation for the airman (and himself) within the serious interior of his outwardly satiric parable. Serious or not, Auden did not neglect his gang.

The airman mentions "the essay club and Stephen," (*O*, 67) and Isherwood is well-represented with the allusions to Uncle Henry and the names of his Mortmere characters in one of the concluding odes. Another ode is for Rex Warner's son. Layard is mentioned as well. Mendelson believes that Auden added the odes as a somewhat more serious—and clearer—postscript for the themes that preceded them.[96] For the reader in 1932, the reckless abandon of *The Orators* superseded its obscurity and this sense of recklessness would be imitated during the decade. The imitators were indirectly flattering the Mortmere stories, which were unknown to all but perhaps a few of them. Other than Upward and Auden, it is unclear who else may have heard of Mortmere. Among the imitators would be Isherwood and Auden themselves in collaboration for their three plays in 1935, 1936, and 1938. However, less than a year later in 1933, the very first imitator of *The Orators* would be Day Lewis in his *The Magnetic Mountain*, which is a deliberate homage dedicated to Auden. In 1932 another important publication was the anthology, *New Signatures*, which championed the activist poet. One of the new poets who attracted the most attention was Stephen Spender, whose first volume of poems would be published the next year.

WORLD WITHIN WORLD: SPENDER'S POEMS

Spender visited Isherwood frequently in Berlin for long periods. Isherwood describes their teacher-pupil relationship with a little bit of mischievous wickedness: "The pupil, striding along the brisk, large-headed little figure of the mentor, [Spender was seven inches taller than Isherwood] keeps bending his beautiful scarlet face downward, lest he shall miss a word, laughing in anticipation as he does so. The pupil already has a stoop, as all tall people who are eager to hear what the rest of the world is saying. And maybe the mentor, that little tormentor, actually lowers his voice at times, to make the pupil bend even lower"(*CK*, 56). Spender freely acknowledged this teacher-pupil deference and was learning so quickly that he would shortly achieve literary success ahead of his mentor. Before either was critically recognized, Isherwood and Spender had their brief falling out.

Isherwood was wary of Spender's cloying nature, which was based on

Spender's insecurity and great need for approval. Isherwood, also insecure, felt that Spender was too intrusive into Isherwood's life as regarded his homosexuality and wanted a little more distance. Spender, becoming aware of Isherwood's irritation, suggested they see less of each other. In *Christopher and His Kind* Isherwood confesses that he was trying to get Spender to go back to England because "Christopher regarded Berlin as his territory. He was actually becoming afraid that Stephen would scoop him by writing Berlin Stories of his own and rushing them into print" (*CK*, 107). The fact that Day Lewis had preempted Auden had probably been noted by Isherwood. They quickly made up, although there was one permanent bit of fallout: in Spender's first volume of poems he left out his intended dedication to Isherwood, and though he reinserted it for later editions, the first British edition is without it.

Spender's first books of poems and stories would not be published until 1933 and 1935 respectively. They were, however, written from 1927 forward while he was befriending Isherwood and Auden. Spender's themes are the Isherwood-Auden themes. Before his art was published, Spender was writing book reviews. In one of his earliest, written in 1930, one sees the practice of his generation to use the essay, even those on art, to express non-artistic views. In a review of Desmond MacCarthy's *Portraits,* which was MacCarthy's recollections of public figures he had known, Spender associates MacCarthy with the dread, Poshocratic past: "There is no evidence that the author . . . has read any writer outside the great nineteenth century tradition except Proust. . . . We do not have to read many pages of this book before we learn that the author was educated at Eton and Cambridge. We are then not entirely surprised to discover that . . . he has an enormous, though concealed, respect for everything that is dull, pompous, and traditional in an uninspired way." Noting a particular MacCarthy anecdote, Spender writes: "The story is an example of the obscene silliness of a certain type of don whom Mr. MacCarthy is only too willing to admire." After these admonitions, Spender does find something to praise—MacCarthy's chapter on Henry James. Spender regarded James highly, as did Auden, at a time when James' reputation was in eclipse. Two years later Spender would contribute to a James' revival and Spender's 1935 book *The Destructive Element* would proclaim James to have been the first modern writer. Spender quotes MacCarthy who "knew James personally." The choice of the quotation tells as much about Spender as it does about Henry James:

> It occurred after a luncheon party of which he had been, as they say, "the life." We happened to be drinking our coffee together while the rest of the party had moved on to the verandah. [James said] "What a charming picture they make. . . ." In his attitude . . . I divined such a complete detachment, that I was startled into speaking out of myself: "I can't bear to look at life like that. . . . I want to be in everything. Perhaps that is why I cannot *write* [fiction], it makes me feel absolutely alone." The effect of this confession on him was surprising. . . . "Yes, it is solitude.

If it runs after you and catches you, well and good. But for heaven's sake, don't run after *it*. It is absolute solitude.[87]

MacCarthy's sense of a "complete detachment" in James sounds like the cypher-witness approach to writing, which is one of passive observation to be undertaken in an "absolute solitude." This does not mean physical solitude, but rather a solitude that reflects the inner detachment of the private sphere in order to observe the public chaos. More importantly, while the writer observes outwardly from within this sanctuary of inner solitude, he understands that each person observed in a public role also has an inner life that is separate from his outer life. (Ironically, James cited Hawthorne as the first modern writer to incorporate the solitary observation of another's duality.)

For Spender the conflict of an inner and outer life needs to be, if not always resolved, at least understood. Spender's art would also observe the conflict of inner and outer as reflected upon in solitude. Sometimes he would be the cypher-witness observing others; sometimes he would be a more contemplative cypher-witness observing himself in order to learn from what he sees. In Spender's 1951 autobiography, appropriately titled *World within World*, he looks back at his conception of the poet as it evolved for him in the late 1920s and through the 1930s: "The poet now became for me someone who rejects the preoccupations of the day, news, struggles for material gain, the machinery of society and even the apparatus for scholarship, by which men add stature to themselves, and who makes for himself a world out of timeless things, nature, and the beauty that he can create with his own imagination. He creates by virtue of the power that comes from the fullest realization of his own being. He does not add anything external to his personality: only that which will develop his inner life. However, my view of the poet was not solipsist. For I remember the thought striking me that to realize oneself to the fullest extent of one's powers means an entering into that which is beyond oneself" (*WW*, 91).

The inner life became the governing principle of Spender's art. The inner life is not a retreat from the outer life; but command of the private sphere can come only when one no longer fears participating in the public chaos. This sense of detachment from worldliness on a material level allows one to be of the world but not in it. It is a mystical detachment that has often been misconstrued as indifference. The detachment aspired to by a mystic does not cut himself off from the world, but allows him to suffer less from the effects of the world. Inner calm allows one to have a greater participation in the world, not less, because one is no longer submitting the vulnerable ego for the world's approval. In this state, Spender said, the poet

> was now a translator of the world which man projects around him through the actions of his will, back into language of the inner life of dreams and phantasy which he has projected this materialistic external actuality. I believed now that everything which men make and invent is to some degree a symbol of an inner

state of consciousness within them, as they are conditioned by their generation.
Poetry was a use of language which revealed external actuality as symbolic inner
consciousness.

> I began to realize that unpoetic-seeming things were material for poetry. . . .
> What excited me about the modern movement was the inclusion within new
> forms of material which seemed ugly, anti-poetic and inhuman. . . . At Oxford I
> started writing poems containing references to gas-works, factories and slums. I
> understood the significance beneath the affectation of Auden saying that the most
> beautiful walk in Oxford was that along the canal, past the gas-works, and that the
> poet must go dressed like "Mr. Everyman." (WW, 95)

Spender's "Mr. Everyman" acknowledged that simplicity and reality—or Huxley's
Wholly-Truthful art—were the keys to the new poetry: "It was as though the twen-
tieth-century writer had extended the range of his material, but in doing so had
made the external world an object of interior sensibility. He had cast away the husk
of its outwardness in attempting to digest it in his mind, and he had often become
sick in the process. *The hero of this literature was inevitably the exceptionally sensitive
person,* [italics mine] that is to say he who was most capable of receiving a wide range
of impressions, most conscious of himself as a reviewer of impressions, and most
likely to make use of his impressions as a means of cultivating himself rather than of
acting upon the world (WW, 96).

The "sensitive person" who would "become sick in the process" of digesting
the world was the antihero who underwent the trials of maturing from Truly
Weak to Truly Strong. The writers of the 1930s did not create the Truly Strong
and sensitive person; he had appeared already in the works of authors they admired
such as James. They did, however, define this person as a model to be written about
in their art and emulated in actuality. Auden's airman learned little from the external world until he understood that his inner world was one connected to an undifferentiated unity of a collective consciousness. The authors of the 1930s would not
only display sensitivity, but would, through parable-art and didactic essays, analyze
the psychology of what "sensitive" meant. Could the sensitive man prevail over his
weaknesses in order to become Truly Strong or would he remain "sick" and Truly
Weak from the excess of the world and succumb to that excess? The implications of
this view are metaphysical, but Isherwood, Auden, and Spender were not yet ready
to make the leap into the spiritual. That would come later.

Spender's early poems reflect the view of poetry that he ascribed to them in
1951. In them, public issues and private feelings are intertwined with the ambiguity that a sensitive person (or highbrow) feels when struggling with his environment, especially an environment as tumultuous as the 1930s. The conflicts of
inner and outer, public and private, hero and antihero, Truly Weak and Truly
Strong, are reflected in Spender's poems. His first volume begins with very pri-

vate poems and gradually turns to more public poems. Spender's poems, whether public or private, whether comments on the external world or introspection upon his internal self, are always about *his* perceptions. The world Spender depicts, inner or outer, is *his* world. Spender's self-portraits are a declaration of autonomy from his two best friends. Auden and Isherwood at this time were still writing as objective witnesses using the third person to imply a detachment that was not the case in actuality. Spender does not hesitate to be subjective and take blame or credit. The first person "I" is the definitive part of his repertoire.

The opening poems of the volume have been called the "Marston" poems. "Marston" is the male object of Spender's unrequited affection and is based on a real acquaintance. Spender recounts actual incidents with Marston. Isherwood and Auden, even when portraying themselves, did so most often in the third person, which obfuscates personal responsibility. Spender is not so cagey. He talks about the physicality of the body, invoking the image of a real body that enemies can attack and thus symbolizing the anxieties created by the ego; conversely, any positive gesture by the person whom one cares for can inspire new lines of poetry, which, in fact are written because Spender is afraid to say what he feels to the object of his desire. Instead he and his object walk the rolling hills, and "And this climbing was a monumental sign of country peace" (*SP,* 10).

By the next day, however, doubt overcomes peace and Spender claims that the emptiness of his room "All splintered in my head and cried for you" (*SP,* 12). Later there is a return to peace that includes Auden-esque urban-industrial images stimulated by a mere accidental touching of hands that triggers enough power to "give a city power, or drive a train" (*SP,* 13). More images from Auden country are also represented with images of soldiers, boundaries, rebels, mutinies, cigarettes, prisoners, bombs, machines, and that Auden staple, "gasworks" (*SP,* 53).

Spender's "I" is not necessarily an egotistical "I" but a self trying to find its way among other selves. He suggests An 'I' can never be truly great as too much "I" is a measure of the ego's insecurity. Within the self are more than one "I." There is the "I" that eats, the "I" that loves, or gets angry, or excretes, or tries to make friends or find a lover. Yet each "I" can never be at peace if "I" can only think of "I." When the ego is abnegated then "all those other 'I's' . . . long for 'We dying'" (*SP,* 17).

The egotistical "I" is Truly Weak; the "I" who can also say "We" learns how to seek unity instead of separation and is Truly Strong. The ego is also an obstacle to love: "Ambition is my death. . . . (*SP,* 32). Spender wonders how the temptation of materialism could ever obscure "The palpable and obvious love of man for man" (*SP,* 48).

There is another poem that intimates that the child is father to the man, and that the unhappy child is father to a Truly Weak Man. Spender as a child hears his parents arguing in the next room, which causes him to weep: "I am your son and from bad dreams arise" (*SP,* 21). This image depicts a very personal past. The collective haunted past also pervades other poems. One escape route from the forbidding past or equally forbidding present is the creation of secondary worlds: "This writing is my only wings away" (*SP,* 44). There is also sympathy for the unemployed who hang out on street corners: "I'm haunted by their emptiness" (*SP,* 30).

Then there is recognition of Germany's new order and its victims. Spender writes that these real Tests are rather more serious than schoolboy sports. Swimming and climbing are the Tests of the Truly Weak. In the new world of fascist threats these Tests are rendered foolish as understood by the Truly Strong Man. Compared to fascist oppression, swimming and climbing are not Tests, but games.

Two poems are particularly lucid on the theme of the Truly Weak and Truly Strong Man. In "What I expected," Spender states that he thought Tests—such as climbing, swimming, rugby, motorcycling—would make him strong; but he learns that these Tests were weakening his will instead of fortifying it. He realizes that pointless Tests of daring are for the Truly Weak when compared to the stoic suffering of the poor. Conversely, in the second poem, titled, "I think continually of those who are Truly Great," Spender recognizes the Truly Strong whose only ambition is to sing of the joy found in the human spirit. The will of the Truly Strong should never allow the noise of the material world to drown out the call of the spirit, and when the Truly Strong complete their journey into spirit, they will leave, "the vivid air signed with their honor" (*SP,* 46). Isherwood's editorial intervention led to this final line, which was inserted in place of "the air signed with vivid honor." He would say so forty-four years later with great pride.[88]

Spender's *Poems* continue to describe the shift that Auden depicted in *The Orators.* Humanity will not find salvation in hero-worship, state-worship, or self-worship that is ego-generated. Salvation will come when the egoless worship of the collective Vedantic Self asserts its detachment from the material world's "noise and fog" that impede "the flowering of the spirit." To find this path, the individual must open his mind to the whole world, and not just the sense world that satisfies the body only. To do so, one must be sensitive to his inner life in order to pass through a learning process that begins in ego-bound weakness and ends in egoless strength. For Spender, the antihero had arrived to stay for the rest of the century.

In 1932, both Auden and Spender were famous. Their figurative older brother still was not. Isherwood was not yet ready to say goodbye to Berlin.

THE SENSITIVE MAN

Spender's success was not quite as celebrated as Auden's, but his poems were regarded as much more accessible than Auden's work. Spender's more personal poems dealt with the same landscape as Auden's, but his prevalent use of the personal "I" connected more substantially with readers, who became the personal "you" of the I-you writer-reader relationship. The cypher-witness of Auden's poems was mysterious and challenging; but the "I" of Spender's poems was more viscerally appealing. Day Lewis, in his *Transitional Poem,* had also abstractly considered the maturation of a young man.

Day Lewis's next long poem, *From Feathers to Iron,* was published in 1932 and was more personal. This work was also about a man in transition. The man passes from the single man of *Transitional Poem* to make new transitions as a sensitive lover, husband, and father. In this poem, the "I" of Day Lewis also becomes a "we." The poem is traditionally pastoral in style while being dominated by Auden-country images as embellishments and homage. The poet celebrates the man's new family life but also hints at the growing public apprehension that has begun to encroach on private spheres. The poem makes clear that to respond to these contemporary issues, the poet must use contemporary terms to deal with a new world of action, politics, and propaganda. The title of the poem comes from preceding epigrams by Auden (feathers) and Keats (iron). That Day Lewis would pair them was homage enough. In the poem, the man's observations are keenly sensitive, often didactically so. He is aware of the divided mind, but more so in others, since he himself is now more single-minded to match his new family responsibilities: " negative's made positive. . . / positives change to negative" (*F,* 74). In stanza 8, there is an alternation of male and female voices designated by "He" and "She" that signify equality. This stanza concludes with the unity of a last verse "Both," in which they speak together as one entity (*F,* 72).

In stanza 13, the man knows that his private world is not separated from the whole world and that he, even "when in love's air," shares that same air with "absolute dictators" who "close a door between the closest hearts" (*F,* 77). Later he speaks to his unborn child, much as Auden spoke to the just-born child of their mutual friend Rex Warner in an ode from *The Orators.* He hopes the child can learn how to "be metal to bore through / The impermeable clay" of life's tribulations (*F,* 81). For his life, his wife, and his child, love is all: "Faith may move mountains; but love's twice as strong" (*F,* 82). The epilogue of *From Feathers to Iron* is a "Letter to W. H. Auden," about whom Day Lewis says that he has written "on heaven a new signature." (*F,* 101)

The term "new signatures" would be the title of a subsequent 1932 anthology edited by Michael Roberts for John Lehmann at the Hogarth Press. This anthology confirmed that there were new voices demanding to be heard. The Auden Generation was becoming aware of itself as an ideological entity. The new gang's leader by acclamation was Auden,[89] which meant their cues came from the Isherwood-Auden schema. Roberts's introduction makes the case for the new poets as iconoclastic, left-leaning activists in a troubled world. This is not to say they were an organized movement. Still, Auden's gang had read more politics into Auden's work than he had ever intended, and they were imitating the intentions he never had. Their poems were calls for action. Auden, meanwhile, was moving on to the metaphysical, which, in fact, he had never left. The gang, however, would be so successful at their activism, that even Auden had to back up and join them with his play *The Dance of Death* in 1933, and the three plays with Isherwood in 1935, 1936, and 1938. As political as these plays are, the metaphysical aspects of the Truly Weak and Truly Strong Man are still paramount.

1933 saw publication of Day Lewis's third long poem, *The Magnetic Mountain,* which is an homage to *The Orators.* This poem reflects the new literary activism and is a statement by Day Lewis that poetry and revolution are compatible. In it, the mountain, compelling in its magnetic attraction, is the symbol of a new life calling to the sensitive man. The poem is evocative of *The Orators* in that it satirizes the sick members of a sick society in a non-realistic narrative that carries within it a more serious moral message.

A young man journeys to leave his sick country and exhorts others to go with him: "Then I'll hit the trail for that promising land / . . . with Wystan and Rex my friend" (*MM,* 111). During the journey Day Lewis acknowledges public turmoil and the conflicts of dead life against new, us against them, evil against good. The Truly Strong Man appears in a stanza that begins, "Let us now praise famous men / Not your earth-shakers, not the dynamiters" (*MM,* 117). This line recollects Spender's poem that begins: "I think continually of those who are truly great" that is also a tribute to the Truly Strong. Day Lewis intended a similar message as that of *The Orators,* but while *The Orators* was an obscure parable, *The Magnetic Mountain* is didactic propaganda.

THE ORATOR AS ESSAYIST

Even though the poets of the 1930s never formed an organization or held a single meeting, they were joined together by their private responses to the public chaos. Since the public events were known to all, and in that sense shared, their responses were similar in subject matter while being distinct in each poet's style and personality. Art reflects the temper of its period even when the art does not necessarily directly comment on the period itself. Poetry is the symbolic and symptomatic response of how one feels about what one knows; it does not, if it is good parable-art, describe the known, but reacts to it. Essays, conversely, are not consciously symbolic and usually not meant to be parables.[90] The fact that essays can be both symbolic and parables unconsciously is certainly true as one can see in Spender's essay. Essays give the writer an opportunity to express what he knows and how he feels about what he knows. The artists of the 1930s took advantage of the opportunity. The writer as essayist wrote on many issues. He was sometimes iconoclastically bombastic to match a certain revolutionary fervor, or he was thoughtfully introspective to reflect the psychoanalytically sensitive man. He also took turns at each and sometimes was sensitively bombastic or bombastically sensitive in the same essay. From 1930 forward Auden as artist and essayist was the exemplar to whom his peers looked for direction. Here are excerpts from essays Auden wrote from 1930 to 1934 that intimate or directly state aspects of the Isherwood-Auden schema. The concept of private and public faces, Auden now sees as duality:

> Duality is one of our oldest concepts; it appears and reappears in every reli-
> gion, metaphysic, and code of ethics. (1930)[91]

Self-consciousness leads to the duality of public and private faces. Communication
tries to unify the faces and speak to others:

> At some time or other in human history . . . man became self-conscious; he
> began to feel, I am I, and you are not I; we are shut inside ourselves and apart from
> each other.
>
> The urge to write, like the urge to speak, came from man's growing sense of
> personal loneliness, of the need for group communication. . . . The writer is like a
> schoolboy who carves his initials on a desk [or into a park bench as in *Letter to
> Wound*]; he wishes to live forever. . . . When we read a book it is as if we were with
> a person. (1932)[92]

Duality includes one's nature as a leader or follower.

> Before a man wants to understand, he wants to command or obey instinc-
> tively, to live with others in a relation of power. (1932)[93]

The old school remains a source of dualistic conflict.

> Don't think you can behave as you like at a liberal school—a little recalci-
> trance, yes that is amusing. But a will of your own! Make no mistake about that.
> (1932)[94]

Duality includes choosing power or passivity.

> The trouble is . . . that man's nature is dual, and that each part of him has its
> own conception of justice and morality. In his passionate nature man wants lord-
> ship, to love in a relation of power to others, to obey and to command, to strut and
> to swagger. He desires mystery and glory. In his cerebral nature he cares for none
> of these things. He wants to know and be gentle; he feels his other passionate
> nature is frightening and cruel. (1932)[95]

In the above passage, Auden tacitly connotes the differences between the Truly
Weak and Truly Strong Man; the former swaggers while the latter has sensitive
virtues. In an essay published two years later, Auden denotes his meaning explicitly
for his generation. For Auden, to be Truly Strong is to be sensitive and a highbrow.
"What is a highbrow? Someone who is not passive to his experience but who tries
to organize, explain and alter it, someone in fact, who tries to influence history"
(1933).[96]

Auden also considered the true basis upon which a highbrow succeeds: "[The
book of Talbot] shows more clearly than anything I have read for a long time that
the first criterion of success in any human activity, the necessary preliminary,
whether to scientific discovery or to artistic vision, is intensity of attention or, less

pompously, love" (1933).[97] The highbrow and sensitive Truly Strong Man acts from love; conversely, the Truly Weak Man acts from fear:

> To me [T. E.] Lawrence's life is an allegory of the transformation of the Truly Weak Man into the Truly Strong Man, an answer to the question "How shall the self-conscious man be saved?" and the moral seems to be this, "self-consciousness is an asset, in fact the only friend of our progress. . . ." But a misinterpretation of absorption [self-consciousness] is one of the great heresies of our generation. To interpret it as blind action without consideration of meaning or ends, as an escape . . . that is indeed to become the Truly Weak Man, to enlist in the great Fascist retreat. . . . Action and reason are inseparable; it is only in action that reason can realise itself, and only through reason that action can become free.
>
> [Lenin] and Lawrence . . . exemplify . . . a synthesis of feeling and reason, act and thought. (1934) [98]

Is this Auden's call to action? It is as close as he would get at this time. In this review of the Lawrence biography by B. H. Liddell Hart, Auden said that he believed in action, but only if that action was tempered by the calm reason that signifies a Truly Strong Man who is pure in heart. A man must be aware of his true Self so that his private and public faces are the same. When reason makes action free; that is, when the actions are derived not from an ego-bound self, but an egoless Self, the contemplative man does not withdraw, but he goes among the people, or as Auden said: "Consciousness necessitates more action not less.[99] The Bhagavad-Gita expresses the same ideal. Isherwood's study of the Gita will be examined in part 2.

Auden's gang were admirers of his art and essays and took him very seriously as an ideologue. If Auden talked about a reasonable and sensitive Truly Strong Man of action, this had an impact. However, the call for action was heard first; the call to be Truly Strong and the understanding of what this meant would take a little more time. Auden was the star of his peer group. Meanwhile, his best friend, the Watcher in Spanish remained in Berlin. Hitler, once thought merely an uncouth buffoon, was demanding that attention be paid him, and Isherwood, the cypher-witness, was recording the action.

THE REAL WORLD INTRUDES

As the 1930s developed, the schema of the Truly Weak and Truly Strong Man evolved in response to the complexities of changing events. The clear demarcation of Weak and Strong, Others and Anti-Others had once reflected Isherwood's old school days and then his life as contrasted between the Mangeots' world and his mother's world. In Berlin Isherwood was confronted by external circumstances that no longer allowed his world to be so egocentric, nor so clearly divided. Isherwood saw a new world emerging and witnessed how people reacted to this world in terms of their personal survival. When the concept of Truly Weak and Truly Strong was only concerned with generational and psychological conflicts, lines could be drawn with clear distinctions because these differences were created internally and the enemy was symbolic only. Now there were external forces and real enemies acting upon real people. Mortmere's symbolic guns and bombs had been replaced by real ones directed at actual human beings. The psychological gamesmanship of Mortmere or *The Orators* had featured cartoon spies and secret agents. Now there were more serious games being played by real spies and secret agents in the service of Nazism, communism, and capitalism. These players were both overt and covert. The Nazis had their brown-shirted overgrown boy scouts with fists and clubs intimidating onlookers and terrorizing Jews. The communists had meetings and rallies. Behind these public displays were the covert operatives. Some worked for a cause; others worked for money with allegiance going to the highest bidder. In this new world the instinct for survival took precedence over scruples, and the dichotomy of Truly Weak and Truly Strong was no longer a parlor game but a blurred dilemma involving real people who were faced with making choices that were literally about life and death. Isherwood the narcissistic artist now would shift his focus away from himself and towards the people who were caught up in the events he witnessed. The first subject that he chose to expose was Gerald Hamilton. Gerald Hamilton was a real person who became the basis of the title character of Isherwood's third novel, *Mr. Norris Changes Trains,* in 1935. Like the original, the fictional duplication of Hamilton was a nefarious, amoral, sociopathic, manipulative conniver, who was not only a criminal, but did not hesitate to use or abuse friends and enemies alike. Nonetheless, the real Gerald Hamilton and the fictitious Arthur Norris were always disarmingly charming so that one did not notice being stabbed in the back until after the damage was done. Like John Layard, Hamilton served as a negative object lesson for Isherwood.

Isherwood and Auden considered Layard's failed suicide attempt as evidence that he was a faux Truly Strong Man who had turned out to be more Weak than Strong. They were disappointed but learned from this experience. Layard was a moral person aspiring to be Truly Strong but was not as Strong as either he himself or Isherwood and Auden had hoped. Isherwood and Auden learned that within each person the Weak and Strong aspects of the psyche fight for dominance; more often than not, the Weak aspect succumbs to the ego's self-interested influence. The aspiring Strong Self is weighed under by the temptation to conform rather than stand alone. Layard's botched suicide along with the rising political turmoil in Berlin made Isherwood and Auden see that Weak and Strong were not clearly demarcated choices, but necessary opposites from which the fission of evolving consciousness develops. One cannot know what it means to be Truly Strong if one cannot compare this to having been Truly Weak. In *The Memorial* and *The Orators* the antihero and the hero were not separate figures, but dual poles within the same person. This person cannot learn to have belief until he has first confronted, then overcome, doubt, or disbelief. For the aspiring Truly Strong Man the circumstances of life and the people he encounters are seen as opportunities to learn about himself.

Isherwood learned much in Berlin and he would make another leap in his writing about the events there and the people he met. Arthur Norris understood that a lowbrow could be Truly Weak simply out of ignorance and would take advantage of that ignorance. Isherwood learned that an oversensitive highbrow aesthete like himself could also be Truly Weak even while he aspired to be Truly Strong and that a Norris could take advantage of him as well. In Norris a new figure is added to the equation. Now Isherwood is depicting a highbrow, Norris, who ignores the difference between right or wrong to serve his own ends. This is not to say that Norris is unaware that there are moral choices. He just ignores them in order to serve one primary concern—himself. For Norris there are no secondary concerns: if one is gullible enough to be deceived by one of Norris's schemes, it is not Norris's responsibility. Isherwood provides little explanation of the charming crook's motivations. The cypher-witness had been done one better; he would now describe a cypher-subject.

The guidelines for analyzing whether one is Truly Weak or Truly Strong became very fuzzy with Norris. While the majority of people in Berlin had needed to adjust to their new era of Nazi-induced paranoia, Norris found that the new era had adjusted to him; it suited his dark inclinations, which thrived on the paranoid environment. In *Christopher and His Kind* Isherwood said, "Christopher first met Gerald Hamilton in the winter of 1930–31." Isherwood notes that Hamilton had a double standard when judging others while making excuses for himself: "He was well aware of his own double standard and couldn't help giggling in the midst of his solemn sincerities. . . . It seems to me that Christopher 'recognized' Gerald Hamilton as Arthur Norris, his character-to-be, almost as he set eyes on him. When William Bradshaw (the I-narrator of the novel) meets Mr. Norris . . . Hamilton and Norris are . . . identical" (*CK,* 73–74).

Isherwood describes the real Hamilton as a living caricature of the soft British gentleman, fleshy, self-indulgent, and proud of his expensive wig. Isherwood thought "Gerald was enchantingly 'period.'" Isherwood also introduced him to his friends who were equally charmed: "No doubt [Gerald] realized that these naive young men who marveled at his wig, his courtly mannerisms, and his police record were unconsciously becoming his accomplices" (*CK,* 75). Isherwood describes Hamilton's willfully amoral attitude:

> On one occasion, a fellow Hamilton connoisseur remarked to Christopher, "It seems that Gerald has had a moral lapse;" to which Christopher replied, "Gerald having a moral lapse is like someone falling off a footstall at the bottom of the Grand Canyon." Christopher was pleased with this *mot* and repeated it to

Gerald, who giggled . . . *"Really!"* Like all deeply dishonest people, he made the relatively honest look hypocritical and cowardly. Only a saint could have remained in contact with him and not been contaminated. . . . Gerald didn't look evil . . . but, he was an icy cynic. Looking back on Gerald's career, I find his misdeeds tiresome rather than amusing. His dishonesty was tiresome because it was so persistent; he was like a greedy animal. (*CK*, 75–77)

Written after Hamilton was dead, Isherwood regards the con artist as if he had been an annoying dog lurking about the dinner table to wait for its chance to snatch a scrap. In fact Hamilton was far more clever and consciously unscrupulous. In the late 1930s when Isherwood was trying to spare his lover, Heinz, from being conscripted into the Nazi army, he desperately gave Hamilton a large sum of money for bribing anyone who could help. It did not help, and Isherwood later suspected Hamilton took the money and made no effort on Heinz's behalf.

Isherwood's fictional character, Mr. Norris, however, seems only an aging dandy, easily unnerved just by being asked for his passport—or at least this is how he appears to William Bradshaw on their first meeting. Bradshaw regards him with condescension. Norris appears to be a harmless caricature of the bachelor British uncle. He seems well-meaning, but clumsy and gullible. After the passport scene, Bradshaw recalls: "I felt more than ever protective towards him at that moment. This affectionate protectiveness, which he so easily and dangerously inspired in me was to colour all our future dealings" (*N*, 9). Norris is an actor who intuitively performs a role in response to whatever he thinks his audience needs to hear. Norris believes in the part he plays— whatever it is—even though his role shifts from moment to moment.

Norris encourages Bradshaw to visit him in Berlin, and when Bradshaw arrives at Norris's flat, there are two adjacent doors with matching brass nameplates. One says *Arthur Norris, Private,* while the other reads *Arthur Norris, Export and Import.* Upon entering, Bradshaw realizes that both doors lead into only one flat; there is no real distinction between public and private, except on a superficial level. The doors symbolize the blurring of inner and outer. They also symbolize that Norris consciously contributes to this confusion as he works best under cover. Unknown to Bradshaw, and perhaps to the reader at this point, is that the clue of the two doors is a warning, which goes unheeded by the once condescendingly smug but actually naive narrator. Norris befriends Bradshaw and, even though Bradshaw slowly begins to see that Norris is a shady character, he regards Norris as a naughty child and is charmed by him. This is exactly what Norris intends, to lure the gullible Bradshaw into his intrigues by deliberately taking advantage of Bradshaw's psychological need to feel protective towards Norris. Bradshaw's weakness becomes Norris's strength.

After Norris has introduced Bradshaw to a Baron von Pregnitz, knowing that the Baron will fall for the young Briton, Norris asks Bradshaw to accompany the

Baron to Switzerland as bait for a deal. While the homosexual attraction is tacit, the hints suffice. The deal fails and it is only through the intercession of a local communist party leader, Bayer, that Bradshaw escapes possible arrest. Bayer tells him the truth about Norris: "do not make yourself reproaches. You have been foolish. . . . Never mind; we are all sometimes very, very foolish. You have done nothing to be ashamed. . . . now you will be more careful with whom you make a friend" (N, 158). Bayer, who is later killed at Spandau, serves as an example of a Truly Strong Man. Or does he? He helps Bradshaw, but is he sincerely motivated or will this be a favor to be cashed in later? Bradshaw, angry at Norris but still under his spell, forgives him: "I don't condemn you. As for my standards, if I ever had any, you've muddled them up completely" (N, 161). This was the case for both Bradshaw and Isherwood, who, after meeting Hamilton and also surviving his other adventures in Berlin, saw that people would alter their different masks to match whatever new scenario they found themselves in. This included himself.

The last chapter forecasts the stories that would make up *Goodbye to Berlin*. Bradshaw and the reader tacitly realize that, compared to the Nazis, Norris has actually been a petty player. Isherwood captures the pervasive panic and paranoia that the Nazis brought with them: "The whole city lay under an epidemic of discreet, infectious fear. I could feel it, like influenza in my bones. When the first news of the house-searchings began to come in, I consulted with Frl. Schroeder about the papers which Bayer had given me. We hid them . . . under the wood pile" (N, 181). Isherwood understood that Berlin was far removed from his Cambridge days, and living there was an exam he could not Camp. There would be real consequences for making the wrong moves.

Isherwood's clearly divided us-against-them righteousness from his old school days no longer applied. He would become more understanding of how the instinct for survival created shades of gray that often superseded the issue of Truly Weak and Truly Strong. Isherwood also became more tolerant and forgiving of others who wore masks as he recognized that he was one of the mask-wearers himself. As for Hamilton, Isherwood would say later that "what was the most enduring bond between Gerald and Christopher, [was] their homosexuality. When it came to breaking the laws which had been made against the existence of their tribe, Christopher was happy to be Gerald's fellow criminal" (CK, 78).

THE PLAYS WITH AUDEN

Although they were not published until 1937 and 1938, the events described in the stories of the *Goodbye to Berlin* collection actually took place in the early thirties and Isherwood related them at that time to Auden and Spender. Back in England the latter two were recognized leaders of the new wave of writers, while Isherwood remained in his self-imposed exile and obscurity. Auden, pure in heart and wanting to at least aspire to be Truly Strong, sought to rectify the injustice of his mentor's lack of recognition.

In 1933 Auden had written the play *The Dance of Death*. Britain's newly emerging Group Theatre wanted more from Auden, who was the icon of the avant garde. Auden began writing a new play. He discussed it with his literary elder brother, who made substantive suggestions. Auden decided that Isherwood should get credit and co-write the play with him. There was some resistance from the Group Theatre as well as from T. S. Eliot at Faber and Faber. Auden would not yield. The result was *The Dog beneath the Skin*.

"Dogskin," as they called it, is a satirical farce like *The Dance of Death*. The latter, according to the announcer's opening statement, is "a picture of the decline of a class, of how its members dream of a new life, but secretly desire the old, for there is death inside them. We show you that death as a dancer" (*DD*, 185). While this play was influenced by the Berlin night life, its themes are still dominated by those of *The Memorial* and *The Orators*. The announcer says: "Comrades . . . We must have revolution" (*DD*, 196). A chorus agrees. Later, the announcer says: "Revolutionary worker / I get what you mean. / But what you're needing / 'S a revolution within" (*DD*, 205). Written a year after *The Orators*, in which the airman had also concluded that change must come from within, Auden was still straddling the fence of political activism or metaphysical activism. When the dancer appears, the announcer says he is "known simply as Pilot. His ambition is no less than to reach the very heart of reality" (*DD*, 207). After various farcical machinations and allusions to different groups seeking to exert their influence on him, the dancer dies. Karl Marx then appears stating that "The instruments of production have been too much for him" (*DD*, 218). The play ends and it is unclear if Marx and communism are supposed to be part of the solution or part of the problem. Auden did not believe the answer rested in politics alone. Auden had learned from an intense personal experience that occurred during the writing of this play that change would need, indeed, to come from within and work its way out from there to the rest of the world. *The Dance of Death* was written during the summer of 1933. In June of that summer, Auden had a spiritual experience that shaped the rest of his life:

> One fine summer night in June I was sitting on a lawn after dinner with three colleagues, two women and one man. We liked each other well enough but we were certainly not intimate friends, nor had any of us a sexual interest in another. . . . we had had not drunk any alcohol. We were talking quite casually about everyday matters when, quite suddenly and unexpectedly, something happened. I felt myself invaded with a power, which, though I consented to it, was irresistible and certainly not mine. For the first time in my life I knew exactly—because, thanks to the power, I was doing it—what it means to love one's neighbor as oneself. I was also certain, though my conversation continued to be perfectly ordinary, that my three colleagues were having the same experience. (In the case of one of them, I was later able to confirm this.) My personal feelings towards them were unchanged—they were

still colleagues, not intimate friends—but I felt their existences themselves to be of infinite value and rejoiced in it.

I recalled with shame, the many occasions on which I had been spiteful, snobbish, selfish, but the immediate joy was greater than the shame, for I knew that, so long as I was possessed by this spirit, it would be literally impossible for me deliberately to injure another human being.[100]

Auden wrote this account many years later; however, he did write a poem about his experience at the time, "A Summer Night." In this poem Auden describes—but does not name—the mystical vision of agape, the transcendent love for all existence.

In the 1930s Auden was looking for some metaphysical meaning that could merge private and public spheres. From his mystical experience he believed that this was possible but had no map of how the one or the many might achieve this goal. His mystical vision of transcendent brotherly love had given Auden a new reference point for the concept of being pure in heart. The vision of agape is one that can come to a sensitive man if he makes room for it by removing his ego. While Auden was in the embrace of this power, he literally believed his faults fell away, his ego was suspended, and his love made him, albeit fleetingly—Truly Strong. Auden told Isherwood of this experience and it influenced their view of the world in general and their plays in particular. Moreover, although Isherwood was not yet as mystically inclined as Auden was at this time, he would later surpass his friend.

The quest saga was the parable form that Isherwood and Auden implemented for the three plays that they wrote in collaboration. The questers, whether satirical as in *Dogskin* or serious as in *The Ascent of F6,* would venture into the public chaos on a metaphorical search for inner peace in the private sphere. The plays were explicitly political, tacitly metaphysical. The villains are Truly Weak; the heroes are Truly Strong. In fact, they are also one and the same.

The Dog beneath the Skin evolved from an earlier, unpublished and unproduced play of Auden's called *The Chase. Dogskin* would be a parable of current events using humor to satirize the serious issues "beneath the skin" of the farce. The two former players of *The Waste Land* game got their title from the line "the skull beneath the skin" from Eliot's "Whispers of Immortality." *Dogskin* owes much to Gilbert and Sullivan as well as to Brecht's plays, *Threepenny Opera* and *The Rise and Fall of the City of Mahogany.* Isherwood would later translate lyrics for the former and Auden, with Chester Kallmann, would translate all of the latter. *Dogskin* became a Mortmere story with absurd content barely masking rebellious intentions. Edward Mendelson notes: "The pattern introduced beneath the wanderings of the hero amounts to a parabolic lesson in history. This takes the form of a progress from innocence, in both the hero and his native village, to experience, of two opposed kinds: the revolutionary awakened in the hero and the reactionary hysteria that emerges in the village."[101] Auden and Isherwood had made their own progress from innocence to experience as witnesses to the Nazi terror in Berlin.

The play's hero, Alan Norman, is selected by his village to search for a missing heir, whose return might bring some stability back to the town. Alan is sent off with pomp and circumstance across the border and into unknown frontiers, where he has burlesque adventures. Norman sets out with the village's favorite "dog" as a companion. Alan returns home with the heir Francis, who in fact had disguised himself as the "dog" years before, and had been in the village all along. Alan and Francis find that their village has become a fascist enclave with the concomitant fear and paranoia this entails. Throughout the play a chorus comments on the action in the didactic mode. In the play's prologue, the chorus invokes the idyllic and pastoral British past and compares it to the Depression present. Then a duet version of a Big Brother-like Watcher in Spanish recites:

> You are the town and we are the clock.
> We are the guardians of the gate in the rock.
> The Two.
> On your left and on your right,
> In the day and in the night,
> We are watching you.

(DS, 15)

The town's vicar, another ancient Other, as in *The Memorial* and *The Orators*, exhorts the village to select a quester who will preserve the past by bringing back the "missing" heir, Sir Francis Crewe. Alan is sent off as the hero-saviour with jingoistic fervor: "Yes! / Set off for Germany and shoot them all!" (DS, 31). His search includes the usual Isherwood-Auden staples of spies and secret agents. The play's left-leaning implications suggest that capitalists are bad while socialists and communists are good. A visit to a red light district includes a stop at the Cosy Corner, the name taken from the gay bar Isherwood and Auden had frequented in Berlin. In addition to the red-light foray, Norman and the "dog," named Francis after the subject of their search, meet, among others, two journalists, a King, a crooked financier (a Hamilton type), a surgeon and his students in a medical school (Isherwood's input, no doubt), and the inmates of a lunatic asylum who are led by "The Voice of the Leader." This leader spouts rabid fascist nonsense. After the asylum, they go to Paradise Park. Norman asks a poet he meets in the park if he knows the missing heir. The poet, pointing to his head, answers: "Here. Everything's here. You're here. He's here. This park's here. This tree's here. If I shut my eyes they all disappear" (DS, 95). The poet reminds the audience of the ephemeral nature of the search and the illusory status of the human condition, which the poet attempts to reflect in the "here" of his imagination. After Norman and the dog take a nap in the park, the chorus states: "Dear sleep, the secretary of that strange club / Where all are members upon one condition, / That they forget their own importance. . ." (DS, 112). Whether in dreams or in life, only when the ego is suspended are people truly equal.

The satire belies the serious undertone of the Isherwood-Auden schema.

There is little difference between the various groups encountered. The lunatics are no more paranoid than normal people. Negative behaviors are a result of living in a capitalist world that produces inevitably deleterious conditions. These conditions are perpetuated by a devotion to the past that ignores current crises, such as the depression and fascism. As postulated by the park poet, reality is in the eye of the beholder. Nothing exists outside each mind's uniquely self-designed perception. This individual perception is distorted by the cultural compulsives or the collective subjectivity of societal attitudes and pervasive propaganda. These attitudes are the obstacles Alan encounters on his quest (Test) over the Northwest Passage. Norman learns, just as Auden's airman learned, that solutions are not to be found externally. Answers must be found within.

In a long monologue the "dog" confesses to what the audience already knows, that he is Francis. He explains that he had taken on his dog disguise to "sever all ties with the past." Masked, he had observed the foibles of human nature as a spy amidst the subjects of his study: "Small children misunderstood by their parents rubbed tearful cheeks against me and whispered their secrets to doggie" (DS, 146). Francis describes his past associations with humans from a dog's eye view. From this view he learned that all were playing at "charades" of self-deception and wearing their public masks in both public and in private. People acted and spoke in front of a "dog" as they never would have in front of people. He learned that people form masks because they are overwrought with neuroses and psychoses that make them easy prey to outside influences. Echoing the Paradise Park poet, Francis says, "Too many ideas in their heads! To them I'm an idea, you're an idea, everything's an idea" (DS, 146). These archetypal ideas, once pure, are now tainted by societal influences that have "subjectivized" them so that they have come to supersede the reality of immediate experience. After this quasi-metaphysical lecture to the audience, the dog also confesses to Alan that he is indeed Francis.

Alan and Francis (as himself) return to their village for the last scene. The chorus precedes the final scene by saying: "Do not speak of a change of heart, meaning five hundred a year and a room of one's own, / As if that were all that is necessary. In these islands alone, there are some forty-seven million hearts" (DS, 155). Bourgeois comfort and complacency are not enough to bridge the gaps created by separate egos who should otherwise strive for an ego-less undifferentiated unity. Each of the forty-seven million hearts is another island within the islands; each wears a mask as a shield to conceal vulnerability, but while these shields try to prevent pain, they also deny love access. The chorus continues with a reiteration of the Isherwood-Auden schema:

> Man divided always and restless always: afraid and unable to forgive: /
> Unable to forgive his parents. / An isolated bundle of nerve and desire, suffering
> alone, / Seeing others only in reference to himself: as a long-lost mother or his
> ideal self at sixteen. / Dreaming of continuous sexual enjoyment or perpetual
> applause. Some turn to . . . solutions of sickness or crime: some to the . . . sport

of the moment. / Some to good works, to a mechanical ritual of giving. / Some have adopted [a] system of beliefs or a political programme, others have escaped to ascetic mountains. / Or taken refuge . . . among the boys on the bar stools, on the small uncritical islands. / Men will profess devotion to anything; to God, to humanity, to Truth, to Beauty: but their first thought on meeting is 'Beware!' / They put their trust in Reason or feelings of the Blood but will not trust a stranger with half-a- crown." (*DS*, 156)

The "feelings of the Blood" refer to the obsolete "life-worship" of D.H. Lawrence, once an Auden favorite but now considered by Auden as a false hope. After this litany of the Truly Weak, the chorus suggests that the only hope for each individual is a transformation from within. This is followed by a transcendent merging into the undifferentiated unity that is engendered by the mystical vision of agape: "Unite. / Your knowledge and your power are capable of infinite extension: / Act" (*DS*, 157). With this exhortation, the chorus represents Everyman (or at least Isherwood and Auden) and sets the stage for the play's conclusion.

Norman and Francis return to the village only to find that it has succumbed to fascist influences. The vicar makes a long speech of patriotic cant warning of what will happen if the enemy succeeds. The vicar's speech is reminiscent of Huxley's 1932 novel, *Brave New World:* "No family love. Sons would inform against their fathers, cheerfully send them to the execution cellars. No romance. Even the peasant must beget that standard child under laboratory conditions. Motherhood would be by licence. Truth and Beauty would be proscribed as dangerously obstructive. No books, no art, no music" (*DS*, 167). A villager who lost both her sons in a previous war responds that this kind of patriotic cant will get more children killed.

Francis, having revealed himself, tells them: "I've had a dog's-eye view of you for the last ten years. . . . I was horrified and fascinated by you all" (*DS*, 172) He continues with a scathing evaluation that amounts to Isherwood speaking for himself—in part because Isherwood wrote the prose passages:

> I thought such obscene, cruel, hypocritical, mean, vulgar creatures have never existed before. . . . As a dog, I learnt with what a mixture of fear, bullying, and condescending kindness you treat those whom you consider your inferiors, but on whom you are dependent for your pleasures.
>
> My diary was my greatest friend. I worked away at it like a scientist. . . . then, slowly, the horror and pseudo-scientific interest wore off. . . . I began to feel I had been foolishly wasting my time. Hadn't it all been a romantic escape. . . . Wasn't it Life itself I was afraid of, hiding in a dog-skin. . . . I don't hate you anymore. I see how you fit into the whole scheme. (*DS*, 172–74)

Isherwood is describing his own self-realization. The play ends with Francis declaring he will join the Anti-Others of the world to spread the truth about The Others.

He departs with his first recruits including Alan, and the chorus concludes with a paraphrase of the communist dictum: "To each his need: from each his power" (*DS*, 180).

The Dog beneath the Skin turns the Isherwood-Auden schema into a blend of parable and didacticism. The themes that dominated their individual works coalesce in collaboration: the duality of private and public, inner and outer is broadly manifested by Francis as "dog" and then Francis as rebel. Norman's quest is a Test beyond the borders and over the Northwest Passage. Nothing is learned from this quest except the realization that external quests and Tests are for the Truly Weak. Realization is circular, not linear. One must return to his inner self. Before the quest, Francis had been in the village all along, just as the answers to society's problems are hidden in each individual all along if one turns inward to seek them. *Dogskin*, even though staged by the Group Theater as a burlesque aiming for political laughs, is another metaphysical exercise signifying Isherwood and Auden's call for a change of heart. This change is sought by the sensitive man who wishes to become Truly Strong. With *Dogskin* as a warm-up, Isherwood and Auden's next play would explore the same themes more seriously and the metaphysical intentions would be front and center. In *The Ascent of F6* the hero/antihero Michael Ransom represents what Isherwood and Auden had learned in their lives and through their work over the previous ten years. Ransom would be the symbolic star of his decade and the antihero role model for the future.

THE METAPHORICAL MOUNTAIN

Michael Ransom's very name carries with it the implication of a man held hostage. Ransom is a captive of the past who becomes a victim of it when that past inflicts its inexorable will on him through The Others. In *Dogskin* the burlesque still had one foot in the pseudo-fascism of the old school with the other foot stepping towards the new school of real-world fascism. *The Ascent of F6* has both feet firmly rooted in current history, and the old school was no longer a source of satire in light of these events. Hitler's rise had given Isherwood a good reason to flee Berlin and, after the success of *Mr. Norris Changes Trains* and *Dogskin*, he also had a motivation for returning to England—for visits only, however, since he still lived elsewhere for much of the decade. He had finally achieved recognition as Isherwood the artist and was not going to miss out on the praise and attention. Isherwood had caught up to his younger literary siblings Auden and Spender, who were glad to have him back. Their peers welcomed him as the mysterious, almost legendary figure from Berlin who had all the inside information on Hitler's Germany. His recollections of Berlin in the early 1930s would become the stories in *Goodbye to Berlin*, even though these tales would wait until 1937, 1938, and 1939 to be published. The first two plays with Auden would come before the Berlin stories, as Isherwood and Auden felt an urgency about current events that demanded tangible responses in the more public forum of the theatre. The success of *Dogskin* had made them viable as dramatists and their next work was much anticipated. In their view the next play was a Test of their mettle to match expectations. The play itself is about the pressure of expectations in the political milieu; Isherwood and Auden were "metaphorizing" their own pressure of expectations in the artistic venue. For ten years they had developed a personal vision and this was the time to present it without satire and jokes—no more Mortmere or airman to hide their angst and anger. In his 1934 essay on T. E. Lawrence, Auden explicitly stated the dichotomy of the Truly Weak and Truly Strong Man. Until then this dichotomy had only been expressed through tacit parables. In *The Ascent of F6* the Truly Weak and Truly Strong Man are defined explicitly and T. E. Lawrence is the role model for both.

The listing of the play's characters "in order of their appearance" begins with "Michael Forsyth Ransom," followed by "Sir James Ransom (his twin brother)." The twinship is a metaphor. They are actually, as Isherwood had also said of his characters in *The Northwest Passage,* "two halves of the same person." The play begins with Michael Ransom's existential monologue that is inspired by Ransom having just read in Dante that men "were not formed to live like brutes, but to follow virtue and knowledge." Ransom, a weary cynic like Isherwood, says of Dante, "a crook speaking to crooks" (*F6,* 11). After calling Dante an aristocratic Other, Ransom asks, "who was Dante to speak of virtue and knowledge?" (*F6,* 12). Ransom suggests that, to Dante, "virtue and knowledge" really meant a quest for power. As Ransom continues he sounds like Eric in *The Memorial* secretly despising the world of his own upper class: "the generals and industrial captains: justifying every baseness [of their] schoolboy lives" (*F6,* 12). Eric had rejected his own class by doing good works among the "enemies" of the upper class—the poor. Ransom has retreated into the solitude and Tests of mountain-climbing.

Ransom speaks bitterly that it would be better to be dead or ignorant than be caught in the "web of guilt that prisons every upright person . . . oh happy the foetus that miscarries and the frozen idiot that cannot cry 'mama!'" (*F6,* 14). Ransom may have been an aesthete who had been tormented by hearties. He may have also been an aesthete who had disguised himself as a heartie and suffers the guilt of having conformed instead of fulfilling his true Self. He speaks of the guilt that only the upright person can feel because it is only the upright who have consciences and can know guilt. Isherwood had learned in Berlin and with Gerald Hamilton that those without an inner voice of conscience know no guilt. Ransom is a cynic; he is Francis Crewe without the satire. From the hero's disappointment with life, the antihero is born.

The scene shifts to a typical middle-class British couple at home and describes their middle-class routine as one of stultifying, spirit-killing ennui. They are listening to the wireless: Mr. A: "I'm sick of the news. All you can hear is politics. . . ." Mrs. A: "They will ask for our children and kill them; sympathise deeply and ask for some more." Mr. A: There is "Nothing to make us proud of our race. . . . Nothing to take us out of ourselves. Out of the oppression of this city. . . . Give us something to live for. We have waited too long" (*F6*, 17–18). This middle-class couple will appear frequently as a contrast to the behind-the-scenes manipulations of The Others. Mr. and Mrs. A represent the anonymous Public who know only what they are fed by a manipulated media.

The next scene emphasizes the contrast of Mr. and Mrs. A with The Others by shifting to, as per the stage directions, "*Sir James Ransom's room at the Colonial office. On the wall . . . hangs a large boldly-printed map showing British Sudoland and Ostnian Sudoland. The frontier between the two colonies is formed by a chain of mountains: one peak, prominently marked F6, is ringed with a red circle. . .*" (*F6*, 19). Sir James, the evil twin, speaks as a stereotypical Other about the Sudoland problem. This British colony, with socialist Ostnia's influence, has been yanking at its colonial chains. The Others denounce socialism and Lord Stagmantle proudly boasts: "We were out to smash the Labour Government . . . and, by God, we did" (*F6*, 21). In "by God" lies a hint of a church-sanctioned imperialist hypocrisy. James forms a plan to inflame public opinion into wanting to keep Sudoland for the British: an expedition will scale the previously insurmountable mountain, F6. Propaganda will arouse British pride and the public will wish to defend their prize, F6, and this means retaining control of British Sudoland at all costs. F6 is also known as the "Haunted Mountain," and Lady Isabel recalls that it is reputedly protected by a "guardian demon" (*F6*, 23). The General retorts that this is a "fairy-tale." James, however, always the politician, responds: "A fairy-tale is significant according to the number of people who believe in it. . ." (*F6*, 24). He is suggesting that propaganda can manufacture nefarious "fairytales" to suit a hungry public starved for self-serving news. James tells The Others that he will recruit his bother, the famous climber, to lead the expedition. The General still has his doubts about James's plan calling it a "wild goose chase" (*F6*, 26). From this line, Rex Warner would write his *Dogskin* -esque novel of the same name.

Next the audience watches Mr. and Mrs. A listen to the first wave of propaganda on the wireless: "The haunted mountain [is] inhabited only by monks [who] practise a mysterious cult . . . and there are wonderful tales of their mystical and psychic powers" (*F6*, 29). Isherwood and Auden foreshadow the metaphysical messages to come later in the play.

In scene 3 we return to Michael Ransom and meet his climbing fellows: the Doctor, Lamp, Shawcross, and Gunn. Ransom is the magnetic leader; Shawcross and Gunn are his devoted followers. The former is an Eric Vernon type who climbs more to please Ransom than to please himself. Shawcross is jealous of Gunn who is a cross of Maurice and Edward Blake. Gunn is a jokester, conniver, and compulsive Test-seeker. Shawcross is a fawning worshiper, even offering to polish Ransom's boots. He is a derivation of Sladen from "Gems of Belgian Architecture." Gunn is a court-jester worshiper, appealing through humor. Shawcross is judgmental of Gunn and a snitch when Gunn is caught in some petty connivance. Shawcross and Gunn are still living as honor system schoolboys in the old school mentality; they are the younger boys trying to please the older leader of the senior class. Shawcross and Gunn are Truly Weak. Ransom understands this undercurrent and is suitably patient with each. Still, recalling his opening monologue, he himself has his own undercurrent of stark cynicism towards his fellow men.

The Others, led by James, visit Michael and his gang to persuade Michael to surmount F6. Lord Stagmantle is intrigued that James's brother is both "a scholar and man of action: an unusual mixture" (F6, 39). James tries flattery on Michael: "In all humility I say it—my brother is a great man" (F6, 39). Michael sees through this, recalling their childhood when James would whine and wheedle for what he wanted. He tells James to cut the subterfuge and get to the point. James starts off: "In the name of His Majesty's Government, I have come to make you an important proposition——." Michael does not want to hear it and interrupts, "Which I unconditionally refuse" (F6, 40). The invocation of king and country is enough to repel him: "I know your propositions James: they are exceedingly convincing. They contain certain reservations. They are concerned with prestige, tactics, money, and the privately pre-arranged meanings of familiar words. I will have nothing to do with any of them. Keep to your world. I will keep to mine" (F6, 40). The Others and the opposing Anti-Other are clearly in conflict, with The Others manipulating their world through a secret code of "familiar words." Michael speaks for the antihero father, Frank Isherwood, and rebuts the upper class that had sent Frank to war. James tempts Michael the mountain climber by telling him that the goal is F6. Michael inquires: "What does your world have to with F6? Since boyhood, in dreams . . . F6 is my fate. . . . But not now, not like this" (F6, 40–41). Lady Isabel tries to manipulate him by shamelessly impugning his manhood: "I see it in your eyes, you are afraid." She confronts Michael with a Test. He does not succumb to the bait. "I am afraid of a great many things. . . . But of nothing which you in your worst nightmares could ever imagine. . ." (F6, 41). This alludes to his angst in the opening monologue. Ransom realizes that he has inner demons spurred by some hidden guilt. In his efforts to be Truly Strong and refuse this Test, like anyone else, he is also Truly Weak; otherwise he would feel no temptation. Speaking of temptation, The Others pull out their ace. There is a knock on the door. James says: "Here is somebody who may be able to persuade you. . . ."

> Ransom [*with a cry of dismay*] Mother!
> Mother [*advancing to* Ransom] Michael, I am so proud——
> Ransom [*recoiling*] You too! No, it isn't impossible! Your shadow adds to theirs, a trick of the light. (F6, 42–43)

His mother—another Mrs. Lindsay or Lily Vernon (both based on Kathleen)—knows no bounds for laying on guilt and shame. Michael tells her that when he and his brother were boys she neglected him in favor of James, of whom he was jealous.

This rejection by his mother leads to his guilt and retreat into solitude. She invokes the memory of their father, saying that James is like him: "he cannot live an hour without applause. . . . But you, you were to be truly strong who must be kept from all that could infect or weaken; it was for you I steeled my love deliberately and hid it. Do you think it was easy to shut you out? But I won. You were to be unlike your father and brother, you were to have the power to stand alone. . . . There was a mother who crucified herself to save her favorite son from weakness" (*F6*, 45). On this pathetic note Michael gives in.

His mother, in her twisted effort to make Michael Truly Strong, had succeeded superficially, but left him with a core of vulnerability, as seen in the bitterness of his opening meditation in act 1. The past lurks always in the psyche to disturb the present. The great irony is that his mother, who claims she withheld her love to make him strong so he could "stand alone," will not let him. Mrs. Ransom gives back the love she withheld, but, since this is only a ploy to make him Truly Weak and accept this Test, she contradicts herself. Here, more so than in Isherwood's first two novels that dealt with the Truly Weak and Truly Strong theme less explicitly, the requirements of the stage demanded a stark directness that enunciated the themes succinctly and viscerally. The Auden Generation was no longer decoding a veiled Isherwood-Auden schema; the dramatists were making it palpably apparent.

After having succeeded in their entrapment of Ransom, The Others leave, and Ransom has a dream (or nightmare) that punctuates his own particular mother-son conundrum: Michael hears his mother tell him she will be with him always, right to the top of the mountain. Her son's tormented voice is heard "*Far off, frightened,* It's the demon, mother!" (*F6*, 53). The line is deliberately ambiguous, since it could refer to the mountain as a demon or to the mother as a demon.

Act 2 begins "*in a monastery on the Great Glacier.*" Shawcross tells Michael that Gunn "steals." Michael laughs, calling a Gunn an essentially harmless "magpie" (*F6*, 57–58). Ransom also notes to Shawcross that he has not changed much since he was captain at school, meaning that he epitomizes the old school's faults. Shawcross fawns some more while still slipping in his derision of Gunn, whom he refers to as being fearful of F6. Michael tells him it is the fear that pushes Gunn: "being frightened is his chief pleasure in life" (*F6*, 60). Gunn is like Edward Blake. Shawcross knows that only two climbers can actually reach the summit of F6 and begins his campaign to be chosen. He jealousy calls Gunn a "neurotic" (*F6*, 61). Shawcross and Gunn are Truly Weak, only differing in approach. Shawcross needs approval from his hero Ransom to validate himself. He endures Tests for Ransom's sake. As Auden previously said concerning *The Orators,* "no secular saviour can equal the hopes of his youthful followers." Gunn needs Tests for his own sake.

Gunn wonders if the monks communicate by "telepathy" in some secret code known only to themselves (*F6*, 62). The monks are a metaphysical gang with their own secret language. The monks unnerve Gunn because his instinct tells him that they understand that his compulsion to live dangerously is a weakness. The monks have a magic crystal into which one can glimpse his future, if not necessarily realize what that future means. The reflections are also omens of death.

Alone together, the monastery's abbot and Ransom philosophize. This dialogue signifies Isherwood and Auden's shift away from the distracting public chaos and into private spheres where the only true salvation can be found. Ransom reveals to the abbot that when it had been his turn to look into the crystal he saw the "ragged denizens" crying out for help and wonders if their cry was for him to save them. The abbot tells him "Only God is great" (*F6*, 68–69), implying that if fate chooses him to be a saviour, so be it, but he cannot put this burden on himself if he is doing so as a compensation for some secret guilt. The abbot warns Michael not to let his Western sensibility discount the idea of a demon on the mountain, telling him that the peasants, unencumbered with the veneer of civilization, "see it more clearly than you or I. For it is a picture of truth. The Demon is real. Only his ministry and his visitation are unique for every nature. To the complicated and sensitive like yourself . . . his disguises are more subtle. . . . I understand your temptation. You wish to conquer the Demon and then to save mankind." The abbot continues:

> Nothing is revealed [in the crystal] but what we have hidden from ourselves. . . . Your temptation . . . is written in your face. You could ask the world to follow you and it would serve you with blind obedience; for most men long to be delivered from the terror of thinking and feeling for themselves. . . . And you would do them much good. Because men desire evil, they must be governed by those who understand the corruption of their hearts. . . . but woe to the governors, for by the very operation of their duty, however excellent, they themselves are destroyed. For you can only rule men by appealing to their fear and lust; government requires the exercise of the human will: and the human will is from the Demon. (*F6*, 70–72)

And the demon (the ego) is a metaphor for the neuroses and psychoses that result from the conflict of trying to shake off the shackles of the past. Ransom asks the abbot what choice he has but to climb the mountain. The abbot answers: "There is an alternative, Mr. Ransom; and I offer it to you. . . . The complete abnegation of the will" (*F6*, 72). Ransom asks what this means, but they are interrupted before the abbot can explain.

In the mystic's view the "abnegation of the will" is the eradication of the willful ego's lower-case self in favor of Vedanta's transcendent upper-case Self. Auden's "Summer Night" vision of agape encouraged the possibility of this mystical viewpoint. But can any ruler abnegate his will? Isherwood and Auden understood that even the well-meaning man becomes corrupted by the process of ruling. Hero-worship entails that a hero fill the needs of the Truly Weak. The amorphous public will objectify the hero and give him an image that no man can possibly live up to. The hero feels compelled to try and match their image of him. A Truly

Strong Man, if asked to be a leader, would wish to maintain his private face in public places, but he would find that this private face may not be the face his public expects or wants. The Truly Weak Man who becomes a leader does not have this problem; his mask is always in place to fit the vision others have of him and indeed need of him.

After he and the abbot are interrupted, Ransom wonders: "Is it too late for me. . . . There was a choice once . . . I made it wrong, and if I choose again now, I must choose for myself alone, not for these others" (*F6*, 74). He implores some greater power to help him: "Save us from the destructive element of our will, for all we do is evil" (*F6*, 74). The term, "destructive element," came from the title of Stephen Spender's 1935 book of literary criticism.

In his critical study, Spender asserts that the technique in the middle and late novels of Henry James is a prelude to literary modernism. Spender argues that James uses interior monologues to tacitly express beliefs in absentia through stating unbelief; that is, by having the characters reject certain ideas, readers infer new ideas antithetically. Further, Spender analyzes James, Yeats, Eliot, and D. H. Lawrence as exemplars of unbelief from which the astute reader should connote new beliefs.[102] Spender declares that there must be a tearing down of the old before there can be a building up of the new. In *F6* Isherwood and Auden convey their understanding of this process, having spent ten years tearing down the influences of the past. The building up of new beliefs must have some underlying metaphysical basis so one can act in the world as a Truly Strong Man, uninfluenced and unimpeded by the needs of the individual ego. To know this is to know also that the public will resist the ideals behind such a theory. Further, what are the beliefs that will supplant the unbelief: socialism? communism? mysticism? These are only words if the private face cannot find its balance in the public chaos. In 1937 Isherwood and Auden were not yet certain of the answers, but they knew enough to pose the questions.

After Ransom's plea goes unanswered, he later asks Gunn if he has considered the aftermath of reaching the peak and then coming down to the trumpeted celebrations of the Public as orchestrated by The Others: "Have you loathed them, and even as you were loathing them, begun to like it all?" (*F6*, 75). Gunn the attention seeker would love it, not loathe it. As they climb a skull is found and, like Hamlet, Ransom speaks to it. Hamlet is Ransom's literary role model; both are internally conflicted concerning their mothers and driven by forces they cannot control or fully understand. As with Hamlet, Ransom's angst will supply ample blood sacrifices. In *F6* the first to die is Edward Lamp from an avalanche. Ransom says of Lamp: "The first victim to my pride" (*F6*, 86). Back in England Lamp is lionized by the media as the newest martyr for the cult of the dead.

Ransom decides that Gunn, not Shawcross, will go with him to the summit. Ransom tells the doctor that Shawcross cannot deal with the Test because he is a nervous wreck and the climb is too psychologically connected with his self-esteem. This makes him a risk. Ransom informs Shawcross, who does not take the decision well: "I'm no damn good. . . . You're all better men than I am. I had a pretty fine opinion of myself, once. I imagined I was indispensable. Even my admiration of you was only another kind of conceit. You were just an ideal of myself. But F6 has broken me; it's shown me what I am—a rotten weakling. . ." (*F6*, 98). Shawcross, unable to bear what he considers to be his failure, jumps to his death. Shawcross saw in his hero Ransom what his lack of self-esteem prevented him from seeing in himself. No actual hero can live up to such a follower's ego-derived vicarious need.

In the next scene Gunn dies of exhaustion as he and Michael are just short of reaching the summit. Ransom thinks that this is Gunn's good luck for he has achieved the release of death that "extricates you now from the most cunning trap of all," which is life (*F6*, 102).

Ransom continues on, nears the summit, and collapses. At the summit he sees a veiled, but as yet, unidentifiable figure. The chorus is in the background wearing the monks' cowled robes. They recite: "When shall the deliverer come to destroy this dragon?" (*F6*, 106). After a fanfare of trumpets, James Ransom appears as the dragon. He spews propaganda. Michael rises and steps into the circle of light around the dragon. James signals and life-size chessmen appear. Their ensuing debate is a matter of gamesmanship. All of the play's characters encircle the twin brothers. The middle-class couple grumble about their dull lives. The general tells them that they have it easy compared to the brave climbers. Maybe so, but in Wholly-Truthful art one's egocentric everyday life goes on; the individual persists as did Spender's figure of "I eating," "I excreting." Mr. and Mrs. A can only suffer for themselves. They cannot feel what the climbers felt or what another feels. For Mr. and Mrs. A, as for any individual, one's own existence is paramount. Another's suffering may be apprehended intellectually, but it is an abstraction, even to one who is well-meaning and tries to empathize. One's intellect cannot live in another's body. Lady Isabel joins the general in admonishing Mr. and Mrs. A. Of course, the rich Others find it easy to chastise others not so rich. Lord Stagmantle shallowly asserts that money is not everything: "I know there are far too many people who have too little. It's a damned shame, but there it is" (*F6*, 110).

Mrs. A asks, "Why were we born?" She does so in despairing ennui, not as a philosophical inquiry. James misinterprets her meaning and sarcastically mimics Michael's scholarly bent by responding with ad hoc nonsense about the "immensity of the universe" (*F6*, 110), in which the life of the individual has no importance but to pass the torch, die, and be forgotten. Michael protests that this is a twisted paraphrase of how he truly feels. His thoughts were distorted, just as a controlled media manipulates propaganda. James taunts him, repeating what Michael had said to him in act 1: "Keep to your world. I will keep to mine" (*F6*,

111). The chess game commences. Michael wins. James falls dead and is eulogized by The Others, who continue their patriotic cant and accuse Michael of murder.

The abbot appears in a judge's wig and robe. Michael cries out that he is innocent and that the demon gave the sign for his brother's death. The abbot calls as witnesses the victims of Michael Ransom's pride. Shawcross appears and implicates the former subject of his hero-worship. Gunn and Lamp follow and are also of no help to their friend. The abbot asks Michael if he wishes to appeal to the all-seeing crystal. The abbot looks into it and tells Ransom that the demon was not the temptation. Ransom realizes his pride was the temptation. He is found guilty to a chorus of "Die for England!" and "*All lights are extinguished below; only the* [veiled] Figure *and* Ransom *remain illuminated. Ransom turns to the* Figure, *whose draperies fall away, revealing* Mrs. Ransom *as a young mother*" (*F6,* 117).

Then, darkness hides the stage. The sun rises; the stage is empty, except for the body of Ransom at the summit. He has been dead or near death all along. The preceding scene was an illusion, or perhaps the dream-vision of one dying. After his death, Ransom is praised by The Others as, indeed, having died for England. James says: "He had many sides to his character and I doubt if anyone knew the whole man. I as his brother certainly did not. He had an almost feminine sensibility which, if it had not been allied to great qualities of soul and will-power and a first class intelligence, might easily have become neurotic—" (*F6,* 121). James did not know him. What he said of his brother is true, but a misinterpretation reversing the real meaning. If his brother was "neurotic," it was not due to a "feminine sensibility" or sensitivity. This sensibility had more likely ameliorated his mental illness instead of worsening it—that is, at least until he had given in to the temptation of his masculine side, which led him to charge up F6. Had his feminine sensibility been stronger, he might not have let his manly pride push him to accept the mission that killed him and his friends. His past, in the symbolic form of his young mother, overcame the common sense of his sensitive, feminine side.

Ransom failed because he gave in to the public chaos instead of listening to his private sphere. His inner Self had an intuition for mysticism as revealed in his conversation with the abbot. The abbot had told him that the secret to his salvation would be in the "abnegation of the will," but Ransom could not resist his ego and he succumbed to the temptations of worldliness that his mother represented. Isherwood and Auden created a character who was the defining figure for their generation. Michael Ransom was an aspiring Truly Strong Man who was overwhelmed by Truly Weak temptation. He was a realistic antiheroic hero; his divided, angst-filled mind was "upright," meaning he had a conscience. Ransom cared—too much! Had he cared less and not been so vulnerable, he might have ignored the appeals of The Others and acted more in self-preservation as would have a Mr. Norris. Ransom was the sensitive man who had an intuition that it is in the world of the spirit where answers might be found. His intuition, however, became clouded by his ego.

For Isherwood and Auden, Michael Ransom's quest represented their own quest. Ransom was their last hope for the 1930s. Metaphorically, his failure would signify the futility that would overcome their iconoclastic generation when it was unable to prevent World War II. This generation, with all its activism, had not been able to save the world. When the decade ended, all that was left for them to do was to try and save themselves by somehow turning inward.

The success of *The Dog beneath the Skin* and *The Ascent of F6* were responded to in the usual manner of the 1930s: they were imitated. The imitations all shared the Isherwood-Auden theme of a conflicted man trying to reconcile his private sphere in public chaos by maturing from Truly Weak to Truly Strong. Day Lewis, in 1936, wrote the play, *Noah and the Waters*, a didactic parable leaning more heavily on the didactic. Noah is an antihero conflicted about saving the world and whom to save. In 1937 Louis MacNeice's satire, *Out of the Picture*, has a sensitive artist as antihero conflicted over the integrity of his art versus the bourgeois world of which he is a member. Also in 1937 Spender's *Trial of a Judge* features a conflicted antihero who has to choose between truth and political expediency. All these plays gave homage to Francis Crewe and Michael Ransom. They also exhorted that something could still be done to save the world. In that regard, 1937 turned out to be a very bad year.

AUDEN: *LETTER TO LORD BYRON, LOOK, STRANGER, SPAIN 1937*

The Isherwood-Auden plays were explicitly political, tacitly metaphysical. Auden, while writing the plays in 1935, 1936, and 1938, was also expressing himself politically in poetry and essays. He was caught up in the era's activism and encouraged by his peers to be an activist. Auden participated in current events but always with some reluctance. Novelist Storm Jameson wrote of Auden's attendance at a 1934 meeting of the Writer's Committee of the Anti-War Council. She describes the contrast of Auden with an older, vocal communist: "I looked [at] the thin tired twisted face of the middle-aged Communist who was there to keep us straight, and W. H. Auden's face, with its extraordinary patina of age.[Auden was twenty-seven.] I have never seen so old a young face, it might have been overhanging a mediaeval cathedral during centuries of frost and sun. He hardly spoke."[103]

Auden's reticence was not habitual. He just was not comfortable at a political meeting. Rabid oratory, even for a just cause, only reminded him of the old school cant and rant. Propaganda of any kind did not suit him. Auden would later say in 1939: "Beware of . . . the dictator who says 'my people': The writer who says 'my public.'"[104] Throughout the 1930s Auden could not decide if art as propaganda should serve a political cause or not. His intuition leaned against it but, in writing the plays and in certain prose and poems, particularly *Spain,* Auden became caught up in the activism of his peers. By March 1939 Auden finally made a choice after giving his first and last political speech: "I suddenly found I could really do it, that I could make a fighting demagogic speech and have the audience roaring. And . . . it is so exciting but so absolutely degrading. I felt just covered with dirt afterwards. It isn't that one shouldn't do any 'social' work but one must do something that is in one's nature to do, and for me that means 'teaching.'"[105] For Auden this meant teaching through parable-art. Before reaching his conclusion in 1939, Auden wrestled with his dilemma by thinking through his pen. Along with writing the plays, Auden wrote three works that concern his internal conflict: *Letter to Lord Byron* (1936), *Look! Stranger* (1936), *Spain* (1937).

Edward Mendelson writes: "*Letter to Lord Byron* is a discursive poem in five parts, urbane, conversational, *au courant,* tolerantly amused by the literary scene, savagely amused by the political one. The poem is splendidly funny, but it has none of the uncontrolled slapstick of *The Orators.* Auden adds a note of comic self-mocking irony whenever the poem gets didactic, but he is more didactic than in anything he wrote before. He claims at the end to have reached only 'the rather tame conclusion / That no man by himself has life's solution.'"[106]

Auden began *Letter to Lord Byron* a few months after completing *The Ascent of F6.* The play, a meditation on man's public and private spheres, was a prelude for Auden to have a further meditation on his own public and private spheres. According to Mendelson, "it was while writing *The Ascent of F6,* that he realized he must someday leave England."[107] Consequently, *Letter* is a summing up of Auden's life in England as well as Auden's history of English life. This long poem is an homage to Byron and written (more or less) in Byronic style. It is alternately satirically serious and seriously satiric. After the grandiloquently serious *F6,* Auden wished to lighten up and chose Byron's "airy manner" to do so (*CP,* 97).

Obscurantist no longer, Auden would be didactic and explain himself clearly, directly, and to great effect. Auden puts himself in the middle of British history—not in a chronological sense, but as the current product incorporating all of that history simultaneously. The product he depicts is a British middle-class intellectual and artist. Auden ruminates on the conflicts derived from being an artist in the modern world. Mendelson considers *Letter* to incorporate three his-tory lessons: (1) the changes in English society; (2) the modern and romantic concept of the hero-artist and his isolation in society; (3) Auden's autobiography of his own art and class. While exploring these three "histories," Auden reiterates the Isherwood-Auden schema of a haunting past and the Truly Weak and Truly Strong Man. He does so with greater compassion, seeing England, not with the hawk's vision of an alienated cypher-witness, but as a citizen among citizens. He does so even though he cannot always agree with or even understand some of his fellow citizens: "You can't change human nature, don't you know!" (*CP,* 92). Auden also praises the common man who is Truly Strong and wants to be like him: "I am like you," he says, "and you, and you" (*CP,* 98). What he is not like is The Others.

In part 3 Auden explains the dilemma of the postromantic artist who now lives in an age of flux. He is without roots in a time of socioeconomic instability. Neither he nor his readers, who are among the alienated herd within the Public, have a mutual ground for understanding. The artist cannot be sure of the temper of his times, so he cannot be sure about his art. Consequently, the conflict arises about what to say and how to say it. Should the artist transcend propaganda or succumb to it? As he considers his answer, Auden writes: "I'm more intuitive than analytic" (*CP,* 97). He would later rely on intuition, mistrusting the "analytic" as leading one astray, saying: "To me Art's subject is the human clay (*CP,* 100); the background, natural or otherwise, is just something humanity stands in front of. Humanity's actions are more important than the scenery behind which these actions take place. The background should not take precedence over the human story, without whom there is no background. An artist, "like a secret agent must keep hidden his passion. . ." (*CP,* 102). The artist should not preach, but teach through parable. His passion must be hidden behind his parable because of the lowbrow Public's mistrust of highbrows, which has been inculcated in them by "the management." Didactic artists are easy targets to either use or subvert as necessary. The result may be a time when the independent, iconoclastic highbrow becomes extinct and a child may ask in the future during his history class what was "An intellectual of the middle classes?'" (*CP,* 105). Auden understands the pressure to conform, saying that for the sake of normality "What murders are committed in thy name" (*CP,* 108). Auden spares the old school in his *Letter* but only because "I've said my say on public schools elsewhere" (*CP,* 109). He does, however, recall youthful influences, Layard, Lane, D. H. Lawrence, and Gerald Heard, who taught him to abhor any one who chose art over "Life and Love and being Pure-in-Heart" (*CP,* 111). Older and wiser, Auden is more bemused about his previous enthusiasms; he does not reject them, but tempers them with a greater understanding of life's contingencies. *Letter to Lord Byron* is in itself pragmatic and didactic, but always with tongue-in-cheek. After the histrionics of *F6,* the *Letter* was also a respite from neo-tragedy.

Look, Stranger, also published in 1936, was Auden's first collection of poems since the 1932 second printing of his first volume. Included in *Look, Stranger* is "A Summer Night," which was written three years earlier. The dedication is to Erika Mann, whom Auden married so she could remain in England after fleeing Germany. This volume's poems have neither *F6*'s histrionics nor, conversely, the satirical airy manner of *Lord Byron.* These poems are more introspective and meditative. Yet all three works examine similar themes, but from different angles of

Auden's perception. The American title *On This Island* is a clue that Mendelson notes is the focus of Auden's mid-1930s perspective: "In the early 1930s Auden dreamed of innocent islands. He woke on a guilty one. From the end of 1935 to the end of 1938, whenever he needed an emblem for his separation from responsibility, audience, love, history, all that is real outside the mind's inner chambers, he invoked the solitary island. . . . The island supplanted the border as Auden's geographical sign of entrapment and enclosure. [Auden] carried his isolation with him."[108]

If an island had become an emblem of isolation, an island could also be a haven for salvation. Just as one sometimes feels alone in a crowd wherever he may be, one can also find a haven wherever he may be. For the mystic, the kingdom of God is within, and all existence is integrally unified if one chooses, as the mystic does, to believe this. The center of the universe for a mystic is wherever he happens to be. This center is a shelter from life's hurricane. The goal is to remain fast to the center and not get caught up in the spin of external reality. Auden's experience on that "Summer Night" had been some evidence that an island can be a blessing as well as curse. One escapes from a solitary island, but one can also escape to an enlightened island. The question remains: where is the enlightened island? Isherwood and Auden spared no energy in looking for it. The poems of *Look, Stranger* continue Auden's search.

"A Summer Night" was inspired by Auden's mystical experience and his reading of the *Book of Talbot,* which he believed to be a supreme expression of unconditional love. This book was a statement of romantic love as a manifestation of Eros, spiritual love for one person. *The Book of Talbot* was written in the past. For Auden the ghosts and traditions of the past were no longer exclusively evil. The past can also guide a search for love in the present. One must learn to select knowledge from the past with sensitive discrimination. The balance of poems in the volume signify a shift for Auden away from being an unreserved Anti-Other to having a more tolerant and even appreciative view of at least some of The Others. The 1930s in some ways had been too independent, leaving members of this generation with little to lean on from the past it disclaimed. During the period when many of the poems were written, Auden was a teacher (master) at the Downs preparatory school. Geoffrey Hoyland was the school's progressive headmaster and Auden dedicated "A Summer Night" to him. By many accounts Auden's tenure at the Downs was the happiest period of his life in England. John Duguid, a student of Auden's at the Downs, recalled that his teacher was "jolly" and inviting, enjoying his charges a great deal.[109]

As in *Letter to Lord Byron,* the verse in *Look, Stranger* is more of an analysis and less of an attack. The poem "Our Hunting Fathers" asserts that these fathers explained the fable "Of the sadness of the creatures." Auden gives credit to the "fathers" for trying to teach, but that their message became distorted by the pressures of public chaos that they reacted to with individual and collective egotism.

The result is "sadness," as love was overcome by guilt (*CP,* 122). This poem follows "A Summer Night" as a contrast. In the former, love exists if one seeks it by "an abnegation of the will"; in the latter, the will did not abnegate and love has been lost, but it can be found again by overcoming guilt.

Throughout these poems there are islands to escape from and the hint of islands where one might escape to if obstacles are overcome. There is a gulf between the inexorable pull of public chaos and possible peace in the private sphere. Auden considers how the gulf can be bridged. In *Early Auden,* Mendelson cites five possible escape routes: (1) erotic: sexual love leading to the vision of Eros and then agape, (2) redemptive: save mankind by example or direct cure, (3) didactive: teach through parables to unlearn hatred and learn love, (4) world-historical: solutions by determined altruistic forces, and (5) escapist: flee to an island refuge of the mind in fantasy.

Before 1933 Auden's obscure anonymity as a cypher-witness revealed to him that taking the Northwest Passage to distant frontiers makes nothing happen within, where real change must begin. People will change one at a time through a change of heart. Only then will civilization follow. Gerald Heard's vision of a unified collective consciousness stated that people can erase ego-generated societal divisions through what Heard called "intentional living." For Heard to live intentionally began with recognizing that the ego is the enemy to serenity. Heard taught a secular version of what the world's religions had long advocated, particularly the mystical exponents in each case. With all the wrestling in these poems, Auden ultimately rejects the solitary island for an island in the heart; one that is to be found in contemplative silence. Auden's intuition was moving him back toward a mystical version of his childhood high Anglican Christianity that he had never really forsaken. Still, there would be some more wrestling with the public chaos against his private sphere. In 1937 Auden would write *Spain.*

Spain is the best poem that Auden wished he had never written. He revised it in 1939 for the volume *Another Time;* kept it in his *Collected Poems* of 1944, regretted it, and banned the poem from any future collections beginning with *Selected Poems* in 1957. *Spain* is brilliant poetry, so why did Auden disavow it? He realized that, regardless of his original good intentions, his sincere support of the anti-fascists loyalists in the Spanish Civil War, and his masterful artistry, he had written propaganda. An argument has been made that Auden was too hard on himself. At the time George Orwell believed Auden deserved to be hard on himself. Orwell's criticism may have been a catalyst for Auden's self-criticism. Orwell's admonition concerned the end of the poem.

The opening of *Spain* is structured to signify Auden's idea of inclusive time as a perpetual continuum. He begins with alternations of "Yesterday" and "Today" then a focus on "Today" followed by alternations of "Tomorrow," and "Today." The past is the present is the future. The themes elucidated within this structure represent a concise version of the same themes in *Letter to Lord Byron* and *Look, Stranger:* the influence of history for good or ill, public and private spheres, responsibility for one's inner life. The first six stanzas summarize the history of the world. The last three of these six stanzas begin with "Yesterday" followed by a succinct capsule of an historical epoch, and each ends with "but-today the struggle." On the visceral level "the struggle" is the Spanish Civil War as the symbol of anti-fascism. The more subtle implication is the struggle of man attempting to place himself in the current context by asking of the past that it explain the present. Auden talks about history as that which operates and organizes, calling it "Time the refreshing River."

"Time the refreshing river" is the time that heals all wounds. This line is sonorously appealing and a wonderful image. Scientist Joseph Needham, a great admirer of Auden, would use this line as the title for a book of essays in 1943. However, Auden's intention for this line is not quite so positive. Time as a river is a linear view of time. Man tends to favor the past and postpone changes needed in the present until faced with dilemmas that those changes might have prevented, in this case, the advent of fascism. Auden moves away from the man-devised illusion of linear time and toward a sense of time as the mystic understands it. A succinct definition of mystical time comes from Thornton Wilder: "It is only in appearance that time is a river. It is a vast landscape and it is the eye of the beholder that moves."[110] Time has no divisions; yesterday, today, and tomorrow are seen as one picture. This picture may be too large for the eye to encompass in a single glance, but it is still one image, not many divided.

Nonetheless, in 1937, today is today, and there is a crisis to be overcome. How will it be done? Who will find justice? Auden's protagonist says that he will, even if that means death. Spain is personified as he who must stand up and take responsibility for this crucial juncture in history, even if that means he must be sacrificed. This point in time has arrived as a result of past influences that confuse present minds. The past has become the present. Auden then contrasts today with the expectation that tomorrow will still come just as the today of the poem is yesterday's tomorrow. He lists items both magnificent and mundane because in Wholly-Truthful art the magnificent and mundane arrive in tandem. After a litany of tomorrows Auden's first point is that, yes, tomorrow will be better than today, but his second point is that tomorrow will forget the past and not learn from it. If so, the past will repeat itself. Then Auden says again that for today there is only struggle. The possibility of death by conflict is great as well as the guilt that comes with causing deaths that are inevitable. These deaths will be determined by the use of power and propaganda. Nature will be ashamed to witness such deaths, but expediency requires that murder be done. All that will be left to the vanquished victims is a history that, in the poem's last words, "May say alas but cannot help nor pardon."

Auden's conclusion is that history, as an abstract monolith, does not give a damn. "In *Spain*'s final words," Mendelson believes, "Auden indicates how deeply he abhors the idea of history in his own poem. What purposive history cannot give is *pardon,* a word that carries special force in Auden's vocabulary. Pardon has nothing to do with vague notions of courteous tolerance; it is the means by which one who is isolated by guilt or circumstance may be restored to wholeness and community. Other needs are vital—hunger and love—but as Auden implied before in 1934 [in his review of *The Book of Talbot*], it is 'our greater need, forgiveness, that matters most.' With all its powers, History cannot help nor pardon; and the sense of the final two lines of *Spain* is that history cannot help nor pardon the defeated, those whose need for pardon is greatest of all."[111]

History did not pardon the victims of the Spanish Civil War. In 1938, George Orwell, who fought in Spain, did not pardon Auden for writing about war in the abstract: "Mr. Auden can write about 'the acceptance of guilt for the necessary murder' because he has never committed a murder, perhaps never had one of his friends murdered, possibly never even seen a murdered man's corpse."[112]

Auden apparently agreed. In his foreword to *Collected Shorter Poems,* 1966, he writes:

> A dishonest poem is one which expresses, no matter how well, feelings or beliefs which its author never felt or entertained. . . . I once wrote:
>
> History to the defeated
>
> may say alas but cannot help nor pardon.
>
> To says this is to equate goodness with success. It would have been bad enough if I had ever held this wicked doctrine, but that I should have stated it simply because it sounded rhetorically effective is quite inexcusable.
>
> In art as in life, bad manners, not to be confused with a deliberate intention to cause offence, are the consequence of an over-concern with one's own ego and a lack of consideration (and knowledge of) others. Readers, like friends, must not be shouted at with brash familiarity. Youth may be forgiven when it is brash or noisy, but this does not mean brashness and noise are virtues.[113]

On one hand, Auden *was* being too hard on himself. Mendelson believes that all of *Spain* expresses the dilemma faced by Auden and his generation: "By speaking for the Republic, he accepted a degree of complicity in the actions done in its name, actions that included political and judicial murders. Other poets of the Spanish war had no trouble ignoring this uncomfortable truth; Auden insisted on facing it. Divided between the moral revulsion and what he felt to be his public obligations, he chose, almost despairingly, the 'conscious acceptance of guilt.'"[114]

On the other hand, although Auden accepted his complicity for the fact that others had killed or been killed, he had not volunteered to fight. Ultimately, Auden had used art for propaganda or, in his nomenclature, "black magic." He had gone against his intuition and allowed the public sphere to motivate his ego into writing a poem that his private sphere could not accept. In Auden's perception, he had not been pure in heart; consequently, he had been Truly Weak. Perhaps as an atonement, in 1939 Auden would make a journey to a war with Isherwood. Before they did, however, it was time for Isherwood to say *Goodbye to Berlin*.

HERR ISSEYVOO: THE SUBTLETY OF WHOLLY-TRUTHFUL ART

In his preface to *Goodbye to Berlin* Isherwood explains that the six episodes in it, as well as his novel about Norris, were originally parts of a long epic, *The Lost*, about a barely pre-Hitler Berlin from 1930 to 1933. *Mr. Norris Changes Trains* was published in 1935, and the Berlin stories individually in 1937 and 1938 before they were collected as the novel *Goodbye to Berlin* in 1939. By then the term pre-Hitler had been introduced as a contrast to the post-Hitler reality. In 1939 the stories, inspired by Isherwood's diaries, seemed presciently poignant to readers who were giving them a historical perspective that enabled readers to believe they were seeing Nazis between every line. Considering recent events this was not unreasonable. The British government had been giving out gas masks and practicing air raid drills for six years. Nonetheless, when Isherwood wrote the stories, the Nazis were an encroaching threat, but they were not yet the all-consuming threat that readers knew them to be in the late 1930s. Since Isherwood's diaries were the source for the stories, the stories are less about history and more about Isherwood and the people he meets. The characters are the focus, not history. Biographer Finney writes that "the only facts to be found in the novel are those which impinged on the narrator's consciousness. This is why . . . political events only surface towards the end of the novel—because Isherwood himself only became politically conscious during the last part of his Berlin sojourn."[115]

The stories are staged chronologically from "Autumn 1930" to "Winter 1932–33," and depict memorable characters based on real people. Lurking within these characterizations are the symptoms of a sickness. Berlin itself is sick and Berliners react to the sickness. Isherwood describes their reactions but does not necessarily explain them. He is the first-person narrator and cannot read the minds of his characters, just as he could not read the minds of the real people these characters represent. In turn, readers cannot read Isherwood's mind either. Since Christopher Isherwood is both the author of the novel and the novel's protagonist, readers and critics have speculated on his true narrative intentions. Finney summarizes the confusion:

> Any discussion of the function of "Christopher Isherwood" within the novel is bedeviled by an unintended ambiguity. . . . Isherwood has repeatedly explained his reasons for creating what he called a "demi-character" [in *CK,* 142] —his artistic need to be true to his own intuitive perception of life, his decision to use his pseudo-self as a scanning device, and his consequent need to avoid drawing attention to the narrator as a character in his own right (and to avoid his homosexuality in particular). The narrator consequently hovers on the edges of the dramas he

has witnessed like a character in limbo. Whenever he seems about to enter the action as a participant, Isherwood closes the scene or extricates his fictive counterpart from self-exposure, as if it was he (which for the main part it was) and not a narrator within his control who was about to reveal himself in his true colours. . . . Invited by the author to identify with "Christopher Isherwood," yet constantly thwarted by his passivity and reticence, the reader tends to project on to the narrator feelings outside the control of his creator. Moreover, far from drawing no attention to himself, the narrator's enigmatic withdrawal from any commitment positively invites the reader to concentrate on "Christopher Isherwood's" hidden responses and attitudes to the bizarre life he is witnessing.[116]

Readers and critics are "bedeviled" because they cannot put aside that the author and the narrator have the same name, and that this name comes with a biography they are aware of. Is the "Isherwood" depicted by the author a fictional character whose background is unknown until it unfolds one page at a time? Or is this the Isherwood who really lived in Berlin, and is reporting on what he saw there? If one knew the latter to be true, the former is impossible. If readers think the narrator is a fictional character, why does the author give him his own name? Conversely, if this is autobiographical, why does the author seem not to fully explain himself and the events he witnessed? Instead, Finney says, he is "intruding into and withdrawing from the action [which has caused] critics to read far more significance into the personality and function of 'Christopher Isherwood' than is justified within the context of the novel."[117] One can pose different interpretations to explain this ambiguity. Has he succumbed to the sick city's illness, reducing him to an enervated bystander? Is he the isolated, neurotic artist unable to have real human contact except through metaphor? Or does he not wish to reveal too much of himself for fear of criticism or even ridicule? Finally, is he actually hiding his acute sensitivity and vulnerability behind a pose of indifference? Finney believes that "such conflicting interpretations are the result of projecting onto the narrator a meaning and function beyond that intended by Isherwood. Nevertheless, Isherwood is at least partly to blame for such misunderstandings by continually drawing attention to the narrator but withholding much of the information he would supply as a matter of course in the case of his other characters."[118]

Although Isherwood may be partly to blame, Finney is correct in saying that readers are reading more into the narrator than Isherwood asked them to do. Much of the speculation might be moot if Isherwood the author had called Isherwood the narrator by another name. If the narrator is Mr. Jones, a debate over what Mr. Jones knows or does not know, says or does not say, would not seem quite as important. However, once Isherwood inserted his external reality into the reader's view, the reader could not truly enter into this fiction without recalling that it might not be fiction at all. Why does Isherwood choose to intrude on his reader with such a conceit? Because he wanted attention and approval in his usual pattern. Yet, if this is so, then why did he not truly play the narcissist and give himself a more central role? Isherwood did not do so because he was uncertain who Christopher Isherwood was. Self-exposure required a self-confidence he did not have. If one is sensitive and vulnerable, it is safer to conceal rather than to reveal a great deal of personal insight. The more one offers opinions, the more one can be criticized for having them. By his reticence Isherwood did not provide fuel for possible contradiction. He wanted attention—but not too much. Isherwood was not yet ready to confront himself. He would not ask the hard questions that called for hard answers. Rather, he just described what he saw and let readers provide the historical context.

I History intrudes itself on lives gradually with its full meaning delayed for historians and artists to analyze. When Isherwood wrote *All the Conspirators* and *The Memorial,* which were about how the shadow of World War I affected his generation, he was writing retrospective parables of cause and effect. Conversely, the Berlin stories were written concurrent with history, not after it. These stories required a new technique. Isherwood would master the art of the Wholly-Truthful by describing daily reality as it occurred at the tea-table. In his first two novels Isherwood's youthful narcissism is the centerpiece psychologically, but he gives himself pseudonyms. He does not in the Berlin stories, although he equivocates somewhat in *Norris* by calling himself William Bradshaw, his two middle names. In the first two novels his angst existed on every page and he revealed himself much more under assumed names than he would as "Bradshaw" or "Isherwood."

In Berlin Isherwood was much less concerned with, even ignorant of, the collective history that was being made. He was more concerned with telling the stories of his characters. In the immediacy of experience as a person lives it, one's particular existence takes precedence over universal existence, at least until the universal begins to inflict itself on the particular. In Berlin, history was creeping forward insidiously, sneaking up on the innocent bystanders who inhabited Isherwood's Berlin world. From Isherwood's point of view the stories are not primarily about Berlin; Berlin just happens to be where he and his characters were living at the time. As Auden said: "Art's subject is the human clay / landscape's but a background to a torso."

The Berlin stories are taken from the particulars in the author's diaries of 1930 to 1933. Readers of 1937 to 1939 could not help but embellish these past particulars with their present knowledge of the rabid fascist threat. In the opening story Isherwood writes: "I am a camera with its shutter open, quite passive, recording, not thinking." This famous line has been misinterpreted to mean indifference and contributed considerably to the debate over the narrator's role. Isherwood disputed the importance that others gave to this sentence. In an interview Isherwood said that this sentence was not a statement of the author's overall approach to the book but just the narrator's feeling at that moment in one story.[119] However, if not for the author and narrator being the same, the line might not have been misconstrued. When Isherwood said he was not "thinking," he did not mean he was not feeling. In Berlin he felt daily life on the visceral level in the same sense of Spender's "I eating," "I excreting." Daily events are reacted to by each person as an "I." The "we" of historical introspection comes later. Wholly-Truthful art details I-you relationships. Characters do not begin to seriously reference public chaos until the chaos starts to affect their private spheres in some tangible way. Isherwood's Berlin stories enact the tea-table technique to perfection because he does not overlay the tea-table conversations with too much inner meaning, but just replays these conversations from real life, which includes more of the mundane than the magnificent and leaves much of the interpretation to the reader.

In a drama such as *The Ascent of F6,* tragedy is highlighted as isolated peaks in the characters' lives. They are conveyed with a minimum of the Wholly-Truthful before-and-after exigencies of daily existence. In prose fiction, there are more details and the characters are not continually sustained in peaks of tragedy but their lives are interrupted by these peaks. Between the heights and depths are those mundane daily activities and conversations that occupy the great majority of a person's time. Wholly-Truthful art is the art of the common man who goes about his business without pomp and circumstance and to whom the level plain between the peaks and valleys has just as much value as the ups and downs. In the streets of the Berlin stories, the downside dominates. In those streets and the homes that lined them, people had to cope somehow. Personal survival was the only scruple to follow by whatever means. Yet one also finds heroes—the common men and women who persevere, adapt, survive. Isherwood depicts Berlin in his understated tea-table manner. The reader sees and hears characters as they are; there is very little thinking out loud by them. Readers learn about them gradually, just as Isherwood did. He speculates about their motivations, but he cannot pretend to know their secret thoughts. Isherwood could observe their actions, but only imply motivation. Readers do the same. The reader engages each character at four levels of comprehension: what the author knows; what the narrator knows; what a character knows (or does not know), and what the reader knows (or does not know). In a historical sense, characters know less than readers do. Isherwood intimates to readers the symptoms of the sick city and how the city affects the characters. The characters react to the symptoms with little or no analysis of their underlying causes. Isherwood the narrator describes much more than he explains. He does express beliefs but implies them by their absence. One sees how not to behave. In Spender's *The Destructive Element,* belief is built up after unbelief is torn down. Spender asserted that the modern literary artist does not tell readers what to believe, but teaches through parable. The writer presents

a moral vacuum that readers intuitively fill with beliefs of their own. The characters' actions and reactions speak for themselves and readers judge them.
Readers arrive at meaning instead of being told meaning. Consequently, what
some critics have called Isherwood the narrator's passive detachment is more a
matter of his getting out of the way to let readers observe the characters and form
impressions of them on their own. By making judgments based on these impressions, readers are creating belief out of unbelief.

As for Isherwood the narrator's so-called passivity, is he really so passive? Or
has this been overstated as a "result of projecting on to the narrator a meaning . . .
beyond that intended." Critics also note the characters' passive resignation as they
succumb to the sick city's disintegration. Are the characters really so passive? In
their personal actions they seem to keep fairly busy attending to the exigencies of
daily survival. Do they seem passive because they are not actively addressing the
social, economic, and political ills of the sick city? Why would they? At the time,
or at any time, the majority of people are not activists and are only marginally
interested in the news until that news compels them to pay attention because
their lives are being tangibly impacted. Finney says of *Goodbye to Berlin,* "It is
precisely because no one really takes the Nazis seriously that they are able to seize
power at the climax of the book."[120] Since 1939 readers have projected their
knowledge of the Nazis on to the narrator and his characters by thinking that
they should have known more than they knew. Much criticism of their passivity
seems almost to blame them for not being prescient enough to have prevented
the sickness of their city and then the Nazi takeover. Their Berlin is an impover-
ished nightmare of unemployment and bitterness. Optimism is nil. There are just
choices of anger or despair, with the despair being interrupted only occasionally
by the anger. Malaise is rampant, relieved infrequently by humor and the frantic
night life of clubs, drugs, alcohol, and sex. Isherwood is the outsider, a witness to
overwhelming desperation. Survival is not a given. For the poor, maintaining
minimal subsistence is a day to day goal. As severe as the depression was for
Europe in general, Germany suffered more, having paid crippling postwar repa-
rations since the end of World War I. Berlin is numb and Isherwood's images of
sickness, death, hysteria, and hallucination pervade the novel. Despite the gloom,
he shows great compassion for his characters, even though he sometimes loses
patience with them for their indifference, their denial of life, and their participation in the city's sickness. Isherwood understands that human nature succumbs
to adversity more often than it overcomes adversity. Readers must consciously
put the characters in their context. For one to merely survive in Berlin—in whatever manner, even a seemingly unsavory one—deserves to be acknowledged if not
necessarily commended. Isherwood seems to have more compassion towards his
characters than some readers have had.

Alan Wilde calls Otto Nowack a "sexual sponger, indiscriminately prostituting
himself to women and men."[121] "Sponger" makes it sound as if Otto is content to be

a bisexual prostitute. He is not. This is a humiliation to him. There is no other work and his mother has tuberculosis that requires attention. Indeed, Otto is sick of himself and Isherwood feels sorry for him even when Otto is annoying. Paul Piazza writes, "Isherwood's characters are neither comic nor clowning, but pathetic, infected with the whimpering nihilism of T. S. Eliot's "The Hollow Men.""[122] This description may in part fit Sally Bowles or Bernhard Landauer (although much of their whining comes from an angst that to some extent is generational and similar to the whining of Isherwood and his peers in England), but "whimpering nihilism" seems harsh applied to the working-class Nowacks who cannot find work or the struggling landlady Fraulein Schroeder and any of her roomers. Finney understands that Isherwood is portraying behaviors that have been created by the prevailing hardships: "'The Nowacks' explores the economic origins for the sickness afflicting Otto and his kind. . . . He lives in a slum where poverty breeds disease, tuberculosis in the case of his mother, contempt for life and the business of living in his own case. . . . Otto's injury is psychological. Poverty and unemployment have turned him into a life-long actor who can believe nothing beyond the scene in which he is participating at any one moment. His mercurial changes of mood subtly suggest the degree to which he has become alienated from himself." His moods also suggest how much he is ashamed of himself. Otto's shame precipitates paranoia, nightmares, and "an amateur attempt at slashing his wrists in a heightened moment of self-pity."[123] These were very, very hard times. Along with Finney, Lisa Schwerdt takes a less critical position toward these characters, suggesting that Isherwood "had been forced to live among the poor who now were portrayed heroically, yet unthinkingly, existing rather than romantically living as Mr. Norris had been." Schwerdt then cites instances when Isherwood the narrator "understands that there are limits to what one can do" to escape overwhelmingly adversity: "We see Isherwood's increasing awareness of just how much influence the individual has in the world. . . . the presentation in fact underscores his increasing belief in the future."[124] If individuals in Berlin can still show some hints of humanity under the harsh circumstances, this seems a miracle to Isherwood that must be recognized as hope. In the face of an unspeakable environment and its moral vacuum, Isherwood finds some belief to counter unbelief. If there are even the faintest hints of a remaining humanity in Berlin's dehumanization, the few exceptions offer the slightest rebuttal against the otherwise prevailing horror and despair.

In a "Berlin Diary (Autumn 1930)," Isherwood introduces his landlady, Frl. Schroeder and her roomers. Schroeder is a great stoic, telling Herr Isseyvoo that there had been a time when she was better off and would have been insulted to do her own housework. "But you get used to it. You can get used to anything" (GB, 3) as Huxley said. "Acceptance is also heroic" and forbearance is a virtue. Isherwood and his landlady make tangential references to the political and economic situation, but these observations are just conversation starters like talking about the weather. Isherwood does the same when he teaches English to nineteen-year-old Frl. Hippi

Bernstein, of whom he says: "Hippi never worries about the future. Like everyone else in Berlin, she refers continually to the political situation, but only briefly, with a conventional melancholy, as when one talks about religion. It is quite unreal to her" (*GB*, 17). The situation is unreal for now because it does not as yet touch Hippi's life directly. Since Frl. Bernstein is Jewish, this would change.

The next story is "Sally Bowles," which would be adapted into the play *I Am a Camera* in 1951 and the musical *Cabaret* in 1967. Sally is another survivor. She is not so much a stoic as oblivious, pretending that nothing matters. She acts the part of over-confident narcissist. However, like many seeming egotists, she is actually hiding her vulnerability in a prickly skin of surface obnoxiousness. Many of Isherwood's characters in these stories are the same: their public faces hide their private identities. Sally recounts her libidinous adventures, but are they true? Isherwood and readers regard Sally with bemused frustration as she is alternately likable and annoying. He often laughs out loud at her preposterousness. Her pose as worldly gold digger is transparent. She is not very good at it, being taken advantage of more than taking advantage of others. Sally often talks in order to shock. Isherwood at first is shocked but soon sees through her act:

> "[W]hen you talk like that it's really just nervousness. You're naturally rather shy with strangers I think: so you've got into this trick of trying to bounce them into approving or disapproving of you, violently. I know, because I try it myself, sometimes. . . . Only I wish you wouldn't try it on me, because it just doesn't work and it only makes me feel embarrassed. If you go to bed with every single man in Berlin and come and tell me about it each time, you still won't convince me that you're *la Dame aux Camilias*—because, really and truly, you know you aren't."
>
> "No . . . I suppose I'm not—." (*GB*, 33)

After this conversation, Sally likes and trusts Christopher even more as a friend because he told her the truth. Others had not and would not. The scene is not histrionic but a tea-table conversation where the most truth is revealed. Isherwood calmly tells Sally what she needs to know for them to continue their friendship on a more equal basis. He has no expectation that this conversation will change her behavior in general; he is only concerned that her behavior changes in relation to him.

In Wholly-Truthful art, events are interruptions of life, but they do not necessarily transform the lives being interrupted. Christopher, Sally, and her new boyfriend Clive watch a funeral procession from a hotel balcony. As it goes past, Sally prefers to notice a "marvelous sunset":

> She was quite right. We had nothing to do with those Germans down there, marching, or with the dead man in the coffin, or with the words on the banners. In a few days, I thought, we shall have forfeited all kinship with ninety-nine per cent of the population of the world, with the men and women who earn their living, who insure their lives, who are anxious about the future of their children.

Perhaps in the middle ages people felt like this when they believed themselves to have sold their souls to the devil. It was a curious, exhilarating, not unpleasant sensation: but, at the same time, I felt slightly scarred. Yes, I said to myself, I've done it now. I am lost. (*GB,* 49)

Isherwood understands that one is always self-absorbed in his own consciousness as a single "I" separated from the many "yous." This is a startling revelation for him, but also a first step to greater self-realization. By realizing that the separation exists, he can seek a bridge to cross it. If one knows he is lost and without belief, one searches for a shelter in new belief.

When Sally needs an illegal abortion, her platonic friend Christopher is a rock of support. Tacitly, they are only friends because Christopher is homosexual. They even share a bed, but just to sleep. She tells Isherwood of some regret over her abortion, though Sally knows there was not really an alternative. Sally is quite as human and vulnerable as Isherwood has intimated to the reader all along. This does not mean that Sally will change her ways. She does not. Isherwood has learned that people, including himself, do not change their natures overnight, even in the face of personal traumas. Sally is who she is. Only more experience and maturity will gradually change her, but not by the end of this story. In Berlin, Isherwood learned to be more accepting of others' weaknesses especially under stress. One cannot be so zealous in looking for perfection in others when one recognizes his own imperfections.

The next narrative, "On Ruegen Island" is about a vacation from Berlin with Isherwood, his British friend, Peter, and Peter's bisexual lover, Otto Nowack, a working-class young man of primal attractiveness and intuition. Peter is a nervous wreck fraught with insecurity. Isherwood describes Peter's background, which is much like his own, particularly as pertained to a hated mother. Peter is in constant psycho-analysis and Otto is amazed at how much he pays his doctors, offering to be a good listener for far less:

> Otto wasn't being altogether preposterous when he offered to take the analyst's place. Like many very animal people, he has considerable instinctive powers of healing—when he chooses to use them. At such times, his treatment of Peter is unerringly correct. Peter will be sitting at the table, hunched up, his downward-curving mouth lined with childhood fears: a perfect case-picture of his twisted, expensive upbringing. Then in comes Otto, grins, dimples, knocks over a chair, slaps Peter on the back, rubs his hands and exclaims fatuously,: *"Ja, ja . . . so ist die sache!"* And in a moment, Peter is transformed. He relaxes, begins to hold himself naturally; the tightness disappears from his mouth, his eyes lose their hunted look. As long as the spell lasts, he is just like an ordinary person.
>
> Peter tells me that before he met Otto, he was so terrified of infection that he would wash his hands with carbolic after picking up a cat. Nowadays, he often drinks out of the same glass as Otto, uses his sponge, and will share the same plate. (*GB,* 83)

Peter the tidy hypochondriac reminds Isherwood of himself. Peter's problem is that he is neurotically jealous when Otto is not around and quarrels with him constantly when he is. Eventually this drives Otto back to Berlin. Otto needs Peter's money but can show some genuine compassion for Peter despite the nature of their master-servant relationship. Otto's animal-like primal intuitiveness can be a boon to Peter when Otto is not annoyed with him. Otto forbears a great deal, but there is a limit. He chooses to leave Peter and his money rather than put up with Peter's self-indulgent paranoia. In this narrative there are references to the increasing Nazi influence, not as analysis, but through casual conversation. The background is moving inexorably closer to the foreground.

In "The Nowacks" Isherwood, short of cash, briefly moves in with Otto's family. Otto's mother has tuberculosis and is another stoic, loving her family while complaining about them in a teasing repartee. Isherwood, more so than Auden and Spender, actually lived with the working class and admired their primal attitudes that centered on the fact that they were too busy merely surviving to be self-absorbed with narcissistic angst. One son, Lothar, has joined the Nazi party. Frau Nowack says of him: "I often wish he'd never taken up with them. They put all kinds of silly ideas into his head. It makes him so restless. Since he joined them he's been a different boy altogether" (*GB*, 109). Lothar is one of many among the unemployed working class susceptible to the Nazi propaganda, and his mother one of many mothers who regret it. The powerless gravitate toward any form of empowerment. Otto leans more towards the communist party. Isherwood contrasts Frau Nowack with the upper middle-class matrons whom he tutors in English so that they can discuss the novels of Aldous Huxley and D. H. Lawrence. His preference for the Nowacks is clear.

The next narrative is about the Landauers, a rich Jewish family that owns Berlin's leading department store. Natalia Landauer is a schoolgirl of eighteen who desperately wants Isherwood's approval to the point of giving him the impression that she demands it. She wants to be regarded as an equal intellectually and not just as a spoiled girl who is adoringly treated as such by her father. Isherwood thinks her sometimes haughty when she is just insecure. Natalia is like Sally. In different ways, each demands that attention be paid. Natalia wants to be respected on her own terms, and Sally just wants to shock on any terms. Isherwood introduces Sally to Natalia and the meeting is a disaster. Sally is at her most offensive with her "endless silly pornographic talk. . . . From this meeting I date the decline of my relations with Natalia" (*GB*, 162–63). However, Isherwood does meet her cousin Bernhard who is thirty-two and manages the store.

Bernhard Landauer is a subdued Michael Ransom. Both seem to hate the world, but with a weary cynicism that always bears with it a deflecting condescension. Bernhard plays the inscrutable martyr acting the part of the seer tempered by the wisdom of pain. All others know nothing about life compared to him. This is a pose. Bernhard is just as vulnerable—in fact more so—than the people he is condescending towards. He even affects a philosophical predilection for the east, wearing a kimono and displaying Oriental art. Isherwood seems to see through the masks that Natalia and Bernhard wear, but they annoy him nonetheless: "It was a complicated simplicity, the negation of negation. Oh dear, I sighed to myself, shall I ever get to the bottom of these people, shall I ever understand them? The mere act of thinking about the Landauers' psychic make-up overcame me, as always, with a sense of absolute, defeated exhaustion" (*GB*, 165). Bernhard's martyr pose is one that Isherwood himself had taken up in the years after Cambridge and Isherwood may have been exhausted by the reminders of his own act, which he had performed to hide his vulnerability.

Bernhard tells Isherwood of some of the Landauers' family tragedies, not the least of which is the difficulty of being Jewish. Bernard wants sympathy but conveys his story as if an aloof clinician, without apparent feeling. He tells Isherwood that their conversation is part of an experiment to see how he will react. Bernhard says, "You are a little shocked. One does not speak of such things, you think. It disgusts your English public-school training. . . . You like to flatter yourself that you are a man of the world and that no form of weakness disgusts you, but your training is too strong for you. People ought not to talk to each other like this, you feel. It is not good form" (*GB*, 171). Bernhard does not realize that Isherwood, who has seen quite a bit in Berlin and will talk to anyone about anything, is not shocked at Bernhard's story, but irritated by Bernhard's condescension. Isherwood is sympathetic to the fact that being Jewish in Berlin requires a defensive posture. Still, Bernhard and Natalia, while having good reason to affect a pose of martyrdom, could have shown a little less self-indulgence and a little more forbearance. The new Isherwood, the one who told Sally the truth, does the same with Bernhard: "I'm getting rather tired of what you call your experiments. To-night wasn't the first of them, by any means. The experiments fail, and then you're angry with me. I must say, I think that's very unjust. . . . But what I can't stand is that you show your resentment by adopting this mock-humble attitude. . . . Actually, you're the least humble person I've ever met" (*GB*, 172).

As with Sally, Isherwood is not afraid to confront behaviors that are derived from being Truly Weak. Sally and Bernhard shield their vulnerability with an attitude that the best defense is a good offense. The maturing Isherwood now saw through the masks others wore because he recognized in them the masks that he himself had worn, and still wore. While this did not yet mean that Isherwood himself was Truly Strong, he was at least able to identify when another was Truly Weak. From this came some idea of how one might aspire to be Truly Strong. In recognizing Truly Weak behavior Isherwood has sympathy for it, knowing it too well in himself. This did not mean he ignored it; Isherwood had learned that, by letting others stay in a martyr-pose, they were trying to steal his pity and prevent their own self-realization—as well as his own. Yet he also knew that his honesty would not help them if they were not ready or willing to be helped; they, in fact, would use him if he would let them, but he does not let them. The ego-bound narcissism of martyrdom—Sally's, Natalia's, Bernhard's—is sometimes all one has to cling to. This narrative leads into the last story, in which Isherwood deals more directly with the increasing Nazi threat because that threat was now impacting the lives of his characters. His narrative ends with his leaving Berlin for good.

The Berlin stories are indicative of Isherwood's greater awareness of private spheres, his own and those of others. He is more cognizant from his own experience of how needy people are emotionally, and that his particular neediness is not quite so unique as he had once thought, but universally recognizable in others. Isherwood more readily sees himself and others as parts of a whole. What he is still trying to determine is how the whole relates to its parts. He did not as yet have a clear view of the big picture, but he knew that when the picture did clear what he would see would have something to do with the dichotomy of the Truly Weak and Truly Strong Man.

1937: THE TURNING POINT OF A "LOW, DISHONEST DECADE"

The Ascent of F6 debuted at the Group Theatre on 26 February 1937. The rest of the year went downhill from there. The Auden Generation, which had been loudly vocal in art and essays, was abruptly rebuffed by events that seemed to have rendered their activism futile. The Spanish Civil War was a front-page horror that proved that the fascists would fight in Europe. Until then that potentiality had been feared but unrealized. Recruits from all over Europe and America had gone to fight the fascists and were lionized because they had acted on principle. British writers Christopher Caudwell, Ralph Fox, and John Cornford died, becoming martyrs. George Orwell fought and, after the war, wrote a book about his experience, *Homage to Catalonia*. He reported in detail what had been leaking out gradually. The fascists had won, less because of their own superiority, but more from the disorganization of their opponents, who were split into numerous factions. Orwell blamed the Moscow-directed Spanish Communist Party for seeming to put control of the various factions ahead of defeating the enemy. Back in England and America the socialists and communists were not pleased at this attack on the Soviet Union. A second blow to their staunch support of Russia came from another book, André Gide's *Return From the U.S.S.R.* Gide, a militant communist, went to Russia as a disciple but returned disappointed. He reported that Stalin's Soviet Union was light years removed from the high hopes of Lenin's revolution and that the new Russia was heavy-handed and quashed individuality in the name of the state. Scientists, historians, and artists all conformed to the will of the Soviet—or else. 1937 was a year of profound disappointment for the Auden Generation's would-be iconoclasts. Coming events would do nothing to reinvigorate their pre-1937 enthusiasm.

In 1938 Isherwood and Auden's last play together, *On the Frontier,* reflected the enervation of their peers. This play was a rote exercise of didactic leftist propaganda, but the passion was missing. After more than ten years of protest against the ways and means of the capitalist infrastructure and the society it had produced (including a fascist enemy), their voices seemed to have gone unheard. War was coming, and the high hopes for the Soviet Union as a secular heaven were dashed as just another "God that Failed." Spender would contribute to a book with this title after World War II detailing his generation's seduction by communism and their despair at Stalin's betrayal of communist principles.

In 1938 Isherwood's primary concern was to save Heinz from conscription into the German army. They lived in various places outside of Germany, but Heinz was unable to get permanent residence anywhere. If found with his temporary visa, he would eventually be returned to Germany. Isherwood even brought Heinz home with him to visit Kathleen. In his diary, the son is still conflicted concerning his mother: "It is amazing—the barrier, even now, between us. Mostly of shyness. But in getting older, she seems to have got heavier and harder. I'd imagined myself falling on her neck, appealing to her to forget and forgive the past, to regard Heinz as her son—but all that, in her presence, seems merely ridiculous. She is infinitely more broad minded, more reasonable, than she was in the old days—I like talking to her, in fact I talk to her better and more amusingly than to anyone else; but the ice is never broken. To Heinz she is pleasant, gracious, chatty. She treats him—in a perfectly nice way—like one of the servants" (CK, 247).

Kathleen may have been condescending, but she accepted her son's sexual orientation. Isherwood continued to act on Heinz's behalf; this included the aforementioned desperate appeal to Gerald Hamilton to no avail. It would be Kathleen who paid for Hamilton's nonservices at one thousand pounds, equal to perhaps ten thousand dollars today. Kathleen did not stint on trying to help her son, regardless of how he perceived that she treated Heinz.

In 1937 Auden and Spender visited Spain as observers. Isherwood dared not go since he feared what might happen to Heinz without his protection, and he certainly could not take Heinz with him. At Auden's departure for Spain, Isherwood said: "This was a solemn parting despite all their jokes. It made them aware how absolutely each relied on the other's continuing existence" (CK, 264).

Meanwhile, Isherwood was finishing Lions and Shadows, which meant his schema of Tests and the Truly Weak and Truly Strong Man were prominent in his mind. He also began the last play with Auden, of which he said: "In a sense, it was about the Heinz situation: lovers who are separated by a frontier" (CK, 288). In his diary he wrote: "Heinz is always the last person I think of at night, the first in the morning. Never to forget Heinz. Never cease to be grateful for every moment of our five years together. I had better face it. I shall never see him again." He believed this because Heinz had been deported and jailed for his relationship with Isherwood, who felt very guilty over it. He hoped to learn from the experience: "Here, alone, I am at any rate stronger. I want, above all, to be strong—to give protection like a tree. This isn't mere conceit. It is part of my deepest nature" (*CK,* 289). Later, in commenting on this diary entry, Isherwood writes: "Should he have ever taken Heinz out of Germany? Was Heinz now cursing him for this in his prison cell? (Fifteen years later, when Christopher next saw Heinz, in Berlin, Heinz assured him that he wouldn't, for anything, have missed their travels together. But Heinz was then speaking with the maturity and generosity of an extraordinarily lucky survivor who served in the German Army on both the Russian and the Western fronts and come out of the war with a whole skin. He alone had the right to blame Christopher. It had never occurred to him to do so.)" (*CK,* 290). Heinz's generosity of spirit was pure in heart and Truly Strong.

JOURNEY TO A WAR

From January to July of 1938 Isherwood and Auden went to China to write their collaborative book on the Sino-Japanese War, *Journey to a War:* Auden wrote the poems, among his best, while Isherwood wrote most of the prose, including this self-assessment: "Christopher was in masquerade as a war correspondent. He may have looked the part—correspondents can be a bit absurd—but he must often have betrayed his amateur status by his nervousness. The threat of air raids kept him keyed up, especially when he was on a train. If they were ordered to leave it and take cover, he couldn't restrain himself from hurrying. Wystan never hurried. . . . Were the two of them ever in serious danger of being killed? Two or three times perhaps" (*CK,* 301–302). Isherwood understates his concern. This exposure to real danger lent some reality to his perception of war, one which would further alienate him from the political activism of the preceding years. War was no longer an abstraction to be thought of in slogans and banners:

> A pause. Then, far off, the hollow, approaching roar of the bombers, boring their way invisibly through the dark. The dull, punching thud of bombs falling, near the airfield. . . . The searchlights criss-crossed, plotting points, like dividers; and suddenly there they were, six of them, flying close together and high up. It was as if a microscope had brought dramatically into focus the bacilli of a fatal disease. They passed, bright, tiny, and deadly, infecting the night. The searchlights followed them right across the sky; guns smashed out; tracer-bullets bounced up towards them, falling hopelessly short, like slow-motion rockets. The concussions made you catch your breath; the watchers around us on the roof exclaimed, softly, breathlessly: "Look! look! there!" It was as tremendous as Beethoven, but *wrong*—a cosmic offence, an insult to the whole of Nature and the entire earth. I don't know if I was frightened. Something inside me was flapping like a fish. If you looked closely you could see dull red shrapnel-bursts and vicious swarms of red sparks, as the Japanese planes spat back.

Over by the aerodrome a great crimson blossom of fire burst from burning hangers. In ten minutes it was all over, and they had gone. (*JW,* 60–61)

> I slept very badly that night, dozing in only five minute snatches until dawn. . . . Meanwhile, in the opposite bed, Auden slept deeply, with the long, calm snores of the truly strong. (*JW,* 75)

During this period Isherwood was thinking about *Lions and Shadows,* in which he would define the Truly Weak and Truly Strong Man. *Journey to a War* is dedicated to Isherwood's Truly Strong role model, novelist E. M. Forster.

The air raid was war at a distance. Isherwood and Auden would get a closer look: "We then went into a Chinese military hospital—actually a square of miserable, windowless huts. . . . The wounded lay . . . on straw—three men beneath a single blanket. The orderly told us that they hardly had any dressings or antiseptics, and no proper surgical instruments at all. . . . In one hut the sweet stench of gas-gangrene from a rotting leg was so violent that I had to step outside to avoid vomiting" (*JW,* 93). Rickshaws transported the wounded and the dead. Later, the war reporters boarded an overnight train for their next destination in China: "I slept uneasily that night—in my trousers and shirt: not wishing to have to leave the train and bolt for cover in my pyjamas. Auden, with his monumental calm, had completely undressed" (*JW,* 120). While they are on the train, a Japanese plane flies over and there is concern over a possible air attack: "Auden, of course, was certain that nothing would happen. 'I *know* they won't shoot' he kept repeating. . . .' After all was clear: 'You see,' said Auden. 'I told you so . . . I knew they wouldn't . . . . Nothing of that sort ever happens to *me.*' 'But it does to *me,*' I objected; 'and if it had this time you'd have been there, too.' 'Ah, but it didn't you see.' 'No, but it might.' 'But it didn't.'" Isherwood concludes: "There is no arguing with the complacency of a mystic. I turned over and went to sleep" (*JW,* 128–29). The humor relieves the tragic images of the war.

While this *Journey* describes places, faces, and events, Isherwood and Auden the mystic were moving away from politics and returning to introspection, which in fact they had never left. Finney observes: "The book opens with Auden's sonnet to Forster whose promise—'still the inner life shall pay'—provides the perspective from which both writers proceed to view China at war. Like Forster they insist upon a creed of personal relationships and see China in wartime not as a battleground of political and economic forces, but as a condition of modern man, an image of mankind overtaken once more by the indiscriminately destructive forces of war."[125]

In addition to Auden's opening sonnet in *Journey to a War,* there is his astonishing sonnet sequence *In Time of War,* of which Mendelson writes:

> *In Time of War* . . . is Auden's most profound and audacious poem of the 1930s, perhaps the greatest English poem of the decade. . . . he achieved monu-

mental dignity and strength. The harsh crude textures of its verse, its emotional clarity in the face of disaster, the rigor and inclusiveness of its moral logic, contribute to the poem's extraordinary weight and force. Auden accomplished all this partly by abandoning the large loose forms he had earlier preferred in writing about history. . . . Instead he used the sonnet form he had reserved mostly for love poems, and brought his writing on public themes the same conviction he brought to his writing on Eros. . . . Each sonnet presents the history of a human type—farmer, poet, scientist—as if it were compressed into a single individual who experiences centuries of change in one lifetime. Auden achieves this metaphoric connection between the general case and the particular example by portraying figures who are not quite allegorical, since their relations with others are not allegorical relations, and not quite exemplary, since their experience is more extensive than any exemplar's could be. . . . Auden's figures are neither villains nor heroes nor larger than life. They are representative men, fallible and complex, as bewildered as everyone is by the outcome of their choices.[126]

Auden himself was one of the bewildered men. Yet, his bewilderment is not about confusion that leads to indecision. His bewilderment is more of a mystification at human nature's inexorable consistency. His puzzlement comes not from a misunderstanding of humanity but from understanding human behavior too well. Hence, his representative figures are timeless; they are of the past, present, and future simultaneously. The puzzle is how little human nature has changed. The enigma is not about what choices human beings make or why they make these decisions; rather, the puzzle is that humanity seems to face the same choices and chooses in the same manner—over and over and over. Herein lies the direction of Auden's future art, a direction that would include his return to the Anglican church. He would augment the Anglican ritual with his own unique blend of Kierkegaardian existentialism and Christian mysticism. Life for Auden was now about choice and freedom. The Test was now about how every new Adam and new Eve is faced with choices that are object lessons from which one can choose to turn away from God, and remain Truly Weak, or turn toward God, and aspire to be Truly Strong. Consequently, history is not really about history. The stuff of history is merely put before humanity in order for individuals to choose their direction. One chooses consciously or unconsciously. The Bhagavad-Gita says: "There are some who have actually looked upon the Atman [God], and understood It in all Its wonder. Others can only speak of It as wonderful beyond their understanding. Others know of Its wonder by hearsay. And there are others who are told about It, and do not understand a word."[127] For Auden history is the means to one end: the evolution of humanity's consciousness toward spirit. History is the background to a torso. What the torso chooses to do or not do in the face of history is a measure of human spiritual progress. Compared to spiritual progress, material progress is unimportant. Auden had questioned humanity's role in the world for ten years. *In Time of War* became his answer: the individual can only live for his spirit and serve the world from this basis; if he lives in ignorance of his spirit and only serves himself, he is lost.

The inner life was also on Isherwood's mind, but he could not yet define his own relation to a metaphysical universe: "as a person I really don't exist. That is one of the reasons why I can't believe in any orthodox religion: I cannot believe in my own soul. No, I am a chemical compound, conditioned by environment and education. My 'character' is simply a repertoire of acquired tricks, my conversation a repertoire of adaptations and echoes, my 'feelings' are dictated by purely physical, external stimuli" (CK, 305). Isherwood later said that what he really meant by this comment at the time was that he could not "believe in his own individuality as something absolute and eternal; the word 'soul' is introduced, quite improperly, as a synonym for 'person.'" He continues, referring to himself in the third person:

> A year later . . . in California, he would have long talks on the subject with Gerald Heard (Gerald Heard . . . together with Aldous and Maria Huxley had left England for the states in April 1937.) Christopher would find himself able to believe—as a possibility, at least— that an eternal impersonal presence (call it "the soul" if you like) exists within all creatures and is other than the mutable non-eternal "person." He would then feel that all his earlier difficulties had been merely semantic; that he could have been converted to this belief at any time in his life, if only someone had used the right words to explain it to him. (CK, 306)

Isherwood's comment in 1976 benefits from retrospective nuances. Looking back on 1938, Isherwood suggests that, even if he had not been "aware that he needed such a belief, he may have been feeling the need subconsciously" (CK, 306). His subconscious need had made itself apparent in his writing.

On the way back from China before returning to England he and Auden traveled and ended up in New York City. The New York visit intrigued them and they began to plan a return of a more permanent nature. He would have to tell Kathleen. "On October 7, 1938, Kathleen had become seventy years old. Up to then, Christopher had remained vague about her age. I can still remember the shock which the news gave him; she always looked much younger than she was. He told her jokingly that no doubt her youthfulness was due to his never having treated her as an old lady; this was his way of apologizing for his past unkindnesses" (CK, 331). With this expiatory statement the Isherwood who had begun to consider metaphysical issues and the Isherwood who had learned to have more patience with the faults of others had turned his camera on himself. What Isherwood saw was that his view of life was changing: "Alone with Wystan, he was able, literally, to speak his mind—to say things which he hadn't known were in it: 'You know, it just doesn't mean anything to me anymore—the Popular Front, the party line, the anti-fascist struggle. I suppose they're okay but something's wrong with me. I simply cannot swallow another mouthful.' To which Wystan answered: 'Neither can I.' Those were not their exact words, but, psychologically, it was simple as that" (CK, 333).

Isherwood's new attitude was prompted by his awareness that Heinz had been forced to return to Germany and would become a member of the German Army. Isherwood's previously blind hate for the Nazis was now complicated by this dilemma:

> Suppose . . . I have a Nazi Army at my mercy. I can blow it up by pressing a button. The men in that Army are notorious for torturing and murdering civilians—all except for one of them, Heinz. Will I press the button? No. . . . Once I have refused to press the button because of Heinz, I can never press it. Because every man in that army could be somebody's Heinz and I have no right to play favorites. Christopher was forced to recognize himself as a pacifist. . . . Christopher had nothing but a negative decision—if war came, he wouldn't fight. He was aware, of course, that pacifism had its positive obligations—you had to do something instead of fighting. Heard and Huxley were the only two articulate pacifists he could contact. (*CK*, 335–36)

Isherwood and Auden departed for the New World. Both were searching for something to replace the disappointment they left behind in their private and public lives of the 1930s:

> This is where I leave Christopher, at the rail, looking eagerly, nervously, hopefully toward the land where he will spend half of his life. At present, he can see almost nothing of what lies ahead. . . . I will allow him and Wystan to ask one question—I can already guess what it is—and I will answer it.
>
> Yes, my dears, each of you will find the person you came here to look for—the ideal companion to whom you can reveal yourself totally and yet be loved for what you are, not what you pretend to be. . . . You, Wystan will find him very soon, within three months. You, Christopher, will have to wait much longer for yours. He is already living in the city where you will settle. He will be near you for many years without your meeting. But it would be no good if you did meet him now. At present, he is only four years old. (*CK*, 339)

Auden would find Chester Kallmann. Isherwood would find Don Bachardy.

For the first eleven years of his life, Christopher Isherwood had been nurtured and protected until his world was shattered. For the next twenty-four years he rebelled against everything that he associated with his childhood trauma. In the course of his rebellion he escaped into secondary worlds. At first these worlds were unconscious reactionary symptoms of his anger: i.e., the Mortmere stories. Later they would be more conscious paths to self-discovery about his inner nature. Even in his anger Isherwood knew that there was something missing in his psyche that needed to be found, something that would reassert the balance that he had lost at age eleven. In America he would find his balance—slowly. First he would talk to Heard and Huxley who would introduce him to Swami Prabhavananda. When he was ready, fate would further introduce him to Don Bachardy, the four-year-old who would grow up waiting to be found by his lifetime companion.

In England Isherwood had rebelled against and torn down all the traditional beliefs of the past. His mind had become empty in a process of unbelief. This moral vacuum could not stand; something, some belief would have to be built up. Vedanta would fill the void first, then Don Bachardy. In this process of unbelief becoming belief, Isherwood was actually searching for that elusive persona within himself that he had always longed for: the Truly Strong Man.

PART 2

VEDANTIC: THE BUILDING UP, 1939–1986

PREFACE TO PART 2

From the year that Christopher Isherwood was stranded then abandoned in 1915 his life was one of continual searching. Through friendships, affairs, and fiction he wished to fill a void he had felt since St. Edmund's. His emptiness was caused by the death of his father and his mother's emotional retreat. His rebellion amounted to a cry for approval, a desperate plea to regain the nurturing womb-cocoon of his early childhood. Isherwood tried various vicarious substitute milieus and poses, both artistic and amatory. Isherwood played the rebel, the friend, the artist, the martyr, the older brother, the satyr, the lover—all of which were aspects of a natural maturation process with the nuances reflecting his country, his class, and his gang. Different masks were worn to hide his private escape into secondary worlds based on his fear of the primary world as constituted by the Public, particularly The Others. To flee across the border of the primary world into the frontiers of secondary worlds was a quest for belief to replace unbelief. The primary world must be torn down to the psyche's bare walls of unbelief in order to make room for new belief. But what beliefs would fill the vacuum?

Over time his guises would slowly melt away, as his private identity and his public face became one and the same. In sun-filled California, Isherwood would see the light and become a Vedantist and aspiring mystic. There would still be Tests, but he would learn that, instead of seeing them as Truly Weak obstacles, Isherwood could regard them as object lessons from which the aspiring Truly Strong Man could learn about himself and others. He had begun to do so in the Berlin stories when he was able to see who Sally Bowles and Bernhard Landauer really were behind their masks. He recognized that their particulars mirrored his own particulars, which were not really particulars at all, but universals replicated in the perpetual continuum of evolving consciousness. In the Berlin stories Isherwood was coming to understand this universal worldview intuitively within the Isherwood-Auden schema. In America he would learn how to fit this intuitive schema into an all-encompassing schema of Vedantic cosmology, within which the particular and the universal are indivisible in an ocean of undifferentiated unity. The Isherwood-Auden schema, and every other metaphysical and philosophical schema preceding it, have been intuitive reactions to Vedantic cosmology, which Aldous Huxley said was the basis of *The Perennial Philosophy*. The Isherwood-Auden schema that had resulted from a tearing down of old belief, could now be fit into a superior logic of Vedantic belief. This was the direction in which he had been unconsciously headed all along. In the scheme of Vedantic beliefs that Isherwood adopted, all of humanity is headed in this same direction—very slowly.

Part 1 detailed the evolution of the Truly Weak and Truly Strong Man as an influence on the Auden Generation. This generation of antiheroic rebels became icons for the rebels of the 1950s and 1960s to admire and emulate. In 1958 Isherwood said in reference to *All the Conspirators:* "Could the author of this novel conceivably be described as a prehistoric Angry Young Man? Well—as a young man, he was certainly angry—God help us if the time ever comes when young men aren't. . . . Today's Angry Young Man . . . is angry with society and its official representatives; he calls them hypocrites, he challenges the truth of what they teach. He declares that a social revolution has taken place of which they are trying to remain unaware. He accuses them of reactionary dullness, snobbery, complacency, apathy." While Isherwood goes on to say that his generation was somewhat different as to how it expressed its anger, he still concludes that, "Nonetheless, there is always an emotional solidarity between rebels. And if the Allen Chalmers of my story could have been taken to see John Osborne's plays he would have been sympathetically thrilled by their anger, just as I am in middle age today."[1]

If this had been written just a few years later, Isherwood could have also said that in the 1960s some of those rebels turned to Eastern mysticism, just as he had done years before in a Vedantic circular pattern. He would have recognized their efforts to make the transition from Truly Weak to Truly Strong.

With the duality of the Truly Weak and Truly Strong Man established in part 1, part 2 will focus primarily on Isherwood's growth as an aspiring Truly Strong Man in his life and in his fiction. His diaries make it apparent that his life informed his art. Since his life in America was devoted to Vedanta, then it is Vedanta that informed and transformed his art. The metaphysics Isherwood intimated in his European years now had a nomenclature and a guide: Vedic scripture and Swami Prabhavananda.

4 ESCAPE TO AMERICA
Themes Vedanticized: The Real Guru and His Disciple

Careful, careful, my dear—if you keep going on like that, you'll have *such* a conversion, one of these days.

> Auden, to Isherwood, just before they left for America.[1]

I think we all sensed that this was a long goodbye. M. cried when I left, I cried. . . . As the train pulled out . . . Auden and I exchanged grins—grins which took us back, in an instant, to the earliest days of our friendship. Suddenly, we were twelve and nine years old. "Well," I said, "we're off again." "Goody," said Auden.

> Christopher Isherwood[2]

Actually, in my sane moments, I love this country [America]. I love it just because I *don't* belong. Because I'm not involved in its traditions, not born under the curse of its history. I feel free here. I'm on my own. My life will be what I make of it.

> Isherwood[3]

I must balance my acts of treason by acts of affirmation. Our ideal should be to accept unlimited liability for all acts of our fellow human beings. We are all members with another. . . .

> Isherwood[4]

Isherwood's allusion to childhood was appropriate. America was another womb-cocoon escape in a series of escapes. He left Europe as a recently converted pacifist. He came to America to see Gerald Heard and Aldous Huxley, who were pacifists of longer standing. Isherwood wanted to learn from them not just how to say no to war, but how to say yes to peace. He wanted a method to his madness. Vedanta would become the method.

Isherwood's published diaries detail his American years from 1939 to 1960. He describes his conversion to Vedanta, which was just as dramatic as Auden warned him it would be. Auden experienced his own religious conversion, returning to the high Anglican church of his youth. In Isherwood's last book, *My Guru and His Disciple* (1980), he combines autobiography with a biography of Swami Prabhavananda in a most heartfelt rendering of his life as an American Vedantist. The reader who compares this book to Isherwood's diaries will see in the former work passages that are verbatim adaptations from the latter. Both make it clear that Isherwood had learned that the kingdom of the Truly Strong Man is within. The

Truly Strong Man—with the Swami as his role model—is at the center of life's hurricane, calmly observing life's frantic storm without getting caught up in it and dizzied by the spin. From 1939 until 1945 Isherwood would not write another novel, choosing instead to immerse himself in his conversion and learn about Vedic scripture. This included a co-translation of the Bhagavad-Gita with the Swami. By the time he did publish *Prater Violet* in 1945, Isherwood the artist had become Isherwood the Vedantist who also happened to be an artist. For one to fully appreciate Isherwood's art after 1939, one must follow his absorption in Vedanta and correlate these beliefs to the fiction written thereafter. In tracing this path, one realizes that Isherwood and his readers are always just a few steps behind the Truly Strong Man, the figure that Isherwood had been looking for all his life. The only difference was that in America his unconscious search had become a conscious one. This does not mean that it was an easy one. In his diary entry dated 19 January 1939 Isherwood writes: "If I were writing a novel—trying, that is to say, to persuade a reader that I was telling him something psychologically plausible—I would have great difficulty at this point. Because now I have to describe a state of mind which introduces a new period in my life." He then describes this new period:

> I realized I was a pacifist.
>
> Maybe it would be more exact to say: I realized I had always been a pacifist. At any rate, in the negative sense. How could I have ever imagined I was anything else? My earliest remembered feelings of rebellion were against the British army, of which my mother and myself were camp followers, and against the staff of St. Edmund's school, who tried to make me believe in a falsified and sentimentalized view of the 1914 war. My father taught me, by his life and death, to hate the profession of soldiering. I remember his telling me, before he left for France, that an officer's sword is useless except for toasting bread, and that he never fired his revolver because he couldn't hit anything with it, and he hated the bang. I came to adore my father's memory, dwelling always upon his civilian virtues, his gentleness, his humor, his musical and artistic talent. (*D*, 5)

In turn Isherwood hated the world that killed Frank, who, in Isherwood's memory, had become the Truly Strong Man.

Isherwood and Auden arrived in New York and were greeted as celebrities. For their benefit, "A small group of actors produced *The Ascent of F6* in the Village" (*D*, 13). Auden, however, had mixed feelings about his celebrity: "Wystan says, however, that he hates all this. But he's unwilling to return to England, because there, he's the center of even more attention" (*D*, 11). Auden no longer wished to be the focal point or the de facto leader of anyone or anything. He wished only to get inside himself and write about what he found. This retreat would be detailed in his *The Prolific and the Devourer* (1939), an exercise in philosophical aphorisms of a Mandarin style such as Lao Tzu's *The Way of Life*.

Auden's first volume of poems in America was *Another Time* (1940), dedicated to his newfound love, Chester Kallman. The dedicatory poem announced Auden's new focus. He states that the "I" must abnegate its selfish will so that it can merge into the "we." When this happens, "Then all I's can meet and grow."[5] This poem is about "the abnegation of the will"; it echos Spender's meaning of the "I" that needs to merge into the "we." This became Auden's primary theme in America. It would become Isherwood's as well, but at this point he still needed some more direction with respect to his newly acquired pacifism.

Isherwood sought counsel and headed for California to seek advice from Aldous Huxley and Gerald Heard. Heard, with his naturally ascetic demeanor, was now a Christ-like, blue-eyed Irishman with the gift o' blarney, which meant that he could philosophize glibly: "Gerald was different. He was one of us [i.e., a homosexual]. He spoke the same language. He might be theatrical, affected, vain, eccentric, but he certainly wasn't crazy" (D, 25). Heard believed in "this thing" (D, 26), which was how he referred to God without using conventional language so that he would not scare off new recruits, such as Isherwood, who were still recoiling from traditional Christianity:

> Life, said Gerald, is for awareness. Awareness of our real nature and our actual situation. The day-to-day, space-time "reality" is, in fact, no reality at all, but a cunning and deadly illusion. Space-time is evil. The process of meditation consists in excluding, as far as possible, our consciousness of the illusory world and turning the mind inward, in search of the knowledge which is locked within itself—the knowledge of its real nature. Our real nature is to be one with life, with consciousness, with everything else in the universe. Supposed knowledge of individuality, separateness and division is nothing but illusion and ignorance. Awareness is increased through love . . . and weakened by hatred. Hence, all positive feeling toward other people is in one's deepest interests, and all negative feeling and action finally harms oneself. . . . our present problems are created by our past deeds and thoughts. Free will consists simply in this: that we can, at any moment, turn inward or away from the search for our real nature. (D, 26–27)

One can either engage in actions that turn him towards "this thing," or one can engage in actions that turn him away from "this thing." With Heard as his mentor Isherwood wrote that he could turn towards "'this thing'—mystical religion—with the aid of a brand-new vocabulary, one uncontaminated by association with bishops' sermons, schoolmasters' lectures, politicians' speeches" (D, 29). Isherwood could retreat into another secondary world that had its own proprietary language. He was not unaware of the correlation this new religion had to art: "Religion is the struggle for greater awareness of reality, deeper understanding of the nature of life. Art, also struggles for awareness and understanding. The goal is identical. Art, rightly practiced, is a form of religion. The better the art, the more religious its

Isherwood (left) and Swami Prabhavananda in the sitting room of the Hollywood Vendanta Society, 1944. (Vedanta Society of Southern California Archives)

Swami Prabhavananda (left) and Gerald Heard, 1946. (Vedanta Society of Southern California Archives)

character" (*D*, 30). In this equation, Isherwood the artist realized that, by his having consciously practiced art, he had also, in a manner of speaking, been Isherwood
the mystic.

Mysticism includes meditation and Isherwood's diaries detail his first awkward
attempts at meditation with Heard's guidance. At first this meant to sit still for
fifteen minutes a day and try to contemplate "this thing" in a self-comforting manner. It was not easy. He wrote that "the first obstacle is self-consciousness" (*D*, 38),
or the obstacle of the ego's lower-case self blocking the upper-case Self from merging into undifferentiated unity. Heard introduced Isherwood to Swami
Prabhavananda to enhance Isherwood's study: "He talks gently and persuasively. His
smile is extraordinary. It is somehow so touching, so open, so brilliant with joy that
it makes me want to cry" (*D*, 43). This feeling and affection would never waiver and
the guru had a new disciple. The Swami gave him some guidance for meditation:

> 1. To try to feel the presence of an all-pervading existence.
> 2. Send thoughts of peace and good will toward all beings. . . .
> 3. Think of the body as a temple, containing the reality.
> 4. Meditate on the Real Self.
> The Self in all beings.
> I am infinite Existence, infinite Knowledge, infinite Bliss. (*D*, 44)

Isherwood did not find the first three immediately conducive, but he did find the
fourth helpful as he could relate it to his writing: "When I think in terms of writing, I can easily see that the writer taps a great store of universal knowledge" (*D*, 44).
The correlation of art and "this thing" began to make more sense to Isherwood. He
compared his past unbelief to his present, aspiring belief:

> I can't remember any time in my life when I seriously believed in God. At
> Repton, when I got confirmed—before I met Edward—I was a cautious diplo-
> matic hypocrite. While I was constantly with Edward at Cambridge, I achieved a
> more or less continuous state of awareness which was religious in character,
> although we expressed it in terms of art. . . . Then came Wystan, preaching Homer
> Lane. I made more contact with the outside world. And when my books were pub-
> lished, I really felt I was doing what Life had made me for. In actual fact, I was only
> giving a performance of the Ego as Artist. "To create, to love, to suffer." The "love"
> part of it was pretty phony. But still those legs and arms and bodies were parts of
> people. The people, when I got to Berlin, belonged to a certain class—poorer than
> mine. I had to spend money on them, and therefore doubted the love. So I became
> political. Marxism said, "I'll remove the barriers."
>
> Marxism also said, "I'll kill the ego"—but it didn't—even in the noblest of
> my revolutionary friends. So I despaired, and started to pretend that the Ego didn't
> exist. But the Ego did exist, and became stronger than ever. It ate up all the "love"
> and even began to paralyze the creative powers. It grew weary of itself, loathing its

own tricks—so weary that, when I finally did get loved, the Ego was so nauseated by its own flattering, distorted mirror image, that it had to turn away. It was afraid of being found out. That's my position now. And . . . nothing has changed—except the way out has become dimly visible. But what a way out! The Ego shivers. It smells the wind of its destruction.

"I love you," says the Ego, doggedly. How well I know that tone! It means, "I hate you and mean to torture you." (*D*, 47–48)

For Isherwood, the tearing down in Europe had led to his present position. He understood that the process of a rebellious tearing down was Truly Weak, but a necessary prelude to the process of building up. One must unlearn before one can learn. Isherwood was not yet Truly Strong but knew that the building up had begun. He was learning about his true Self, his Vedantic Self.

Nonetheless, "real life" required that he make a living. Hollywood was very convenient for a well-known writer to get work writing screenplays. This meant participating in the Hollywood scene—that fantasy world of egos resplendent. The naked display of egos was so transparent that this actually helped Isherwood in his own quest for egolessness.[6] The Hollywood contrast between ego-full and ego-less was blatantly unambiguous. For Isherwood, this fantasy world was so absurd that going home in the evening to meditate was a welcome relief:

> Only the true sage . . . really knows what things are, and never forgets it. He can own a car and not be hypnotized by the idea, "car." The tragic American, on the other hand, sees his car as a symbol. Different makes of automobile, in ascending order of luxury, are the punctuation marks in his success story. . . . They are only unreal counterparts of the things and people they represent. They are no longer important, primarily in themselves—but only as symbols in a scale of imaginary social, erotic, autohypnotic values. This state of autohypnosis—in which my possessions have value as possessions, not as intrinsically serviceable objects—is called "Real Life." One may recognize this absurdity—but it is all too fatally easy to slip back into the autohypnotic condition. Every advertisement, every radio commercial, every popular movie or magazine story potentially resembles the small object which the hypnotist uses to focus his patient's attention.
>
> I have found myself repeatedly slipping into the "Real Life" trance.
>
> The most advertised, and the most fantastically inflated and distorted values in "Real Life" are "Sex" and "Love." (*D*, 60)

Isherwood then explains that, since he was making a great deal of money as a screenwriter, the temptations of "Real Life" were even more tempting because they were affordable. He certainly was spending his earnings on himself and his boyfriend Vernon. Of this, he said facetiously: "Day in the life of an autohypnotist: Got my paycheck, got a Renoir, did the sights, did a matinee, had supper, had my wife" (*D*, 61). Isherwood could now see himself and his actions for what they were—the ego giving in to the temptations of Maya, the Vedantic name for the illusion of the mate-rial world. This was progress over having no clue at all.

More clues would come from his friendship with Aldous Huxley: "How kind, how shy he is—searching painfully through the darkness of this world's ignorance with his blind, mild, deep-sea eye.[7] He has a pained, bewildered smile of despair at all human activity. 'It's inconceivable,' he repeatedly begins, 'how anyone in their senses could *possibly* imagine—' But they *do* imagine—and Aldous is very, very sorry" (*D*, 77).

After World War II began in Europe, Huxley, Heard, Isherwood, and Auden were all "very sorry" that they were being lambasted in Britain as deserters. In partic-ular, Isherwood reacted to a doggerel verse that he said was "going around London":

> The literary erstwhile Left-wellwisher would
> Seek vainly now for Auden and for Isherwood:
> The dog beneath the skin has had the brains
> To save it, Norris-like, by changing trains.

> Why does this sting me so? Simply because it is really clever. It succeeds in making me look ridiculous—My vanity is hurt. Yes, I had better admit it. I am not in the least ashamed of myself, but I feel foolish.

> I'll try to be absolutely honest about this. Am I a coward, a deserter? Not according to my standards. If I were told that somebody else had "run away from England," I should ask, What did "England" mean to him? "England" to me meant a place that I stayed away from as much as possible during the last ten years. From a strictly patriotic standpoint, you can be "disloyal" in peace as well as in war. Yet no one blamed me then. And I certainly didn't blame myself.

> Am I afraid of being bombed? Of course. Everybody is. But within reason. I know I certainly wouldn't leave Los Angeles if the Japanese were to attack tomor-row. No, it isn't that . . . If I fear anything, I fear the atmosphere, the power which it gives to all the things I hate—the newspapers, the politicians, the puritans. . . .

> Am I being disloyal to my friends [in Britain]? My friends don't seem to think so. (*D*, 83–84)

Isherwood's diaries had always been a means for him to observe somewhat objectively himself and his place in relation to others and The Others. He was recording in them the results of his daily meditations in the sense that they were a deliberate withdrawal from a pseudo "Real Life" into the Ultimate Reality, which is real life from the Vedantist's viewpoint. Returning from these inner safe havens of daily meditation, Isherwood was able to observe himself as the center of his own hurricane. He gives a very concrete example of this effect:

> This morning, lying in bed, half-awake, I had a very strange experience. I remembered—or rather, relived, with extraordinary vividness—an instant of a cer-tain morning, four years ago. I was sitting in a small park in Amsterdam, with

Gerald Hamilton. . . . Not only did I relive this instant . . . but, for a couple of seconds, I actually *was* the Christopher of 1936. I was—and yet I wasn't; because,
standing aside from the experience, I was also aware of the present-day Christopher.
I can't, of course, in the least describe the difference between the two personalities—
that of 1936 and that of 1940—but . . . I was intensely conscious of it. I could hold
the two selves separate, comparing them—and in doing so, I caught the faintest
glimpse of something else—that part of my consciousness which has not changed,
will never change, because it is part of [the Ultimate] Reality. (*D,* 91)

This sense of a simultaneous vision of multiple Isherwoods would become a dominant theme in his future art. Isherwood also recalled that the moment was not permanent because "Real Life" intruded and brought him back to the unreality of Maya
and the world of the senses. Still, it was a moment that proved that these instances
of mystical awareness could exist, and were worth attempting to replicate in the
future: "Saw Gerald . . . We talked about the enlargement of consciousness. Three
stages: first, you see something—some single object—as it really is, 'in its own right';
then, you see that the object is part of a plan—its position in time and space is
inevitable—it isn't there by accident; then, in the highest state of illumination, you
see beyond objects altogether—you trace, as it were, the line which connects them
all with a single focal point, the absolute reality. Experience of the first stage is quite
common to artists and other observant people" (*D,* 95). "Observant people" meant
highbrows. Isherwood was giving a theoretical context to his "very strange experience" of seeing his 1936 Self simultaneously with his 1940 Self.

Isherwood would later write about Vedantic theory in essays and in his last
book, *My Guru and His Disciple,* some of which was taken from his diaries. The
complete diaries, however, allow one to learn about Vedanta as Isherwood did—
as a process over time. One can learn along with him and see how Vedanta would
later influence his art. Hints of the Truly Strong Man as a Vedantist also emerge
slowly. When Isherwood thought about how he and Auden had been punching
bags in England for their "desertion," he said, "As long as Wystan and I are here,
taking the blame, the smaller escapists are safe from notice" (*D,* 101). He thought
that he and Auden were covering for those less capable of defending themselves.

Isherwood was also learning about the illusion of time as a man-made construct that is an obstacle to knowing the Ultimate Reality. The all-encompassing
nature of the Ultimate Reality does not exist in time because "time" does not exist
in it: "All evil is in time. Like animals we cannot see a thing when it is moving
slowly. We can't experience horror as evil until its movement is speeded up. If ten
people die within six months, each in a different manner and in a different place,
we don't care much. If ten people die within six seconds, all together in an automobile accident, we are shocked" (*D,* 102). Within the Ultimate Reality's perpetual continuum, the past, present, and future are continuously, contiguously,
and simultaneously to be envisioned as a single tapestry of a "vast landscape."

Two days after this entry Isherwood put into practice Vedantic renunciation after learning that his childless Uncle Henry had passed away, meaning the estate would go to Frank's eldest son. However, several weeks before, on hearing of his uncle's last illness, he had written to "M." that his brother Richard was to have everything, which meant Kathleen would benefit as well. Isherwood had chosen not to be a hypocrite and take over an estate in a country he had always rejected. Two days later, as a coda to his decision, Isherwood records a lecture given by Huxley:

> He pointed out that power comes into the organism from above and from below—up through the animal level and down through the spiritual. But it can't circulate, because it is checked by the Ego—the level of self-consciousness, which is in the middle. "Animal grace" is the functioning of the organism in accordance with the laws of physical being: the lilies taking no thought for tomorrow. "Spiritual grace" is the functioning of the organism in accordance with the laws of its spiritual being: we are all a part of absolute reality. "Human grace" is pseudo-grace. It is only a projection of the Ego—into patriotic nationalism, for example. It may seem selfless, but it never really is. The whole problem of the spiritual life is to keep the self-conscious Ego quiet. To stop it from interfering on the two other levels and allow them to function naturally.
>
> The Ego wants to interfere. It commits original sin—the setting up of its own self-conscious power against the natural powers of body and soul. On the animal level, this interference produces physical disease; on the spiritual level, spiritual disease . . . such as pride. If you can only quiet the Ego, the soul and body begin to function of themselves, in spiritual and physical health, and the aim of yoga is achieved. The Ego is the eternal wiseguy, the Mr. Fix-It. It dances about in its impatience at the slowness of nature—and yet, with its fussing, it holds up everything.
>
> Beware, says Aldous of confusing spirit and public spirit. The most diabolical people are often the most public-spirited—e.g., Hitler. (*D*, 104–105)

From these kinds of spiritual sessions with Huxley, Heard, and the Swami, Isherwood always made connections to his art, sometimes with a little tongue-in-cheek added to the lessons learned: "Prayer for writers: Oh source of my inspiration, teach me to extend toward all-living beings that fascinated, unsentimental loving and all-pardoning interest which I feel for the characters I create. May I become identified with all humanity, as I identify myself with these imaginary persons. May my art become my life, and my life my art. Deliver me from snootiness and the Pulitzer Prize. Teach me to practice true anonymity. Help me to forgive my agents and my publishers. Make me attentive to my critics and patient with my fans. Stop trying to use the conscious will. Free the Ego from its attachments with expert gentleness, like a surgeon. Remember that the strangulated Ego is everything you hate in others—so how can you hate anybody? You are only hating yourself" (*D*, 106).

Within the Ultimate Reality there is no separating duality. Everyone and everything is integrated continuously, contiguously, and simultaneously. In Vedantic terms, Isherwood and every other "Other" were, are, and will be one and the same person made indivisible by "this thing." Isherwood tried to see people as mirrors of himself in order to identify with their imperfections. Then these "Others" (who were not really others) seemed more like himself with his own imperfections: "It is only when I have laid my finger on a weak spot that I can really admire anybody" (D, 110). Thus, they became equals through their mutual frailties.

As for potential perfection Isherwood was given a definition of immortality from the Swami, which simply entailed that immortality is when the spirit gets "beyond time and causation" (D, 112). The perfect spirit is not the body; the body is merely a suitcase carrying the spirit around. The spirit exists before it enters a particular body, and it will continue after it is freed from that particular body. Then it becomes universal again as in fact it has always been. The Swami also gave Isherwood "new and more elaborate instructions" for meditation: "First, I am to think of people all over the world—all kinds of people, at all kinds of occupations. In each of them, and in all matter, is this Reality, this Atman, which is also inside myself. [The Atman is the Vedantic Self in the individual body which is always integrated with the Larger Self of all existence called Brahman. This is not a duality; Atman and Brahman are a two-way mirror.] And what is 'myself'? Am I my body? Am I my mind? Am I my thoughts? What can I find inside myself which is eternal? Let me examine my thoughts and see how they reflect this reality—for I can only know it by its reflection. And let me think of this reality as seated in the top of my head. . . . I am infinite existence, infinite knowledge, infinite happiness. . . . Meditation night and morning. It is much easier now . . . because I can begin with the external world and work inward (D, 116–117).

By meditating night and morning, and thus fortified, Isherwood could go into the Hollywood fantasy world and then come back from it to detoxify: "My chief effort is to stand outside the Ego, to try to catch a glimpse of the world with a non-attached eye. . . . It is terribly difficult, but the mere discipline of trying brings its own rewards—cheerfulness, long periods of calm, freedom from self-pity. . . . Guard against feelings of self-congratulation or holiness. Self-congratulation is of the Ego. The real self can't boast of its advance toward wisdom: it is wisdom. As Gerald says: 'Love God without fear and without hope'" (D, 119).

One must eliminate the duality of fear and hope, regret or anticipation, for there is no real duality; everything is integrated. Isherwood began to understand that this also applied to individuals: "The cult of a great teacher and saint only seems to be dualistic. The dualistic approach is just a convenient way to realization of oneness, identity. That's why it doesn't matter in the least if the real historical Christ never existed. He'll exist in you, if you want him too" (D, 122). Nor can one pretend to run away from the pain in the world since all of the world is wherever one happens to be: "How much unhappiness there is in the world! No need to search for it across the ocean, in bombed London, or China, or Greece. The other evening, outside my window, a little boy cried to his mother: 'You don't want *anyone* to play with me!' Even the most trivial unkindness is heartbreaking, if one weren't so deaf and blind. Every sigh, every tear, every cross word is really the last straw which break's humanity's back. If we could be conscious, every minute, of the dreadful predicament of life, we should handle each other with the greatest gentleness" (*D*, 124).

He also recorded some notes from the Swami's lectures:

We make the mistake of seeking perfection outside ourselves. We want to achieve completeness by creating something, or by accumulating possessions, or by recognizing a part of the external work. But completeness is within us.

The aim of life is to be reborn in spirit as we were born into flesh . . . to attain transcendental consciousness.

It's no good just saying, "I have faith," and leaving it at that. Faith in someone else's revelation is not enough. It will get you nowhere. . . . What is *your* experience? Do *you* see any light? Experience, empirical knowledge, are what really matter in religion.

The universe according to Vedanta philosophy:

I. The ultimate reality. This, for convenience, has two names: *Brahman* (God transcendent, all around you) and the *Atman* (God immanent, within you).

2. *Ishwara:* The reality united with its power to create, preserve, and destroy the universe. This does not imply a philosophical dualism, because the reality and its power are inseparable, like fire and heat. Brahman, the Reality, by definition, has no attributes. Ishwara has attributes: it is "the personal God."

3. *Prakriti, or maya:* the effect of all Brahman's power, the basis of all mind and matter. Modern physics recognizes the principle of Prakriti in saying that the universe is composed of different arrangements of identical units, Prakriti can be roughly translated as "nature."

4. Prakriti is said to be made up of three *gunas,* three forces.

(a) *Sattva:* the quality of fineness, beauty, purity, calm: the power of self-revelation in any object.

(b) *Rajas:* the quality of action, reaction, repulsion: the power which holds an object together.

(c) *Tamas:* obstruction: the power that veils and obscures an object's identity. Psychologically, sattva creates the mood of peaceful, clear understanding. Rajas brings restlessness, hate, rage, aggression, and desire to enjoy. Tamas brings laziness, dullness, obstinacy.

All three gunas are present in everything, in different combinations, one or the other predominating. To see the Reality, we must go beyond the gunas, even sattva.

> The mistake of the West is the mass application of all its standards. . . . It dis-
> criminates between different types of people and the different approaches which
> are helpful for each.
>
> You cannot approach a Sattvic man as you would approach a Rajasic man.
> (D, 127–28)

Just as there are three gunas, there are three possible paths of spiritual devotion
to suit different personalities: The Jnana yogi pursues ultimate reality through intellectual knowledge; the Bhakti yogi offers love and devotion through prayer, song,
and ritual; the Karma yogi chooses good works. Just as the gunas correlate in different proportions, an aspiring yogi, or aspiring Truly Strong Man, combines the three
paths in proportion to meet the needs of his personality. The yogi learns that all of
life is always with us. Past, present, and future are not distinct: "When 'peace'
returns, let me never again say that suffering is not always with us. This war is not
unique. During the gayest periods of my life, people were being killed and starving
and dying in agony" (D, 137). Conversely, current events, such as the war, should
have been dealt with before they reached the crisis stage. "Why do we fool ourselves
that we can suddenly behave like heroes and saints after a lifetime of cowardly thinking, daydreaming and hate? The acts of 1941 will be the thoughts of the past ten
years" (D, 133).

After talking with Heard, Isherwood considers how the constructs concerning evil and the devil" were just synonyms for the ego's selfishness: "Gerald said
that lately he's been very conscious of his [the ego's] presence; not as someone ter-
rifying, but as unwearying Watcher—a presence which is always waiting its
chance, bold and impudent and brutally cynical. . ." (D, 142). Isherwood had
known about the this type of devil since Cambridge, where it was made manifest
under the alias of the Watcher in Spanish.

Isherwood came to realize that, "Real Happiness is the absence of pain" (D,
155). Real happiness is also the recognition of the Ultimate Reality: "If this Force,
which is behind all life, could ever become the consciously controlling factor in
myself—if I could ever surrender myself to it completely and fearlessly—then my
life would be the most amazing adventure. . . . in fact, it wouldn't be my life anymore. I should be an instrument, absolutely dedicated, absolutely safe. . ." (D, 177).

With this goal in mind and the Swami as his primary guide, Isherwood
made great strides towards his dedication and safety. This is not to say—nor
would he himself have said—that he was nearing nirvana—far from it. He had
many doubts, many misgivings about his new life, but he had more doubts and
more misgivings about his old one. The old life had to go. This new one seemed
more likely to help than anything else he could come up with. The path to salvation is neither steady nor certain, but a positive direction is better than none.

In October 1941 Isherwood became a Karma yogi by doing good works in a
Quaker-run camp for German refugees in Haverford, Pennsylvania. He was to teach

them English. He learned quickly that he needed to be much more than just an English teacher: "The lessons were not really lessons, they were psychiatric sessions. You had to give all your time, confidence, faith, courage, to these badly rattled middle-aged people whose lifeline to the homeland had been brutally cut, and whose will to make a new start in the new country was very weak. The giving wasn't confined to lesson times" (D, 188). While he gave, he also received; a good teacher learns from his pupils. He had become attuned to learning from the psychological resonances of the people he was with. Isherwood had infused all of his art with psychology. In the Berlin stories, he not only understood his characters, he could tell them when they were being annoying. Isherwood, who had so adroitly looked into his own particular psyche, now could take what he had learned from himself to realize that there is a collective universal psyche and that individual psyches are integrally related to this collective psyche. In the refugee camp, Isherwood realized that his needy charges were not so different from himself, Sally, Bernhard, or anyone else; it was just that there were more of them and their multiplicity only confirmed their sameness rather than their differences.

By September 1942 Isherwood had returned from Haverford. He began working with the Swami on a new translation of the Bhagavad-Gita and was also trying to be classified as a conscientious objector. He succeeded at both. The translation was a long process of very intense study and concentration upon the most important Vedic scripture. The Gita synthesizes all the wisdom of Vedanta succinctly. This process of working closely with the Swami in understanding the text's most profound intentions did more than anything else to convince Isherwood that, despite his backsliding and imperfections, Vedanta was the right path for him. One need not be perfect to be a Vedantist; one need only know that perfection is worth striving for. Everything in existence, imperfect or not, derives from and is integrated with the Ultimate Reality, about which Huxley said, as recorded by Isherwood: "I came to this thing in a rather curious way, as a reductio ad absurdum. I have mainly lived in the world of intellectual life and art. But the world of knowing-about-things is unsatisfactory. It's no good knowing about the taste of strawberries out of a book. The more I think of art, I realize that though artists do establish some contact with spiritual reality, they establish it unconsciously. Beauty is imprisoned, as it were, within the white spaces between the lines of a poem, between the notes of music, in the apertures between groups of sculpture. This function of talent is unconscious. They throw a net and catch something, though the net is trivial. But one wants to go further. One wants to have a conscious taste of these holes between the strings of the net. . ." (D, 246–47).

Huxley and Isherwood wanted to fill the holes in the net, and while Isherwood worked on the Gita, Huxley was a sympathetic sounding board. During this same period Huxley was working on his anthology, The Perennial Philosophy, which would be a compilation of knowledge from all of the world's spiritual and moral systems from the purview of the mystics within each discipline. His intent was to show that there are common tenets underlying the whole body of mysticism and that Vedanta, as the first recorded system of mysticism, was the seminal source of these common beliefs. To this end Huxley posited a Minimum Working Hypothesis of four tenets that fill the holes in life's interstices. Huxley first stated these tenets in the introduction to the Isherwood-Prabhavananda translation of the Bhagavad-Gita:

1. the phenomenal world of matter and of individualized consciousness—the world of things and animals and even gods—is the manifestation of a Divine Ground, within which all partial realities have their being, and apart from which they would be non-existent.

2. human beings are capable not merely of knowing about the Divine Ground by inference; they can also realize its existence by a direct intuition superior to discursive reasoning. This immediate knowledge unites the knower with that which is known.

3. man possesses a *double nature*, a phenomenal ego and an eternal self, which is the inner man, the spirit, the spark of divinity within the soul. It is possible for a man, if he so desires, to identify himself with this spirit and therefore with the Divine Ground which is of the same or like nature with the spirit.

4. man's life on earth has only one end and purpose: to identify himself with his eternal self and so come to unitive knowledge of the Divine Ground of all existence.[8]

In his Minimum Working Hypothesis, Huxley summed up the essence of Vedantic existence. This essence depended on intuition. Isherwood had intuited "this thing" long before his intuitions were to have a basis and nomenclature. He had done so while struggling with that devil, the ego, for supremacy over his mind. At this point in his new life, he at least could identify his ego as the enemy, which was more than most people could do. Isherwood knew that winning the struggle against the ego was worthwhile; he also knew that the Truly Strong Man of his intuition was the Vedantic mystic who was integrally at peace with himself and his world. Huxley asked why this peace is valuable to the mystic and to those who know one:

What is the mystical experience? I take it that the mystical experience is essentially the being aware of and, while the experience lasts, being identified with a form of consciousness, of unstructured transpersonal consciousness which lies, so to speak, upstream from the ordinary discursive consciousness of every day. It is non egoistic consciousness, a kind of formless and timeless consciousness, which seems to underlie the consciousness of the separate ego in time.

Why should this consciousness be regarded as valuable? First, it is regarded as valuable because of the self-evident sensibility of values. . . . It is intrinsically valuable, just as the experience of beauty is valuable because as a matter of empirical experience it does bring about changes in thought and character and feeling which the experiencer and those about him regard in him as manifestly desirable. It makes possible a sense of unity and solidarity with the world. It brings about the possibility of that kind of unjudging love and compassion which is stressed so much [in scripture]. The mystic . . . is able to understand organically such portentous phrases, which for the ordinary person are extremely difficult to understand— phrases such as "God is love." As for the three words which are the basis of virtually all Indian religion and philosophy: *Tat Twam Asi* (Thou art That, That art Thou), the sense being that the deepest part of the soul is identical with the divine nature . . . it is the idea of the inner light, the scintilla animae (spark of the soul); the scholastics had a word for it, the "synderesis."[9]

For the balance of this study, the reader must submit to his own synderesis, even if temporarily. The reader must believe what Isherwood believed, or at least believe that Isherwood believed it.

THE WISHING TREE

In addition to translating the Gita, Isherwood was editing and contributing to the Vedanta Society's monthly publication, *Vedanta and the West*. His essays included "How I Came to Vedanta," "What is Vedanta," "What Vedanta Means to Me," and many more. These essays detail the letter of Isherwood's learning, but to understand the spirit of his learning, one must read his very short story, "The Wishing Tree,"[10] Isherwood's first fictional work after his conversion. In it the Isherwood of past, present, and future, child and man, appears in a succinct parable that became the cue for all of his future art. Children listen to an old uncle who tells them about a magic tree that grants wishes:

> The children are skeptical, half impressed. Truly—it'll give you anything you ask for? Anything? Yes, the uncle assures them solemnly: anything in the world. . . ,
>
> But this is too much of a good thing. . . . "He's just fooling us!" they exclaim, indignantly. And they scatter again to their play.
>
> However, children do not forget so easily. . . . They have been trained by their parents to believe in wishing. . . . The Kalpataru tree listens attentively to the children's wishes . . . and in due time, it grants them all. Most of the wishes are very unwise—many of them end in indigestion or tears—but the wishing tree fulfills them, just the same: it is not interested in giving good advice.
>
> Years pass. The children are all men and women now. They have long since forgotten the Kalpataru tree and the wishes they told it—indeed, it is part of the tree's magic to make them forget. Only—and this is the terrible thing about the Kalpataru magic—the gifts which it gave the children were not really gifts, but only links of a chain—each wish was linked to another wish, and so on. The older the children grow, the more they wish; it seems as if they never wish enough. At first, the aim of their lives was to get their wishes granted; but later on, it is just the opposite—their whole effort is to find wishes which will be very hard, or even impossible, to fulfill. Of course, the Kalpataru tree can grant any wish in the world—but they have forgotten it, and the garden where it stands. All that remains is the fever it has kindled in them by the granting of that first, childish wish.

You might suppose that these unlucky children, as they became adults, would be regarded as lunatics, with horror or pity, by their fellow human beings. But more people have wished at the Kalpataru tree than is generally supposed. The kind of madness from which the children are suffering is so common that nearly everybody has a streak of it in his or her nature—so it is regarded as perfectly right and proper. "You want to watch those kids," older people say of them, approvingly: "They've got plenty of ambition. . . ." And these elders, in their friendly desire to see this ambition rewarded, are always suggesting to the children new things to wish for. The children listen . . . believing that they must be the best guides to the right conduct of one's life.

Thanks to these helpful elders, they know exactly what are the things one must wish for in this world. . . . For this wisdom of past generations has forever decided what is, and what is not, desirable and enjoyable and worthwhile. Just obey the rules of the world's wishing game and you need never bother about your feelings. As long as you wish for the right things, you may be quite sure you really want them, no matter what disturbing doubts may trouble you from time to time. Above all, you must wish continually for money and power—more and more money, and more and more power—because, without these two basic wishes, the whole game of wishing becomes impossible—not only for yourself, but for others as well. By not wishing, you are actually spoiling their game—and that, everybody agrees, is not merely selfish, but dangerous and criminal, too.

And so men and women who were shown the Kalpataru tree in the garden of their childhood, grow old and sick and come near to their end. Then, perhaps, at last, very dimly, they begin to remember . . . how all this madness of wishing began. . . . they exclaim: "All my other wishes were mistaken. Now I wish the wish to end all wishes. I wish for death."

But, in the garden, long ago, there was one child whose experience was different from that of all the others. For, when he had crept out of the house at night, and stood alone, looking up into the branches of the tree, the real nature of the Kalpataru was suddenly revealed to him. For him, the Kalpataru was not the pretty magic tree of his uncle's story— it did not exist to grant the stupid wishes of children—it was unspeakably terrible and grand. It was his father and his mother. Its roots held the world together, and its branches reached behind the stars. Before the beginning, it had been—and it would be, always.

Wherever that child went, as a boy, as a youth, and as a man, he never forgot the Kalpataru tree. He carried the secret knowledge of it in his heart. He was wise in its wisdom and strong in its strength; its magic never harmed him. Nobody ever heard him say, "I wish," or "I want"—and for this reason, he was not highly thought of in the world. As for his brothers and sisters, they sometimes referred to him, rather apologetically, as "a bit of a saint," by which they meant he was a trifle crazy.

But the boy himself did not feel that he had to apologize or explain anything.

He knew the secret of the Kalpataru and that was all he needed to know. For, even as an old man, his heart was still the heart of that little child who stood breathless in the moonlight beneath the great tree and thrilled with such wonder and awe and love that he utterly forgot to speak his wish.[11]

When it came time for the spirit of the little boy in the old man's body to leave his corporeal suitcase, the spirit that left his body was that of a Truly Strong Man. The simple wisdom of "The Wishing Tree" was a postscript to what Isherwood had learned before 1943 and a prelude for not only his next novel but for the rest of his life.

PRATER VIOLET

After six years of immersion into Vedanta, Isherwood, the sometimes screenwriter but full-time disciple, returned to his first love—the novel. *Prater Violet* would be deeply influenced by his life and learning of the previous six years. The Bhagavad Gita would be *Prater Violet*'s inspiration and resonate profoundly within the novel. What did his publisher think of this? On the jacket of the first edition the blurb explains that the writer of the Berlin stories had been in a "virtual literary retirement" as he had become a "disciple of the Vedanta Society, a cult." However, "in his new novel, *Prater Violet,* there is no trace of mysticism." Either Random House did not understand the underlying mystical intentions or was disowning them for fear of alarming the readership.

The readership would not have been as alarmed as the publisher might have feared, since in 1944 and 1945 there was a renewed interest in mysticism. A measure of this is seen in the popularity of the Isherwood-Prabhavananda translation of the Bhagavad-Gita, Huxley's *The Perennial Philosophy* as well as his mystical novel, *Time Must Have a Stop,* and the Witter Bynner translation of the Taoist handbook, Lao Tzu's *The Way of Life.* Right after World War II it seemed that highbrows wanted a new direction, one that turned inward and away from the external reality of the preceding years.

In *Lions and Shadows* Isherwood had written about his 1928 discovery of the pure-in-heart man as explained to him by Auden, who was interpreting Homer Lane via John Layard: "The pure-in-heart man became our new ideal. . . . He was essentially free and easy, generous with his money and belongings. He would let you brush your teeth with his toothbrush or write with his fountainpen. He was a wonderful listener, but he never 'sympathized' with your troubles; and the only advice he ever gave was in the form of parables—stories about other people which you could apply to your own problems, if you liked. He was entirely without fear. . ." (*LS,* 304–305).

In 1943 Isherwood translated the Bhagavad-Gita, which is itself a parable; his translation included this passage:

A man who is born with tendencies toward the divine, is fearless and pure in heart. He perseveres in that path to union with Brahman [God], which the scriptures and his teacher have taught him. He is charitable. He can control his passions. . . . He practices spiritual disciplines. He is straightforward, truthful, and of an even temper. He harms no one. He renounces the things of this world. He has a tranquil mind and an unmalicious tongue. He is compassionate toward all. He is not greedy. He is gentle and modest. He abstains from useless activity. He has faith in the strength of his higher nature. He can forgive and endure. He is clean in thought and act. He is free from hatred and from pride. (*BG,* 152)

One can see in comparing these two passages, written fifteen years apart, that Isherwood unconsciously, then consciously, had been moving towards the Truly Strong Man in the Vedantic sense. In his 1945 novel *Prater Violet,* with the lessons of the Gita as a philosophical basis, and "The Wishing Tree" as a parabolic precursor, he tells a tale of an aspiring Truly Strong Man in a real world scenario.

Claude J. Summers astutely introduces his analysis of this short novel in a chapter whose title is taken from a phrase in *Prater Violet,* "The Pain of Hunger beneath Everything": "Within its brief compass, *Prater Violet* explores themes as diverse and as weighty as the role of the artist in modern society, the search for a father, the problem of identity, and finally the quest for transcendence. Unobtrusively informed by its author's newly discovered faith in Vedantism, *Prater Violet* is ultimately a religious novel. For all its obvious similarities to the earlier works, the book signals a departure for Isherwood and a new beginning."[12] It is a departure because the metaphysical themes that Isherwood had previously dealt with intuitively now had Vedanta for their basis; it is a new beginning for the same reason—Vedanta is now the purpose of the novel and its teachings are conveyed through parable.

The novel takes place in 1933 London and is a fictionalized account of Isherwood's real-life experiences working with the Austrian director Berthold Viertel. Isherwood, as his own revisionist historian, looks back on those events and examines them from a more mature perspective that is framed in Vedanta. Isherwood's choice of setting his first novel written in America in his British past points to his declaration of independence from that past but not with rebellious anger. This look at the past is not about revolution, but evolution. Isherwood, always a "sensitive man" in Spender's terms, was now also an aspiring Truly Strong Man on his own terms. Isherwood was no longer just reacting against the past negatively but seeing the past as the links of a chain in his own personal continuum and, more importantly, seeing his own continuum as linked to the universal perpetual continuum of Vedantic cosmology. The past is the precursor to the future, something to be learned from, not just cursed. All events—positive or negative—are not obstacles, but lessons to be encountered as steps towards the Ultimate Reality. "In this yoga," according to the Gita, "even the abortive attempt is not wasted. Nor can it produce a contrary result"

(*BG*, 45). How one reacts to events is more important than the events themselves. Acceptance is also heroic. There can be no success or failure—only more knowledge of the Ultimate Reality. The Gita also says, "The will is directed singly toward one ideal" (*BG*, 45). The ideal is "this thing" that supersedes in importance the history that comes and goes. The progress of the spirit is permanent. History, in Vedantic terms, is only the record of that spiritual progress.

Within the permanence of the spirit is the flux of the material world. In Isherwood's new world, the aspiring Truly Strong Man who is pure in heart sees the totality of the world and all those in it equally, whether they have complete understanding, a desire for understanding, have heard about the possibility of understanding, or do not have a clue. Each human being, in whatever category, has integral value, a concept akin to Auden's vision of agape recorded in "A Summer Night." In *Prater Violet* Isherwood's vision of totality is the hawk's vision, which sees the universal within the particular as well as the particular in the universal. Yet, this hawk—a Bergmann or an Isherwood—is not a silent cypher-witness; he is not aloof or unconcerned; this witness is of the world, not above it.

The narrator in *Prater Violet*, named Christopher Isherwood, is the screenwriter for a film directed by Austrian director Friedrich Bergmann, who is consumed by fears for his wife and daughter who are still in Vienna with Hitler's shadow over them. This portrait intimates the real life relationship of a guru (the Swami) and his disciple when Christopher says of Bergmann, "He was my father. I was his son." The Gita emphasizes work as a form of devotion to "this thing." The devotion is the goal, not attachment to the fruits of the labor: "Perform every action with your heart fixed on the Supreme Lord. Renounce attachment to the fruits. Be even-tempered in success and failure. . . . Work done with anxiety about results is far inferior to work done without such anxiety, in the calm of self-surrender. . . . Those who work selfishly for results are miserable" (*BG*, 46). The results of work—whether it is the product itself or the remuneration gained from the product—cannot become the goal without forming negative attachment:

> Thinking about sense-objects
> Will attach you to sense-objects;
> Grow attached, and you become addicted;
> Thwart your addiction, it turns to anger;
> Be angry, and you confuse your mind;
> Confuse your mind, you forget the lesson of experience.
> (*BG*, 49)
> Man deluded by his egoism, thinks: "I am the doer."
> (*BG*, 57)

God is the doer and this lesson of experience is the one about working only for God as the goal in itself; the results of the work are almost incidental to that ultimate purpose.

The Gita teaches that it is the process of work, not the product of the work that brings wisdom; it is the means that matter, not the end. In *Prater Violet* Bergmann fights his fear and despair concerning his family in Vienna by throwing himself into the making of what is intended to be a lightweight, escapist film and turning it into an entertainment with a sociopolitical message. Isherwood learns from Bergmann (based on Prabhavananda) that a man must proceed with his duty in the face of calamity. *Prater Violet* is a parable of Isherwood's experiences during the war: he chose a new life which gave him the structure of moral values and security he craved; he chose to be a conscientious objector, which would lead him to Pennsylvania and a Quaker-run camp where he taught English to war-escaping refugees; he chose these steps to make strides in his quest to be pure in heart and Truly Strong. In the effort, he also came to realize that learning to be Truly Strong only comes when one understands that it is the ego that keeps one Truly Weak. According to Summers, "This discovery of the ego as the source of the Truly Weak Man's neurosis marks a critical stage in Christopher's emergent maturity. . . . Christopher glimpses beyond the neurosis to its cure in the Vedantic renunciation of the self."[13] Isherwood renounces the self in order to embrace and merge with the greater Self of the Maya-transcending Ultimate Reality. Still, to understand that the ego is a nemesis is not to entirely make it go away, but the knowledge allows one to confront the ego when backsliding threatens to stall spiritual progress. Consequently, for Isherwood, the opposites of weak and strong, public and private, inner and outer, hero and antihero are now grounded in a realistic context: A man seeks perfection by overcoming imperfections; these imperfections are Tests meant, from the Vedantic viewpoint, as lessons, not obstacles. The divided mind is comprehended as standard operating procedure, and one cannot become a hero and Truly Strong until one knows that this is the flip side of having been an antihero striving to be Strong while still Truly Weak.

Prater Violet opens with Isherwood at home with his mother and his brother, Richard. The phone rings and it is Mr. Chatsworth of Bulldog Pictures with a screenwriting job. After hanging up, Isherwood is coy: "'Was that Stephen?' my mother asked. She generally knew when I needed a cue line" (*PV,* 5). There is this allusion to Spender and a later one to "W. H." (*PV,* 38). He tells her the news, and she and Richard are excited. In this scene there is familial repartee that is warm and delightful, certainly a much kinder view of the "female relative."

Isherwood meets Bergmann and they are simpatico since both speak German. This gives the director an ally. Isherwood the involved hawk sees in the particulars of Bergmann the universal that he recognized in the Quaker refugee camp: "Of course we knew each other. The name, the voice, the features were inessential, I knew that face. It was the face of a political situation, an epoch. The face of Central Europe" (*PV,* 17).

Bergmann is thoroughly charming. He is sensitive towards others, willing to listen as well as talk. He can be volatile, such as when he is concerned about his wife and daughter in Austria or when he perceives insensitivity in others. He does not suffer fools gladly. Isherwood is not a fool and Bergmann is paternal towards him: "His voice dropped; he looked deeply and affectionately into my eyes. 'I am sure we shall be very happy together. You know, already, I feel absolutely no shame before you. We are like two married men who meet in a whorehouse'" (*PV,* 23). This allusion to secret knowledge makes Bergmann and Isherwood another gang of two.

The sensitive Bergmann even reads *The Memorial* and praises it to his new symbolic son with fatherly pride. Of this recognition, Isherwood writes, "I was absurdly pleased and flattered" (*PV,* 27). Bergmann tells Isherwood that he will teach him the business of film making.

In giving Isherwood his first lesson on film, Bergmann asks: "'Do you know what the film is?' Bergmann cupped his hands, lovingly, as if around an exquisite flower. 'The film is an infernal machine. Once it is ignited and set in motion, it resolves with an enormous dynamism. It cannot pause. It cannot apologize. It cannot retract anything. It cannot wait for you to understand it. It cannot explain itself. It simply ripens to its inevitable explosion'" (*PV,* 30–31).

The progress of a film is a metaphor for the evolution of the Vedantic universe, which is also an "infernal machine" that moves forward inexorably. In Vedic scripture and in the Swami's lessons, a flower is often metaphorized as a microcosm of the world's macrocosm. The "inevitable explosion" alludes to the triple metaphor of the finished film, an individual's spiritual enlightenment, and the world's ultimate enlightenment. The next day, Isherwood the disciple paraphrases for his mother and Richard Bergmann's (his guru's) metaphor. In doing so, Isherwood demonstrates his understanding that the disciple's path is to become a guru for new disciples. The Gita says "Whatever a great man does, ordinary people will imitate; they follow his example" (*BG,* 56). Isherwood's diary says: "The only worthwhile thing we can do for each other is to set an example" (*D,* 280).[14] Isherwood's life as recorded in his diaries, became his art.

Isherwood the artist of 1945 does not spare Isherwood the novice screenwriter of 1933. When the novice has trouble writing working-class dialogue, he at first rationalizes his difficulty, declaring the work beneath him, and calling it "essentially false, cheap, vulgar." Yet he knows this is a weak excuse. "Nonsense. I didn't believe that either. It isn't vulgar to be able to make people talk. An old man selling sausages isn't vulgar, except in the original meaning of the word, 'belonging to the common people.' Shakespeare would have known how he spoke. I was a snob. I didn't know how anybody spoke, except school boys and neurotic bohemians" (*PV,* 34–35). He would learn. When Bergmann senses Isherwood's doubt, he teaches his disciple as does the pure-in-heart man—

through parable: "You know what my wife tells me when I have these difficulties? 'Friedrich,' she says, 'Go write your poems. When I have cooked the dinner, I will invent this idiotic story for you. After all, prostitution's a woman's business'" (*PV,* 36–37).

Another woman assumes an important role when the guru and his disciple go to their usual restaurant for dinner where Bergmann despairs over the European situation: "And while he was in the midst of his horrors, his glance around the room generally discovered a girl or woman who interested him, and diverted the stream of his imagination. His favorite was the manageress of the restaurant, a handsome blonde with a very sweet, motherly smile, about thirty years old. Bergmann approved of her highly. 'I have only to look at her,' he told me, 'to know that she is satisfied. Deeply satisfied. Some man has made her happy. For her, there is no longer any search. She has found what we are all looking for. She understands all of us. She does not need books, or theories, or philosophy, or priests. She understands Michelangelo, Beethoven, Christ, Lenin—even Hitler. And she is afraid of nothing, nothing. . . . Such a woman is my religion'" (*PV,* 44). Bergmann's description of the woman parallels the teaching of The Gita, which says that "A man [or woman] who is born with tendencies towards the divine, is fearless and pure in heart" (*BG,* 152):

> The manageress would always have a special smile for Bergmann when we came in; and, during the meal, she would walk over to our table and ask if everything was all right. "Everything is all right, my darling," Bergmann would reply; "thanks to God, but chiefly to you. You restore our confidence in ourselves."
>
> I don't know exactly what the manageress made of this, but she smiled, in an amused kindly way. She really was very nice. "You see?" Bergmann would turn to me, after she had gone. "We understand each other perfectly." (*PV,* 43–44)[15]

For Bergmann (and Isherwood) the manageress is a figure of spirit-inspired intuition. The Gita asks: "How does one reach true Religion?" And it answers: "Not by argument. Not by scriptures and doctrines, they cannot help. The path to religion is trodden by the saints" (*BG,* 25). Whether she realizes it or not, the manageress— or intuitive priestess and seer—is pure in heart and Truly Strong.

The scene with the madonna-manageress is followed directly by a contrasting Bergmann epiphany about the Nazis. When Bergmann's secretary says: "Those Nazis aren't human," Bergmann answers: "That is how they wish you to imagine them, as unconquerable monsters. But they are human, very human, in their weakness. We must not fear them. We must understand them. It is absolutely necessary to understand them or we are all lost" (*PV,* 47). In Berlin Isherwood had witnessed the seduction of the weak-willed innocents by Hitler. The Truly Strong and pure in heart would know that even the bitterest enemy is ego-dominated in an effort to hide the fact that he is actually Truly Weak, and that an individual's self-centered subjectivity can become collective self-centered subjectivity, as in the case of the Germans who rallied around Nazism. One cannot always change the human nature of the individual or the many, the personal or the collective ego, but one can forgive.

Later Isherwood dismisses his own screenplay with the excuse that its subject does not interest him; this really means he is having trouble writing it. Bergmann sees through this: "You are wrong. . . . It is not uninteresting. It is not unreal. . . . It is highly contemporary. And it is of enormous psychological and political significance. . . . And the reason you refuse to see this, the reason you pretend it is uninteresting, is that it directly concerns yourself. The dilemma of [the character] Rudolph is the dilemma of the would-be revolutionary writer or artist, all over Europe. . . . His economic background is bourgeois. He is accustomed to comfort, a nice home. . . . he now has to make a choice" (PV, 49–50). The choice concerns learning enough from the past to take it into the future without bitterness. One must see the past as necessary lessons that make the future possible. Bergmann calls the film a "symbolic fable" (PV, 50) from which Isherwood can learn about himself. Prater Violet is a symbolic parable about the Gita from which readers can learn about themselves.

One can also learn from Lawrence Dwight, a "film-cutter," (editor), who is a career pragmatist. He complains to Isherwood about screenwriters' romantic ideas:

> "all you bloody writers have such a romantic attitude. . . . We need technicians. . . . I'm a cutter. I know my job. As a matter of fact, I'm damned good at it.
> . . . It's all Chatsworth's fault [the studio head]. He's a romantic too. . . . The only people who really matter are the technicians. They know what they want."
>
> "And what do they want?"
>
> "They want efficiency."
>
> "What's that?"
>
> "Efficiency is doing a job for the sake of doing a job."
>
> "But why should you do a job anyway? What's the incentive?"
>
> "The incentive is to fight anarchy. That's all Man lives for. Reclaiming life from its natural muddle. Making patterns."
>
> "Patterns for what?"
>
> "For the sake of patterns. To create meaning. What else is there?" (PV, 66–70)

Like the manageress, Dwight is another player in Vedantic cosmology. The manageress as priestess and seer represents the spiritual leader who inspires by example, or sets patterns for the technicians to follow. The technicians follow the patterns efficiently for the sake of the whole. Dwight has pride in his work that he sees as essential to the big picture, literally as a film and figuratively as a wholistic philosophy. The Gita urges believers into self-controlled action, like that of the technicians:

> Activity is better than inertia. Act, but with self-control. . . . The world is imprisoned in its own activity, except when actions are performed as worship of

God. Therefore you must perform every action sacramentally, and be free from all
attachments to results (*BG*, 53).

Every wise man acts according to the tendencies of his own nature. It is better to do your own duty, however imperfectly, than to assume the duties of another
person, however successfully, if it is not one's true inclination. (*BG*, 57–58)

You must learn what kind of work to do, what kind of work to avoid, and
how to reach a state of calm detachment from your work. (*BG*, 63)

Dwight cannot be the manageress nor can the manageress be Dwight. Isherwood
could not be a Cambridge don or a medical doctor. His destiny began as a writer in
childhood, and a writer he would be while learning how to teach parables about the
progress of the aspiring Truly Strong Man.

The Vienna uprising occurs and Bergmann is beside himself with worry.
Isherwood tries to console him, but Bergmann is beyond solace and considers going
back to Austria. Isherwood reminds him that he left because of his leftist politics and
a return would be dangerous. Bergmann is ashamed that he is in safety. Isherwood
assures him that this is exactly where his wife and daughter want him to be and that
his return might compromise them more than help them. An encounter with a
reporter who asks Bergmann about Austria makes matters worse, especially after the
reporter reacts to the director's tirade with, "'after all . . .' he said defensively, with
his . . . insensitive smile, 'you must remember, it isn't our affair. I mean, you can't
really expect people in England to care. . .'" (*PV*, 103). Then Bergmann really
explodes. Isherwood responds to this incident by examining the superficiality of his
own political sympathies:

I knew what I was supposed to feel, what it was fashionable for my generation to feel. We cared about everything: fascism in Germany and Italy, the seizure
of Manchuria, Indian nationalism, the Irish question, the workers, the Negroes,
the Jews. We had spread our feelings over the whole world; and I knew that mine
were spread very thin. I cared—oh, yes, I certainly cared—about the Austrian
socialists. But did I care as much as I said I did, tried to imagine I did? No, not
nearly as much. I felt angry with [the reporter]; but he, at least, was honest. What
is the use of caring at all, if you aren't prepared to dedicate your life, to die?

Bergmann must have known what I was thinking. "You are tired, my child,
go to bed." (*PV*, 104–105)

Even after Bergmann receives a letter from his wife saying that she is well, his foul
mood continues and he is sinking the picture. Bergmann is rescued from his despair
by a most unlikely source for a Truly Strong Man—Chatsworth, the studio head.
Dwight did say Chatsworth is a romantic, a fact that implies that an individual
should not be judged by his work, but for himself, or his inner Self.

Chatsworth summons Bergmann and Isherwood and half cajoles, half extorts,
new passion from Bergmann by appealing to the director's pride. Isherwood is

astounded and charmed at Chatsworth's genuinely sensitive tact in re-energizing the director so that Bergmann believes it is his own decision to continue. The director is in charge of his emotions again—and in charge of his motion picture: "Bergmann inspired us all. His absolute certainty swept us along like a torrent. Bergmann knew exactly what he wanted. We took everything in our stride" (*PV*, 120). Bergmann's revival suggests yet another parallel to the Gita, which suggests that "Whatever a great man does, ordinary people will imitate." The cast and crew finish the picture exhilarated from a stirring accomplishment. Even Dwight the efficiency expert is impressed. After the picture's wrap party, Isherwood, exhausted, returns home near dawn:

> It was that hour of the night at which man's ego almost sleeps. The sense of identity, of possession, of name and address and telephone number grows very faint. It was the hour at which man shivers, pulls up his coat collar, and thinks, "I am a traveler. I have no home. . . .
>
> What makes us go on living? I supposed vaguely, that it was a kind of balance, a complex of tensions.
>
> Death, the desired, the feared. . . . Not the fears that are advertised. More dreadful than those: the private fears of childhood. . . . And behind them, most unspeakably terrible of all, the arch fear: the fear of being afraid.
>
> It can never be escaped. . . . Not if you run away to the ends of the earth . . . not if you yell mummy, or keep a stiff upper lip.
>
> But if it is mine, if it is really within me . . . Then . . . Why, then . . . And, at this moment, but how infinitely faint, how distant, like the high far glimpse of a goat track through the mountains between the clouds, I see something else: the way that leads to safety. To where there is no fear, no loneliness . . . I glimpse it. For an instant, it is even quite clear. (*PV*, 122–26)

And though only for an instant, Isherwood the character of *Prater Violet* and more so, Isherwood the author of *Prater Violet*, feels that warm touch, sees the brilliant light, hears the moan of the universe—the eternal Om that is the sound of God, and wants to come back for more . . . forever.

As for Bergmann:

> Beneath outer consciousness, two other beings, anonymous, impersonal, without labels, had met and recognized each other, and had clasped hands. He was my father. I was his son. And I loved him very much.
>
> Bergmann held out his hand.
>
> 'Good night my child,' he said." (*PV*, 127)

Bergman and Viertel were indeed loved by Isherwood, but the real-life figure behind them both who actually said "good night my child" was the Swami. *Prater Violet* is a parable of the Gita, and of the Swami, who had brought the warmth, the light, and the sound of God into Isherwood's life.

The novel was an act of devotion; Isherwood did his duty in the form of sacra-
mental writing based in love. *Prater Violet* is an achievement in itself and fully satisfactory to any reader, Vedantist or not. To a Perennial Philosopher, however, it is a
remarkable philosophical parable. On 19 December 1943 Isherwood wrote very
clearly that this was his intention: "To be a monk and to be a writer are the same,
there's no clash of purposes. Dedicate everything to Him" (*D*, 328).

One should not think that Isherwood's devotion to Vedanta had become too
solemn. Indeed, the satirical inspiration of Mortmere was always lurking nearby.
This parodic impulse is apparent in the 26 March 1943 entry of his diary:

> Dishwashing is always a pleasant part of the day. I make up verses to amuse
> the girls—particularly Sarada, who is very sensitive to words. The charm of this
> sort of humor is simply that it is so specialized like the jokes of Airmen or scien-
> tists. . . . Some specimens:
>
> With many a mudra and mantram, with mutterings and mouthings and
> moans,
> The rishis flew into a tantrum and rattled the avatar's bones.
> Or:
> Never smoke before the Swami
> For he hates a bad cigar, Water pipes would be pretentious—
> They are for the avatar:
> Only saints may stoop to cigarettes, Only rishis dare to chew,
> Therefore if you see the Swa-ami
> Hide that Camel underne-eath the pew. (*D*, 278)

During the post-war years the Isherwood gang of Auden and Spender were also
maturing and turning inward. In the summer of 1947 Isherwood and Spender vaca-
tioned in New York with Auden while the poet worked on *The Age of Anxiety*, a long
poem that would win a Pulitzer Prize. Auden's poem was about the spoken meditations of four people in a bar as a metaphor of Jung's four aspects of personality:
thinking, feeling, intuition, sensation. In it the divided mind, now split into four
parts, not just two, is posited as the natural condition of humanity in the new post-
war world order. It is the divided human psyche that causes anxiety; psychoanalysis
is an attempt to alleviate this anxiety. The isolated neurotic of the 1930s is no longer
the exception but the rule with one important distinction: the individual can
acknowledge his neuroses without shame and seek to change.

The sensitive Stephen Spender composed *Poems of Dedication* (1947) to the
memory of Margaret Spender, his brother Humphrey's wife, who had died on
Christmas Day 1945. She had had a protracted incurable illness since 1939 and her
body wasted away slowly, but her spirit, according to Spender, never wavered.
Margaret had been his confidant and comforter when Spender's first marriage dissolved:

Margaret touched my forehead with her skeleton-like hand, and at that moment, I realized as I identified my misfortune with hers the egotism of my demand for sympathy and of my claim to be unhappy.

I am astonished that there are people who boast of being egotists, because actually the consciousness of egotism is like a sour taste on the tongue. Now Margaret's gesture, which spoke of her far more serious unhappiness, brought back to me the truth of various remarks which had been scattered through the years, all pointing to the thought that unhappiness is a condition which few people have the right to claim. I remember Auden's remark when we were at Oxford that if I were in love, had good health and sufficient income, I ought to consider myself happy.[16]

To Spender, Margaret was a kind of manageress. Later, Spender wrote: "she died, confident that death was only a temporary separation from those she loved, whom she would soon meet again."[17]

Isherwood was not evolving alone; his gang was evolving with him.

BACKSLIDING IN SOUTH AMERICA

From 1939 to 1945 Isherwood had embraced Vedanta with the fervent zeal of the recently converted. He had been devoted, almost celibate and monk-like—but not quite. He was a true believer; he never doubted his belief in God or the Swami, but after six years, Isherwood did doubt if he could be a full-fledged monk and actually undergo the initiation that entailed always living at the temple and celibacy. He had tried but failed to steel himself for the requirement of celibacy. He knew he needed companionship outside the Vedanta temple as well as inside it. The writing of *Prater Violet* had been the culmination of his six years of study. The novel was also a signal that Isherwood needed to be in the world again. He informed the Swami of his decision to be a lay follower. The Swami was supportive and understanding; he would let Isherwood evolve in his own time and in his own way, which from the Vedantic standpoint, might mean more than one lifetime. Their mutual devotion to each other never wavered. Isherwood continued to study with the Swami and assist him with more translations of Vedic texts.

Isherwood's diary from 1939 to 1945 recorded his conversion in 380 detailed pages. He would later say of his diary writing in general: "I shall not try to forestall criticism by apologizing for the many absurdities, inaccuracies and errors of judgment which will probably be found in my work. A diarist ought to be able to make a fool of himself, sometimes. He aims at being impressionistic and spontaneous, rather than authoritative."[18] Although Isherwood's diaries managed to be all three, the former two qualities are what make them so compelling. The latter sense of authority came from the sincerity of feeling rather than any structured argument. Isherwood's "I am a camera" line from the Berlin stories seems applicable to his diary writing: he was feeling before thinking, although a

great deal of cogent thought can still be extracted from these relatively unstructured descriptions of his feelings.

After Isherwood's decision to be a lay devotee, he wanted to make up for his
monk-like years by being rather unmonk-like and pursuing one relationship after
another. From early 1945 to late 1947 there are no diary entries. Perhaps this was
a reaction to six years of copious entries. The omissions may also have reflected
some guilt over his inability to come to terms with his decision not to become a
monk; he may have thought this a form of failure. If he did not write in his diary,
he would not have to analyze or confront himself. He did maintain a list of events
during this period, mainly of people he met but no comments whatsoever.
Isherwood had not let go completely of his need to validate his existence by writing it down, however cursorily.

During this period Isherwood's most consistent relationship was with the
younger William Caskey towards whom Isherwood could continue his paternal-
fraternal inclinations. In 1947 Isherwood and Caskey, a photographer, traveled to
South America in order to write a travel book, *The Condor and the Cows,* with
Isherwood's text and Caskey's photos. The resulting book was less like Isherwood
and Auden's *Journey to a War* and more like Huxley's travel books, *Along the Road*
(1925), *Jesting Pilate* (1926), and *Beyond the Mexique Bay* (1934). In Huxley's works
the trips seemed almost an excuse for providing caustic philosophical commentary.
Isherwood's entry for 9 April 1947 was written aboard a ship bound for South
America: "It is time to wake Bill Caskey. He is asleep in the upper berth, his head
burrowing in the pillow, his lips emitting short angry-sounding snores. Caskey wal-
lows in sleep, as if in a hot bath, and wakes slowly, his face flushed, swollen, furious.
He is twenty-six years old, Kentucky-Irish. . . . His friends often compare him, not
unkindly, to a pig. I needn't add any epithets of my own. He will probably describe
himself, by degrees, as the account of our journey continues. He is a photographer
by profession, and is coming along to take pictures for this book. He speaks a little
Spanish as I do, and has only been abroad once before, on a short trip to Mexico
City." Isherwood is being somewhat disingenuous, sounding as if Caskey was a hired
hand. Caskey was along as Isherwood's companion and would have been whether
he knew how to work a camera or not. Later they go to the ship's dining room:

> We share a table with a married couple from New York. They are cruise pas-
> sengers, booked for the round-trip. . . . He is a lawyer and an amateur footballer,
> in his early thirties; a huskey good-looking Jewish ex-college boy who is growing
> fat somewhat apologetically. She is Spanish-Irish, and still very attractive.
>
> They have been married about ten years, have children, seem happy. This is
> their first trip alone together since their honeymoon. It was almost certainly her
> idea. He's a little unwilling. He can't quite relax. For him, as for so many Americans
> of his kind, a pleasure journey is just another sort of investment. . . . With his puz-
> zled collegiate frown, he is perpetually trying to assess the whole undertaking in

terms of value and service. He isn't in the least stingy—all his instincts are generous—but he is determined not to be gypped. . . .

She is equally determined—to enjoy herself and to make him enjoy himself
too. The energy which she brings to this task is really beautiful and touching. (CC,
7–8)

The wife is another manageress. Isherwood surmised his psychological interpretations of the couple by observing them. Before and after encountering Vedanta, he
had always recorded the people he encountered in whatever world he was in. Only
the degree of insight he could add to his observations changed.

After the South American expedition Isherwood visited England in 1947 for
the first time since 1939. This trip stirred up old feelings—mostly negative. This
could not have helped his relationship with Caskey, which was tumultuous as the
latter had a temper and Isherwood had not yet mastered his own sensitivity
enough not to react with equal emotion. The fact that neither refused attention
from other admirers could not have helped. During this time the aspiring Strong
Man seemed to be missing in action. What had happened to the man who almost
became a monk? His objective mind was still a believer, but his subjective body
could not resist temptation. The policy of this period seemed to be: do as I say,
not as I do. According to Katherine Bucknell in her preface to these years in the
Diaries, "As his relationship with Caskey grew more strained, Isherwood's diary
keeping became more regular. . . . But their lives were increasingly in conflict,
with Isherwood professing he wanted a settled domestic routine, which would
permit him to work during the daytime, and Caskey preferring to drink and have
spontaneous parties, and loud music. . . . Gerald Heard, Aldous Huxley, and the
Swami—admonished Isherwood about his way of life; the drinking and the
promiscuity could not be entirely blamed on Caskey's influence" (D, 388).

Since Isherwood was now forty-four and Caskey twenty-nine, blame could
not fall only on the younger man. Was this a middle-aged crisis? In part it was,
but only in part. From 1939 to 1945 Isherwood had been consumed with
Vedanta, which answered many of the questions that he had sought in his past
metaphysical inclinations; however, Vedanta could not help him answer the one
question he had been asking since he had gotten his own flat after first leaving
his mother's nest so many years before—his need for a lover who could also be
his friend. In Lions and Shadows Isherwood said that his first bachelor apartment
was his symbol of compulsive neatness, a tidiness that was covering up for what
he really wanted—a lover as soul-mate. Vedanta taught Isherwood a great deal;
however, he was not yet capable of making this knowledge into a life in and of
itself. Isherwood was still only an aspiring Strong Man who had in his middle age
discovered that, as wonderful as Vedanta was for him, he needed a sympathetic
lover to share his experience. Neither Caskey nor the various other substitutes
were the right ones; they were only object lessons so that when Isherwood met

the right one, he would be more prepared for him. At this time, however, Isherwood still did not realize that the right one—who had been four years old when Isherwood came to America to stay—was still living nearby, still unknown, still only sixteen years old.

5 SEEKING CALM IN THE *AGE OF ANXIETY*
Themes Developed: The Aspiring Truly Strong Man

[Isherwood speaking of Gore Vidal:] He wanted advice on "how to manage my career." He is very jealous of Truman [Capote], but does not want to quarrel with him because he feels that when a group of writers sticks together it's better business for all of them. (He got this moral from the Auden-Spender-Day Lewis-MacNeice-Isherwood gang, he says.)

Diaries, 4 April 1948

What I am really trying to run away from is myself.
What I am trying to impose under the guise of "reasonableness"—is my own will. "Nothing burns in hell except the self,"[1] and I am miserable because the self is burning. In the simplest, most terrible manner I am being taught that no other kind of life [meaning Vedanta] is possible for me. The monastery is *here,* is wherever I am.

4 April 1951

Without some awareness of God or some movement of the will toward him, everything is madness and nonsense. It's far better to feel alienated from God than to feel nothing at all.

29 August 1951

I must confess, I want to be looked after. I want the background of a "home." I see now how well the arrangement [at Kathleen's] suited me the last year or so in England (much as I complained about it. . . .) I had the snugness of a bedroom and breakfast.

6 May 1951

A little stirring of sex today. Not much. It occurs to me that, of all the sensual pleasures, sex is the only one that depends on reciprocation. That's its power. Imagine if an orange said: "Darling, I was just longing for *you* to eat me. I was so afraid that horrible old man would. He's not at *all* my type.

5 May 1952

When I typed out the title page of the Patanjali [translation] this morning, I put "by Swami Prabhavananda and Christopher Isherwood," and Swami said, "why put *and* Chris? It separates us." It's impossible to convey the sweetness and meaning with which he said this. All day long, he fairly shines with love.

19 May 1952

I feel a special kind of love for Don [Bachardy]. I suppose I'm just another frustrated father. But this feeling exists at a very deep level, beneath names for things or their appearances.

6 March 1953

Made it! Fifty—the unimaginable age. And now comes what might be the most interesting part of my life—the twenty years till seventy [or eighty-two].

27 August 54

When one peruses Isherwood's *Diaries,* it seems that he knew everybody—or at least everybody worth knowing. Many gravitated towards him as an icon of the iconoclastic 1930s, including young writers like Gore Vidal and Gavin Lambert, who were fans who became friends. As the west coast representative of the Auden Generation, Isherwood had a special status for a post-war contingent of new rebels, particularly fellow members of his tribe. After the war Isherwood was temporarily a semi-lapsed Vedantist—believing in spirit but lapsing in practice because the body was weak. His relationship with the Swami remained an anchor that pulled him back to sanity when the world was otherwise too much with him. Middle age did not agree with Isherwood.

MIDDLE-AGED CRAZY

When Isherwood turned forty in 1944, this seemed to be the beginning of his new period of restlessness. In his diaries he observes that neither he nor his peers were the raging youth of the 1930s any longer. After seeing Auden on 28 April 1948, he writes: "As for Wystan [at 41], he's quite middle-aged, with a thick waist and such a sad anxiously lined face. We sat together this morning on the boulevard in the sunshine and suddenly it was like a scene from Chekhov, I thought: 'Here we are, two old bags—and only a moment ago, it seems, we were boys, talking about our careers. Like Truman and Gore. How sad.'"

In his 14 December 1949 diary entry, he tries to make sense of his mid-life transformation: "I think there is no doubt about it, I'm going through the change of life. . . . Certainly, my mind is softening, weakening. I have so little coordination that I putter around like a dotard." Moreover, in the *Diaries* Isherwood would flagellate himself constantly for the laziness and procrastination that blocked his writing. Isherwood also wrote copiously of his difficulties with Caskey but did not seem to make the correlation that perhaps it was the related stress that was making him feel old, since being forty-four years of age need not have been so debilitating.

Despite his feelings of advanced age the "dotard" started a new novel in 1949, although he would not finish it until 1953. Isherwood had great difficulty right from the beginning with *The World in the Evening.* He had trouble finding the right voice for his protagonist and comments on this repeatedly through the next few years; for instance, he records his search for the proper voice in his 17 August 1949 entry: "[The character] 'Stephen Monkhouse' has got to be me— not some synthetic Anglo-American. The few circumstances can be so easily imagined—his ex-wife, his Quaker background, etc. But it must be written out of the middle of *my* consciousness." If his own voice was muddled by the stress of not having the domestic bliss he craved, his novel's antihero did not benefit from the angst either. Isherwood was also concerned about the coming Korean War and its potential effect on Caskey and all other young American men.

At least money was not a concern. A boon to Isherwood's financial situation was the success of John Van Druten's 1951 Broadway adaptation of the Berlin stories, *I Am a Camera*. The play reintroduced Isherwood to new admirers outside the almost cultish cognoscenti, such as Vidal. This financial stability helped, but his precarious psyche, troubled by his self-perceived advancing age and a lack of a snug home life, raged at the barest slights—real or imagined—that seemed to trip him up. He knew he was overreacting and could rationally analyze why but could not stop himself from worrying. Isherwood would let himself be affected by worldly anxieties too easily. He writes on 22 September 1951 that a friend said to him: "'I want to be lucky and carefree and gay.'" Isherwood's comment on this remark was that the "statement depressed me profoundly, because it is the kind of thing that is only said by the weak, the hopelessly hopelessly weak." Isherwood's evaluation reflected his own frustration. At that moment Isherwood was appalled by his own weakness. Life, however, would soon change for the better.

On 13 September 1952 Isherwood had a dream:

> My father, in uniform, at a table. I'm sitting beside him.
> "Are you lonely here, Daddy?"
> "Yes."
> "So am I. But never mind. You get used to it."
> I pat him on the shoulder, rather deliberately, never having done this before but feeling that it's right. A very strong feeling of rapport, between us.
> Woke up happy. This was a good dream.

Isherwood believed in omens. This may have been one. Shortly afterwards he would meet Don Bachardy.

The first diary entry concerning Bachardy is on 6 March 1953: "I feel a special kind of love for Don. I suppose I'm just another frustrated father." This indicates a relationship already underway; however, this is the first time Bachardy is noted in the *Diaries*. Perhaps Isherwood had been psychologically cautious, not wanting to declare himself in his diary as being in love before being confident that his love was reciprocated. After this Bachardy is mentioned substantially. Isherwood was deeply in love with a young man thirty years his junior. Bachardy had struggled with a strained home life and needed a paternal-fraternal figure to make up for it. Isherwood, in his terrible middle age, tried to be this figure. This was not always easy, as Bachardy—like any troubled eighteen-year-old—was fraught with insecurities that the almost equally insecure Isherwood coped with as best he could. Even when they were at odds, however, Isherwood persevered; he was not letting go of this relationship.

On 22 September 1953 Isherwood recorded the following entry: "I'm very happy in my father relationship with Don, except that he makes me feel so terribly responsible." Bachardy did become a responsibility, and despite some bumps in their road, Isherwood was done with his second tearing down and had begun his second reawakening and his second building up. He would chronicle these steps consciously and unconsciously in the novel he had been having trouble finishing, *The World in the Evening*.

THE WORLD IN THE EVENING

Brian Finney writes in his biography of Isherwood: "When it was published in June 1954, *The World in the Evening* received a primarily hostile reception from the critics. Even Upward, Lehmann and Spender felt compelled to express reservations about it in their private correspondence with Isherwood. As for Isherwood himself, he accepted the general verdict and subsequently became one of the book's most perceptive critics. '*The World in the Evening*, is a failure,' he wrote to Upward . . . 'but an interesting one, I hope, and a necessary one I'm *sure* for me.'"[2]

Failure is too severe. Uneven seems more appropriate, for it is sometimes brilliant, sometimes helpless. The antihero Stephen Monk is an aspiring Truly Strong Man. He speaks in the first person and sounds best when he is ruminating to himself. When he does, Monk is the Isherwood who said that this character had to come from "out of the middle of *my* consciousness." These are the brilliant parts. When Monk talks with some of the other characters concerning matters that Isherwood is not quite so sure of, these dialogues sound stilted, coy, wooden, and artificial. When Isherwood said it was a "necessary" failure, this is the crux of the novel's importance for his own evolving consciousness and that of the Truly Strong Man. The novel is a description—or story within a story—of Isherwood's first and second reawakenings: It details a character—based on Isherwood—who tells his life story concerning a process of tearing down unbelief and undertaking an internal journey of building up new belief. This is a replay of Isherwood's first awakening in 1939. The novel also forced Isherwood to take stock of his disrupted life since leaving the temple in 1945, after which he underwent the process of a second tearing down and a second building up. After leaving the temple, he had questioned his ability to remain true to his Vedantic beliefs while he struggled with the temptations of the body. Over the next seven years he slowly learned to be more accepting of the balance one needed to be a Vedantist in the material world. In 1939 his life was changed by meeting the Swami. In 1953 his life would be changed again by meeting Don Bachardy. In *The World in the Evening*, both the entire story of Isherwood's life and the chapter concerned with his post-temple years are told as a parable.

Isherwood makes the purpose of his parable plain by having three sections: "An End," which is the end of the tearing down of his old life; "Letters and Life," where Monk evaluates his past life in order to begin the process of building up a new life; and "A Beginning," which is the start of his new life of belief. The theory of this plan is sound; the implementation is not as sure. Stephen Monk's name itself indicates Isherwood's more heavy-handed approach to this novel. Is it meant to be ironic, since Monk, when the novel begins, is not a monk, or is it an omen for the path this character would take by the book's end? Unlike *Prater Violet*, which seamlessly delivered its parable of the Bhagavad-Gita, the messages of *The World in the Evening* are more patchwork and sometimes clumsily didactic. Compared to *Prater Violet*, there are fewer scenes such as the description of the manageress, or of Chatsworth's deft handling of Bergmann's angst. Nor do the scenes flow as smoothly from one to the next. Even with these criticisms, the novel has enough good scenes among those of Monk's introspective ruminating to sustain the reader through some of the less convincing dialogues. It also dares to do what Isherwood had not done before. As Summers said of the novel, "it pioneers in a genuinely felt expression of homosexual militancy and in a famous articulation of a homosexual aesthetic, 'High and Low Camp.'"[3] For the first time—and in the bland 1950s—Isherwood came out of the closet, at least through his characters. Isherwood made the first gesture toward the rest of his tribe to be pure in heart and Truly Strong. His choice to be open about the issue could only have been welcomed in the homosexual community.

The first section, "An End," begins in 1941 at a Hollywood party. Stephen Monk is thirty-seven and rich. At the party he discovers the infidelity of his second wife Jane. This motivates Stephen to leave the false glitter of Hollywood. He retreats to the Monk family estate in Pennsylvania and to his Aunt Sarah who raised him from childhood after he lost his parents. She is a Quaker who raised Stephen to be one, although he has long lapsed. His former home reminds him too much of the past. Monk, not wanting any reminders, attempts to leave surreptitiously in the middle of the night and is hit by a truck, which leaves him injured and back in his old home. Isherwood implies that this may have been a suicide attempt. In the long middle section, "Life and Letters," Monk, while recovering from his injuries, reconsiders his life, the catalyst being the reading of his first wife's letters. Thirty-four-year-old Elizabeth Rydal was a novelist and twelve years older than Stephen when they met. She was fragile physically from a weak heart. While he reads the letters, Stephen is nursed by Gerda Mannheim, a young German refugee. She is concerned about her husband who is still in

Isherwood overdressed with his Sherlock Holmesian deerstalker cap, early 1950s. (Vedanta Society of Southern California Archives)

At a devotional meal (prasad), dramatist John van Druten (upper left); Isherwood to the right of Van Druten; the Swami to his right. (Vedanta Society of Southern California Archives)

Isherwood at work at the temple and monastery, early 1950s (Vedanta Society of Southern California Archives)

Germany and has not been heard from. Elizabeth's letters prompt Monk's retrospective evaluation of his past. He recalls his wife's miscarriage, her failing health, his brief tryst with a homosexual friend who loved Stephen one-sidedly, an affair with Jane during Elizabeth's last illness, Elizabeth's death, and his second marriage.

In the last section, "A Beginning, " Gerda's husband is found to be safe in Switzerland, and Monk comes to terms with himself, his past, and Elizabeth's memory. Declaring himself a pacifist and conscientious objector, Stephen becomes a civilian ambulance driver in North Africa.

Monk's internal journey parallels Isherwood's. Monk represents Isherwood himself in different stages of the author's life. Sometimes Monk also becomes other people in Isherwood's life, such as his younger lovers, Caskey or Bachardy. Indeed, Bachardy's name is mentioned directly in the novel. Isherwood reiterates his past by giving much of his own history to Monk. He also features a character named Mary Scriven, who appears as the very same persona from Isherwood's 1932 novel, *The Memorial*. Isherwood does so to connect his past and present symbolically. In its way, *The World in the Evening* is another roman à clef for the gang to decipher. Isherwood's gang now included American friends, particularly the members of his tribe. The best parts of the narrative are those when Monk paraphrases from Isherwood's diaries, such as this early passage in "An End": "Somehow or another, I'd wandered into this gibbering jungle of phonies and here I was floundering stupidly in the mud of my jealous misery and sinking deeper with every movement. I hadn't even the consolation of being able to feel sorry for myself. I couldn't get out of the swamp. I tried to think of Elizabeth and what she would have said, but it was no good. Elizabeth wasn't here. I was all alone. I should go on struggling and sinking. I had no control over what was going to happen" (*W*, 8). This sounds like any number of diary entries between 1947 and 1953 and one could substitute the Swami for Elizabeth.

Monk returns to Aunt Sarah in a Pennsylvania Quaker enclave similar to the one near the refugee camp of Isherwood's Haverford experience. Sarah speaks in "thees" and "thous," of which Monk says: "It was like talking in a secret language after a long time, a language you thought you'd forgotten. The Sarah-Stephen language had its limitations; there were many things you couldn't say in it at all. But how comforting and safe it was, for that very reason" (*W*, 24). Just as safe as the Isherwood-Upward language or the Isherwood-Auden language, which were created to insulate themselves from The Others. Monk thought: "This was really a fresh start. . . . I had come back to the room I was born in, bringing nobody with me, nothing except a suitcase. Now at last, I told myself with apprehension and excitement, I've actually done it. I've cut all the life lines, kicked away all the props. From here on in, whatever happens, I'll be entirely on my own." (*W*, 30) Monk's words are reminiscent of Isherwood's arrival in America.

Speaking to Gerda and Stephen, Sarah compares Stephen to his late father, noting: "they had deep spiritual values in common. . . ." And Stephen thinks: "My stomach gave a big turn" (*W*, 33). He knew his father would not have been pleased with his son's life up to now. For Isherwood the father figure is still a conflicted issue. Though Stephen was born in America he went to live in England at age five. When Stephen tells Gerda that he gets homesick for people instead of countries, Gerda responds: "There are some people who are *like* countries. When you are with them, that is your country and you speak its language. And then it does not matter where you are together, you are home" (*W*, 38). Gerda means her husband; Stephen means Elizabeth; Isherwood means the Swami, or Upward, or Auden, or Spender, or Bachardy.

After Gerda and Sarah leave Stephen alone, he has a vision of Elizabeth: "Elizabeth, tell me was I crazy to come here? What am I getting into? [She answers] Don't worry, Darling. Just be patient. You'll find out" (*W*, 43). And he will—slowly—as a Vedantic unfolding of inner truth. On 27 October 1956, Isherwood writes in his diary of imagined conversations he holds with the Swami: "I think about him all the time and have conversations with him in my mind." When Monk tells Elizabeth he is unhappy, she responds: "You needn't be. . . . Nobody need be" (*W*, 44). Then Stephen recalls how, at a Quaker Friends Meeting, a woman testified: "My self-will comes between me and the light that is within me. I know that. . . . But . . . my will doesn't *have* to be self-will. My will is a necessary part of me. I need it. And God needs my will, to draw me to him" (*W,* 45). When the spell of Elizabeth's vision subsides, however, the memo-ries that Monk finds in his childhood home are almost too wholesome to bear comparison to his guilt at having been seduced by the Hollywood glitter. Conflicted between the two worlds, Stephen tries to flee again, and is hit by the truck. So ends "An End." This can only mean a new beginning is ahead.

"Life and Letters" begins with Stephen being nursed by Gerda. These scenes include therapeutic dialogue for both Monk and Isherwood. Stephen tells Gerda that Sarah's ways remind him of his childhood, which he does not wish to remember. Gerda understands this but tells him, "some part of you is still a kid. . . . This kid I can see in you I like. . . . Only Stephen, you know children can be cruel sometimes, by not thinking. You must not be cruel to Sarah. She loves you. You love her too. You must show her too" (*W,* 52). Isherwood might have been thinking of himself and Kathleen, whom he had last seen in 1947. Gerda is another manageress dispensing wisdom. She suggests to Stephen that he should be more sensitive to the inner awareness that is latent within him. Stephen real-izes his vision of Elizabeth was meant to tell him the same thing.

A Swami figure in the guise of Dr. Charles Kennedy comes to see Monk. Stephen thinks, "His mere presence was almost hypnotically protective. . . . If there was any worrying to be done, I felt, he would take care of it all" (*W,* 54). Kennedy alludes to the possibility that Stephen's accident was not accidental and Monk side-steps the issue. The doctor's friend Bob Wood joins them. Readers will learn that Charles and Bob are lovers. As Chris Wood was Gerald Heard's companion, Bob and Charles may have been counterparts. Charles is concerned about Bob going to Korea to fight in the war, just as Isherwood was concerned about that possibility for Caskey, and later Bachardy.

Alone, Stephen acknowledges to himself—and to the reader—that he lied to Kennedy about his "accident." He begins to read Elizabeth's letters that were written to himself and to others, particularly Mary Scriven. Stephen says to Elizabeth's aura, "now you've got me. . . . I'll listen to you now. I'll try and face up to whatever you want me to know. Just tell me what I am to do next" (*W,* 63). Monk, through Elizabeth's letters (and Isherwood's diaries), reconstructs his life for examination. In one of her letters, written before she met Stephen, Elizabeth describes the writing of an early novel involving a mother-son relationship. The relationship depicted is a combination of Kathleen to Christopher and Isherwood the father to Bachardy:

> The mother, so utterly, angrily alone with her tragedy—nobody else under-stands it, and it cuts her off, even, from her own son. She sits watching him, sadly, quite objectively, almost with a kind of mocking hostility. She longs to break down the barrier between them, to get through to him and make him share what she feels, somehow, even if she has to hurt him. And the boy, absorbed in his play, answers her probing, teasing questions with that strange obstinate inner certainty that children sometimes have. You try to warn them about life, all its pain, its

cruelty—and they simply won't believe you. . . . They're so absurdly, idiotically, heartbreakingly confident. You're sure they're wrong—they must be—and yet, you wonder uneasily, *are* they? The older generation, still sitting under the shadow of the past war [WWI]—disillusioned, bereaved, resentful—and watching this new generation at play. Trying desperately, to warn it of its doom, the doom of its dead fathers, and being answered with this absurd heartbreaking innocent cynical confidence. . . . jazz, Dadaism, flappers, night clubs—that's what they all mean. "I can look after myself . . . mother. . . . Why can't you leave me alone?" (*W,* 67)

Isherwood's tone here is more conciliatory towards his mother's generation and a little more caustic concerning his own. Stephen says that "at the time of this letter—the first week of November, 1926—I was still over in Germany" (*W,* 68). Monk then details the disgust he felt for the world right after leaving Cambridge. The twenty-two-year-old Stephen pursued sex in Germany, even though he felt guilty for betraying Sarah's principles. One woman he met in Germany makes it clear to him that she had other men friends beside himself. This is what Isherwood had experienced, only he had switched the genders.

Monk reads another of Elizabeth's letters, in which she describes a character named Adrian from a later novel that was written after she met Stephen. Stephen realizes Adrian is himself. Adrian also could have been Isherwood, or Spender in the past, or Bachardy in the present: "On the surface, this polite, guarded boredom, this self-protective vagueness. And inside —flashing out of him at moments—a really startling joy. . . . And suddenly, he's a little boy" (*W,* 79). Monk recalls that when he first met Elizabeth he pugnaciously refuted his youthful Quaker beliefs. She had been very patient with his rebelliousness, understanding it to be natural to his age. He then tries, like Sally Bowles, to act "grown-up" by shocking her with his adventures in Berlin and Paris. Stephen, speaking to her supernatural presence, recalls that instead of being shocked, Elizabeth "just smiled and looked indulgent and abstracted, like a mother who listens to her child telling her about the dog having puppies" (*W,* 84). Yet at the time when he had talked to her about specific people he had met in Europe, he recalls "You asked me dozens of questions. I could see you projecting yourself into their lives. You translated everything into terms of individual human beings. You taught me so much. . . . I'm sure you weren't even aware that you were doing it" (*W,* 85). Just like Bergmann or the Swami, Elizabeth, even as a vision, is teaching by example.

Stephen recalls how he had been insecure around Elizabeth's intellectual friends, just as Bachardy was in similar company. Monk thought: "I regarded these people as my natural enemies. I imagined them looking through and through me, judging me, dismissing me. . ." (*W,* 86). He imagined slights and finally blew up over one. Elizabeth patiently comforted him. After this Elizabeth and Stephen realized they were in love and this temporarily assuaged his insecurity.

Returning his thoughts to the present, Stephen has an early morning rumination. He thinks that he is able, when first waking, to recall all of his thoughts and actions since birth but not as memory in bits and pieces, rather as "total, instantaneous awareness" (*W,* 94). His following description is like Isherwood's vision of being himself in 1940 while also being able to see himself simultaneously in 1936:

> Everything particular was on the outside; and what was aware of this was a simple consciousness that had no name, no face, no identity of any kind. If there was a purgatory . . . it would probably be something like this. You'd be set face to face, inescapably, with what you'd made of yourself. . . . And I could never wipe any of it out. I could never atone for it. I could never be sufficiently ashamed. But consciousness wasn't ashamed, because consciousness wasn't I. It refused to accept the least responsibility for what I'd done or been. It felt no relation to my acts. It knew no feelings, except the feeling of being itself; and that was the deepest, quietest, most mysterious kind of happiness.
>
> Within this happiness were absolute safety, entire peace. (*W,* 94–95)

Isherwood is also describing those moments during meditation, which, however fleeting, intimate that, if one could abnegate the will and surrender to total awareness, the bliss of "this thing" could be achieved. For Isherwood this total awareness is represented by his overall scheme for the novel itself. He would use this scheme again in his next novel *Down There on a Visit.* Isherwood's life is a macrocosm. The immediately preceding years within his life are a microcosm within that macrocosm or the reiteration of a cycle within a cycle that is a circular reminder of a bigger picture. For Stephen the vision of Elizabeth is the center of his life, around which his circular path is connected continuously and contiguously. The circle is unbroken; all of existence is integrated within it. Even when Gerda and Sarah are present, Stephen feels that when he is in this morning mood of total awareness, Elizabeth is also present as his manageress, directing his re-education.

Another aspect of Isherwood's bigger picture was his decision to deal with homosexuality directly—the tacit years were over. Bob Wood visits and reveals to Stephen that he is not only homosexual but militantly so. When Bob, who is somewhat defensive, unfairly implies that Stephen is being patronizing to him, Monk responds, "Oh, Bob, don't be stuffy about this, please!" Wood answers:

> "That's what you heterosexuals always say. We'll run you out of town. We'll send you to jail. We'll stop you getting another job. But please don't be stuffy about it."
>
> "I only mean don't be so aggressive. That's what puts people against you."
>
> "Maybe we ought to put people against us. Maybe we're too damned tactful. People just ignore us, most of the time, and we let them. So this whole business never gets discussed, and the laws never get changed. There's a few people right here in the village who really know what the score is with Charles and me, but they won't admit it, not even to themselves. We're such *nice* boys, they say. So whole some. They just refuse to imagine how nice boys like us could be arrested and

locked up as crooks. They're afraid to think about it, for fear it'd trouble their tender consciences. Next thing you know, they might get a *concern* . . . and then they'd have to *do* something."

Then Stephen reveals: "Let me tell you something, Bob. There was a guy *I* liked, once. In that way I mean. . ." (*W,* 105). Isherwood was making a bold statement for 1954. His novel was not aimed at the avant garde or a cult audience—this was a mainstream book. It also found its way to the people it was intended for, the fellow members of his tribe who welcomed the candor.[4]

Stephen's candid remark to Bob will later become another motivation for a flashback to Elizabeth. Before this, however, Monk discusses with Kennedy the concept of Camp. This comes after a talk about Quakers and their "plainness" (or squareness). Charles says "they've no notion of elegance":

> "Plainness doesn't exclude elegance; it only makes it all the more necessary. Anyhow, 'elegance' isn't quite what I mean. . . . In any of your *voyages au bout de la nuit,* did you ever run across the word 'camp'?"
>
> "I've heard people use it in bars. But I thought. . ."
>
> "You thought it meant a swishy little boy with peroxided hair, dressed in a picture hat and a feather boa, pretending to be Marlene Dietrich? Yes, in queer circles, they call *that* camping. It's all very well in its place, but it's an utterly debased form. . . ." Charles eyes shone delightedly. He seemed to be in the best of spirits, now, and thoroughly enjoying *this exposition.* "What *I* mean by camp is something much more fundamental. You can call the other Low Camp, if you like; then what I'm talking about is High Camp. High Camp is the whole emotional basis of the ballet, for example, and of course Baroque art. You see, true High Camp always has an underlying seriousness. You can't camp about something you don't take seriously. You're not making fun of it; you're making fun out of it. You're expressing what's basically serious to you in terms of fun and artifice and elegance. Baroque art is largely camp about religion. The ballet is camp about love. . . . Do you see at all what I'm getting at?"
>
> "I'm not sure give me some instances. What about Mozart?"
>
> "Mozart's definitely a camp. Beethoven . . . isn't."
>
> "Is Flaubert?"
>
> "God, no!"
>
> "And neither is Rembrandt?"
>
> "No. Definitely not."
>
> "But El Greco is?"
>
> "Certainly."
>
> "And so is Dostoevski?"
>
> "Of course he is! In fact, he's the founder of the whole school of modern Psycho-Camp which was later developed by Freud." Charles had a sudden spasm of laughter. "Splendid, Stephen!"

"I don't know if I have it or not. It seems such an elastic expression."

Actually, it isn't at all. But I admit it's terribly hard to define. You have to meditate on it and feel it intuitively, like Laotse's *Tao*." (*W,* 110–111)

For Charles and Isherwood Camp cannot be defined but must be felt with an intuitive
awareness, a similar innate awareness as the one needed to feel "this thing."

A correlative type of awareness, that of relating the particular to the universal, becomes the subject of a later discussion between Stephen and Gerda about
Elizabeth's last novel, *The World in the Evening*. Gerda could not believe that a
novel written in 1934 that takes place in the late 1920s did not refer at all to the
rise of fascism. It seemed to her that Elizabeth did not care about the suffering of
other people. Stephen responds that "Elizabeth transposed everything she wrote
about into her own kind of microcosm" and did not deal with "big-scale
tragedies." Rather she tried to reproduce "the essence of them." In effect, she
would take the big picture—a massacre—"and tell a story about two children
stoning a cat to death. . . . And she'd put into it all the pain and disgust and horror she felt about the things the Nazis do" (*W,* 119). Elizabeth told parables.
Monk explains that Elizabeth, being of the previous generation, lost touch with
the coming younger writers of the 1930s, who were politically didactic.
Isherwood was one of those younger writers, and he, along with Auden, ultimately rejected didacticism in favor of parable, which is the art form of choice
for the pure in heart and Truly Strong.

Another flashback has Stephen and Elizabeth in England where he meets his
new wife's old friend Mary Scriven. Her home has a "pleasant air of bohemian
vagueness [as did Olive Mangeot's home]." Mary, unlike some of Elizabeth's
intellectual friends, "accepted us as a matter of course as an established couple,
who might have been together for years. No one had treated me like this before,
so I felt an extravagant gratitude to Mary. . ." (*W,* 139). Scriven was the principal recipient of Elizabeth's letters.

One of these letters is about Elizabeth-as-Isherwood and Stephen-as-
Bachardy: "How strange and sad it is this business of ages. Deep down, it doesn't
matter, it has no significance at all: love, on that level, it is so simple. It asks no questions. But up on the surface, where we spend so much of our time, there's a perpetual, tragic frustration. We have to wear masks, and keep pretending to be what
we seem at that particular moment" (*W,* 146).

Enter briefly Michael Drummond, who is eighteen years old. His first visit
is short. His second will be longer and more vital.

In another letter to Mary Scriven, Elizabeth writes about the 1930s threat of
war—and also answers Gerda's concern about the lack of current events in the
1934 novel: "At a period like this, it's hard to believe that art has any value at all.
. . . What's the use of this game with words and shades of meaning and feeling?
Oughtn't I to be *doing* something to try to stop this hate-disease. . . . this very

feeling of guilt and inadequacy is really a symptom of the disease itself. The disease is trying to paralyze you into complete inaction, so it makes you drop your own work and attempt to fight it in some practical way, which is unpractical for you because you aren't equipped for it—the only way I can fight the disease effectively is to go on with the work I understand" (*W,* 171). Elizabeth is reiterating the Gita-inspired lesson from *Prater Violet* that one can only do the duty for which one is suited. Near the end of this letter Elizabeth mentions that Michael Drummond has returned after seven years.

Elizabeth identifies that Michael is under some "terrible strain." She does not realize that the cause is his love for Stephen. Michael and Stephen have their affair and Michael confronts Elizabeth with the news, thinking Stephen would leave her for him. Monk never intended to. Instead, Michael leaves, crushed. Elizabeth admonishes Stephen by describing to him a trait Isherwood knew well: "You have the power to hurt. . . . What I am trying to say is that it would be so much better if you'd realize that and be frankly vain. . . . you're not nearly vain enough—you still feel in some mysterious way inferior—and that makes you cruel. You can't resist using your power. You have to keep proving to yourself that you're attractive" (*W,* 211). The gender toward whom Stephen was cruel made no difference to Elizabeth. To her, only "unkindness shocks" (*W,* 213). In a later letter Elizabeth writes: "Oh yes, believe me, the living have their ghosts, too. And they're much more intimate, much more boldly aggressive, than the other kind" (*W,* 221).

During Elizabeth's last illness Stephen secretly began his affair with Jane. The guilt of his betrayal while Elizabeth was dying would follow him to the present. In the past Elizabeth had told him that, even though she was sometimes afraid, she can assure him of the safety of the present: "I promise you, it isn't necessary. We only get afraid because we cling to things in the past or the future. If you stay in the present moment, you're never afraid, and you're safe—because that's always" (*W,* 247). On the same night, just after saying this, Elizabeth died. Stephen was not ready to understand her last message to him at the time she said it. Now he is.

At the end of "Life and Letters" Stephen writes a long letter to Jane that is a combination of expiatory confession, an apologia, and self-realization. Monk, like Isherwood in 1953, finally accepts responsibility for himself and is ready to move on. For both Stephen and Isherwood the last section, "A Beginning," is exactly that.

A new start means a new appreciation for Sarah. Even though Stephen has always loved Sarah, he never truly appreciated her Quaker beliefs. Thanks to Elizabeth his new awareness has taken hold. Stephen finally gives Sarah her due: "The look in her eyes wasn't hers. I had an uncanny feeling—it was very close to fear—that I was 'in the presence'—but of what? The what-ever-it-was behind Sarah's eyes looked out at me through them, as if through the eyeholes in a mask. And its look meant: Yes, I am always here" (*W,* 293). For Stephen, Sarah's eyes are the mirror in which he sees where he himself needs to go. Isherwood, since age eleven, had wanted to receive, and also to give, the sense of a presence to embrace him and for this same presence within him to have someone to embrace in return. Sarah is the Swami—the giver who is always there. Isherwood became the giver to Bachardy. Isherwood made Sarah a Quaker instead of a Vedantist because Quakers were more familiar to the general readership. Isherwood also believed that "the Society of Friends is . . . the Christian sect which comes closest to agreement with the teachings of Vedanta."[5]

The World in the Evening is not Isherwood's best work but is a prelude to his best. This novel is very important as a personal affirmation and, more importantly, as a public declaration by Isherwood at age fifty of three important parameters in his bigger picture: he restated his Vedantic beliefs as the means for his personal well-being; he asserted the rights of his tribe as part of these beliefs; he was in love for the last time.

The World in the Evening is transitional. It marks "An End" to the Isherwood who had been, to some extent, still trapped in his British past. He had even set *Prater Violet* in the Britain of 1933, even though it was a Vedantic parable about what he had learned in America. In the years from 1945 to 1954 he did not live at the temple, which had previously been his buffer and safety net, because he wanted to stand on his own. With great struggle he retained his inner awareness of "the presence" and began to distance himself, finally, from the pain originally engendered by his youthful feelings of rejection. Isherwood began this process in *Prater Violet,* but at that time, he had still been in the temple's womb-cocoon, leaning on the Swami. He continued the process in *The World in the Evening,* but did so without training wheels—unsteady—but on his own. The novels and plays before *Prater Violet* and *The World in the Evening* were about tearing down unbelief, but they offer no specific alternative beliefs to fill the void, although there were intuitive intimations that these beliefs would be metaphysical. The earlier works were about specific times and places—rungs of a ladder trying to look up at the big picture—but not quite seeing all of it. *Prater Violet* and *The World in the Evening* were "A Beginning" of how Isherwood's inner awareness as a Vedantist was also becoming his inner awareness as a writer. Each looked at specific years and places as incidents from which the hawk's vision suspended time while Isherwood oversaw the parts as links to a cosmic whole. He looked down from the top of the ladder and saw all the rungs inclusively as the bigger picture of total awareness. For the writer as Perennial Philosopher there are no parts—only the whole. This writer's vision is not linear but circular; he intuitively feels in the presence of the whole and fuses the parts as seamless lessons in a perpetual continuum that leads to transcendent knowledge. Isherwood's future work would be his best work. This author argues against the prevalent view of critics that Isherwood was principally a thirties writer, with the Berlin stories as his pinnacle. Isherwood's personal F6 was still in front of him. At age fifty—and looking forward to the the next twenty years—Isherwood was ready to come into his own in the decade that was made for him—the 1960s.

THE PAIN OF HUNGER BENEATH EVERYTHING:
DOWN THERE ON A VISIT

In his diary entry for 1 March 1955, Isherwood writes: "After Maria's funeral, I cried all the way to the studio, and I was really crying for myself." Isherwood was referring to Maria Huxley, who had died after a long bout with cancer that she had faced bravely. On 21 March 1955, Isherwood wrote that Heard recalled how Maria had said to him calmly: "I'm perfectly happy, except that I have a little cancer." Isherwood and many others had been very fond of her. For Aldous, she had been his manageress. Isherwood does not define his tears in the diary, perhaps feeling they were self-explanatory. For anyone, the death of a friend becomes another mirror for self-reflection, forcing one to ask himself, who am, I? whom ought I to become? Isherwood had cried for himself and for the recognition of all the different lives he had lived up to this point in time. Another question Isherwood may have asked himself, as did many who knew the Huxleys, was what will Aldous do? Maria had managed his life, leaving him more time to be brilliant, but also leaving him helpless in practical matters.[6]

In the later 1950s Isherwood decided his next book would revisit four of his own different past lives and how they had lead up to his present experience, which included Don Bachardy. Bachardy was a very typical young man with normal anxieties perhaps augmented by a troubled family situation and aggravated by being thirty years younger than his celebrity companion. Isherwood notes Bachardy's insecurity around Isherwood's friends—intellectuals and more celebrities—and was deeply sympathetic and empathetic. He was also certain that he could help Bachardy by assuming the tripartite responsibility of being the lover, friend, paternal-fraternal figure that Bachardy needed.[7] Isherwood saw in Bachardy much of himself as he had been many years before; consequently, he had a growing sense of an inner awareness that was increasingly taking a world view rather than just an Isherwood view. Isherwood began looking into life and its constituents as a mirror in which he saw his past lives looking back at him. These past lives represented a multiplicity of times, places, and disguises that were becoming integrated into a fluid tapestry from which he could observe certain details but not separately. Now the details comprising the bigger picture of his life were all of a piece, with no sense of before or after; the different strands of his past lives were woven together in a continuous and contiguous tapestry. The sensitive man has an inner awareness of himself and others; the Vedantic, Truly Strong Man has an inner awareness of himself, others, and their places in the perpetual continuum of evolving consciousness. This view of consciousness was confirmed every time the disciple saw his guru, the Swami.[8]

Another reminder of the totality of his life took place in September 1959 when Isherwood visited his mother: "Saying goodbye to M.—probably for the last time—didn't bother me much, because of course I won't admit it's the last time. I know I shall mind when she dies—more than I can imagine." The female relative—Kathleen—died on 15 June 1960, and Isherwood minded very much. She was gone, along with the burden of a past he had attributed to her. Both Isherwood and his mother were finally free of that past.

From this perspective Isherwood chose to write of past events for his next novel, *Down There on a Visit*. Even though they were not published in book form until 1961, Isherwood wrote the four sections of this novel in the latter half of the 1950s. These four sections signify the continuing advances of the maturing Isherwood, who had been developing his Vedantist-inspired world view in *Prater Violet* and *The World in the Evening*. In *Down There on a Visit* the continuity of his world view is the book's purposeful theme. On the dust-jacket blurb—which, according to Bachardy, Isherwood wrote himself—the plan is stated:[9]

> *Down There on a Visit* is a novel in four episodes. The "Visitor" who links them together speaks in the first person and is called by its author's name. But who, exactly is he? The twenty-three-year old Christopher Isherwood who visits Mr. Lancaster in Germany [in 1927] is not the same Christopher who spends the summer with Ambrose on his Greek island, five years later. A third and different Christopher witnesses the Munich crisis of 1938 in London with Dorothy and Waldemar. Yet another Christopher becomes involved with Paul in California, during the forties. And all these four Christophers are observed by a fifth, the middle-aged author.
>
> The words *Down There* refer to a nether world within the individual; a place of loneliness, alienation and hatred. Here are people shut up inside private hells of their own making, self-dedicated with a lifelong feud with The Others. The author laughs at and with them often, for even a private hell can be funny; but he cannot sneer at them, knowing how much they and he have in common. His visits to them are also visits to the *Down There* inside himself.

This summary indicates an intended circularity. The different Isherwoods of the past constitute the present author. A character named Waldemar (based on Heinz) appears in all four episodes, with his last appearance not until 1945. He links the four, indicating Isherwood's circular notion of continuity—with Waldemar he begins and with Waldemar he ends.

After his "interesting failure" with *The World in the Evening*, which was also about circularity, Isherwood decided that his next work would return to his strengths. He consulted his diaries and wrote about his own life again, changing all the names except his own. There would be no stilted dialogue made from whole cloth as in *World*, but reiterations of Wholly-Truthful conversations overheard at the tea-table. Isherwood would again take his particulars and make them universal. The four long short stories or short novellas seem almost a sequel to the sequence of *Goodbye to Berlin*. In a sense, they are a sequel, but feature even more insightful maturity and an even greater retrospective sympathy and empathy for his characters. Added to this is a deftly devastating sense of humor heretofore only hinted at in his fiction. Previously, Isherwood's satiric touch had mainly displayed itself in *Lions and Shadows*. In *Down There* Isherwood laughs warmly at the human comedy that is behind "the pain of hunger beneath everything." Nonetheless, he does not "sneer" at his characters or himself. Human nature is what it is and people cannot help themselves. Patience and understanding are required.

The first episode is about "Mr. Lancaster." Isherwood begins with a preface that can be applied to all four episodes:

> Now, at last, I'm ready to write about Mr. Lancaster. For years I had been meaning to, but only rather halfheartedly; I never felt I could quite do him justice. Now I see what my mistake was; I always used to think of him as an isolated character. Taken alone, he is less than himself. . . . I realize I must show how our meeting was the start of a new chapter in my life, indeed a whole series of chapters. And I must go on to describe the characters in those chapters. They are all, with one exception, strangers to Lancaster. (If he could have known what was to become of Waldemar, he would have cast him from the office in horror.) If he could ever have met Ambrose, or Geoffrey, or Maria, or Paul. . . . And yet, through me all these people are involved with each other, however much they might have hated to think so. And so they are all going to have to share the insult of each other's presence in this book. (*DV,* 11)

The plan of circularity is posited and Isherwood begins. He visits his cousin Lancaster in Germany. Lancaster is twenty six years older and the epitome of the stuffy, overbearing, condescending British gentleman whose attitude is one of a personal hand in managing the empire. Lancaster is the ultimately Mortmere-ish Other. Isherwood interrupts his flashback to become once again the "middle-aged author" interpreting himself. He does so in the same manner as Stephen Monk. All of the past is a tapestry to be seen simultaneously in a vision of total instantaneous awareness: "And now before I slip back into the convention of calling this young man "I," let me consider him as a separate being, a stranger almost. . . . he *is* almost a stranger to me. I have [in the middle-aged present] revised his opinions, changed his accent and his mannerisms, unlearned or exaggerated his prejudices and his habits. . . . I doubt he would recognize me on the street. We have in common the label of our name, and a continuity of consciousness; there has been no break in the daily sequence of I am I. But *what* I am has refashioned itself throughout the days and years, until now almost all that remains constant is the mere awareness of being conscious. And that awareness belongs to everybody; it isn't a particular person" (*DV,* 14). Yet this awareness, while belonging to everyone, is latent except to those who choose to uncover it and learn from it.

The middle-aged Isherwood looks back at the younger Isherwood, who seems almost a stranger: "I can only reconstruct him from his remembered acts and words from the writings he has left us. . . . I'll try not to apologize for him, either. After all, I owe him some respect. In a sense he is my father, and in another sense my son." In remembering his former self Isherwood included aspects both of himself and of Don Bachardy, showing sympathy for each. He said of his younger self that he was always "play acting" to hide his inexperience and insecurity. The older Self writes of his younger self: "He dreads the past—its prestige, its traditions, and their implied challenge and reproach. Perhaps his strongest negative motivation is ancestor hatred. . . . He is genuinely a rebel. He knows instinctively that it is only through rebellion that he will ever learn and grow" (DV, 14). Understanding the rebelliousness of his younger self, Isherwood was able to be more patient with Bachardy's own rebelliousness, considering it as part of a normal process of maturation, without which there might not be any maturation. Isherwood's sense of circularity is herein indicated. Past-present-future, father-son, are all interrelated in one integrated picture. They are not linear; that is an illusion. Isherwood of the present says of Isherwood of the past: "I will never apologize for him. I am proud to be his father and son. . . . I keep forgetting that he is as blind to his own future . . . as blind as I am to mine. His is an extraordinary future in many ways. . ." (DV, 15).

However, while in the past with Mr. Lancaster, that future could not yet be imagined and the young Isherwood could only be infuriated with his older cousin's bombastic pomposity that is matched by the man's homeliness: "I reminded myself with approval of one of my friend Hugh Weston's dicta: 'All ugly people are wicked'" (DV, 21). Lancaster's ego-bound insensitive condescension is such that when his younger cousin tells him that *All the Conspirators* is about to be published, Lancaster says that he should be sent a copy so that, he tells Isherwood, he can correct it for him.

Later, Isherwood sees himself in a restaurant mirror and thinks how "a mirror will seem to catch your image and hold it like a camera. Years later, you only have to think of that mirror in order to see yourself as you appeared in it then. You can even recall the feelings you had. . . . I see my twenty-three-year old face regarding me with large, reproachful eyes, from beneath a cowlick of streaky blond hair. A thin, strained face, so touchingly pretty that it might have been photographed and blown up for a big poster appealing on behalf of the world's young: 'The old hate us because we're so cute. Won't you help?'" (DV, 27).

When Lancaster tells Christopher to avoid Berlin because it is the new Sodom, Isherwood thinks: "I decided no matter how, I would get to Berlin just as soon as ever I could and that I would stay there a long, long time" (DV, 35). The older Isherwood explains that, even though it was a reverse motivation, seeing Lancaster helped him to make a decision that would later be life-changing. All things happen for a reason; but not all reasons necessarily have explanations in one's present or even in one's present lifetime.

Slowly the younger Isherwood as character and the older Isherwood as author realize that Lancaster, under his bombast, is merely human and that the bombast is a mask. After listening to some pontificating at dinner, Isherwood "realized the full beauty of this discovery. Mr. Lancaster had genuine delusions of grandeur"[10] (*DV,* 38). Lancaster goes on to talk about writing in a way that Isherwood acknowledges is not so foolish after all: "What I would do . . . is to write a series of stories which do not describe an emotion, but create it. . . . a story in which the word 'fear' is never mentioned and the emotion of fear is never described, but which *induces* fear in the reader. Can you imagine how terrible that fear would be?" (*DV,* 39). Isherwood's interest in his cousin is growing with a perverse fascination: "You had to study him like lessons. I actually made notes of his table talk" (*DV,* 40).

When Isherwood returns to London, he tells Chalmers about Lancaster but cannot quite get a handle on how to explain him: "I just did not have the key to him it seemed" (*DV,* 55). Later in talking to M. he gets the key that explains all. She tells him that Lancaster had been married very briefly, "but that his wife left him. . . . 'Because,' said my mother dryly, 'Cousin Alexander wasn't—so one was given to understand—at all adequate as a husband'" (*DV,* 55). Alexander's impotence is evidence that the public bombast is pathetic compensation for private failure. A few months later Lancaster kills himself. The middle-aged Isherwood looking back clearly understands why. The younger Isherwood did not quite get it at first: "I thought of it as an act of protest against society. I wanted to make a saga around Mr. Lancaster's protest. . . . But I couldn't. I didn't know how" (*DV,* 56). The younger Isherwood did not know how, because he had misunderstood the true cause of his cousin's despair and had not yet been quite ready to fully understand what the older Isherwood, now past Lancaster's age, grasped quite easily.

Isherwood learns from Waldemar, a former office worker of his cousin, that Lancaster "was really fond of you. He never had any son of his own, did he? Who knows, Christoph, if you'd been there to look after him, he might have been alive today" (*DV,* 57). The younger Isherwood thinks: "I see now that Mr. Lancaster's invitation to me was his last attempt to re-establish relations with the outside world. . . . Despair is something horribly simple. . . . Few of us can bear much pain of this kind and remain conscious. Most of the time, thank goodness, we suffer quite stupidly and unreflectingly, like the animals" (*DV,* 57). Or one could, as Isherwood had done, cry after a funeral. The younger Isherwood had been able to narrate his experiences with Lancaster, but the older Isherwood understood them.

"Ambrose" takes place five years later in 1933 and details Isherwood's adventures on a Greek isle with a seemingly batty Briton and an equally eccentric cast of supporting characters. One of them is Waldemar, who serves as the link in the overall narrative chain. Isherwood begins the narrative reminding readers that he is speaking from the vantage point of the middle-aged author surveying himself in retrospect: "I am on a train going south from Berlin. . . . What am I doing here? I suppose I could answer 'escaping from the Nazis'" (*DV,* 61). However, both the older and younger Isherwood realize this is a melodramatic pose that is "heartless and childish [because] on this very train there must be a few people in danger of their lives, traveling with false papers and in fear of being caught and sent to concentration camps or simply killed outright. . . . I have fully grasped that such a situation exists—not in a newspaper or novel—but where I have been living [in Berlin]" (*DV,* 61). Nonetheless, the middle-aged author confesses that the young Isherwood isn't escaping from danger; he is merely escaping into a frivolous vacation, and that this purpose supersedes all other political exigencies. The older Isherwood writes that his 1933 alter ego has changed little since his visit to Mr. Lancaster five years before (*DV,* 62).

In each episode Isherwood deals with one particular period but always drops in reminders that he is never looking at the four episodes as separate entities. He views them as parts of his particular whole; they were object lessons at their respective times that helped him become the persona of the middle-aged author. Isherwood believed that who he was in 1954, the father figure to Bachardy, was meant to be, and was set up by the awareness gained from his previous incarnations. Isherwood always characterized *Down There on a Visit* as a novel, even though it appears to be comprised of four distinct episodes. To him, they were not distinct. The mind that produced them did so from a Vedantic inner awareness, which reduced the concepts of separation, duality, and time to illusions: everything is integrated and, to invoke Huxley's title, *Time Must Have a Stop.* In *Down There* the continuity and contiguity of the author's integrated circular vision is what made this a novel and not anything else.

When Waldemar tells Christoph about late-night parties where gartered ladies "whip" their customers, Isherwood thinks: "Don't the S. A. boys do the exact same thing with their customers—except the whipping is in fatal earnest? Wasn't the one a kind of psychological dress rehearsal for the other?" (*DV,* 69). The 1933 Isherwood thinks of the serious complications fleetingly; he is really only concerned with his own good time. This search for the good time is the quality he loves most in Waldemar: "He has no conscience which forces him to take attitudes and hold opinions. . . . I love him—but somewhat as you love an animal" (*DV,* 70). When Isherwood arrives at the island and meets Ambrose, he writes that, despite his host's nervous ticks, "there was a kind of inner contemplative repose in the midst of him. It made him touchingly beautiful. He could have posed for the portrait of a saint" (*DV,* 71). Isherwood then realizes that he and Ambrose were at Cambridge together. When he tells Ambrose, his host reveals that he had known this all along and when Isherwood asks why he had not said so, Ambrose answers, "with touching sweetness. 'After all, lovey, I'm dead you aren't'" (*DV,* 75). Isherwood is puzzled by this remark but does not inquire of its meaning. He and readers will discover that this is a clue to Ambrose's self-perception, which is that of a refugee from England.

A guest named Geoffrey, a former old school heartie who is a younger version of the bombastic Lancaster, recounts to Isherwood a dangerous prank he had once enacted at school to get even with some Others (although he was an Other himself). Isherwood asks him why one would do such a thing. Geoffrey's convoluted answer amounts to his need to prove himself, thus showing him to have been Truly Weak. In his need to prove himself, he is like Gunn in *F6*. The incident seems to be the clue to Geoffrey's pugnacity, just as Lancaster's impotence was the clue to his particular belligerence.

Isherwood is linking his novel through the cyclical and circular patterns of human nature, revealing how individuals duplicate each other in terms of underlying psychological motivations. Geoffrey is another Lancaster. Moreover, the implied references to the Truly Weak Man contrast with the definition of the Truly Strong Man that Isherwood refers to later in this episode and features in the following episode.

Ambrose, as a fellow tribe-member and the leader of this island expedition, impresses Isherwood even while Isherwood is trying to act unimpressible: "Again and again he reminds me of one of Shakespeare's exiled kings; exiled, but by no means without hope. This is how Ambrose talks about his future kingdom":

> Of course, when we do get into power, we shall have to begin by reassuring everybody. We must make it clear that there will be absolutely no reprisals. Actually, they'll be amazed to find how tolerant we are. . . . I'm afraid we shan't be able to make heterosexuality actually legal, at first—there'd be too much of an outcry. One'll have to let twenty years go by, until all the resentment has died down. But meanwhile it'll be winked at, of course, as long as it's practiced in decent privacy. I think we shall even allow a few bars to be opened for people with those unfortunate tendencies. . . . They'll have to be clearly marked, with police there to warn foreigners what kind of places these are—just so no one will find himself there by mistake and see something that might upset him. Naturally, from time to time some tourist with weak nerves may have to be rushed to the hospital, suffering from shock. We'll have a psychologist on hand to explain to him that people like that do exist, through no fault of their own, and that we must feel sympathy for them and try to find scientific ways of reconditioning them. . . . What most people don't realize is that, when we take over, women will be much better off than they are now. (*DV,* 100)

Behind the satire Ambrose is bitterly sarcastic. When he says that the homosexual tribe would be more tolerant of heterosexuals, he does so with tongue deeply set in cheek. Nonetheless, even though Ambrose may not be altogether sincere about his tolerance, Isherwood implies that a persecuted minority understands what it means to be persecuted and has sympathy for other minorities. Throughout *Down There on a Visit* the references to homosexuality are made with an affectionately realistic banter that ultimately renders them more effective than the less convincing dialogues in *The World in the Evening*. The above passage must have been thoroughly enjoyed by fellow tribe members.

Isherwood makes note of Ambrose's compulsive fastidiousness—it took one to know one: "Ambrose's obstinacy is chiefly expressed by his absolute demand for politeness. He demands it heroically, without the least fear of the consequences. He refuses to be threatened or bullied in any way. If you want him to give you money, you must ask for it nicely or else beat him into unconsciousness and then pick his pocket. One would think it was never too much trouble to say please. But unfortunately, Ambrose is trying to impose his demand on the sort of men and boys who frequent the toughest bars and roughest parts of town" (*DV*, 102). Isherwood admires this heroic trait for its adherence to some standard of civility in a world that is not inclined to be civil. At the bottom of this quest for civility is a corresponding desire to retain, outside of England, the British stiff upper lip that once had meaning back home, but now only masks the vicious hypocrisy Ambrose had encountered at Cambridge, which caused him to flee England. Ambrose explains to Isherwood that at Cambridge he had played the game of fitting into the Poshocracy and he thought he had been accepted by them. He soon learned he had been "living in a fool's paradise and how obscene people are below the surface. They pretend to be so nice and friendly. And all the time, they're *swine-swine*— and how they *hate, hate, hate* everything they don't understand [meaning homosexuals]" (*DV*, 112). The Cambridge incident that brought Ambrose to this bitterness was a complete thrashing of his room by hearties: "They'd even found my little egg-cup that I loved so. It was a present on my fourth birthday; and I kept it hidden away . . . [and] loved it all the more because nobody but me ever saw it. Well, they'd taken it out—this little bit of my childhood—and they'd smashed it. How could they have known that I'd mind that most of all" (*DV*, 112). As with Lancaster, Ambrose had his secret horror that had pushed its way to the surface as eccentric behavioral symptoms.

Just before Isherwood leaves this Greek isle to return to England, he expresses to Ambrose his admiration for him: "You know, I've learned so many things, just by being here with you. I think you're the first person I've ever met who really understands what it's all about. . . . You've made me see how ghastly England is" (*DV*, 133). Ambrose, to his credit, takes no credit, realizing that what Isherwood is misguidedly admiring is nothing more than the nihilistic despair of a man who believes he has no home where home used to be.

The first two episodes of the novel reiterate feelings that Isherwood had during the time the actual events took place. These feelings are also reinterpreted by the middle-aged author who is using this novel to better understand his past in terms of how that past led to the present. The next two episodes continue this process. Unlike the writing of *The World in the Evening* that had been difficult for him, Isherwood had much more confidence in *Down There*. In his diary entry for 4 September 1957, he writes: "My novel is very interesting to me. . . . Something is alive. I'm down near the nerve—as I *never* was in World." His approach is to portray the previous Isherwoods as outsiders looking in at the world, and they only appear to be amenable joiners regardless of how well they act the part. The 12 October 1956 entry reads: ". . . as far as I'm concerned, I not only take it for granted that I'm an Outsider but I am really only interested in modern books if they are written from an Outsider's point of view. An Outsider but not a No Sider. I'm not interested in tales of fey folks who live in trees. The Outsider stands outside the modern conformist world, looking in—but with passion, with sincere involvement, with heartfelt hostility." For *Down There on a Visit* the middle-aged author becomes the Outsider looking in at four versions of his previous self.

"Waldemar" is set in 1938 England and begins with that year's version of Isherwood analyzing himself and his relations to Britain. Of The Others, he says—in a sentiment that recalls Ambrose—"If you have any criticism, they have one unanswerable answer: you can stay off our island" (*DV,* 139). This was exactly what Ambrose and Isherwood had chosen to do in 1933. Isherwood wonders why he has bothered to return to England at all: "I was just passively spinning back on the return arc, like a boomerang. Who throws me? I don't know, and I'm not really interested in finding out or am I afraid to? I refuse to answer that question. All I'll tell you is, I'm spinning" (*DV,* 140).

The boomerang metaphor is apt for this book's circular intent. The younger Isherwood said: "Who throws me?" In 1938, he knew enough to ask the question, if not enough to answer it. The older, Vedantist Isherwood had a much better idea of who had "thrown" the younger one and understood that a boomerang always came back to its origin—the Self—to find inner truth.

The 1938 Isherwood wonders how he appears to his friends: "To judge from the jokes they make about me, they see a rather complex creature, part despot, part diplomat. I'm told I hold myself like a drill sergeant or a strict little landlady; I am supposed to have an overpowering will. Hugh Weston compared it once to a fire hose before which everybody has to retreat. Then again they say I'm so sly; I pretend to be nobody in particular, just one of the gang, when all the time I have the arrogance of Lawrence of Arabia and the subtlety of Tallyrand. Oh, yes—and I'm utterly ruthless and completely cynical. But I do make them laugh" (*DV,* 140).

This is a cynical self-appraisal and the older Isherwood is reminding the reader of the point of view that the younger version brought to all his interactions with the world and the people in it. During the writing of this novel, Isherwood's diaries are filled with references to Bachardy's difficulties as a typical young man adjusting to life as a responsible adult. There are passages describing an angst-filled Bachardy that sound like descriptions of the younger Isherwood. Bachardy was a mirror in which the older Isherwood saw the younger Isherwood as he had been years before.

The 1938 Isherwood, after describing himself, wonders what his personality is a reaction to, and why he takes the trouble to play the roles The Others expect of him: "I suppose the answer is, *I do it to prove I can play their game.* Whose game? The Others' Game. The game for which the rules have been made by The Others. And The Others are all the headmasters of the schools I went to, all the clergymen I have ever known, all reactionary politicians, newspapers, editors, journalists, and most women over forty. Ever since I've been able to talk and read they have been telling me the rules of their game" (*DV,* 141–42). The 1938 Isherwood is the one who has just written *Lions and Shadows.* In this episode the Truly Strong Man would be defined again, just as he had been thirty years before, but for a new generation of the 1960s that was more attuned to recognizing him.

Isherwood's 1938 narrative concerns an old Berlin friend, Dorothy, who is trying to get her German lover into England to escape conscription back home. The lover turns out to be Isherwood's even older friend, Waldemar. Dorothy and Waldemar are based on Isherwood and Heinz, and what follows is their story. When Dorothy and Waldemar attempt to get past customs, discrepancies in his and her stories prevent the officials from giving him any more than a month's stay. Isherwood thinks: "What on earth is going to become of them. . . . And for that matter, what at the end of this *jour sans lendemain* (day without tomorrow), was going to become of us all?" (*DV,* 160).

The term "day without tomorrow" in this context is seen as threatening. The later Isherwood knew otherwise, having learned that the Ultimate Reality exists in an eternal now so that the eternal day has neither a tomorrow, nor a yesterday. The Vedantic Day is circular, an "Is-ness" without beginning or end. The 1938 Isherwood ruminates on his place in the world. He has just returned from his role as a "war correspondent" in China. Isherwood contemplates the differences between the illusion of abstract slogans and the reality of an actual war: "all that seems vivid and poignant is the tragedy of minor actors; the early teen-age conscripts in the trenches, the civilian corpses after an air raid pitted with gravel and sand from the blasts. They make the slogans seem heartless and vile. And yet I still slip into slogan language when I write, and I talk it quite shamelessly on the lecture platform, where I strut . . . playing the hero—for the benefit of anyone attractive who may happen to be in the audience" (*DV,* 161). His thought of "playing the hero" moves him to consider who the real heroes are:

> WHEN the [British] newspapers compare Chamberlain to Abe Lincoln and Jesus Christ, they aren't being in the least sacrilegious, because *their* Lincoln and *their* Christ are utter phonies. . . . The newspapers are moved to tears by the spectacle of

a gentleman standing his ground against a non-gentleman [Hitler]. So they call him "England."

Well, *my* "England" is E. M. [Forster]; the anti heroic hero, with his straggly straw moustache, his light, gay, baby blue eyes and his elderly stoop. Instead of a folded umbrella or a brown uniform, his emblems are a tweed cap (which is too small for him) and the odd-shaped brown paper parcels in which he carries his belongings from country to town and back again. While the others tell their followers to be ready to die, he advises us to live as if we were immortal. And he really does this himself, although he is as anxious and afraid as any of us, and never for an instant pretends not to be. He and his books and what they stand for are all that is truly worth saving from Hitler; and the vast majority of people on this island aren't even aware that he exists (*DV,* 162).

. . . he's far saner than anyone else I know. And immensely, superhumanly strong. He's strong because he doesn't try to be a stiff-lipped stoic like the rest of us, and so he'll never crack. He's absolutely flexible. He lives by love, not by will. (*DV,* 175)

For his new generation of readers Isherwood defines the true hero as the antihero who is pure in heart, Truly Strong, and perhaps not coincidentally a member of his tribe.

While the 1938 Isherwood and his fellow Britons are being fitted for gas masks, he realizes that he is "one of the relatively few people in this city [London] who have been in a modern air raid [in China]." He reminds himself that he "wasn't too frightened then, and I kept assuring my friends (and myself) that we would probably have lots of excitement and even fun— including shelter parties and sex pick-ups in the blackout" (*DV,* 181–82). Right after this, however, he puts matters into a more serious perspective: "I have made another discovery about myself, and I don't care if it's humiliating or not. I am quite certain of this now: as far as I am concerned, nothing, nothing, nothing is worth a war" (*DV,* 184).

In this episode the older Isherwood chooses not to deal with himself and Heinz directly, even though losing Heinz to deportation may have been the single most distressing and influential event in his adult life. For years afterwards diary entries confirm his sense of loss and guilt, which was not assuaged until after the war when he learned that Heinz had not only survived but held no grudge. Perhaps Isherwood had known it would be too painful to tell the complete truth and that it might have affected how he told that truth. It is also possible that, at the time, he was being sensitive to Bachardy, still young, and possibly not yet ready to hear about the previous great love of his partner's life.

The last episode is about Paul and Augustus Parr (who is based on Gerald Heard). It takes place during Isherwood's early years in America. Paul is a famous— at least among the tribe—bisexual hustler who has decided to come down to earth in California. His previous extravagance of lifestyle and personal joie de vivre befit the definition of High Camp put forth in *World.*

A mutual acquaintance of Paul and Isherwood is Ruthie, whom Isherwood describes as "an animal person; she has that cozy quality of a subhuman and therefore guileless creature, she might just have emerged from a warm burrow under a hill" (*DV*, 195). Once again Isherwood refers to a person's "animal" qualities in a way that is obscurely positive. He uses the term for people who react with intuitive feeling, which he considers superior to intellectual reasoning. Is Isherwood being positive? No one was held in greater esteem by Isherwood than the Swami. The 17 February 1957 entry to his diary reads: "He was like a small adorable animal with ruffled fur as he sat on his bed telling us about the early days at the monastery. I don't feel he is altogether a person, any longer. This light seems to flood through him more and more continuously." Isherwood, who had often reproached himself for over-thinking and over-reacting, put great faith in those who felt more and thought less. As Lao Tzu said, "The way to do is to be."

Paul is one who *does*. He seems to react to stimuli like a flower, and bend to whatever direction the light comes from. Paul delivers himself to Isherwood, burnt out from his hell-bent hustling days and in need of some form of psychic repose. From what Isherwood tells him Paul thinks he might be able to find it in Augustus Parr, a former Briton like Isherwood and a neo-yogi who is under a Swami's tutelage. Isherwood is making lots of money as a screenwriter, which ironically comes at a time when he is in a Vedanta-inspired mood of renunciation. He had just renounced his inheritance in favor of his younger brother Richard and denounces the Hollywood money that, perhaps just a year before, he would have welcomed enthusiastically. In this narrative Isherwood thinks aloud about his conversion to Vedanta and writes almost verbatim from his diary the passage about not being able to press the button that might kill Heinz.

Isherwood's pacifism is given a philosophical basis by Parr, whose conversations, as tea-tabled by Isherwood, are affectionately recalled as perhaps long-winded but never less than delightful and illuminating: "How lovable he is. What was most lovable in Augustus was his fearless eagerness" (*DV*, 227). Paul hints at a need for Parr's teachings but cannot resist acting cynical about them. Isherwood defends Parr, his friend and teacher, unaware that Paul is testing him and the degree of his conviction, which Paul desperately wants to share. Paul is like Sally Bowles. He wants to test by shocking. Isherwood, as he had done with Sally (and Bernhard Landauer), does not stand for it: "Ever since we've met, you've been trying every which way to impress me. And every new stunt you try is more idiotic than the last. We're all supposed to fall down on our asses with amazement because you're such a devilishly wicked Dorian Gray" (*DV*, 229). The 1940 Isherwood, the person who provided the definition of a vainglorious Truly Weak Man in *Lions and Shadows*, knew one when he saw one. From this truthful bloodletting, a truce is formed. Both Isherwood and Paul have passed the Test and now respect each other.

Isherwood takes Paul into his home and to Augustus, who says of those in spiritual need: "This is the middle world—we must never forget that. The world that my uncle [a clergyman] called hell—which perhaps isn't after all such an inept name for a state which is probably very much more acutely unpleasant, even if temporary, than we moderns are willing to admit—and what my uncle used to call heaven, imagining a kind of Gustave Dore paradise which would no doubt seem like an absurd picture post card you bought on Brighton pier beside that appalling instantaneity of awareness which the Vedas speak of. *Every* moment is eternity. And at *any* given moment we can break through the web of time. There are three kinds of bondage . . . addiction, pretention, aversion. . . . One's never safe. One's got to be on one's guard every instant. Unwavering recollectedness, unwavering awareness. . ." (*DV,* 229–30). What Parr intimates by "unwavering awareness" is the Vedantic version of the Watcher in Spanish.

Through Parr, Isherwood is moving into the purpose of this episodic novel. Since "*every* moment is eternity," and time stops, these four episodes occur simultaneously in the author's mind and in the world mind of evolving consciousness. The four different Isherwoods are not different at all. The reader is meant to envision them on a four-cornered screen, seeing them all at the same time. Isherwood applies this view to himself and Parr applies it to Paul, of whom he says: ". . . he can't retreat any farther. He *must* advance, in one way or another. Have you looked into his face Christopher? There's a very curious expression in his eyes—you see it sometimes in wild animals at bay. But one also saw something else . . . despair. Not helpless, negative despair. Dynamic despair. The kind that makes dangerous criminals, and very occasionally, saints" (*DV,* 237).

On this note Isherwood decides Paul is to be his project for a mutual redemption and resurrection. Together they will break their bondage from the past. Isherwood, as a gesture to prove to Paul his sincere intentions, gives Paul half of his Hollywood-earned income—ten-thousand dollars. The older Isherwood admits that the younger Isherwood did so to prove that he could act upon the spirit of Vedantic renunciation—and compensate for his guilt over Heinz.

The 1940 Isherwood also writes: "Our friendship was of the sort which naturally evolves its own private jargon; ours was made up principally of misapplications of Augustus's favorite phrases. If we were late for a date . . . Paul might exclaim, 'Boy, we'd better get over there with appalling instantaneity!' Hunting for the can opener . . . I would tell him, 'I'm so near this thing which is so far from me'" (*DV,* 255).

Paul and Christopher are at a camp training to be conscientious objectors for the forestry service. Paul is thought by The Others to have seriously lapsed by having sex with an underage girl. He neither confirms nor denies this charge, amid a great outcry from those who had trusted him. It turns out that the girl's jealous sister had made a false accusation. The damage is done. Paul feels that he cannot escape his past reputation. Later there is a forest fire and Paul's cool head saves himself and two younger foresters. Christopher is proud of him, especially since he and Paul are members of their own tribe, which could now refute The Others who had accused Paul. Life intervenes so that Paul and Isherwood must go their separate ways. One door closes, another opens, and the circle continues.

In 1945 Isherwood receives a letter from Waldemar, who is alive and well. Isherwood's great guilt is overcome, especially when he hears that Waldemar is happily married and has a son named Christoph. This is indeed a resurrection. Conversely, in 1946 Isherwood receives a letter from Paul saying that he is returning to Europe: "You are the only person I have to talk to about it, because you are my sweet baby and you always stood by me" (*DV,* 306). Paul's resurrection has stalled. In 1952 Isherwood learns that Paul died of a heart attack brought on by drug use.

Waldemar survived; Paul did not—at least as perceived in the material world. Paul's place in the bigger picture is another matter—one without definition. This episode is in part about karma, actions bringing about reactions. For seven years Isherwood was guilt-ridden about Heinz, especially since he had not known his fate. Motivated by his pacifism, which had been motivated by Heinz, Isherwood became a Vedantist and made every effort to help Paul. One might think that, in material terms, Isherwood did not succeed with Paul, but in the balance of karma, no actions are without consequence. Isherwood's good will tipped some cosmic scale so even if it seems that he had not been able to help Paul—and that is not for mortals to judge—somehow his effort had helped him atone for Heinz. 1952 was the year before Isherwood met Bachardy. The implication is that one cycle around the circle had been fulfilled, so that the next cycle could begin.

Down There on a Visit is filled with caustic wit and insight. The novel is another parable about Vedantic cycles. Quietly, during the late 1940s and all of the 1950s, Isherwood had been moving towards a very productive 1960s. In the American years before 1961 he had become a friend and de facto influence to many young writers personally, and to many more by reputation. Among the former were Gore Vidal, Gavin Lambert, William Goyen, and among the latter, Reynolds Price, who as a Rhodes scholar at Oxford in the mid-1950s had both Spender and Auden as teachers and now has a picture of them with Isherwood in his study. In the 1960s Isherwood's influence would have a more profound impact when minorities of all tribes asserted their pride and when Eastern mysticism became au courant again. Isherwood was ready to become a tribal icon.

JOUR SANS LENDEMAIN: *A SINGLE MAN*

Down There on a Visit has four episodes that span a period of twenty-four years from 1928 to 1952, when Isherwood learns of Paul's death. Isherwood's next novel, *A Single Man* (1964)—with a title supplied by Bachardy and a dedication to Gore Vidal—covers twenty-four hours and a death precedes the action of the novel. *A Single Man's* compressed time span and focus on George, the single man, seem a radical departure from *Down There,* in which the four episodes are named after four different people. In *Down There* one might think that Isherwood's purpose is to have readers learn about these four individuals. The reader does learn about them but not as ends in themselves. Isherwood reacts to these four people and the reader learns more about Isherwood from his reactions. The characters are a means to this end. Isherwood's real purpose is to explain how his experiences with these people lead to the book's truly dominating persona—the middle-aged author. This persona is off-stage for *Down There on a Visit,* but he becomes the centerpiece of *A Single Man.* On first impression *A Single Man* seems very different than *Down There,* but it is in fact a thematic sequel to it. Isherwood's dust-jacket text states his intentions:

> A single man awakes at the beginning of the novel, sleeps at the end of it. . . . A human presence, *now*—and, through the focus of *now,* back through the years—is made so physically, emotionally, and morally palpable, that the reader has the sense of touching not only another's life but his own.
>
> The single man is middle-aged, an expatriate, an Englishman, a professor of English in a California university. He is a man of intellect and humor, impassioned, gentle, with a benign sense of mischief, an enjoyer and a pessimist. Consumed with grief over the recent death of young man he has lived with, he resolutely persists in the routine of his daily life.
>
> The novel follows him. . . . the alien young neighbors whose attempts at friendliness merely underline his loneliness . . . a roomful of students reacting with serious and respectful imbecility to his lecture on the modern novel, the drunken dinner with a lonely Englishwoman who tempts him with a sentimental vision of England as *home,* the unexpected exhilaration and melancholy of an encounter with one of his students at a waterfront bar. . . .
>
> *A Single Man* is a book about the moment and the act of living. It is . . . about the inescapable loneliness that can be breached only—if at all—by love. It is a portrayal of middle-age, seen as the most protean of all phases of human life—a phase in which one may think and behave like a baby, a wild adolescent, a mature man, a dotard, a madman, all within a few hours.

The figure of the middle-aged English professor of *A Single Man* picks up where *Down There on a Visit* leaves off. *Down There* ends with the death of Paul; *A Single Man* begins with the knowledge that Jim, George's lover, died in an accident shortly before this novel's twenty-four hours begin. *Down There*'s four episodes span twenty-four years; *A Single Man* spans twenty-four hours. For Isherwood there is no metaphysical difference between years or hours: "*Every* moment is eternity," as Parr said. Evolving consciousness exists in a single cosmic moment and the Truly Strong Man is able to see the world and his place in it from this vantage point.

Willa Cather, an author Isherwood admired and was reading during the writing of *A Single Man,* expresses this idea in her 1927 novel *Death Comes for the Archbishop* when Father Latour is near death:

He observed that there was no longer any perspective in his memories. He remembered his winters with his cousins on the Mediterranean when he was a little boy, his student days in the Holy City, as clearly as he remembered the arrival of M. Molny and the building of his cathedral. He was soon to have done with calendared time, and it had already ceased to count for him. He sat in the middle of his own consciousness; none of his former states of mind were lost or outgrown. They were all within reach of his hand, and all comprehensible.

Sometimes, when [others] asked him a question, it took him several seconds to bring himself back to the present. He could see they thought his mind was failing; but it was extraordinarily active in some other part of the great picture of his life. . . .[11]

In *A Single Man*, George, motivated by Jim's passing, takes the same view as Father Latour. Reflecting Isherwood's own attitude, George starts from the inset picture of one day and sends the images and sound waves of that day in all directions—past, present, future—until they rebound and return to him, just like that boomerang Isherwood compared himself to in *Down There*. For the single day of *A Single Man* George is the hub of Vedanta's Burning Wheel of existence—all flows through him, then emanates from him, resonating in the universe to factor into the perpetual continuum of which he is integrally related. Isherwood the Vedantist believed that human devised constructs of duality and time do not actually exist; there is no separation from, nor distinction between, twenty-four hours or twenty-four years. The method in *Down There* is to observe the four past Isherwoods, just as Father Latour views all of his life as one landscape. George's reverse process turns the microcosm of his one day into the macrocosm of all his days. Both books are flip sides of the same coin: each is about continuity, contiguity, and Heard's "instantaneity" of simultaneous awareness. Interpreted from this Vedantic perspective, these two novels are parts one and two of a single novel, changed only by point of view. In *Down There* the middle-aged author is the somewhat objective interpreter of four different subjective Isherwoods; in *A Single Man*, middle-aged George is the subjective interpreter of himself and the characters he encounters.

In *The World in the Evening* the dialogue is sometimes wooden because Isherwood tries to put words into the mouths of characters who had no basis in his real life. In *Down There on a Visit* the dialogue is witty, incisive, and believable because it comes out of the mouths of people Isherwood actually knew. They were either different versions of himself or real people he portrayed fictionally. Their words either came from his diaries or represent words that these personas would likely say. *A Single Man* connects George with Isherwood, since many of George's thoughts come out of the diaries; however, the other characters—Kenny, Charlotte, Doris, Mrs. Strunk—appear to be purely imaginative creations without real antecedents. Or are they?

In *Down There* the author interprets four previous Isherwoods by showing how each one interacts with different characters. Isherwood compresses this technique in *A Single Man*. George has dialogues with composites of people Isherwood has known; he does so in the guises of the novel's other characters. Under their various masks, these characters are having metaphysical discussions with the middle-aged Isherwood. The dialogues in *A Single Man* are equally realistic because Isherwood is acting out all the parts. Isherwood makes this very clear when George has a drunken night out with his student, Kenny. The omniscient narrator describes what George thinks while interacting with Kenny:

> He tries to describe to himself what this kind of drunkenness is like. . . . it's like Plato; it's a dialogue. A dialogue between two people. Yes, but not a Platonic dialogue in the hair-splitting, word-twisting, one-up-to-me-sense; not a mock-humble bitching match; not a debate. . . . In fact, what really matters is not what you talk about, but the being together in this particular relationship. . . . You and your dialogue-partner have to be somehow opposites. Why? Because you have to be symbolic figures—like, in this case, Youth and Age. It's a symbolic encounter. It doesn't involve either party personally. That's why, in a dialogue, you can say absolutely anything . . . the deadliest secret comes out objectively as a mere metaphor or illustration which could never be used against you. . . . more than anything George wants Kenny to understand, wants to be able to believe that Kenny knows what this dialogue is all about. . . . it seems possible that Kenny *does* know. George can almost feel the electric field of the dialogue surrounding and irradiating them. *He* certainly feels irradiated. As for Kenny, he looks quite beautiful. *Radiant with rapport* is the phrase which George finds to describe him. (*SM*, 154–55)

Kenny looks beautiful, as did the young Isherwood who saw himself in the mirror in "Mr. Lancaster." Kenny also looks beautiful, as did Don Bachardy, with whom Isherwood also felt "Radiant with rapport." When Isherwood saw Bachardy, he saw himself as he had been many years before. He also saw that every young man—the previous Isherwood or the Bachardy of 1953 or the Kenny of 1962—has to learn about life as one new Adam at a time.

Kenny represents a younger Isherwood. Kenny is also a Vedantic opposite needing to be reconciled through the "Platonic dialogue." Kenny says he has little use for the past. George responds:

> "you've got the present."
> "Oh, but the present's a real drag."
> "Okay," says George. "The past—no help. The present—no good. . . . you're stuck with the future . . . the future—that's where death is." (*SM*, 156)

The discussion continues with Kenny asking George if there is any benefit to gaining experience:

> "For other people, I can't speak—but personally, I haven't gotten wise on anything.
> Certainly, I've been through this and that; and when it happens again, I say to

myself, Here it is again. But that doesn't seem to help me. In my opinion, I, personally, have gotten sillier and sillier and sillier—and that's a fact."

"I'll be darned. Then experience is no use at all? You're saying it just as well not
have happened?"

"No. I'm not saying that. I only mean, you can't *use* it. But if you don't try to—
if you just realize it's there and you've got it—then it can be marvelous." (*SM,* 160)

George (and, by extension, Isherwood himself) does not mean that one does not
benefit from experience, but that one cannot always look at experiences clinically
and think, "Because this has happened, now I know what life means." In *Goodbye
to Berlin* Isherwood's camera eye does not think while it observes, but it does feel.
Sally does not change her ways after her abortion because she is not ready to learn
from her experiences. The beginning of wisdom comes from the incremental, cumu-
lative reactions that fill the interstices of knowledge very slowly after many years.
One cannot say how one event—no matter how traumatic—changes one directly at
the time it takes place; one may not even be able to say it with certainty even after
many years. One can only know that in ways too mysterious to delineate, knowledge does come, but it cannot be forced upon someone who is not ready for it.
Consequently, what Isherwood (in the fictional guise of George) is really trying to
suggest to Kenny is, "The way to do is to be." *A Single Man* is about being and consciousness. The particular body that happens to be carrying that consciousness
around is George, yet, George's consciousness also resonates with universal
identification for the reader.

When the narrative begins, George's body

has awoken and then lies for a while staring up at the ceiling and down on top itself
until it has recognized *I.* . . . Then to the mirror. What it sees there isn't so much
a face as a predicament. Here's what it has done to itself, here's the mess it has somehow managed to get itself into during its fifty-eight years. . . . Staring and staring
into the mirror, it sees many faces within its face—the face of a child, the boy, the
young man, the not-so-young man—all present still, preserved like fossils on
superimposed layers, and, like fossils, dead. Their message to this live dying creature is: Look at us—we have died—what is there to be afraid of?

It answers them: But that happened so gradually, so easily. *I'm afraid of being
rushed.*

[George's body] is going outside, into the world of the other people. . . . Its
behavior must be acceptable to them.

It knows its name. It is called George. (*SM,* 9–11)

The body does not seem real. In a sense, it does not belong to George; rather, it
seems to belong more to the world of The Others who see George's body much more
than it sees itself. All that it can claim to have independent of the body or of The
Others who look at it is consciousness. This consciousness is principally aware of one

fact: "Jim is dead. Is dead" (*SM*, 13). This is the input that overwhelms George's consciousness in every waking moment and forms the umbrella that all other information crowds itself under with obtrusive rudeness. It is 1962. George cannot yet say openly that his male lover is dead and be allowed to grieve openly. Since George is British, his stiff upper lip is a conditioned non-response to his grief, even though he knows that this particular reaction is a fool's mask. George goes through his own emotional autobiography in terms of psychological parable. In Arlin Turner's biography of Hawthorne, Turner said of his subject's fiction: "He is the most autobiographical of our writers—in his particular way."[12] The dash implies volumes and the same could be said of Isherwood, who uses George in part as a means of conveying his own deep-seated emotions.

In the diaries Isherwood writes of the noisy children he chases away from his home because they disturb both his writing and his serenity. George does the same and is sure they consider him a monster. In his next sentence George also imagines that the father of the children, Mr. Strunk,

> tries to nail him down with a word. Queer. . . .13 But since this is after all the year 1962, even he [Strunk] may be expected to add, I don't give a damn what he does just as long as he stays away from me. . . . But Mrs. Strunk . . . is trained in the new tolerance, the technique of annihilation by blandness. Out comes her psychology book. . . .
>
> All is due to heredity, early environment (Shame on those possessive mothers, those sex-segregated British schools!) arrested development at puberty, and/or glands. Here we have a misfit, debarred forever from the best things of life, to be pitied, not blamed. Some cases, caught young enough, *may* respond to therapy. As for the rest—ah, it's so sad; especially when it happens . . . to truly worthwhile people. . . . (Even when they are geniuses in spite of it, their masterpieces are invariably *warped*.) So let us be understanding . . . there were the Greeks. . . . Let us go so far as to say that this kind of relationship can sometimes be beautiful—particularly if one of the parties is already dead. (*SM*, 27–28)

George is angry and bitter that people like the Strunks would allow Jim to be dead, but not allow George to grieve for him. When George imagines Mr. Strunk nailing him down with the word queer, he imagines Strunk sneering the word in its bigoted American context rather than how it is used more benignly in Britain. This commentary by George is the flip-side version of the declaration that Ambrose made when he described how it would be when the tribe took over. Ambrose had been satirically—and bitterly—rebutting the attitudes of The Others, such as the hearties who had trashed his room at Cambridge. George gives his own tacit rebuttal to the Strunks, which is first prefaced by the reader's knowledge that George has not told his neighbors that Jim is dead, but that Jim is just away. He does not want their textbook pity: "But your book is wrong Mrs. Strunk, says George, when it tells you that

Jim is a substitute I found for a real son, a real kid brother, a real husband, a real wife. Jim wasn't a substitute for anything. And there is no substitute for Jim . . . anywhere" (*SM*, 29).

Many of the episodes are very short—snapshots going by quickly just as one looks at a stack of photographs. They are flash cards of mental pictures that pop in and out of the daily routine. They interrupt the mundane tasks, like George's drive to work. George turns his daily drive on the freeway into an imaginative exercise by looking at other drivers and thinking: *"Idiots—fooled them again"* (*SM*, 33). George tells Kenny in the bar that he, George, could sometimes be very silly—just like anyone else. George even has a recurring Mortmere fantasy starring his alter ego "Uncle George," who would, as the leader of his tribe, exact revenge on The Others with murderous glee (*SM*, 38–39).

George has a long rumination about minorities. His particular minority is linked to other minorities by their common enemy—The Others. For Isherwood, minorities can be glorious, as a concept. It is from minority groups— and highbrows are a minority as well—that the diversity which fuels the evolution of consciousness comes from. Without the contention that comes from diversity—hopefully contention in the form of Isherwood's neo-Platonic dialogues—life would be boring and progress nil. On this subject, Kenny tells George in the bar: "'What's so phony these days is all this familiarity. Pretending there isn't any difference between people—well, like you were saying about minorities, this morning [in class]. If you and I are no different, what do we have to give each other? How can we ever be friends?'" And George, delighted, thinks: 'He *does* understand'" (*SM*, 158). To George minorities "are not The Enemy. If they would ever accept George, they might even be allies. They never figure in the Uncle George fantasies" (*SM*, 42).

Life for George is acting, which he does with suitably adjusted nuances and facile smiles for different people and different situations. Behind this acting is the real George—Uncle George—who is metaphorically blowing up The Others, just as Isherwood had done at Cambridge. George wonders what people think of him, just as Isherwood wondered the same thing in *Down There on a Visit*. George wonders if The Others can see through the acting and know that he is homosexual: "Does he know about me? . . . do any of them? Oh, yes probably. It wouldn't interest them. They don't want to know about my feelings, or my glands or anything below my neck. I could just as well be a severed head carried into the classroom to lecture them from a dish" (*SM*, 51). In his play-acting, George refers to himself as a "talking head" (*SM*, 54). When George passes a tennis court, he observes a match between two student-aged young men "stripped nearly naked" (*SM*, 52). One is Mexican and George tacitly roots for him. In class George discusses Huxley's 1939 novel *After Many a Summer Dies the Swan*. Isherwood did teach this book in a college class and draws deftly with great humor from his experience. In this sequence the reader first hears of Kenny: "George suspects Kenny of understanding the innermost meaning of life—of being, in fact, some sort of genius (though you would certainly never guess this from his term papers)" (*SM*, 60). Nor would have anyone suspected Isherwood of any genius when he camped his exams at Cambridge. Kenny always calls George "Sir" to be facilely charming, as the younger Isherwood would have been to certain Others, like his Uncle Henry.

George thinks about Grant Lefanu, "a young physics professor who writes poetry. . . . George rather loves him" (*SM*, 84). This is because Lefanu is a shy radical who quietly stands up for what he believes is right. For example, Grant is a "defense witness for a bookseller caught peddling some grand old sex classic . . . fighting for its right to be devoured by American youth. . . . Grant's heroism on this occasion consisted of his defense of the book at the risk of his academic neck"[14] (*SM*, 85). George is flattered by being included in Grant's confidence as someone who shares his radical politics: "Grant treated George as a fellow subverter. . . . 'What's new?' George asks him, implying what has the Enemy been up to? . . . George laughs in an appropriately sardonic manner, since this is what Grant expects of him. But this gallows humor sickens his heart. In all those old crises of the twenties, the thirties, the war—each one of them has left its traces on George, like an illness—what was terrible was the fear of annihilation. Now we have with us a far more terrible fear, the fear of survival. Survival into the Rubble Age [after a nuclear war]" (*SM*, 84–87). In describing this interaction between George and Grant, Isherwood is drawing on aspects of his own life and character to create both of these characters. Grant's rebelliousness duplicates the George (and Isherwood) of the 1920s and 1930s.

The connection between Isherwood's autobiography and the fictionalized events of *A Single Man* is again apparent in a passage from Isherwood's diaries:

> 29 November 1962: [Isherwood's friend, the actor and director] Charles Laughton was . . . dying of cancer . . . .
>
> He was sleepy and in pain but quite lucid. He said, "The preoccupation is with death, isn't it?" What he really wanted to ask, though he didn't put it directly, was whether or not I approved of his having seen a priest. I told him, I certainly did.

This entry is revisited in *A Single Man*. George goes to see Doris, his and Jim's old friend and a former lover of Jim. She is in a hospital, dying. Once she was the enemy who wanted to steal Jim away. George visits her out of kindness but also with an ulterior motive. He holds her hand, "for the gesture means, *We are on the same road, I shall follow you soon*" (*SM*, 98). The gesture also suggests a connection to Jim in some way beyond the world of dust and ashes. George learns "that Doris has been seeing a priest. (She was raised a Catholic.). . . . Ah, but when the road narrows to the width of this bed, when there is nothing in front of you that is known, dare you disdain any guide? Perhaps Doris has learned something already about the journey ahead of her. But, even supposing that she has and that George could bring himself to ask her, she could never tell him what she knows. For that could only be expressed in the language of the place to which she is going. And that language—though some of us gabble it out so glibly—has no real meaning in our world. In our mouths, it is just a lot of words" (*SM,* 101).

Throughout his life and career, Isherwood always sought the "secret language" that would help him gain entry to his various secondary worlds: Mortmere, *The Waste Land* game with Auden, Layard-Lane, the Isherwood-Auden schema, and Vedanta. The world he was really seeking is beyond language since language is man's symbolic measure of duality and separation. The world of the mystics is beyond words and in that world one does not consciously think in words but intuitively feels without words. When George leaves Doris, "he knew something: that the very last traces of the Doris who tried to take Jim from him have vanished from this shriveled mannequin, and with them, the last drop of his hate. . . . That has been the bond between him and Doris. And now it is broken. And one more bit of Jim is lost to him forever" (*SM,* 102).

That night, in his sadness, George decides he does not want to eat alone; yet, he realizes: "But to say, I won't eat alone . . . isn't that deadly dangerous." He knows this could be a prelude to thoughts of despair and sleeping pills. He thinks: "Damn all food. Damn all life" (*SM,* 113). In a concession to his fear of being alone he decides to have dinner with his friend Charlotte, another British expatriate. George is not always keen to see her because she wants to replace Jim. They slowly become drunk, about which George feels "this utterly mysterious unsensational thing—not bliss, not ecstasy, not joy—just plain happiness." And he attributes this feeling to "Charley" who creates it "astonishingly often; this doubtless is something else she isn't aware of since she can do it even when she herself is miserable" (*SM,* 123). Charley is a manageress of some mystical quality, who can give comfort to others in a manner that transcends definition.

George recalls Charlotte's enormous kindness to him when Jim died. Charley has suffered her own heartache with men, but of the "leaving" kind. As they have more wine Charley reminds George that their present separate homes are too big for one person. She knows he is attached to his home and assumes that behind this attachment is a desire to honor Jim's memory. This is true, but George also likes his home and the independence it gives him. Wine-fortified, Charlotte moves on to plan B, nostalgia for England: "'How can you pretend not to love it?' She is asking him, with a teasing, coquettish reproachfulness. 'And you miss it—you wish you were back there—you *know* you do!'" George has been back to England many times but with no wish to return there permanently. George admits to her that he liked it better each time he returned because "Everything's changed, and yet nothing has"

(*SM,* 131). The positive sense of change results from the addition of minorities, such as Negroes and Chinese, as part of the English nation. The negative sense of change results from the cult of the past, an overdetermination of history that is evident when Charley makes George tell her again about how the house he was born in had been built in 1649. George tells her of the updating of the house with modern conveniences, which she rebuts as an affront to the past; he counters that the house had been falling apart. Charley then talks about her sister Nan, who is back in England:

> "There's another thing about going back home—it's the past; and that's all tied up with Nan, too. Sort of going back to the place where I turned off the road, do you see?"
>
> "No, I don't see."
>
> But, Geo—the *past!* Surely you can't pretend you don't know what I meant by that?"
>
> "The past is just something that's over. . . . The past is over. People make believe that it isn't, and they show you things in museums. But that's not the past. You won't find the past in England. Or anywhere else, for that matter." (*SM,* 141)

In Vedantic terms George is not rejecting the past because there is no past to reject. The present moment includes the past simultaneously, not separately. One who is chained to the past neurotically—like a Lily Vernon—poisons the present and negatively affects those trying to have their own present, such as Lily's son Eric. George, as a fictionalized stand-in for Isherwood, is having a dialogue with Charlotte, as another fictionalized stand-in for Isherwood and also for Kathleen. This is Isherwood's last debate on the issue of England and all the angst that England had once invoked in him. After this last debate concerning England and Kathleen, there is some absolution for both George and, by extension, Isherwood.

When George is leaving, Charley "kisses him full on the mouth. . . . It's one of those drunken long-shots. Do women ever stop trying? No, but because they never stop, they learn to be good losers. . . . He kisses her on the forehead. She is like a child who has at last submitted to being tucked into her cot" (*SM,* 145). Charley's submission is also a metaphor of how Isherwood's anger toward the past is finally being put to bed. Isherwood would prove this point emphatically when he immersed himself in his parents' past to write *Kathleen and Frank.*

After leaving Charley, George decides he is not ready to go home; too much of what is on his mind is centered in his house. Instead he heads for "the tribal encampment" (*SM,* 148)—i.e., the gay bar at the beach. This is where George and Kenny will have their Platonic dialogue. George is surprised to see Kenny there since he thinks that Kenny has a girlfriend. When George sees him at the bar, he says, "I didn't expect to see you in this neck of the woods." Kenny answers that he has gone there because "one of the kids told me you're in here a lot." George senses "something not quite in order." Kenny reveals he has no ride home. George reads this as a sexual invitation: "A voice inside George says, *You could invite him to stay the night at your place. Tell him you'll drive him back in the morning.* What in the hell do you think I am? George asks it [the voice]. *It was merely a suggestion,* says the voice" (*SM*, 152–53). George does not ask Kenny—at least not yet—but they do get drunk. George gets increasingly drunk, as he adds to the drinks he has had at Charley's. In his drunken state George experiences his aforementioned contemplation upon the Platonic dialogue he is now having with Kenny, and by Isherwood's extension, the rest of the universe. This includes Kenny's question about "experience" and George's answer about getting "sillier and sillier." Kenny, suspicious of how silly George could actually be, asks him to go for a swim in the ocean and is shocked when he agrees. Kenny responds: "Oh—that's terrific! . . . It was a test. I thought you were bluffing, about being silly" (*SM*, 161). George, however, is not bluffing. They have a child-like romp in the surf, leaving George exhilarated. They then walk to George's home nearby. Kenny tells George about his girlfriend, Lois, who is Japanese:

> "She says she won't marry a Caucasian. She says she can't take people in this country seriously. She doesn't feel anything we do here *means* anything. She wants to go back to Japan and teach.
>
> "She's an American citizen , isn't she?"
>
> "Oh, sure. She's a Nisei. But, just the same, she and her whole family got shipped up to one of those internment camps in the Sierras, right after the war began. Her father had to sell his business for peanuts, give it away, practically, to some sharks who were grabbing all the Japanese property. . . . Lois was only a small kid, then, but you can't expect anyone to forget. . . . She says that they were all treated as enemy aliens. . . . She says the Negroes were the only ones who acted decently to them. And a few pacifists. Christ, she certainly has the right to hate our guts! Not that she does, actually. She always seems to be able to see the funny side of things." (*SM*, 168)

Kenny's monologue serves two purposes. First, like Isherwood himself, Kenny is reiterating lessons about being a member of a scorned minority; it is often from other minorities that sympathy can be drawn. The middle-aged author is replicating a cycle of emotions that repeats perpetually for each new Adam and Eve. Second, George thinks that, like the younger and more manipulative Isherwood, Kenny is being "positively flirty" by talking about a "girlfriend." Kenny offers a coy response: "I don't think you're that much interested [in talking about Lois]. I think you want to ask me something different. Only you're not sure how I'll take it." George is cautious, yet hopeful that this might be the prelude to a pass. Kenny continues, "You want to know if Lois and I—if we make out together" (*SM*, 169). George's hope is unfounded; he realizes that Kenny has come to set him up, but not for a sexual purpose. Kenny needs a place to go with Lois in order to "make-out." Kenny does not ask George directly, but George has enough sense to read between the lines.

Consequently, "Uncle George," the nonconformist who admires other nonconformists and minorities, offers his home to Kenny for one night a week when George will plan to have a regular dinner with Charley.

With the sexual tension now moot, "George felt himself entering a new phase. . . . George transformed: a formidable George . . . An inquisitorial George, seated in judgment. . . . An oracular George. . ." (*SM*, 173). He tells Kenny:

> "What is this life supposed to be *for?* Are we to spend it identifying each other with catalogues, like tourists. . . ? Or are we to try and exchange *some* kind of signal, however garbled, before it's too late?. . . Don't you have a glimmering of how I must feel—longing to *speak?*
>
> "You asked me about experience. So I told you. Experience isn't any *use*. And yet, in quite another way, it *might* be. . . . I know *exactly* what you want. You want me to tell you *what I know*.
>
> ". . . there's nothing I'd rather do! I want like *hell* to tell you. But, I can't. I quite literally can't. Because, don't you see, *what I know is what I am?* And I can't tell you that. You have to find it out for yourself. I'm like a book you have to read. A book can't read itself to you." (*SM*, 174–76)

George continues by warning Kenny not to be a typical, self-absorbed young man. Kenny should try being a more sensitive man. He should not succumb to "'the enormous tragedy of everything nowadays: flirtation. . . . And miss the one thing that might really . . . *transform your entire life*—' For a moment Kenny's face is quite distinct. It grins, dazzlingly" (*SM*, 177). Perhaps George has broken through. Both then fall asleep. While George continues to sleep, Kenny departs, after having put George to bed with fresh pajamas and leaving a note saying so.

George awakens. The experience with Kenny has indeed transformed him by giving him back his will to go forward—if not with Kenny, then with someone else. He would remember Jim faithfully but would no longer cling to his memory as an emotional crutch. George would stay in their home because this was where he had had found Jim and where a new cycle should begin: "Damn the future. Let Kenny and the kids have it. Let Charley keep the past. George clings only to Now. It is Now that he must find another Jim. Now that he must love. Now that he must live. . ." (*SM*, 182).

George returns to sleep. He is merely a body again. His consciousness is suspended in sleep while the body exists on automatic pilot: "But *is* all of George altogether present here?" The narrator draws an analogy:

> Up the coast . . . there are a lot of rock pools. . . . Each pool is separate and different, and you can, if you you are fanciful, give them names, such as George, Charlotte, Kenny, Mrs. Strunk. Just as George and the others are thought of, for convenience, as individual entities, so you may think of a rock pool as an entity; though, of course, it is not. The waters of its consciousness—so to speak—are

swarming with hunted anxieties, grim-jawed greeds, dartingly vivid intuitions, old crusty-shelled rock-gripping obstinacies, deep-down sparkling undiscovered secrets. . . . How can such a variety of creatures coexist at all? Because they have to. The rocks of the pool hold their world together. . . . so over George and the others in sleep come the waters of that other consciousness which is no one in particular but which contains everyone and everything, past, present, and future, and extends unbroken beyond the uttermost stars. We may surely suppose that, in darkness of the full flood, some of these creatures are lifted from their pools to drift far out over the deep waters. But do they ever come back. . . . Can they tell us, in any manner, about their journey? Is there, indeed, anything for them to tell— except that the waters of the ocean are not really other than the waters of the pool? (*SM,* 183–84)

The last two remarkable pages of *A Single Man* are a conjecture about whether the body of George while asleep could also be a body about to die. It does not matter; consciousness is beyond the body. A transcendent consciousness can observe the body independently: "For a few minutes maybe, life lingers in the tissues of some outlying regions of the body. Then, one by one, the lights go out and there is total blackness" (*SM,* 186). This passage was drawn from Isherwood's diary.

On 4 November 1963, while Isherwood was completing *A Single Man,* he saw Aldous Huxley for the last time in the same hospital where he had seen Charles Laughton for the last time the year before. Indeed, Huxley would die of cancer on 22 November 1963. Isherwood records his response to his dying friend and literary brother-in-arms: "Aldous was in obvious discomfort, but there was nothing poignant or desperate in his manner, and he clearly didn't want to talk about death. . . . I touched on subject after subject, at random. Each time I did so, Aldous commented acutely, or remembered an appropriate quotation. I came away with the picture of a great noble vessel sinking quietly into the deep, many of its delicate marvelous mechanisms still in perfect order, all its lights still shining."[15]

From life to diary page to printed page to reader, and into each reader's consciousness, the Vedantic circular motion of Isherwood's poignantly particular moment with Huxley becomes a universal moment at the end of *A Single Man.* Life is art; art is life, and the particular is the universal, continuously, contiguously, and simultaneously.

"*A Single Man* is a quite astonishing *tour de force,*" writes Brian Finney. Finney offers the following assessment of the place of this novel in Isherwood's canon: "Isherwood [liked] it best of all his novels and so did Auden. . . . When it was published in 1964 the book had a mixed reception, but even the most favorable reviews reveal a misunderstanding of what a radical departure from his earlier books this novel represented. . . . Almost everything about *A Single Man* is different—its conception of character, its narrative viewpoint, and its temporal structure. Underlying these changes is the elementary presupposition which the Vedantist shares with anyone who believes that life of some sort continues after death—that the everyday conception of self is an illusion. . . . The Vedantic presupposition is unobtrusively present in this creature's multiplicity of past selves."[16]

Alan Wilde writes that "George is [Isherwood] as he might have been had he not discovered Vedanta. . . . *A Single Man* insists upon the illusion of separateness and the factitiousness of identity. . . . George's day becomes a metaphor for his life and George himself a type of everyman."[17] From this Everyman the reader learns through parable. George does not understand the deeper ramifications of his experience, but Isherwood the middle-aged author calmly, but firmly, asserts the metaphysical implications without naming any specific beliefs. Nonetheless, George does implicitly intuit some manner of transcendence in his conversation with Kenny. Piazza writes: "Isherwood's description of George's late-night encounter with Kenny . . . as a symbolic Platonic dialogue, defines the book's narrative method: a symbolic dialogue between the author as a kind of guru and the reader as a disciple meditating on the ephemera of George's day."[18] Piazza divides George's day in half: "In the first half of the novel, George is certainly the smallest integral division of humanity. Toward the end of the novel, however, the single man advances toward a letting go of consciousness and of self and toward a merging with Being itself."[19]

If George is merging with "Being itself," this explains the narrator's unemotional depiction of the possible death of George's body. A Vedantist does not fear the death of the body. The narrator speaks matter-of-factly because the body's demise is a matter of fact, but it is not an end. If it is not an end, then what is it? Isherwood's choice of narrator gives the answer. His narrator is not the subjective Isherwood who dominates his previous work. That is, the narrator is not subjective in the sense that he does not have Isherwood's name or personality. However, although Isherwood's Vedantic beliefs are implied by an objective narrator, to Isherwood, these beliefs are very subjective.

Lisa Schwerdt adds her view to the critical chorus: "*A Single Man,* a departure for Isherwood in both content and technique, is, as Isherwood's novels inevitably are, closely tied to his private experience. In his earlier works, we saw Isherwood concerned with defining himself as an individual, establishing his identity; in later works determining how that identity could be merged with another. The majority of his novels, however, reflected his primary interests through the namesake narrator. In *A Single Man* Isherwood shifts from concern over self to concern over those who will follow him—to the younger generation beginning careers, trying to find a place in the world. Since the primary preoccupation is no longer with identity, with 'Who am I?' the namesake narrator becomes unnecessary, even inappropriate. Just as Isherwood's relationship to his protagonist changes, so does the protagonist's relationship to the reader."[20]

The protagonist's story is a parable. Isherwood is the guru and the reader is his disciple. The focus has moved away from the "I" of Isherwood's consciousness to the "you" of the reader's consciousness. Isherwood asks his reader, How can this book help you learn about your Self, with a capital "S"? *A Single Man* is Isherwood's most distinctive and perhaps his finest achievement. In 1964 the novel's Vedantic parable was not so readily accessible. Today's audience is more familiar with mysticism. For this audience and even more so for those who know the more subtle forms of mysticism, *A Single Man* is a mystical novel and a great one.

6 INEXPLICABLE HAPPINESS
Themes Fulfilled: The Truly Strong Man

... he's not simply digging up the past, in the sense of recreating it and going over it again, but he's relating it to the Christopher of now. . . . he sees the past as a continuous past which merges into a continuous present, and there is still Christopher now, and something that happened in 1938 or 1945, can tell you a good deal about Christopher now.

Gavin Lambert[1]

The first discovery I made about Swami, and I made it only by very slow degrees, was his tremendous capacity for concern. Before I could think of myself as truly his disciple, I had to understand and believe that I mattered to him, far more than I'd ever mattered to anyone else I'd known, even to mother. What makes this kind of concern so tremendously powerful is that it has no ulterior motive, it isn't in the least possessive, and it isn't adulterated with pathos and sentimentality, like most so-called love.[2]

... you told me that there was a character in a book you'd read about that you used to think about a lot and hope one day you'd meet someone like him. The way you told me made it clear that now you *had* met the someone and it was me—[3]

... it's what you become that matters, not what you cease to be[4]

What unites us is the one and only thing that matters.[5]

Christopher Isherwood (all from *A Meeting by the River*)

If I had known when I was 21, that I would be as happy as I am now, [age 70] I should have been sincerely shocked.

Isherwood (in a letter to Edward Upward)[6]

The early 1960s were transition years for Isherwood. In the United States the civil rights legislation of 1964 opened the door for minority pride, as minorities felt empowered to speak out. Coordinated articulation was power. Speaking out became more focused when there was an opposition and a cause to protest against—the Vietnam War provided both. Once again the enemy was The Others who had started another absurd war to serve their interests. As a minority of one Isherwood had once been an Angry Young Man. His previous three novels, *The World in the Evening, Down There on a Visit,* and *A Single Man,* had concerned themselves with the circular motion of, as friend and fellow novelist Gavin Lambert said, "a continuous past which merges into a continuous present." In his present, Isherwood became an Angry Older Man lending his own voice to a new generation of rebels.

Since 1915 Isherwood's anger at The Others had been—choose one or more of the following—subconscious, sublimated, transferred, fantasized, "diarized," fictionalized, or "sloganized." This rebellious anger had been the basis for his art. His art represented a series of Platonic dialogues that served as self-therapy in his attempt to examine the sources of his anger so he could try to pacify it. The dialogues were therapeutic private conversations that just happened to end up in a public medium. His diaries were written with an eye toward publication; yet, Isherwood would have likely written them anyway out of the dearest need to express himself even without an audience. Isherwood's cathartic release through art was mainly intellectual rather than visceral. However, beginning in the later 1960s and lasting to the end of his life in 1986, Isherwood expressed himself intellectually *and* viscerally. He came out, literally and figuratively, from behind the pages of his books to say whatever he wanted to, complete and unabridged. When the climate for outspokenness presented itself, Isherwood presented himself—militantly so—as if a great wellspring had finally let loose its pressure valve. Isherwood became a spokesman for his tribe and was proud to be a senior member. Moreover, Vedanta was now in vogue. The Isherwood-Prabhavananda translations of the Bhagavad-Gita and Patanjali's aphorisms, *How to Know God,* came out in paperback versions and sold hundreds of thousands of copies.[7] Finally, Van Druten's *I Am a Camera* was put to music and became the successful stage and film musical *Cabaret.* Isherwood was no longer just a cult figure among a limited cognoscenti—he was a full-fledged celebrity. In a sense, Isherwood returned to his pre-1915 childhood womb-cocoon, since he was once again the center of attention.

Gavin Lambert said of Isherwood in a 1976 interview: "he has an enormous theatrical sense. If you've seen him give a lecture . . . He's a star, he is a real star. I used to see him on the Oscar Levant [TV talk] show [in the sixties]. . . . it was a . . . west coast show . . . [Levant] let people really talk and he adored Chris. Chris very often used to recite poetry and reminisce."[8] Isherwood the celebrity was no longer just *Down There on a Visit,* he was also out there on stage. His private thoughts were now in the public domain and the benefits to him were profound. That willful ego he had been trying so hard to abnegate since 1939 was getting a lot of attention—and approval. The more approval Isherwood received, the more his ego stepped aside self-effacingly. Because Isherwood was finally given what he no longer felt compelled to demand, a calming self-approval matched the public approval, which for him was like revisiting the womb-cocoon. His dialogues in diaries and art—conversations with himself—had been a ritual to assert that he had a right to share in the world's consciousness. Diary and art were now easing their way into a more affirmative monologue—the single voice within the voice of humanity that affirmed to him that he *was* collective consciousness. Within a context of contentment his art itself would shift from one final expiatory dialogue of conflict in 1967's *A Meeting by the River* to three non-conflicted monologues of affirmation: *Kathleen and Frank* in 1971, *Christopher and His Kind* in 1976, and his last book *My Guru and His Disciple* in 1980.

His influence was no longer limited to himself, his art, his selected friends, nor even to his readers. Directly or indirectly, Isherwood was part of the movement toward the sensitive man who was pure in heart and Truly Strong. The middle-aged searcher of *Down There on a Visit* and *A Single Man* had looked back at all the previous Christopher Isherwoods and had decided that the current version was the only version that counted. Indeed, with his black leather motorcycle jacket (sans motorcycle), he became a model for that sixties and seventies folk hero, the militant mystic. Lest one imagine that this is hyperbole, evidence is provided by naming just three of the great pop culture icons of the era, *Billy Jack,* from the film of that name, Kwai-Chang Caine, the Shao-Lin priest/mystic of the TV series *Kung Fu,* and the antihero, R. P. McMurphy, played by Jack Nicholson in the film version of *One Flew over the Cuckoo's Nest.* [9] In the 1960s it was not only cool to be kind, but also to speak up for your kind, as Isherwood did by asserting his homosexuality and his spiritual beliefs.

The bedrock bolstering Isherwood's self-esteem was Don Bachardy. Lambert said of Bachardy in 1976: "since Don, [Isherwood has] had a marvelous period. It seems to me to be an extraordinary relationship from every point of view. [Don's] a wonderful person, absolutely wonderful, exceptional, genuinely talented [as a successful portrait artist], which is so gratifying for Christopher."[10] Bachardy's talent would also manifest itself as a co-writer with Isherwood for a stage version of *A Meeting by the River* and a 1973 teleplay, *Frankenstein: The True Story.* When Bachardy also became a Vedantist, the two most important people in Isherwood's life were in agreement.

In 1945, Isherwood had written of the manageress in *Prater Violet:* "I have only to look at her to know she is satisfied. Deeply satisfied. Some man has made her happy. For her, there is no longer any search. She has found what we are all looking for." For the Isherwood of 1945 this was a wish for himself not yet fulfilled. Bachardy fulfilled the wish so that Isherwood also became deeply satisfied. This sense of wish-fullfilment may have contributed to the aforementioned lines in *A Meeting by the River.* "you told me that there was a character in a book you'd read about that you used to think about a lot and hope one day you'd meet someone like him. The way you told me made it clear that now you *had* met the someone and it was me."

Isherwood was appreciated by Bachardy and the satisfaction derived from this approval bolstered his confidence for the role of public figure. The timing was fortuitous since there was much more of a public that was interested in Isherwood. From the late 1960s to 1986 Isherwood gave many more interviews and made many more appearances than in all of his previous adult years combined since 1925.

He was in a position to talk as he had never been able to before. He could

Isherwood and the Swami bound for India, 1963, on the trip that would be fictionalized in Isherwood's 1967 novel (and later play) *A Meeting by the River*. (Vedanta Society of Southern California Archives)

say that he was proud to be queer (his term of choice) on national television. After so many years of covering up his homosexuality, he felt he was no longer required to strive to be Strong privately while his bedeviling ego chafed beneath his public mask; he could now be Strong publicly and let the ego serve him, instead of his true Self being served up to his ego. His ego, a former enemy, was now an ally, giving him the voice to say aloud what he had previously said only to friends directly or implied indirectly through his art. Not only could he now speak in public, but he also became a hero for doing so. Isherwood was letting go of his ego by asserting it. He was no longer disguising his weakness as misplaced anger or neurotic symptoms. His ego was now speaking as the "I" within the "we" of tribal solidarity. Through his new and wider public he was granted a return to that appreciative and nurturing womb-cocoon from which he had thought himself ejected so long ago. W. H. Auden said that the two paramount questions that each person should ask himself are: Who am I? Whom ought I to become? Isherwood's diaries and art had been asking these two questions all his life. His two answers, which initially were wrought with uncertainty had gradually developed into strong responses: I am an aspiring Strong Man. I ought to become a Truly Strong Man. This maturation in his later years was reflected by the art produced during them. This art moved away from the conflicts of expiatory dialogue to monologues of affirmation.

THE LAST DIALOGUE: *A MEETING BY THE RIVER*

In 1963 Isherwood went with the Swami to India for the initiation of a fellow disciple as a full-fledged monk. He went with great reluctance and only out of respect
for his Guru. His misgivings and the details of the trip are recorded in his diaries and
rendered verbatim in his last book *My Guru and His Disciple.* Isherwood's reluctance
was two-fold: he did not want to be away from Bachardy, who had business in New
York, and he had never been attracted so much to the rituals of Vedanta as to the
philosophy and the Swami personally. Isherwood was conflicted with the thought of
being witness to a great deal of bowing and prostrating that he was afraid would
somehow deflate his belief. In *My Guru and His Disciple* he repeats his diary entry
of 16 December 1963, two days before his departure: "Don is in New York. Woke
up in a big flap . . . travel dread gripping me. So I started taking Librium in
advance." On departure day, he added: "About fifty people came to the airport to
see us off. The parting was like a funeral which is so boring and hammy that you are
glad to be one of the corpses" (*GD,* 260). Isherwood deliberated upon how he, as a
lay devotee, was supposed to act: "During this visit, I am playing it very broad. I bow
down even to the most junior swamis. This is partly clowning, partly aggression—
and how it embarrasses many of them! A few retaliate—I have to take a standing
jump backwards, to avoid having them do it to me" (*GD,* 264).

Isherwood's ironic acerbity had not left him, even in this most holy of envi-
ronments. The contrast between the relative comfort of the lay devotee's life and the
stark asceticism of the monk's life likely heightened Isherwood's caustic wit. Nearly
twenty years before in 1945 Isherwood had left the temple because he knew he could
never become a monk. For the next eight years he did his best to live a semi-satyr's
life, as if to prove to himself that he had been right. For the ensuing ten years with
Bachardy, Isherwood had modified his behavior and his attitude towards that behavior. Isherwood accepted that he could not be a saint; yet, he could still devoutly
believe in "this thing" and in his Guru. While in India on New Year's Eve 1963,
Isherwood records the following diary entry:

> Just before going to bed, I started to get the gripes. I shivered a lot and
> couldn't sleep all night. Lying awake in the dark, I was swept by gusts of furious
> resentment—against India, against the senior swamis (not the younger ones),
> against the Swami himself, even. I resolved to tell him that I refuse, ever again, to
> appear in the temple or anywhere else and talk about God.
>
> Part of this resolve is quite valid. I do honestly think that, when I give these
> God lectures, it is Sunday Religion in the worst sense. As long as I quite
> unashamedly get drunk, have promiscuous sex, and write books like A Single Man,
> I simply cannot appear before people as sort of a lay monk. Whenever I do, my life
> becomes divided and untruthful—or rather, the only truth left is in my drunken-
> ness, my sex, and my art. (There are, of course, dozens of audiences which would
> be ready to accept drink, sex and art. To these I could also talk about God without

falseness. They might be embarrassed but they would listen. Such audiences are not
to be found within the Vedanta Society, however.) (*GD,* 272)

In the future, Isherwood would recant this attitude to some extent, but the crux of
his problem remained. He was aware that he was balancing two worlds. He seemed
perfectly willing to do so as long as he was not put into situations he thought others might have considered hypocritical. This is not to say Isherwood thought himself hypocritical. He did not. His attitude was that if the Swami and Bachardy
accepted him as he was, everybody else would either have to fall in line or get out of
the way. Interviewing Gavin Lambert in 1976, Carolyn Heilbrun said to Lambert:
"The only thing that surprised me about Christopher, whom I'd always thought of
as saint-like, is that he can be rather truculent." Lambert responded: "Oh, yes. But
he hasn't a saintly idea of himself, that's the marvelous thing, it's the saint in the
world enjoying the world. That's, in a way, why he is very close to Krishnamurti.
[Krishnamurti] always said it's terribly easy to be good in a monastery or to be pure
in a convent, but the really important problem is how to do it in the world, and they
are very close in that way. I think if sainthood has any meaning at all, that's what it
does mean."[11]

How to do it in the world was the problem for Isherwood. The frustration
of his Indian adventure would end up having a positive side effect. Like so much
of the rest of his often conflicted life, he would write a book about it:

A Meeting by the River is dedicated to Gerald Heard. This novel is ostensibly
about two brothers. Oliver is about to take his vows to become a Hindu Monk;
Patrick is a slick businessman for a publishing firm in Los Angeles. Isherwood
may have not put Patrick directly in the L.A. film scene because he had depicted
the film world twice before in his novels; however, Patrick's glitzy glibness is all
Hollywood. Nonetheless, Isherwood did have Patrick connected with the filming
of one of his book properties. After a long period of silence Oliver writes Patrick
(called Paddy) a letter announcing his spiritual intentions and asks his brother to
inform their mother in some tactful way. So begins the novel that will remain in
the form of letters and diary entries, a new approach for Isherwood. Oliver feels
he should inform his family. He does so only a few days before the ceremony.
This is the first time they hear that he has even been a disciple. He did not want
them involved. He fears any brother-to-brother or son-to-mother conflict might
unnerve him. Patrick, while responding to Oliver in seemingly neutral terms, is
determined to stop his brother from "wasting" his life and goes to India to bring
him home. Their meeting stirs up old resentments and new rounds of self analysis. Patrick's views are written as letters to his mother, his wife Penelope, and his
lover, Tom. Oliver writes only in his diary. Patrick begrudges Oliver for their
mother's favoritism towards him. Patrick also sees Oliver's choice of a spiritual
world as a repudiation of Patrick's own material world. Oliver had loved Penelope,
a dabbler in Eastern philosophy, but lost her to Patrick's ability to provide her with

material comforts. To "save" Oliver, Patrick offers Oliver not only a job in the material world but Penelope as well. Patrick's motives are selfish. If Oliver provides for Penelope and her two children, Patrick can leave her for Tom. By the end both brothers have learned a little more about themselves. They continue their paths as monk and businessman. However, Patrick breaks with Tom to return to Penelope and his children, and Oliver becomes more tolerant of Patrick and Patrick's world. The plot as summarized disguises the novel's actual purpose. The real story is not about two brothers at all; the tale of Oliver and Patrick functions primarily as a symbolic parable.

Isherwood was deeply cognizant of the duality within individuals. In *Meeting by the River* the conflict between the ostensible brothers is really between the two halves of Isherwood's self during his trip to India: saint versus sinner. The saint half (Oliver) wishes to become one while fretting about the temptations of his ego. The sinner half (Patrick) wants to stay one even though his exposure to Oliver's spiritual world gives him pause to reconsider how he lives. Each does not want to be considered hypocritical, just as Isherwood had not wanted to be thought of as hypocritical in India. Standing outside the two halves is the Watcher in Spanish, that great silent arbiter who passively, yet somehow effectively, directs the two halves toward a merger into a third figure: the equitable common sense compromise of body and soul known as the new Christopher Isherwood. This is possible because the two brothers, as counterparts to the two Isherwoods, are not really so different at all. Isherwood points this out in *A Meeting by the River* through an internal dialogue, a technique he had been using since 1928. Brian Finney agrees with this reading: "Oliver believes in God. Patrick is the personification of the ego. . . . Yet, to see the book simply in terms of dichotomies is a falsification of Isherwood's subtle presentation. . . . For a start the two are brothers locked until the finale in a love-hate relationship that emphasizes their similarities far more than their differences. Each . . . claims to detect in the other signs of weariness from the pursuit of his chosen path in life. . . . Their differences, such as they are, are attributed to the rules their mother tried to impose on them. . . . Each shares more of the other's characteristics than at first either dares to admit."[12]

The allegorical struggle between the dueling sides of Isherwood's psyche is made apparent as Oliver writes: "At moments, I can actually feel and think like him, and that scares me. . . . I get afraid that I'll start behaving like him and lose my identity altogether. Patrick can disturb me so terribly because he can make me question the way I live my life. . . . His power over me is nothing but my own doubt and weakness" (*MR,* 115–16). Isherwood often referred to his own ego in the third person as a tormentor. "His power" was really Isherwood's ego and the doubts and weaknesses were his own, for he had felt them throughout his life and particularly in India.

Some have thought that Isherwood gives Oliver an edge over Patrick in the book's debate. Oliver has the advantage of being the spokesman for Vedantic ideals, which in 1967 had become more credible. When one first reads the novel, this impression takes hold. Oliver seems to win out. Yet, as Finney gleaned from reading an interview with Isherwood, "if anything, [Isherwood] is far more Patrick than he is Oliver."[13] The conflict Isherwood felt in India motivated the novel's theme. In India he had gotten the "gripes" because his "Patrick" side had been forced to bump up against the "Oliver" side. Isherwood knew that any pretense of appearing, as he had said, as a "lay monk" bordered on the ludicrous. He refused to be hypocritical. He felt he could not be a hypocrite when the Watcher in Spanish, in the guise of the Swami, was always in his thoughts. Isherwood notes this in *My Guru and His Disciple*: "He [the Swami] is fond of telling people how humble I am about my literary reputation. But he must know perfectly well what my humility really is—the other half of my vanity. It is so cozy and relaxing to play the lowest of the low within his circle—which tends to make me feel all the more sophisticated and superior in my attitude toward uninitiated outsiders, especially when they are literary intellectuals" (*GD*, 328). The ego always lurks nearby to perpetrate its mischief. As he grew older Isherwood understood how the ego acted on him. By analyzing himself, he could exert some control over his ego instead of his ego controlling him.

The debate between the two brothers is a fictionalized replaying of the debates Isherwood had with himself in his diaries. The Isherwood-Auden schema is the map that provides the parameters for the internal dialogues between the Truly Weak and Truly Strong Man. Patrick and Oliver are not really brothers any more than Michael and James Ransom. The mothers of these pairs of brothers are not their mothers but the great symbolic evil archetype mother modeled on Kathleen. This would be the last time Isherwood would do so in anger. Oliver and Patrick's "father died when they were both so young" (*MR*, 20). When the brothers describe each other, Isherwood is depicting his own characteristics. *Patrick on Oliver:* "As a young man, there was an assurance about him, or shall we say a determination, or even a ruthlessness—no, I've gone too far" (*MR*, 60). *Patrick to Oliver on their mother:* "She *lives* for you. And therefore only you have the power to hurt her, which I know of course you'd never dream of doing, intentionally" (*MR*, 32). This is emotional extortion as James Ransom had perpetrated on Michael Ransom. *Oliver on Patrick:* "He's still playing all his old tricks, including that blackmailing sobstuff about mother" (*MR*, 34). *Oliver on himself:* "The truth is that I am unspeakably humiliated and shocked that I, who am supposed to be spiritually advanced . . . still feel these primitive spasms of sheer hatred toward my own brother! *That* stabs my ego in the very heart of its vanity" (*MR*, 35). Isherwood made such pronouncements about his ego repeatedly in his diaries. Further, Oliver writes:

> WHEN shall I get it through my head, once and for all, that the ego, the Oliver in me, never will and never can be anything but a vain little monkey. I ought

to have learned after all this time, after all the Swami's teaching . . . to live with this monkey and refuse to be impressed or shocked by its postures and greeds and rages. Its whole effort is directed toward making me identify myself with it, when I know perfectly well that I ought to be continually dissociating myself from it, calmly and firmly and with complete good humor— if you get angry with it, you identify automatically. That's what self-discipline means. The monkey must be made to face its ugliness again and again. That's why I should keep on with this diary." (*MR,* 36)

Through Oliver, this was Isherwood's affirmation by declaration. Hereafter, Isherwood in his life and last three books was better able to regard his ego "calmly and firmly and with complete good humor."

After an incident in which Patrick particularly annoys his brother, Oliver writes: "When I first realized what Patrick had done . . . I could have killed him, almost. But then I saw this situation was really offering itself as a test" (*MR,* 125). This meant a Test in the Vedantic sense since it is not an obstacle but an object lesson from which one can learn to persevere while controlling ego-generated emotions.

Patrick tells Oliver about his lover Tom in terms that are both confessional and deliberately shocking in the Sally Bowles manner. Oliver understands that Patrick is being narcissistic, yet also somehow devious: "But then I got the suspicion . . . that he was trying to excite me, not himself. . . . it seemed terribly silly of him and somehow sinister—and I was shocked, though less shocked than puzzled" (*MR,* 145). Patrick's lewdness is meant to tempt the soon-to-be-celibate monk with a vision of one aspect of the world that Patrick assumed, from his own standard, one could not possibly give up. Isherwood had faced this crossroad in 1945. In part he left the temple then because he realized that he could not give up sex.

When Patrick later tells Oliver that he has decided to stay with his family out of duty and forsake Tom, Oliver responds that if his family only represents duty to Patrick, he should leave them because it would be more heartless to stay. Patrick then tells Oliver that he had been shockingly frank about Tom for a purpose. His reason was to have Oliver feel that he could be totally frank in return. This is another Test for Oliver. The implication from Patrick is that now Oliver could tell the truth—that is, Patrick feels that his openness has opened the way for Oliver to confess that he does not actually want to be a monk but is doing so out of a perverse jealousy because he could not have Penelope (*MR,* 151). Patrick could not imagine that a man might want to be a monk for his own sake. Oliver does not fall for this ploy. Furthermore, Patrick suggests that Oliver wants power and ambition just like any other "normal" man, but is so much afraid of failing in the material world, that he would rather renounce the world than face possible rejection by it. Oliver does not fall for this trap either. Patrick simply cannot grasp that Oliver's beliefs are as genuine to Oliver as Patrick's love for money is real to him. Through Oliver, Isherwood is also asserting the sincerity of his faith.

Concerning his faith, Isherwood was often frustrated by the persistent refusal among some critics, reviewers, and even friends, who would not accept the sincerity of his beliefs nor acknowledge how these beliefs influenced his life and work. In 1965, while Isherwood was writing *A Meeting by the River,* he published a biography of Sri Ramakrishna, the patron saint of the Vedanta society. Of the reception to this biography, Isherwood notes: "One recurring objection to the book was that I, who had written such worldly novels, was its author. 'It is still a bit difficult to regard Herr Isseyvoo as a guru-fancier.' Such critics had evidently expected that I would handle this subject, also, with irony or treat it as high camp."[14] There was some relief from this dilemma for Isherwood in the 1960s and 1970s when the increased interest in Eastern mysticism added to Isherwood's readership those readers who were intrigued to learn about the art of the man who had done the Vedic translations.[15]

   A Meeting by the River did in fact fare better with the 1960s neo-mystics than with the non-mystical critics. The latter may have had some reservations concerning Isherwood's use of Oliver's diary to express a Vedantic philosophy that they were not familiar with—or that they may have even tacitly disparaged. This was Isherwood's most didactic exposition of his beliefs, which were not yet palatable to everyone, just as they still are not even today.[16] Consequently, when Oliver has a vivid vision of his guru, who passed away the year before, this may not have suited non-believers among readers who were unable to suspend their non-belief even temporarily: "I knew that Swami was 'dead,' and I knew that nevertheless he was now with me—*and that he is with me always wherever I am.* . . . now we are never separated. I woke up actually *knowing* that" (*MR,* 173). For a Vedantist, this is reality. This was Isherwood's reality. There are numerous passages in the diaries that serve as evidence that he made this leap of faith in his life and not just in his fiction.

   Oliver's vision of the Swami gives him back the balance that Patrick had unsettled. Oliver believes the Swami's presence is also "gravely concerned about Patrick. He was like a doctor discussing the condition of a very sick patient— only what he was discussing was Patrick's spiritual, not physical condition. And yet, despite his gravity and concern, he seemed amused and even on the verge of smiling—shaking his head over Patrick, so to speak, with an air of indulgent amusement, as if to say, 'Oh, my goodness, what *will* he be up to next'" (*MR,* 175). This was exactly how Isherwood believed his own Swami perceived him, with total non-judgmental acceptance. Bolstered by his belief in the vision, Oliver accepts Patrick because he now has hope for his brother's future. This omen of the vision is followed by a letter by Patrick to Penelope asking for her acceptance as well: "Penny, dearest, for the sake of our whole future together, I appeal to you—accept me as I am. Will you try to do that?" Patrick continues by sounding like Isherwood in the voice of George from *A Single Man:* "Will you let me be silly sometimes, and show me you know it's only silliness and doesn't matter to you? Let me run off now and then, looking for my teen-age self and flexing my muscles! I can promise you one thing, I shall always return from these idiotic adventures with increased love for you and gratitude—in fact, I can only enjoy the adventures if you sanction them! Can't I quite shamelessly be the child who keeps running home to you, and is always thinking of you even in the midst of his play? When I see us in that relationship it's obvious to me that you can be more central in my life than any mere wife could be to any mere husband" (*MR*, 184). Isherwood is writing about his relationship with Bachardy, although one does not exactly know who played the role of Patrick or who played the role of Penelope, or if they each shared both roles.

Oliver takes his vows with a somewhat chastened Patrick as a proud witness. The ostensible brothers—saint and sinner—have come to a truce with the transcendent aid of Oliver's Swami. The actual Isherwood's soul and body had already come to this truce. *A Meeting by the River* was written after Isherwood's personal acceptance of himself as a mystic in the material world who could laugh at this image with affection. Isherwood had the support of Prabhavananda, Bachardy, his tribe, a new generation of readers, and audiences who applauded his star quality. The idea for the novel had come from his conflicted Indian trip in 1963, but it was written later while he was making the transition to his more even-tempered Self. Colin Wilson wrote of *A Meeting by the River:* "its ending carries deep conviction . . . [it] seems a triumph of decency and common sense more than of religion—and this is surely Isherwood's point. He is not suggesting that the answer to human misery and stupidity lies in sainthood or mysticism—only in decency and common sense, and also a certain optimism. For this is the thing that comes over most clearly from *A Single Man* and *A Meeting by the River:* that Isherwood's integrity is born of hope."[17]

A Meeting by the River is Isherwood's last great internal debate, but one presented more with calm reflection than with anger because he was not fighting himself anymore. Instead, he was affirming himself. He came to realize that The Others had never really been his enemy; he had been his own enemy. All of his art had represented confrontations with the different Christopher Isherwoods. In his late-blooming happiness Isherwood had made peace with himself so that the past no longer hurt him; his contentment began when the hurt of the past had ceased to be painful any longer. Without the hurt, Isherwood could now replace an abusive past with a usable past that he wanted to make peace with. More specifically, it was time to make peace with Kathleen.

THE FIRST AFFIRMATION: *KATHLEEN AND FRANK*, PEACE WITH THE PAST

The last sentence of *Kathleen and Frank* reads: "Perhaps, on closer examination, this book too may prove to be chiefly about Christopher" (*KF,* 510).

Angus Wilson writes that *Kathleen and Frank* is Isherwood's "act of empathy designed to atone for a lifetime of rebellion."[18] Throughout his life, Isherwood had used his art as a vehicle to examine and re-examine himself. Isherwood had a compulsion not only to write about himself in the first place, but to correct himself in the second place. If he thought that during a certain time period, he had not been clear to either himself or to his readers about how he had really felt about particular situations, Isherwood would write his own revisionist history. Much of the revising often stemmed from Isherwood's need to redress wrongs. The Vedantist as sensitive man cannot be one without compassion. Compassion includes the capacity to forgive one's self and one's Self—that is, all others who comprise the indivisible consciousness within which the "I" is the "we." In October 1966, just after completing *A Meeting by the River,* which was about familial healing and forgiving, Isherwood returned to England and the family estate motivated by an idea for his next book. It would be another "official" auto-biography, and he wanted to sort through his mother and father's copious diaries and letters for material. When he did so, his older eyes were compelled to see his parents again, as if for the first time. Isherwood was to be profoundly moved, not only from what he expected to find, but from what he would newly discover about his mother.

Kathleen, once known only as the "female relative," or the pseudo-anonymous "M." had been the terror of Isherwood's psyche. She was, as all myths are, just a human being—albeit a fallible one. As Isherwood read his mother's thoughts—very human and quite sensitive thoughts—the myth faded and Kathleen became his mother again to be judged as such, and not as an evil archetype any longer. Her transformation and the satisfaction Isherwood felt within himself for letting the transformation happen, was of major importance in the coming years, which proved to be Isherwood's happiest. In *A Meeting by the River* the mother-figure was still a nemesis, and this novel was another chapter in Isherwood's long running internal debate. After Isherwood's maternal revelation in England, the demon-mother ceased to be and Isherwood's hurt ended as well. Now Kathleen's past was a usable past, to be regarded as continuously, contiguously, and simultaneously as not the past at all, but integral to a very happy present.

When Isherwood went to England, he had originally had something very different in mind than what became *Kathleen and Frank.* He imagined something on the order of that never-written epic, *The Northwest Passage,* but updated with the latest developments in the Isherwood-Auden schema. He listed his usual themes in planning the new epic: "the home-image, the romance of distant places, loneliness, homosexuality, the cult of being an outsider, the anti-Hero, Vedanta as anti-Religion, high camp."[19] Isherwood intended to blend the main characters of this projected work into a saga based on his personal mythology. Then he read his parents' letters and diaries. The details of his parents' world and the two sensitive people in that world were so poignantly and overwhelmingly

human, that Isherwood knew an epic myth would be a disservice to his parents
and to himself. *He* had created the myth, not his parents; he may have blamed
them for his need for a myth, but their words were the antithesis of myth and his
parents could no longer be held accountable for his mythmaking. Their words
moved him so much that a belatedly loving son decided Kathleen and Frank
would tell their own story in their own words, supplemented by Isherwood's
commentary. This book would not be a mythical epic, nor would Isherwood ever
deal with the Northwest Passage again. With the writing of *Kathleen and Frank,*
Isherwood no longer needed to mythologize. His myths, going back to
Mortmere, had been substitutes for his perceived expulsion from the womb-
cocoon. Discovering his parents' words and world, particularly the words of their
love for him, recreated the original womb-cocoon with which he integrated his
present Swami-Bachardy cocoon to make Isherwood as close to whole as he had
ever been since 1915. He was at peace with the four most important people in
his life, who rounded out both ends of his life; his continuous past had truly
merged with his continuous present. His life was now a very full one.

In part 1, chapter 1 of this study, excerpts from *Kathleen and Frank* were introduced to establish the context of the womb-cocoon since Isherwood's ostracism
from this protective shell had determined the direction of his future rebellion.
Isherwood learned from his "exhumation" of his parents' papers that very often one
does not rebel against his parents because one is unlike them, but rather because one
is too much like them, though he refuses to believe this during the rebellion itself.
According to Finney, Isherwood was "amazed at how his empathy with his parents
helped him to read between the lines of his parents' letters and diaries so that concepts underlying the book virtually declared themselves."[20]

Isherwood gives his supplemental commentary for the book in the third person, which some reviewers thought a conceit. If a conceit is a "fanciful whim,"
then Isherwood was the opposite of whimsical. This was not the first time that
Isherwood had chosen to put himself in the third person. He had always done so
to observe himself almost as an independent witness. Isherwood in the past had
been so hypersensitive to his need for self-confession that to have indulged himself as a subjective "I" might have tempted him toward pathos and bathos. In
addition, the Kathleen and Frank of the letters and diaries were very distant to
the sixty-three-year-old Isherwood. Most of their chronicle was recorded before
his birth and gave a portrait of a late Victorian and early Edwardian England that
he had known only from books. Since he was reading their words for the first
time, their words were almost as novel to him as an actual novel. If he had commented on their words and world in the first person, he would have seemed to
claim more knowledge than he actually had. Isherwood truly thought that their
own first-person narratives made for fascinating reading and to add a third "I" to
their first-person subjective voices would have hindered the prominence of his

parents' personalities. As a third-person narrator, Isherwood, instead of being fanciful, was being self-effacing on his own terms by letting Kathleen and Frank play the leads. His own voice stands offstage only to prompt.

The book is dedicated to "Kathleen and Frank and Richard." This was the first time his mother had been so honored. What follows are his parents' letters and diaries astutely fused between Isherwood's deliberately understated narration. Even though Isherwood's narrative in the total text comprises as much or more of the book than his parents' text, its unobtrusiveness makes it seem otherwise. The words tell about the world his parents lived in, the world Isherwood came to hate when it was an abstraction. Now, in the particulars of his parents' daily reality, Isherwood saw that they were as much victims of the past as he had thought himself to have been. Kathleen and Frank had not consciously dictated their world to Isherwood; their world had, by its inexorable power of class-conscious peer pressure, dictated to them, and they behaved as they were expected to behave. To have done otherwise would have been as obtuse to them as not being a rebel would have been to their son. Isherwood could no longer blame his parents for having been merely human, especially Kathleen.

The other figures in the narrative are also very human, often amusingly so—Isherwood's nanny, his Uncle Henry, his grandparents—but Isherwood regards them with the same bemused affection that Oliver's Swami had regarded Patrick: "Oh my goodness, what *will* he be up to next?" For instance: "One example of Henry's grandeur was his use of the hyphen. He always called himself Bradshaw-Isherwood. Later, when he married Miss Muriel Bagshawe, he legally enlarged his name to Bradshaw-Isherwood-Bagshawe and seemed to find nothing ridiculous in signing himself 'Henry B-I-B.' (Christopher, from his school days on, groaned under the weight of his huge name, and got an aggressive satisfaction from officially dropping the William and the Bradshaw when he became an American citizen in 1946)" (*KF*, 121).

Isherwood discovered that to Frank, Kathleen was "My darling Kitty" and the letters of their courtship were charming examples of Victorian banter—the kind of talk Isherwood had satirized in Mortmere.

In addition to the letters and diaries, Isherwood rediscovered the pages of his childhood "newspapers," which displayed the considerable artistic talents of both parents and a large proportion of proud doting that any other child could have envied. Isherwood, fifty years later, must have understood how much he had been loved regardless of how he had felt afterwards. In the perpetual continuum he was being loved by his parents again. Kathleen's diary of 3 June 1912 demonstrates that Christopher held center stage in his parents' view: "Christopher is having a Shakespeare week at his toy theatre! Tonight it was Macbeth which he read extracts from, different china animals taking different parts" (*KF*, 371).

At the end of the narrative (but before the crucial afterword) Isherwood writes of his last visit to Kathleen the year before her death: "Once she asked him if Vedanta philosophy included a belief in an afterlife. He answered yes; it would have been pedantic and cruel to qualify his yes with doubts about the degree to which the individual personality survives. Kathleen then told him she believed she and Frank would be together again. She said this with conviction; yet she was keeping her indignation in reserve, to be turned against God Himself if necessary—for she added, 'That must be true, otherwise everything would really be too monstrously unfair!'" (*KF,* 499).

Kathleen remained stubbornly herself right to the end. Isherwood, who could also be stubborn, had chosen in this case not to be "cruel" just for the sake of once again being in opposition to her. In the afterword, Isherwood, very Vedanta-like, saw their opposition as having been necessary for the development of his present consciousness and that Kathleen's seeming obstinateness had been for a purpose in the bigger picture. By his reacting to her, he had rejected Kathleen's world and forged ahead to make his own world: "Kathleen's opposition was rooted in obstinacy. . . . [Without it, however,] he would have lost the counterforce which gave him strength. It was Kathleen . . . who saved him from being a mother's boy, a churchgoer, an academic, a conservative, a patriot and a respectable citizen. His friends were all rebels in their different ways, they set him an example and gave him plenty of encouragement; but without Kathleen's counter pressure and the rage it inspired in him, he might still have wavered and lapsed. It was she who made the snug-home-womb [after Frank's death] uninhabitable, despite his desire to hide in it" (*KF,* 508). Isherwood lists possible choices in his life that he rejected because they would have been his mother's choices for him: church, Cambridge, becoming a don or doctor in a safe career, getting married, and providing grandchildren. By opposing the traditional roles he could have taken, he chose the roles which led him to writing, America, the Swami, Bachardy, and ultimately, his late-blooming happiness.

Consequently, even though mother and son had been in conflict, in writing *Kathleen and Frank* Isherwood had finally achieved a Vedantic reconciliation of their opposition, an opposition without which the fission required to advance his evolving consciousness would never have been fueled. The process, as arduous and as heart-rending and as unfathomable as it had sometimes been, had been a purposeful one. The opposition had created a psychic environment for the highbrow, sensitive Isherwood to be challenged by and to learn from. Without his rebellious struggle, there would have been no books to influence readers and no translations to encourage interest in Eastern philosophy. (Indeed, I first read the translations many years ago, and even if I had stopped at that, Christopher Isherwood would have had an impact on my life.) Isherwood's drama did not play out in a vacuum. Many others were, are, and will continue to be affected by it, for the most part unknowingly. One may read *Prater Violet* or the Bhagavad-Gita to one's great benefit while knowing little or nothing about the man behind them. Yet, by reading them, one becomes intrinsically linked to the pattern of that bigger picture that constitutes conscious-ness in the Vedantic sense. One person is always too close to the picture to see and understand it in its entirety, but the sensitive highbrow realizes that, if he could only stand back far enough, he could try to see the vast landscape all at once. One may never be able to do so, but the reward is in the effort. Isherwood made the effort and saw intimations of the continuous and contiguous pattern:

> Christopher saw how heredity and kinship create a woven fabric; its patterns vary, but its strands are the same throughout. Impossible to say exactly where Kathleen and Frank end and Richard and Christopher begin. . . . Christopher has found that he is far more closely interwoven with Kathleen and Frank than he had supposed, or liked to believe. . . . If these diaries and letters were part of his pro-ject, he was part of theirs—for they themselves were a project too. Its nature was revealed by those coy but broad hints dropped by Kathleen and Frank: "Perhaps someone will be glad of it some day," "What a pity your husband's life is never to be written!," "I hope posterity when they read this won't think I am grumbling."
>
> So now Christopher's project has become theirs; their demand to be recorded is met by his eagerness to record. For once the Anti-Son is in perfect harmony with his parents, for he can say, "Our will be done!"

Isherwood concluded that although readers might think *Kathleen and Frank* is "their story rather than his . . . this book too may prove to be chiefly about Christopher (*KF,* 509–10).

THE SECOND AFFIRMATION: *CHRISTOPHER AND HIS KIND,* PEACE WITH HIS "QUEERNESS"

The writing and editing of *Kathleen and Frank* had been a poignant process of self-examination for Isherwood, who came to terms with both of his parents and made up with them in his own metaphysical way. As a Vedantist, Isherwood believed in this reconciliation, cynics be damned. If he could be at peace with his parents and at peace with the Swami and Bachardy, life, indeed, was good, and he did not mind telling people about it. The afterword of *Kathleen and Frank* serves three purposes: (1) as a summary of Isherwood's life; (2) as a didactic explanation of the Isherwood Schema; (3) as Isherwood's coming out in a mainstream book.

In the afterword Isherwood conjectures on how Frank might have dealt with his son's homosexuality had his father survived the war. With this speculation, understated matter-of-factly, Isherwood said explicitly what had been generally known tacitly. In 1971, it was still a brave declaration. Many other tacit homosex-ual celebrities were still wearing the "don't ask; don't tell" mask. In 1972 Isherwood attended the Modern Language Association conference, which had its first-ever ses-sion on gay literature. For the then staid MLA, this was major recognition, at least among intellectuals. As the decade continued, Isherwood became a militant mystic for his tribe, outspoken and unafraid: Isherwood as George was history. The new Isherwood was exemplified in this Vedantic fable, first told by Sri Ramakrishna, and retold by the Swami:

> *The Vedic fable of the Guru and the Snake:* Long ago, in an ancient Indian village lived a reputedly dangerous snake. He was feared but actually was very lonely because no one would go near him except silly children who would taunt him with sticks and throw stones at him until he sometimes had to defend himself by biting one or two so they'd leave him alone—at least temporarily. He approached a reclusive Guru, and this guru was not afraid. The snake asked to be the guru's disciple and was accepted. The snake was very happy. One day, the Guru told his disciple that he had to go away for three months and while he was gone, the snake, no matter how provoked, must not bite anyone. The snake obeyed. However, when the snake would come out of his hole in the ground to find food, the silly children would bother him again, and when the snake steadfastly restrained himself, the children became emboldened and attacked the snake more often and more viciously. The snake could not even come out of his hiding place, but still, he obeyed his Guru. The Guru returned and found his disciple near death from starvation. The snake, weakly, but proudly told his guru that he had never wavered; no matter what, he didn't bite. His Guru answered: " My poor foolish disciple, I told you not to bite; I didn't tell you not to hiss."

Isherwood understood the moral of this fable. If he was going to come out, he was coming out unequivocally. The result would be his "now-the-truth-can-be-told" revisionist autobiography, *Christopher and His Kind*.

After so many years of simmering with the lid on, the opportunity to finally let off steam released much pent-up emotion. For Isherwood, the chance to really express himself was irresistible, and his flair for the spotlight served his outspoken militance. Isherwood made this clear in a 1976 interview just before *Christopher and His Kind* was published. Isherwood was asked: "You've said that you slept with one or two women, but that you didn't really like it." Isherwood answered,

> Oh, but it worked all right. There again of course it's difficult to say whether under other circumstances one might be able to feel romantically about a woman. And then, you see, getting right down to the core of myself, I begin to feel the old obstinacy coming up. I've tried to write about that in this book I've just finished. Then I think, "Well, fuck them all, why should I?" As long as there's pressure, as long as there's this majority saying "that's the way, that's what you ought to do," as long as nearly all the poets, and nearly everybody are going to harp on heterosexuality, I think "No, I won't, I absolutely won't." And I do see that there's a certain streak of perversity in me, of refusal to go along with the others. Somebody was telling me that I said in some interview that I felt that I would certainly have

become heterosexual, if everybody else was homosexual—there's a streak of that in my make-up.[21]

Isherwood indicated that he was not going to be anything less than candid in his forthcoming book and in his forthcoming life. He sounded somewhat like the Ambrose who had facetiously announced what he would do when the tribe took over and how they would be much more tolerant of heterosexuals than the heterosexuals had been of the tribe.

For Isherwood to be asked if he had tried someone from the opposite gender was as problematical to him as if a heterosexual was asked if he or she had been with someone of the same gender. In the former case, the implication was that homosexuality was an aberration as in, "Could there still be hope for you?" The interviewer, Carolyn Heilbrun, was not at all insensitive, but asking a rhetorical question so Isherwood could make his case. In Ambrose's hypothetical world run by the tribe, this silly question could have been asked of the minority heterosexuals who might have reacted just as vigorously as Isherwood did. In 1976 he believed that he should not have to explain his homosexuality. He should just write about it no differently than a heterosexual would write of his or her own life without qualifying the orientation. In the 1970s, coming out was an educative process for the Mr. and Mrs. Strunks of George's world, who wanted to be open-minded but needed some help in overcoming their culturally acquired Judeo-Christian antipathy. Deep-rooted antipathy cannot be overcome with only a passive resistance. Sometimes spokespersons are needed who are not afraid to hiss a little so that attention can be paid. Isherwood—like a Quentin Crisp or Truman Capote—was too old to be bothered with dissembling pretension.

He and other well-known vocal cohorts knew that their celebrity status gave them greater independence and a certain amount of protection that was still not the norm for the majority of their fellow tribe members. Just as Isherwood had said at the outbreak of World War II that his and Auden's status provided some cover for other conscientious objectors, in 1976 he did the same for homosexuals who still were not sure if they could speak out without negative ramifications. This is not to say that presently Ambrose's world has been achieved, but there has been progress for which tribal representatives such as Isherwood deserve much credit.

In part 1, chapter 3 of this study, *Christopher and His Kind* was introduced to reveal Isherwood's real motivation for going to Berlin, which he had not been able to say truthfully in *Lions and Shadows*. He went to Berlin because Auden had told him what he would find there: boys. *Christopher and His Kind* was written in 1976 when Isherwood was age seventy-two and after he had spent sixty years as a homosexual. Isherwood made the most of the opportunity afforded him by a more liberal climate to say what he had never written before for public consumption. If he was going to be a spokesperson for his tribe, he would not let them down.

Christopher and His Kind more than satisfied his tribe. There were not many (mainstream) memoirs before this one that had been so entertainingly truthful from the tribe's perspective. But what did the non-tribal public think? According to Finney, "The publication of *Christopher and his Kind . . .* involved [Isherwood] in a grueling round of press interviews and appearances on radio and television. But to his mild surprise the book was generally well-received on both sides of the Atlantic and had better initial sales than any other book he had written [excluding the Vedic translations]. Because of its frank treatment of homosexual life he had half-expected the kind of vicious attack which in the event only one or two reviewers such as Rebecca West delivered who denounced the book as 'one long symphony of squalor.'"[22] This harsh remark was hardly valid, especially by today's standards. And the fact that West made it—she had been H. G. Wells's longtime adulterous mistress who had been made pregnant by him—was almost humorous. Apparently nonconformist sex was all right as long as it did not involve homosexual liasons.

Perhaps the very British West had expected Isherwood, the former Briton, to be more reserved. By 1976, however, Isherwood had lived in America longer than he had lived in Britain. His British accent had become minimal and his British reserve long rejected. He was an American, a U.S. citizen since 1946. Isherwood explained the difference in a 1976 interview: "There was a time when, I realize now, I saw my sex partners as belonging to a sort of tribe which I was approaching in the spirit of a colonial exploiter. There was also, I suppose, a shyness involved; I preferred having them not only another class, but another race, so they could speak a different language. Talking English to them embarrassed me. But [in the U.S.] all of this disappeared. In that sense, America did not disappoint me; as soon as I got here, I got into a much more Whitmanesque sort of attitude, and in the essential democracy of life here I never again had any of these problems. And most of the people I've really cared about have been Americans."[23]

Isherwood told his story of the 1929 to 1939 years as a memoir of Wholly-Truthful art. Though some thought he had been overly aggressive, there had been heterosexual memoirs equally explicit or more so. But homosexuality was still shocking to a mainstream audience and regarded with caution in the general populace which feared any form of possible—to them—proselytizing. Aggressive is a relative term. At the time, Isherwood himself believed he had been necessarily assertive. He said then that he had been concerned that some people would indeed find the book distasteful. When asked why, he answered: "Because of its aggressiveness. It's not pornographic, not by any standards of nowadays. It would never be banned, at least not in any sort of semi-civilized place. But that's not the point. I think a lot of people would say: 'What's all the fuss about?' The most effective form of annihilation is to say, 'Yes, so he's a fag, what else is new? Some of our best friends are fags and we don't mind.'"[24] Today, *Christopher and His Kind* is still vastly entertaining, but hardly seems aggressive or shocking; that in itself is progress for his tribe, which marked even more progress when a play about the tribe, Tony Kushner's *Angels in America,* won the 1993 Pulitzer Prize. Kushner also wrote a 1994 play about Berlin in the 1930s titled *A Bright Room Called Day.*

In addition to being truthful about Isherwood's life and his tribe *Christopher and His Kind* has a another purpose. During the extended period when Isherwood had researched and then written *Kathleen and Frank,* he found the process an exercise in expiatory fence-mending that left him feeling better about himself. Confession was good for the soul—good enough that he would do more of it in *Christopher and His Kind.* Isherwood finally deals honestly with his homosexuality, which is the major theme. He understood that this was also an opportunity to clarify some issues and make amends for others that had been loose ends not previously accounted for. In 1976 Isherwood had never been more content; there was no better time to feel even more so by disentangling former equivocations. To become Truly Strong, an aspiring Truly Strong Man should have a clear conscience. Isherwood would demonstrate to readers that he could redress wrongs and try to make them right—if not in actuality as regarded history—at least as recorded intellectually for posterity.

Isherwood's tone is on the order of, *This is what I said before, but what I actually meant was,* or, *My ego prevented me from seeing the truth at the time, which I now finally understand.* There are numerous autobiographical revisions. For example, Isherwood felt particularly remiss about his fictional treatment of Bernhard Landauer, who is based on Wilfred Israel. In an interview, he said "as a matter of fact I don't altogether like the attitude toward him that's displayed in the story. . . . As I point out in this new book, he led a life which became incredibly heroic toward the end." Then Isherwood immediately followed this statement with a remark that seemed as if he needed to be clear on a point he had not even been asked: "I couldn't be anti Semitic if I tried, because we're too much in the same applecart."[25] That is, he and Bernhard were both members of much persecuted tribal minorities.

Isherwood's lifelong blending of fact and fiction was hardly known by a great majority of readers who regarded his characters only as that—characters, pure fictions. Consequently, Isherwood's need to revisit these characters with fairer appraisals was a choice of personal, not public, absolution. If he had never said a word about the real Landauer, Wilfred Israel, only he and a handful of his closest friends would have known. By 1976 fewer of those friends were still around. Of those who had passed away, the biggest loss was Auden in 1973. Spender, however, was very much alive, and it had been Spender who provoked Isherwood's conscience about Israel.

In Isherwood's corrective memoir, he writes this of his original portrayal of Landauer: "Again and again, Bernhard is presented as being tired and apathetic"

(*CK*, 65). Isherwood then repeats from the 1938 story what Landauer had said concerning a death threat he had received. Isherwood tells Bernhard to call the police. Bernhard answers: "My existence is not of such vital importance to myself or to others that the forces of the Law should be called upon to protect me." The 1976 Isherwood adds that in 1938 Landauer's answer seemed "a reply which suggests apathy rather than courage" (*CK*, 66). Isherwood follows by saying that in 1938 he had believed his perception to be correct, but that this changed after reading about Israel in Spender's autobiography, *World within World*. Spender describes the fervent plans of a very passionate anti-Nazi Israel in 1932. Isherwood says of Spender's description: "This was no mere theoretical talk. Less than a year later, when Hitler came to power, Wilfred began to show himself capable of great courage and firmness of purpose" (*CK*, 67). Israel was half-British and could have left for England at any time, but he stayed in Berlin until 1939, helping fellow Jews until he himself was one of the last Jews left. Only then did he go to Britain, where he aided refugees. He would be killed in 1943 when Nazi aircraft shot down a passenger flight he was on along with the actor Leslie Howard. In 1976 Isherwood speculates on his 1938 antipathy concerning the Landauer-Israel of 1932 Berlin:

> Christopher suspected that Wilfred was a severely repressed homosexual and that, as such, he condemned Christopher for his aggressive frankness about his own sex life. If Christopher did indeed suspect this, it would have been characteristic of him to be extra frank with Wilfred, in order to jolt him into frankness about himself.
>
> In the novel, it seems to be implied that what Bernhard is hiding is a romantic attachment to "Isherwood." Whether Wilfred was or wasn't homosexual is neither here nor there. Of one thing I am certain, he wasn't in love with Christopher. I therefore find the hint contained in the novel offensive, vague as it is, and I am embarrassed to know that Wilfred read it. (*CK*, 71)

In Vedanta's perpetual continuum it is never too late to practice "right speech" and make amends. Cause and effect in the metaphysical realm work independently of the material world. Karma has no statute of limitations. It did not matter how few people knew that Landauer had been based on Israel; it had only mattered to Isherwood that he himself knew.

Christopher and His Kind also details Isherwood's relationship with Heinz. Readers of "Waldemar" in *Down There on a Visit* find out in *Christopher and His Kind* that the 1938 customs' incident with Dorothy, whose character and situation parallel Isherwood's, had actually taken place earlier in the decade. Readers also find out that it was Isherwood who had been indirectly responsible for landing Heinz in jail and, subsequently, in the German army. Another comparison of *Christopher and His Kind* with *Down There on a Visit* is that the former matches the latter in narrative style and sardonic humor.

Since *Christopher and His Kind* was written immediately following *Kathleen and Frank,* Isherwood continues to be more sympathetic to his mother; he does not overlook her stubbornness, but he also does not overlook his own petulant stubbornness. Isherwood also gives Kathleen credit for her more positive actions concerning him, such as her efforts on behalf of her son the writer by acting as his unofficial agent when he was away, which was often. Kathleen was very proud of her son's books and plays—as a typical mother would have been. She had also given Gerald Hamilton the money that was supposed to help Heinz but did not. Overall, in *Christopher And His Kind,* she is depicted as more of an example of her class who could not help herself, rather than as the demon-mother.

On two counts, *Christopher and His Kind* is another affirmation, just like *Kathleen and Frank.* Isherwood affirms his right to be a member of his tribe and a tribal spokesperson, and he settles up with some of those he felt he needed to put things right with. The book ends with Isherwood on his way to America. His next book would trace all of his American years from 1939 to 1976 with one purpose only. During these thirty-seven years Isherwood learned that the hypothetical aspiring Truly Strong Man of the Isherwood-Auden schema could become Truly Strong because in America he found living proof: Isherwood's attraction to Vedanta was real, but what made it real and kept it real even during his lapsed years from 1945 to 1953 was his Guru. Isherwood believed he could not have had his last years of happiness had there not been so many previous years of unconditional love from Swami Prabhavananda. Throughout these years the Swami had been pure in heart and Truly Strong.

THE LAST AFFIRMATION: *MY GURU AND HIS DISCIPLE,* PEACE WITH GOD AND THE TRULY STRONG MAN

In 1976 Isherwood was asked to describe his first meeting alone with the Swami in 1939. He began his answer by reiterating that after all the British years of anti-religion and pro-tribal membership, Isherwood had needed to know where this Swami fellow stood on the issue of homosexuality: "'Well you see, he's a monk. And his view is that all attachment is attachment, that life exists only for God within one's self and that everything which hinders that is to be kept to a minimum, or sublimated. In a word, he said homosexuality is merely another form of attachment, neither worse nor better, and that was all I wanted to hear. I said all right, good. Now we can understand each other."[26] They did for the next thirty-seven years.

Isherwood's education about "this thing" began hypothetically with Gerald Heard. His belief in "this thing" was confirmed intuitively by the aura of its presence within his Guru: "To have had glimpses of the gradual taking over of Prabhavananda by 'this thing' is almost all I can lay claim to in the way of spiritual experience. Such glimpses may be awesome, even fear inspiring, or they may move you to tears or silly laughter. They are never decorous or sentimental and bear little or no relation to ecclesiastical dogmas and lists of virtues and sins. To communicate this kind of experience to your readers is perhaps beyond the power of words. But no writer who has had it could resist trying to communicate it, because no other subject matter is so challenging."[27] For Isherwood no other subject matter could be as important and personally rewarding.

Going back to 1928, all of Isherwood's work was about Isherwood in various stages of his psychic evolution. In the frantic British years his early writing depicted conflicts without solutions. For the most part, until the plays with Auden and his autobiography, *Lions and Shadows,* Isherwood had posed questions without answers. In the plays, with Auden's influence, there were intimations of some metaphysical answers; yet, those hints were fuzzy glimpses with little additional help for the reader other than that the answers were not to be found without, but within. With this much understood, in 1938 Isherwood was motivated to write his first official autobiography, *Lions and Shadows.* He looked back at his past in order to make sense of his present. Isherwood continued this re-evaluation process for the rest of his life. In *Lions* he posited the schema of the Truly Weak and Truly Strong Man, with E. M. Forster as the exemplar. Isherwood listed the virtues of a Truly Strong Man, which he summed up with the term pure in heart. In 1938, however, he could not yet say how one became pure in heart, or not Truly Weak. He could give no specific directions at the time because he did not have any. Nonetheless, a need for direction was apparent and that direction was west to America.

In the Vedantic years in America, Isherwood would receive direction and inspiration from a very special man. One emphasizes man, since, to this point, notwithstanding his initial quite human description of the Swami's "sometimes cantankerous, sometimes absurd Bengali self," Prabhavananda has seemed a saint. He may have become one but what appealed so strongly to Isherwood about his Guru was that he had been a man with the presence of God within him, but never had this man acted God-like. The Swami was humbled by this presence within him but never presumed he was the actor who commanded the presence to be present. Rather, he was acted upon by the presence and was humbly grateful that he was a vehicle for others to learn about God.

My Guru and His Disciple is Isherwood's homage to the Swami but without the slightest sanctimoniousness. The narrative is derived mainly from his diaries with additional commentary. This approach had served Isherwood well for *Kathleen and Frank.* His diaries were written with an ear for their future publication. They are the writer's rendering of Wholly-Truthful art that combines insight with vastly entertaining reality. *My Guru and His Disciple* is also similar to *Kathleen and Frank* in that both books, while titularly about other people, are "chiefly about Christopher."

Isherwood's last book was written after the Swami died in 1976 and it was a confirmation of how his Guru had changed his disciple's life. The book is also his last affirmation of how much the Guru-influenced changes in his life had given him such happiness, especially after meeting Don Bachardy, who provided the secular stability to augment Isherwood's spiritual world. Just as the Swami had passed the test in 1939 by accepting Isherwood's homosexuality, Prabhavananda also accepted Bachardy wholeheartedly. So much so that Bachardy became another disciple. In its own way this was a love triangle of great satisfaction to all three. Love is exactly the right word. Isherwood loved his Guru as deeply as he loved Bachardy, just in a different context. The Swami gave his love in return unconditionally. When Isherwood was in his post-temple years of temporary dissoluteness, on 23 August 1951 he wrote of the Swami: "he said that both Gerald [Heard] and Aldous had come to him and told him things about the way I am living, and asked him to remonstrate with me. Swami had answered, 'Why don't you pray for him?' I was touched and delighted by Swami's reaction, which I interpreted as a rebuke to Gerald and Aldous. Wasn't he telling them, in effect, 'You'd do better to love Chris more and criticize him less?'" (*GD*, 201–202).

In the Vedantic perpetual continuum a few years in a single lifetime (and even a single lifetime) do not mean as much in their particulars as they ultimately will in the context of a universal bigger picture. Patience is required. The Swami understood that the Isherwood of 1945 to 1953 was reacting to his 1939 to 1945 years of zealous immersion in his conversion by letting loose again. His Guru considered this rebellion part of a necessary process for Isherwood to go through in order to ultimately confirm or deny his faith. Isherwood confirmed his faith while learning that he could have faith and be in the world simultaneously, but without guilt. Consequently, painful as the years from 1945 to 1953 had sometimes been, without them, the contented Isherwood of the subsequent years might not have been possible. Without his Guru's unwavering love for the God within the man named Isherwood, the disciple might not have kept his own faith in God. In *My Guru and His Disciple* Isherwood's accounting of the love for his Guru and the God within his Guru are evident:

> 12 December 1962: Swami when asked about prayer, said that it is good for you and for the person you pray for; and he added: "You see, when you are speaking to God like that, there are not two people, there is only one." He also said that all you needed was faith that the prayer would be answered. You didn't have to be saint. . . . He said this with that absolute compelling confidence of his (*GD*, 250).
>
> 25 June 1963: Swami said that he had "the intense thought that *I am the Self in all beings*, so how can one harm anyone?" It's a wonderful life if you feel like that. . . (*GD*, 255).
>
> 2 November 1967: People who keep imputing deep intentions to Swami understand him very little. . . . Don says, "he works on automatic pilot most of the time." Of course, one may agree—in fact, I think one is forced to agree—that his

sayings sometimes show uncanny insight. But I don't think he is always aware of this. . . (*GD*, 295)

20 September 1967: [Swami told me,] as he has before . . . that I am the Atman [the God within the man] and that it doesn't make any difference whether I am aware of this or not. I am the Atman and that's that (*GD*, 299).

11 May 1971: At the end of the question period in the temple, Swami was asked, "Does the Guru ever withdraw his love from a disciple. . . ." Swami answered, "I don't know yet." (*GD*, 302)

8 March 1972: Vedanta, in its purest form, negates all cults, even cults of divine beings.

On the other hand, I personally am a devotee first and a Vedantist second. I flatter myself that I can discriminate—bowing down to the Eternal which is sometimes manifest to me in Swami, yet feeling perfectly at ease with him, most of the time on an ordinary human basis. My religion is almost entirely what I glimpse of Swami's spiritual experience. . . . I believe a single meeting might have incalculable effects upon an individual throughout his life (*GD*, 309).

15 December 1973: Swami asked me if I had any "experiences" [visions]. That's the word I always use when I ask him the same question. I found myself instantly in a state of strong emotion. I told him that I hadn't had any experiences, but that it didn't matter, because at least I know that, if I hadn't met him, my life would have been nothing. My voice was shaking and tears ran down my face. . . (*GD*, 319)

The Swami died on 4 July 1976 and the epilogue to *My Guru and His Disciple* was written three years later. Isherwood writes that the Swami's physical absence had not mattered to him as much as he would have imagined and that he thought about him as frequently as he always had. He also began to meditate more on "God's female aspect" partly because Swami had done so toward the end of his life, and "partly because I needed a mother figure through whom I can feel a more loving acceptance of my own mother, now that she is dead and my hostility toward her has left me" (*GD*, 335–36). Perhaps as part of an infinite plan, the Swami had helped Isherwood to have peace with Kathleen.

Isherwood wrote this epilogue at age seventy-five. He knew his own death was near and speculated on what that could mean. He was not afraid: "My life is still beautiful to me—beautiful because of Don, because of the enduring fascination of my efforts to describe my life experience in my writing, because of my interest in the various predicaments of my fellow travelers on this journey. . . . All I can offer them is this book, which I have written about matters I only partially understand, in the hope that it may somehow, to some readers, reveal glimpses of inner truth which remain hidden from its author" (*GD*, 337–38). Isherwood's modesty does not obscure that his last book and last affirmation describe how he had met a human being who had not only fulfilled the promise of what it meant to be pure in heart and Truly Strong, but had given his disciple directions for aspiring to become Truly Strong himself.

In Don Bachardy's book, *Last Drawings of Christopher Isherwood,* Bachardy writes of the last three months of Christopher Isherwood's life, which was failing from cancer. The title accounts for the final drawings Bachardy made of Isherwood. Bachardy said these drawings provided healing for both of them in letting Christopher go. In the introduction Bachardy includes journal entries for this period: 25 August 1985: ". . . working with him is not only an ever-growing, fascinating challenge but occasionally a real joy—for us both!" Bachardy writes of the thirty-three years of encouragement Isherwood had given him in his career as an artist and how often Isherwood had told him it was "one of the greatest sources of satisfaction he'd known in his life" (2 December 1985).

Isherwood died on 4 January 1986. Two days later, Bachardy writes:

> While Chris was dying . . . I focused on him intensely. . . . I was able to identify with him to such an extent that I felt I was sharing his dying, just as I'd shared so many experiences with him. It began to seem that dying was something which we were doing together. The shared experience provided me with a greater understanding of what death is and, with it, a diminished fear of my own. Chris's last gift to me was one of the most valuable of many he gave me. It was characteristic of him to be generous, even in the act of dying.[28]

Isherwood the disciple had learned the spirit of concern from his Guru. He passed this on to Bachardy who shared with readers Isherwood's last gesture of what it meant to be pure in heart and Truly Strong.

One can look around and see the representatives of the sensitive, Truly Strong Man in fact, fiction, and film. Today's hero can cry without shame as well as stand up for himself and others. In the past the hero had been stoic, stalwart—and unreal. The present hero, antihero first and hero second, is more prevalent than his more one dimensional ancestors. The line goes back to the 1930s. This study does not claim Christopher Isherwood invented the Truly Strong Man, but that Isherwood helped shape him. This is Christopher Isherwood's legacy. Ultimately, it is less important to ask how much credit Isherwood should get for developing the persona of the Truly Strong Man, than to know that he became one.

NOTES

INTRODUCTION

1. Quoted by Brian Finney in *Christopher Isherwood: A Critical Biography* (New York: Oxford University Press, 1979), 287.

2. Christopher Isherwood, *Lions and Shadows* (London: Hogarth Press, 1938), 19.

3. Ibid., 207.

4. Isherwood, *Mr. Norris Changes Trains* (New York: New Directions, 1947), 13.

5. W. H. Auden, *The Orators* (London: Faber and Faber, 1932).

6. Isherwood, *My Guru and his Disciple* (New York: Farrar, Straus, Giroux, 1980), 5.

7. Ibid., 4–5.

8. Ibid., jacket copy, written by Isherwood.

CHAPTER 1

1. John Lehmann, *The Whispering Gallery* (New York: Harcourt, Brace, 1955), 179.

2. Finney, *Christopher Isherwood: A Critical Biography,* 287.

3. Auden, *The Orators,* 14.

4. Kathleen's willfulness, perhaps generated by her only-child status, manifested itself to Frank even before marriage. After a petty but lingering disagreement about how they should address letters to each other, Kathleen sends one to Frank with no salutation at all, and writes, "You notice my beautiful submission? So may the subject pleased be dropped now? All the same I can't resist the last word, which is that before long I think you will come to take my view of beginnings" (*KF,* 135). Her son inherited her stubbornness, particularly with respect to his relationship with Kathleen herself.

5. Finney, *Christopher Isherwood: A Critical Biography,* 19–20.

6. Samuel Hynes, *The Auden Generation* (Princeton: Princeton University Press, 1976).

7. Katherine Bucknell, introduction to *Diaries: Volume One: 1939–1960,* ed. Bucknell (New York: Harper Collins, 1997), xi.

8. W. H. Auden, "Writing," in *A Certain World* (New York: Viking Press, 1970), 423–24.

9. Auden, "Squares and Oblongs," in *Poets at Work* (New York: Harcourt, Brace, 1948), 177.

10. Auden, "The Liberal Fascist," in *The English Auden,* ed. Edward Mendelson (New York: Random House, 1977), 322–23.

11. Ibid., 323.

12. Ibid,. 323

13. Isherwood, *Diaries,* 756.

14. According to Kierkegaard, "The public is a concept which could not have occurred in antiquity because people *en masse, in corpare,* took part in any situation

which arose and were responsible for the actions of the individual, and, moreover, the individual was personally present and had to submit at once to applause or disapproval. . . . Only when the sense of association in society is no longer strong enough to give life to concrete realities is the press [media] able to create that abstraction 'the public' consisting of unreal individuals who can never be united in an actual situation or organization—and yet are held together as a whole. . . . A public is everything and nothing, the most dangerous of all powers and the most insignificant." See *The Living Thoughts of Kierkegaard,* ed. W. H. Auden (Bloomington, Ind.: Midland Books, 1963), 41–43.

15. Auden, "Letter to Lord Byron," in *Collected Poems* (New York: Random House, 1976), 83.

16. Auden, "Reviews," in *The English Auden,* 317.

17. Auden, "The Dyer's Hand," in *The Anchor Review* (New York: Doubleday, 1957), 295.

18. Bucknell, introduction to *Diaries,* ix.

19. Another author stranded and abandoned at age eleven was Conrad Aiken, whose father shot his mother to death, then killed himself. It was their son who heard the shots and ran to find the aftermath. Like Isherwood, Aiken spent the rest of his life getting over this early trauma, writing prose and poetry that, as confession and expiation, ceaselessly re-examined his evolving psyche. Aiken also struggled with compulsive sexuality and troubled relationships, as did Isherwood. In fact, their lives were very similar psychologically; Aiken's heterosexuality and Isherwood's homosexuality seemed to make very little difference in the way they handled relationships, for better or worse. To read about their trials and tribulations, one might think their failed sexual relationships could be transposed without noticing the change in the gender of their lovers. Perhaps this similarity points out that the physical aspect of a relationship might be the least important, and most ephemeral, difference between human beings–that is to say, sexual preference has much less to do with bodies than with minds. From a Vedantist standpoint this is the case. A major reason for Isherwood's love and respect for Swami Prabhavananda was that his Guru, while seeing sex as an obstacle in freeing the body from the mind, nonetheless was absolutely nonjudgmental about which bodies were concerned.

20. Finney, *Christopher Isherwood: A Critical Biography,* 31.

21. Isherwood, *Lions and Shadows* (London: Hogarth Press, 1938), 13.

22. Auden, "The Guilty Vicarage," in *The Dyer's Hand* (New York: Random House, 1962), 158. Auden took the title of his previous *Anchor Review* essay and used it again for this book of essays (see note 17).

23. Stephen Spender, *World within World* (London: Hamish Hamilton, 1951), 9.

24. Bucknell, introduction to *The Mortmere Stories,* by Christopher Isherwood and Edward Upward (London: Enitharmon Press, 1994), 9–10.

CHAPTER 2

1. T. S. Eliot, "The Love Song of Alfred J. Prufrock," in *The Norton Anthology of Modern Poetry,* 2d ed., ed. Richard Ellmann and Robert O'Clair (New York: Norton, 1988), 482.

2. Aldous Huxley, *Limbo* (London: Chatto and Windus, 1920), 109.

3. Huxley, *Vulgarity in Literature* (London: Chatto and Windus, 1931), 21.

4. "Interview with W. H. Auden," *Antaeus* (spring/summer 1972): 137.

5. Huxley, introduction to *Texts and Pretexts*, ed. Huxley (London: Chatto and Windus, 1931), 4.

6. Auden, "Poets, Poetry, and Taste," in *The English Auden*, 363.

7. The tribe image developed from psychoanalysis—particularly Jungian psychoanalysis—and asserts that the individual's unconscious is derived from archetypal myths and images that permeate his present psyche. The group mentality had more of a sociological and educational basis, particularly since Oxford made the group the focus of a study culminating in a book of essays, *Oxford and the Groups* (London: Blackwell-Oxford, 1934), to which Auden contributed "The Group Movement and the Middle Class." The gang mindset originated with public school identification, which was positive for the hearties, negative for the highbrows like Isherwood. The gang mentality took on darker implications with the rise of fascism, which was not restricted to Germany and Italy but in Sir Oswald Mosley had a leader in Britain who became a character in Huxley's *Point Counterpoint* in 1928.

8. Isherwood, introduction to *All the Conspirators* (New York: New Directions Books, 1958), i.

9. Ibid., iii.

10. "How to Be Masters of the Machine," in *The English Auden*, 315–17.

11. In reading this 1996 recollection by Upward, I was particularly struck by the reference to George Moore. Before writing this study I had read Isherwood's works over a number of years, but had not read George Moore's texts until much later. Having read Moore, I believe that he was someone who may have influenced Isherwood, but I did not know of a reference that suggested this connection. Moore's style of "mythified" realism, (see particularly *Evelyn Innes*) as well as his blurring of autobiographical fiction and fictionalized autobiography (see *Memoirs of My Dead Life*) do indeed seem possible influences for Isherwood.

12. Edward Upward, *Christopher Isherwood: Notes in Remembrance of a Friendship* (London: Enitharmon Press, 1996), 8.

13. Isherwood, *Diaries*, 30.

14. Bucknell, introduction to *The Mortmere Stories*, 11.

15. Auden, "Tennyson," in *Forewords and Afterwords*, ed. Edward Mendelson (New York: Random House, 1973), 230n.

16. Auden, "Review of *Open House*," *Saturday Review of Literature*, April 5, 1931, 30.

17. See David Garrett Izzo, *Aldous Huxley and W. H. Auden: On Language* (West Cornwall, Conn.: Locust Hill Press, 1998).

18. Huxley, "Art," in *The Human Situation* (New York: Harper and Row 1977), 183.

19. Upward, *Notes in Remembrance*, 7.

20. Ibid., 9–10

21. Auden, *The Prolific and the Devourer* (Hopewell, N.J.: Ecco Press, 1993), 10.

22. Auden, "An Outline for Boys and Girls and Their Parents," in *The English Auden,* 305.

23. Auden, "Words and the Word," in *Secondary Worlds* (New York: Random House, 1968), 125.

24. Bucknell, introduction to *The Mortmere Stories,* 9.

25. Ibid. 11.

26. Upward, *Notes in Remembrance,* 5.

27. Quoted in Bucknell, introduction to *The Mortmere Stories,* 21.

28. Isherwood, "The Speckled Band," in *Exhumations* (New York; Simon and Schuster, 1966), 88–89.

29. George Orwell, introduction to *The Complete Short Stories of Raffles: The Amateur Cracksman,* by E. W. Hornung (New York: St. Martin's Press, 1984), 256.

30. Isherwood, "The Horror in the Tower," in *The Mortmere Stories,* 49.

31. Isherwood, "Introductory Dialogue," in *The Mortmere Stories,* 33–47.

32. Isherwood, "The Horror in the Tower," 54.

33. Ibid., 60.

34. Isherwood, "The Greatness of Andy Shanks," in *The Mortmere Stories,* 67.

35. Isherwood, "The Adventures of Fooby Bevan," in *The Mortmere Stories,* 71–73.

36. Isherwood, "The Garage in Drover's Hollow, in *The Mortmere Stories,* 80.

37. Isherwood,"Christmas in the Country," in *The Mortmere Stories,* 95–96.

38. Bucknell, introduction to *The Mortmere Stories,* 16.

39. *Diaries,* 434.

40. Isherwood, "Recessional From Cambridge, " in *The Mortmere Stories,* 163–67.

41. Andrew Mangeot, introduction to *People One Ought to Know,* by Christopher Isherwood, (Garden City, N.Y.: Doubleday, 1982), 2–3.

42. "Crocodile," *People,* 5.

43. "The Javanese Sapphires, " in *The Mortmere Stories,* 97–98.

44. Ibid., 171.

45. Ibid., 111–24.

46. Huxley, "The Subject Matter of Poetry," in *On The Margin* (London: Chatto and Windus, 1923), 26–38; "Tragedy and the Whole Truth," in *Music at Night* (London: Chatto and Windus, 1931), 3–18.

47. Huxley, "The Subject of Matter of Poetry," 32–34.

48. Auden, "Poets, Poetry, and Taste," 329.

49. Auden, "Dyer's Hand," 266.

50. Isherwood, "Christmas in the Country," 103.

51. Huxley, "Tragedy and the Whole Truth, " 14–15.

52. Auden, "Poets, Poetry, and Taste," 329.

Chapter 3

1. Stephen Spender, *World within World* (London: Hamish Hamilton, 1951), 103.

2. Ibid., 128.

3. Quoted by Finney in *Christopher Isherwood: A Critical Biography,* 289.

4. Spender, *World within World,* 102.

5. "Christopher Isherwood: An Interview," *Twentieth Century Literature* 22 (October 1976): 261.

6. "A Conversation with Christopher Isherwood," *Antaeus* 13–14, nos. 2–3 (spring/summer 1972): 370.

7. Auden, "An Outline for Boys and Girls and Their Parents," in *The English Auden,* 305.

8. Isherwood, "Stories," in *Exhumations* (New York: Simon and Schuster, 1966), 170–71.

9. Ibid., 172.

10. Ibid., 173.

11. Ibid., 174. The story is "Evening at the Bay," included in *Exhumations.*

12. Edward Mendelson, "Appendix I," in *The English Auden,* 409.

13. Edward Mendelson, *Early Auden* (Cambridge: Harvard University Press, 1983), 29.

14. Ibid., 33–34.

15. Ibid., 38.

16. Ibid., 47.

17. Ibid., 47.

18. Ibid., 48.

19. Ibid., 54.

20. Mendelson, "Appendix I," in *The English Auden,* 410.

21. Ibid., 412.

22. Isherwood's hypochondria was a nervous reaction to his own insecurities, especially when he felt himself in stressful circumstances. For example, he describes this visit to Oxford while Auden was still a student there in 1927: "This room, these cultured voices still exercised something of their evil, insidious power; they made me feel, yes, competitive. Against my will, against my better judgment, something inside me wanted to stand up . . . to astound them all. And because I wouldn't, couldn't, I sat and sulked. . . . I returned to London next day, with the beginnings of a violent attack of influenza, . . . I cursed the Oxford climate: but Oxford wasn't to blame—it was Weston himself. Henceforward, I caught a bad cold nearly every time we met: indeed, the mere sight of a postcard announcing his arrival would be sufficient to send up my temperature. . . . these psychological attacks became one of our stock jokes. . . . I have never been able to explain them. . . . was the analyst-patient relationship between Weston and myself far more permanent and profound than either of us realized. . . . I record my symptoms here. . . . my modest exhibit in the vast freak museum of our neurotic generation" (*LS,* 216–17).

23. "A Conversation with Christopher Isherwood," 366.

24. Isherwood, introduction to *All the Conspirators,* 9.

25. Claude Summers, *Christopher Isherwood* (New York: Ungar, 1980), 50.

26. Quoted in Finney, *Christopher Isherwood: A Critical Biography,* 63.

27. Auden, "Shorts," in *Collected Poems,* 55–56.

28. Auden, "Taller To-day," in *Collected Poems,* 30. For a specific source for Auden's

"Gas-works," see C. Day Lewis's autobiography, in which he writes that "Often, during the summer of 1927, we walked around Oxford—Wystan's favorite walk was past the gas-works." See *The Buried Day* (London: Chatto and Windus, 1960), 177–79. When Isherwood would visit Auden at Oxford, they made this same walk.

29. Auden, "The Watershed," in *Collected Poems,* 32

30. Quoted in Spender, *World within World,* 57. In his autobiography Spender attributed the introduction to Auden without mentioning Day Lewis, who not only reminds readers in his own autobiography that he and Auden wrote it together, but states that they alternated paragraphs and this paragraph was one of those written by himself. Day Lewis, however, also admits how much he was under Auden's influence at the time in thought, prose, and verse: "Wystan aroused to the utmost my emulative faculty" (*The Buried Day,* 177–79).

31. Spender, quoted in Lee Bartlett, introduction to *Stephen Spender: Letters to Christopher* (Santa Barbara: Black Sparrow Press, 1980), 13.

32. Huxley, *Texts and Pretexts* (London: Chatto and Windus, 1932), 17. In this commonplace anthology, in which Huxley comments on poetry, there are the early stirrings of his mystical inclinations that would eventually culminate in his later anthology, *The Perennial Philosophy* (New York: Harper and Brothers, 1945). In *The Perennial Philosophy,* Huxley comments on the writings of the mystics in all of the known spiritual and metaphysical disciplines and consolidates their wisdom into what he called The Minimum Working Hypothesis. This hypothesis summarizes the basis of Vedanta and would be included in Huxley's introduction to the Isherwood-Prabhavananda translation of the Bhagavad-Gita (Hollywood: Marcel Rodd, 1944). As for *Texts and Pretexts,* Auden referred to it in his own commonplace anthology, *A Certain World.* (New York: Viking, 1970.) He and Huxley based much of their metaphysical ideas of the 1930s and beyond on the theories of their mutual friend, Gerald Heard, who is one of the most unknown, and yet greatest influences on literature and philosophy in this century. He not only influenced Huxley, Auden, and Isherwood directly, but, through them, many others indirectly. Heard can also be linked to the philosopher Michael Polanyi, who is in vogue today, while Heard is virtually, but undeservedly, anonymous. He will, however, factor in the balance of this study.

33. As for Mortmere and Edward Upward, they were still in Isherwood's life. Isherwood and Upward would visit with each other whenever possible: "I found Chalmers' company all-absorbing and sufficient. . . . we seemed to have grown increasingly silly: our favorite game was to chase down bits of toilet paper with walking sticks over the downs. . . . we followed it with yells and Starnese hunting-cries, whirling the sticks above our heads or flinging them, like javelins, at the quarry" (*LS,* 275).

34. Isherwood, *Diaries,* 645.

35. Another view comes from Day Lewis. Day Lewis said that while Auden's "vitality [was] so abundant that, overflowing into certain poses and follies and wildly unrealistic notions, it gave these an authority, an illusion of rightness, which enticed some of Auden's contemporaries into taking them over-seriously. His exuberance redeemed too, for me, the dogmatism, the intellectual bossiness, and the tendency to try to run his

friends' lives for them, all of which were by-products of his excess of life. I found him, and still do, intensely stimulating: it was probably just as well that I was three years older than he, for otherwise his influence might have been too potent for me: as it was, though, I came under the spell. Auden's personality also set up in me a certain resistance, and I instinctively felt, that he was perhaps best taken in small doses. . . . Though I had certain half-conscious reservations about him, I willingly became his disciple where poetry was concerned" (*The Buried Day*, 176–77). Day Lewis imitated Auden's poetry in content, if not technique, and plainly said so.

As for Auden's "exuberance," novelist Glenway Wescott said on first meeting Auden in New York on 2 February 1939, "Auden is in N.Y. and dined here last night, very energetic and amiable—he greatly resembles Vachel Lindsay!" (*Continual Lessons: The Journals of Glenway Wescott* [New York: Farrar, Straus, Giroux, 1990], 49). Lindsay, 1879–1931, was the first great American poet as performance artist; he recited, chanted, added sound effects and was a legend for his prodigious energy.

As for Day Lewis and his "conscious reservations," he was not alone in this attitude; as Auden aged and became more of a curmudgeon, even Spender's view changed from bemusement to begrudgingness at times, as if he would stay friends with the Auden of the past while acknowledging that the Auden of the present could be annoyingly cantankerous. In Spender's *Journals, 1939–1983* (Franklin, Pa.: Franklin Library, 1985), he recounts an occasion of Auden's contrary behavior and his own lack of a response in order to avoid a confrontation. (He also reminds himself of other times when Auden was kind and generous.) He writes: "All the same, not to protest, not to say anything on such an occasion, but just dumbly to go through an absurd farce seemed vaguely humiliating. I felt that if Christopher Isherwood had been in my place he would have objected saying, 'Come off it, Wystan!'" (162). Isherwood likely would have, and because of this, Auden would just as likely not have been so difficult in the first place. Spender, as he himself knew, was too willing to acquiesce. A strong personality like Auden's would take advantage of this, whereas Isherwood, another strong personality, would not back down.

36. Spender, *World within World*, 103–105.

37. Spender, in a letter to Lincoln Kirstein, editor of the American literary magazine *The Hound and Horn*. This passage is quoted in *The Hound and Horn Letters*, ed. Mitzi Berger Hamovitch (Athens, Ga.: Georgia University Press, 1982), 211.

38. Day Lewis, *The Buried Day*, 178–79. Day Lewis, in 1935, writing as Nicholas Blake, published *A Question of Proof*, his first in a series of detective novels featuring the consulting detective Nigel Strangeways, who is obviously based on Auden in all his idiosyncratic charm. The story takes place at a preparatory school.

39. Hynes, *The Auden Generation*, 43.

40. Day Lewis, *Collected Poems 1929–1933 and A Hope for Poetry* (New York: Random House, 1935), 55. It should also be noted that Random House had published Auden's *Poems* the year before and to some extent Auden was still helping Day Lewis and Day Lewis was still emulating Auden.

41. Edward Elton Smith, *The Angry Young Men of the Thirties* (Carbondale, Ill.: Southern Illinois University Press, 1975), 9.

42. Aiken's long poems are *Jig of Forslin* (1916), *Senlin: A Biography* (1917), *Punch: The Immortal Liar* (1921), *The Pilgrimage of Festus* (1924), *Priapus and the Pool* (1925), all in *Selected Poems* (London: Charles Scribner's and Sons, 1930). Aiken was a classmate and friend of T. S. Eliot's at Harvard. Today Aiken is vastly underappreciated because his work was dealing with psychological and metaphysical themes that are better understood now, but were remote when he was writing about them. Aiken was an influence on Eliot rather than the other way around. *The Waste Land*, while eclipsing Aiken, was derivative of Aiken's psychological questing, and *The Four Quartets*, written years after Aiken's work of spiritual and metaphysical introspection, displays Eliot's own "emulative" faculty. (Eliot's play *The Cocktail Party*, seems to be not only, in parts, a pastiche of Witter Bynner's *Cake* but, in other parts, a co-opting of it.) See Edward Butscher's *Conrad Aiken: Poet of White Horse Vale* (Athens: Georgia University Press, 1988), and Ted Spivey's *Time Stops in Savannah* (Macon, Ga.: Mercer University Press, 1997).

43. Hynes, *The Auden Generation*, 43.

44. Day Lewis, *Collected Poems*, 19.

45. Ibid., 45.

46. Ibid., 53.

47. Ibid., 18.

48. Auden, *Collected Poems*, 8.

49. Day Lewis, *Collected Poems*, 16.

50. Ibid., 11.

51. Auden, "Consider," in *Collected Poems*, 61.

52. Day Lewis, *Collected Poems*, 9.

53. Auden, *Collected Poems*, 38.

54. Day Lewis, *Collected Poems*, 14.

55. Auden, "XXVIII," in *Poems* (London: Faber and Faber, 1930), 76.

56. Day Lewis, *Collected Poems*, 21.

57. Ibid., 19.

58. Isherwood and Spender were never overly warm to Day Lewis. (Spender did leave out Day Lewis when he discussed "Auden's" Oxford preface in *World within World*, for which he was chastised by Day Lewis in *The Buried Day*.) Isherwood wrote in his diary for 8 August 1958 that, after a fan asked him about "the gods of his youth—Auden, Spender, MacNeice, Day Lewis," Isherwood responded to the fan while "nobly refraining" from telling the fan what he thought of Day Lewis's poetry.

59. Day Lewis, *Collected Poems*, 49.

60. Ibid., 56.

61. Auden, *Collected Poems*, 36.

62. Mendelson, *Early Auden*, 13–14.

63. Gerald Heard, *The Emergence of Man* (London: Jonathan Cape, 1931), 21. The idea of a psychic evolution is not so rare today in this new age milieu but was rather unusual when Heard wrote this study. Heard was very well known in Britain and even had a BBC radio program, *This Surprising World*, which put science, philosophy, and metaphysics into layman's language. Heard influenced Auden with his theories, which

now—if anyone would read Heard—would make more sense than they did in his time. The world has caught up with him. Heard also befriended Huxley and Isherwood, introducing the latter to Vedanta in America. Isherwood said of him in a 1972 interview: "He was one of the most astounding people I ever met. He was a wonderful mythmaker. It was something approximate to knowing Jung. He saw the great archetypes that govern life to an extraordinary extent." See "Christopher Isherwood," in *Writers at Work: The Paris Review Interviews, Fourth Series* (New York: Viking, 1974), 229–30. Heard was so compelling a personality that he became a major character in four novels: Dr. Miller in Huxley's *Eyeless in Gaza* (1935) and Mr. Propter in Huxley's *After Many a Summer Dies the Swan* (1939); Larry Darrell in Maugham's *The Razor's Edge* (1944), and Augustus Parr in Isherwood's *Down There on a Visit* (1962).

64. Mendelson, *Early Auden*, 8.

65. Ibid., 7.

66. See *The Living Thoughts of Kierkegaard*, 25.

67. Mendelson, *Early Auden*, 22.

68. Auden, "II," in *Poems*, 40

69. Auden, "A Free One," in *Collected Poems*, 40.

70. Auden, "1929, II," in *Collected Poems*, 46.

71. Auden, "Never Stronger," in *Collected Poems*, 35–36.

72. Auden, "Too Dear, Too Vague," in *Collected Poems*, 38.

73. Auden, "Between Adventure," in *Collected Poems*, 39.

74. Auden, "XIV," in *Poems*, 53.

75. Auden, "1929, I," in *Collected Poems*, 45.

76. Auden, "1929, III," in *Collected Poems*, 49.

77. The flashback and forward time order was also featured in another novel published in 1932, Conrad Aiken's *Great Circle*, which was influenced by Freud. Aiken's intent was to show that the neurotic behavior of the adult protagonist (Aiken) was shaped by a childhood murder-suicide, something that had actually happened to Aiken. In *Great Circle* Aiken uses the phrase "eyeless at Gaza" (175) and a variation "eyeless in Gaza" (243), which are allusions taken from Milton. The second, "eyeless in Gaza," became the title of Aldous Huxley's 1936 novel, which took time-shifting to even more complex variations. Huxley's choice of title may have been an homage to Aiken, whom he knew when the latter lived in England. See *The Collected Novels of Conrad Aiken* (New York: Holt, Rinehart and Winston, 1964). Freud himself admired *Great Circle* so much that he kept it in his waiting room along with Thornton Wilder's *The Bridge of San Luis Rey*.

78. Summers, *Christopher Isherwood*, 55.

79. Auden, "Preface," in *The Orators*, rev. ed. (London: Faber and Faber, 1966), 7.

80. Auden, *The Orators*.

81. Quoted in Mendelson, *Early Auden*, 97.

82. Ibid., 100.

83. Ibid., 101.

84. Ibid., 103.

85. Ibid., 104.

86. *The Orators* is much more complex than can be described here since my intent is only to connect Auden's themes to the themes of this study. For the complete analysis, as in all things Auden, I defer to Edward Mendelson.

87. Spender, "Review of Portraits by Desmond MacCarthy," *Criterion* 11 (April 1932): 554–57.

88. Isherwood, *Christopher and His Kind* (New York: Farrar, Strauss, Giroux, 1976), 118.

89. Spender would later say: "In a sense one might describe the Thirties as a leader—Auden—with a following but no movement. Movements have meetings, issue manifestoes, have aims in common. The Thirties poets never held a single meeting. . . . However, Auden did have certain characteristics of a leader. He was in several ways very much ahead of his colleagues; he had very definite views about certain subjects of whose very existence his colleagues often first heard from him. He had a tactician's sense of a map which was the time in which we were living and on which, in his mind, all the poets, past and present, had definite places. He was also conscious of the current condition of literature within which he and certain of his friends would belong to the winning future. He was also much cleverer than the others of us, conscious of being so, and without the slightest trace of inferiority complex." See the introduction to *The Thirties and After.* (New York: Random House, 1978), 8–9. Auden did not have an inferiority complex concerning his intellectual ability, but like most human beings, he was not always so sure of himself as concerned human relationships. Much of his later dour gruffness has often been attributed to his disappointments in matters of the heart, which even his great intellect could not master.

90. That the essay can be a medium for satiric parable is evidenced by, among many possible examples, Swift's "A Modest Proposal," and William Golding's "Thinking as a Hobby." George Orwell's "Shooting an Elephant" may not be a satire, but it is certainly a parable.

91. Auden, "Review of *Instinct and Intuition: A Study in Mental Duality,* by George Binney Dibblee," in *The English Auden,* 301.

92. Auden, "Writing," in *The English Auden,* 303.

93. Auden, "Private Pleasure," in *The English Auden,* 313.

94. Ibid., 313.

95. Auden, "Problems of Education," in *The English Auden,* 315.

96. Auden, "VII," in *The English Auden,* 317.

97. Auden, "Review of The *Book of Talbot,* by Violet Clifton," in *The English Auden,* 319.

98. Auden, "Review of *T. E. Lawrence,* by B. H. Liddell Hart," in *The English Auden,* 320.

99. Ibid., 321.

100. Auden, "The Protestant Mystics," in *Forewords and Afterwords* (New York: Random House, 1976), 69–70.

101. Mendelson, *Early Auden,* 274.

102. Spender, *The Destructive Element* (London: Jonathan Cape, 1935). In *The Auden*

Generation, Samuel Hynes explains: "The 'destructive element' of the title is the phrase from Conrad's *Lord Jim,* but that is not Spender's immediate source. As he explains in his introduction, he took the phrase, and the argument of which it is part, from [I. A.] Richards' *Science and Poetry,* and specifically from that influential footnote on *The Waste Land.* Richards had said that, "by effecting a completer severance between his poetry and all beliefs, and this without any weakening of the poetry, he has realised what might have otherwise have remained largely a speculative possibility, and has shown the way to the only solution of these difficulties. 'In the destructive element immerse. That is the way'" (162–63).

103. *Journey From the North: Autobiography of Storm Jameson* (New York: Harper and Row, 1969), 306–7.

104. Auden, *The Prolific and Devourer* (Hopewell, N.J.: Ecco Press, 1993), 4. Auden wrote this in 1939.

105. Auden, as quoted in Mendelson, preface to *The Prolific and the Devourer,* vii-viii.

106. Mendelson, *Early Auden,* 286.

107. Ibid., 286.

108. Ibid., 333.

109. David Garrett Izzo, "The Student and the Master: A Pupil Recollects W. H. Auden," *Carolina Quarterly* 3 (summer 1996): 29–38.

110. Thornton Wilder, *The Eighth Day* (New York: Harper, 1967), 395.

111. Mendelson, *Early Auden,* 320.

112. George Orwell, quoted in *Early Auden,* 321n.

113. Auden, forward to *Collected Shorter Poems* (New York: Random House, 1966), 15.

114. Mendelson, *Early Auden,* 321.

115. Finney, *Christopher Isherwood: A Critical Biography,* 145

116. Ibid., 144–45.

117. Ibid., 146.

118. Ibid., 146.

119. Ibid., 145.

120. Ibid., 148.

121. Alan Wilde, *Christopher Isherwood* (New York: Twayne, 1971), 70.

122. Paul Piazza, *Christopher Isherwood: Myth and Anti-Myth* (New York: Columbia University Press, 1978), 94.

123. Finney, 150–51.

124. Lisa Schwerdt, *Isherwood's Fiction* (London: Macmillan, 1991), 86–87.

125. Finney, *Christopher Isherwood: A Critical Biography,* 168.

126. Mendelson, *Early Auden,* 348–49.

127. *The Song of God: Bhagavad-Gita,* trans. Isherwood and Prabhavananda, (Los Angeles: Marcel Rodd, 1944).

PREFACE TO PART 2

1. Isherwood, introduction to *All the Conspirators,* 2.

Chapter 4

1. Isherwood, *Christopher and His Kind,* 306.
2. Isherwood, *Diaries,* 4.
3. Ibid., 94.
4. Ibid., 179.
5. Auden, *Another Time* (New York: Random House, 1940), dedication page.
6. The most detailed and delightful rendering of Hollywood's eccentricities in the 1930s and early 1940s is *Down But Not Quite Out in Hollow-Weird: A Documentary in Letters of Eric Knight* by Geoff Gehman (Lanham, Md.: Scarecrow Press, 1998). Knight was a screenwriter who created *Lassie* and also wrote the anti-fascist novel *This Above All.* Knight was killed in 1943 when the Nazis shot down the plane he was on, thus meeting the same fate that also killed Wilfred Israel (the real Bernhard Landauer) and the film actor Leslie Howard.
7. When Huxley was sixteen, he was afflicted with an eye disease that left him blind for a year and his vision remained seriously impaired for the rest of his life.
8. Huxley, introduction to the *The Song of God: Bhagavad-Gita* (Los Angeles: Marcel Rodd, 1944), 7.
9. Huxley, "Man and Religion," in *The Human Situation* (New York: Harper and Row, 1977), 212–13.
10. All of Isherwood's writings on Vedanta have been compiled in *The Wishing Tree: Christopher Isherwood on Mystical Religion* (San Francisco: Harper and Row, 1987).
11. Ibid., 205–208)
12. Summers, *Christopher Isherwood,* 70.
13. Ibid., 76.
14. Isherwood, *Diaries,* 17 April 1943: "We can *do* nothing to help each other, nothing whatever. We help each other only by *being,* by setting an example, by giving forth the light of God inside ourselves. Nevertheless, the hospitals must be kept open, and the blueprints must be drawn—not to cure or house the patients, which is utterly immaterial and unimportant, but in order that, by offering all this activity to God, we come nearer to him . . . and may attract others to his light" (*D,* 283). In Lao Tzu's *The Way of Life* (New York: John Day, 1944), the sage says: "The way to do is to be."
15. The manageress may have been based on another of the Swami's disciples, who was called Sudhira by him. On 5 February 1943, Isherwood writes: "Sudhira's name was Helen Kennedy. She was a trained nurse. . . . She was an Irish Californian: one of the most beautiful women I have ever met—in the same class as Garbo and Virginia Woolf. Her beauty wasn't so much in her features or her figure as in her manner, her voice, the way she carried herself: she was physically aristocratic. . . . I suppose that, within the limitations of our respective neuroses, we were in love with each other. I had a kind of metaphysical feeling about her—especially after I had been sick a couple of times and she'd nursed me. To me, she was the universal cosmic Nanny; the beautiful, mysterious figure whom we meet twice in our lives, at the entrance and the exit. Sudhira exercised what was really a most dangerous kind of fascination over me" (*D,* 269).
16. Spender, *World within World,* 261.

17. Ibid., 310.

18. Isherwood, introduction to *The Condor and the Cows* (New York: Random House, 1947), 4.

CHAPTER 5

1. This phrase is a variation from Meister Eckhart's *Theologica Germanica* and a phrase that Huxley was fond of saying.

2. Finney, *Christopher Isherwood: A Critical Biography,* 215.

3. Summers, *Christopher Isherwood,* 79.

4. Years before, in England, Isherwood's hero, E. M. Forster, the older master, had shown the young novelist the manuscript of *Maurice,* Forster's story of two men in love, which could not be published at the time without legal consequences. Perhaps Isherwood recalled this injustice and decided, in his fashion, to redress it in his own way and honor Forster by doing so. According to Brian Finney in his biography of Isherwood, "When Forster died [in 1970], he left Isherwood the rights to *Maurice. . . .* In accordance with Forster's wishes, Isherwood promptly made over the royalties earned by the book to the National Institute of Arts and Letters in the States for the establishment of a fund to help British writers travel to America" (271).

5. Isherwood, *An Approach to Vedanta* (Hollywood: Vedanta Press, 1963), 46.

6. Aldous Huxley would remarry less than a year later, finding it too difficult to be alone. Laura Archera had befriended both Huxleys before Maria died and there was a tacit sense among them and their friends that Maria had selected and sanctioned Laura as her replacement.

7. One can get the sense of Isherwood's deep paternal feeling for Bachardy from the *Diaries.* See, for example, the entry for 9 April 1955: "If only I could help Don more! All my sympathy and understanding, all my quite genuine knowledge—through my own past experience—of what he is feeling—no, they just don't help. I'm not him." On 20 May 1955, Isherwood writes: "As for Don—all that part of my life couldn't be happier and more harmonious. I've started reading aloud to him before we go to sleep. . . ." Isherwood reiterates his paternal relation to Bachardy on 26 July 1955: "My job is very simple—i.e. provide a background of security for Don at the same time leave the door open for him to issue forth from it anytime he wants to. . . . I've taken on this project and I obviously have to do my best. And I do want to do my best. I'm not being noble about that. It is a genuine vocation. Don is by far the most interesting person I've ever lived with. Why? Because he *minds* the most about things."

8. See Isherwood, *Diaries,* 24 June 1956: "Don and I went to tea at Vedanta Place . . . with Swami, Aldous and Laura. It was rather a success. Swami seems to have accepted Don's relation to me as a matter of course. He said to Don, as we were leaving: 'Come again—every time Chris comes.'" Isherwood's entry for 27 October 1956 reads: "Going to see Swami is like opening a window into my life. I have to keep doing this or my life gets stuffy." On 24 September 1957, he writes: "Let me write this down clearly and definitely: I believe that there is something called (for convenience) God, and this some-

thing can be experienced (don't ask me how), and that a man I know (Swami) has had this experience. . . . All this I believe because my instinct, as a novelist and connoisseur of people, assures me, after long, long observation, that it is true in Swami's case."

9. In a letter to myself on 6 June 1998, Don Bachardy confirmed that "Chris invariably wrote (or at least rewrote) the blurbs for the dust-jackets of his books. *Down There on a Visit* I'm certain about, and *A Single Man,* too."

10. Indeed, in some ways Lancaster's pompous grandeur also sounds like that of the novelist George Moore's, as recalled affectionately by his peers and demonstrated in his own memoirs. Isherwood and Upward had read *Esther Waters* to each other at Cambridge.

11. Willa Cather, *Death Comes for the Archbishop* (New York: Alfred A. Knopf, 1927), 293.

12. Arlin Turner, preface to *Nathaniel Hawthorne: A Biography* (New York: Oxford University Press, 1980), 7. Moreover, Harry Levin said "that while Hawthorne creates a world of his own, it is *his own* that we should emphasize rather than a *world.* To consider his work as a whole is to watch the recurrence of certain thematic patterns so obsessive . . . they might well be regarded as complexes." See Levin, *The Power of Blackness* (New York: Vintage Books, 1958), 147. It would seem that Isherwood and Hawthorne have something in common.

13. In 1962, "gay" was the generally preferred term for describing homosexuality; however, Isherwood always chose to say "queer." While he used the term *queer* mainly to get reactions from heterosexuals, he did so in the same way that some African Americans use the word "nigger," to display a certain aggressiveness and to rob the word of its ugliness. When Mr. Strunk uses the word (or, more precisely, when George imagines Mr. Strunk using the word), he is not using it in the way Isherwood in real life used it. Rather, this American character is using it to express contempt.

14. Joseph Sheridan Lefanu, 1814–1873, wrote a classic novella, *Carmilla,* which in some modern interpretations has been considered a lesbian love story with a vampiress seducing the heroine.

15. From Isherwood's diary, as recounted in his last book, *My Guru and his Disciple,* (New York: Farrar, Strauss, Giroux, 1980), 259–60. Huxley died the day President Kennedy was assassinated and his passing was only marginally noticed.

16. Finney, *Christopher Isherwood: A Critical Biography,* 251.

17. Wilde, *Christopher Isherwood,* 128.

18. Piazza, *Christopher Isherwood: Myth and Anti-Myth,* 150.

19. Ibid., 153.

20. Schwerdt, *Isherwood's Fiction,* 163.

CHAPTER 6

1. Carolyn Heilbrun, "An Interview with Gavin Lambert," in *Twentieth Century Literature* 22 (October 1976): 338.

2. Isherwood, *A Meeting by the River* (New York: Simon and Schuster, 1967), 78.

3. Ibid., 85.

4. Ibid., 129.

5. Ibid., 120.

6. Quoted by Finney in *Christopher Isherwood: A Critical Biography,* 280.

7. Aldous Huxley's last novel, *Island* (New York: Harpers, 1962) was reprinted in 1968 and sold almost one million copies. It was Huxley's program for a utopian society, which was based on what now would be considered the cutting edge of new age thinking. At the core of the program is the Perennial Philosophy.

8. Heilbrun, "An Interview with Gavin Lambert," 335.

9. If one refers back to the chart in the introduction, the sensitive, Truly Strong anti-hero first surfaced dominantly in the 1930s and was imitated thereafter. In 1958 Isherwood cited the plays of John Osborne and could have noted many more examples. The Auden Generation was an inspiration to the highbrow artists of the 1950s, who, even as a minority, were creating the art that would be preserved from that decade to inspire their imitators in the following decades. In theater, the avant-garde protest plays of the 1930s, British and American, preceded plays by Osborne, Arthur Miller, Rod Serling, Samuel Beckett, Eugene Ionesco, among others. These artists of the 1950s, as so many more in all the art forms, were the new rebels and pathfinders who forecast the near future. In the 1960s the general rebellion of the "new" rebels looked back to give homage to the "old" rebels who were their role models. This psychology of pseudo-deification was earlier demonstrated by Isherwood's nod to Sherlock Holmes in Mortmere, Auden's litany of heroes in *The Orators,* and the co-opting by both of T. E. Lawrence as Michael Ransom. Ransom was replicated in the 1950s on stage and film with Marlon Brando, James Dean, and Montgomery Clift. These actors were alternatives to the traditional leading man. In the late 1960s into the 1970s, this type of actor became the standard leading man: Dustin Hoffman, Gene Hackman, Jack Nicholson, Dennis Hopper, Peter Fonda. Numerous examples can be cited in whatever art form one might choose; arguments can be made for the inclusion or exclusion of particular examples, but this only proves a universal pattern exists.

10. Heilbrun, "Interview with Gavin Lambert," 336.

11. Ibid., 336.

12. Finney, *Christopher Isherwood: A Critical Biography,* 260.

13. Ibid., 263. The interview that Finney was referring to was, "An Interview with Christopher Isherwood," in *Journal of Narrative Technique* 2 (March 1972): 143–58.

14. Isherwood, *My Guru and His Disciple,* 287.

15. I also feel that all of Isherwood's work after 1939 has been underestimated by reviewers, even when it was praised, because the continuous weave of Vedanta in this work has not been fully appreciated. In large part, this was often due to either a total ignorance of Vedantic philosophy, or only a cursory understanding of it. (Conversely, critics such as Brian Finney, Claude Summers, Alan Wilde, Paul Piazza, and Lisa Schwerdt have explored the influence of Vedanta in their studies of Isherwood.) One might argue that literature should be appreciated only through the words as they appear on the page, without any special knowledge of the author's beliefs. This can be true to some extent since no one can become an expert on the various biographical influences that may or may not impact an author's writing. On the other hand, one cannot discount

how much more is brought to Isherwood's post-1939 work when its Vedantic resonances can be appreciated by those who already do know or care to learn about their sources. Moreover, Isherwood himself, that purveyor of "secret languages," would have appreciated the effort. As for readers who discovered Isherwood the artist after having first met Isherwood the mystic, I am one of them.

16. Resistance to mysticism in general and mysticism in literature particularly is still strong; however, the recent surge in postmodernist theory, which shares features with Vedanta cosmology, has somewhat softened the opposition.

17. Colin Wilson, "An Integrity Born of Hope: Notes on Christopher Isherwood," *Twentieth Century Literature* 22 (October 1976): 331.

18. Quoted by Finney in *Christopher Isherwood: A Critical Biography*, 276

19. Ibid., 268.

20. Ibid., 273.

21. Carolyn Heilbrun, "Christopher Isherwood: An Interview," *Twentieth Century Literature* 22 (October 1976): 256.

22. Finney, *Christopher Isherwood: A Critical Biography*, 280.

23. Heilbrun, "Christopher Isherwood," 257.

24. Ibid., 262.

25. Ibid., 257.

26. Ibid., 262.

27. Isherwood, *My Guru and His Disciple*, jacket.

28. Don Bachardy, introduction to *Last Drawings of Christopher Isherwood*, (London: Faber and Faber, 1991).

BIBLIOGRAPHY

WORKS BY CHRISTOPHER ISHERWOOD

BOOKS AS AUTHOR

All the Conspirators. New York: New Directions, 1958.

An Approach to Vedanta. Hollywood: Vedanta Press, 1963.

Christopher and His Kind. New York: Farrar, Straus, Giroux, 1976.

The Condor and the Cows. New York: Random House, 1949.

Diaries: Volume One, 1939–1960. Edited by Katherine Bucknell. New York: HarperCollins, 1997.

Down There on a Visit. New York: Simon and Schuster, 1962.

Exhumations. New York: Simon and Schuster, 1966.

Goodbye to Berlin. New York: New Directions, 1947.

Kathleen and Frank. New York: Simon and Schuster, 1971.

Lions and Shadows. London: Hogarth Press, 1938; Norfolk, Conn.: New Directions, 1947.

The Memorial. London: Hogarth Press, 1932; Norfolk, Conn.: New Directions, 1946.

A Meeting by the River. New York: Simon and Schuster, 1967.

Mr. Norris Changes Trains. New York: New Directions, 1947.

My Guru and His Disciple. New York: Farrar, Straus, Giroux, 1980.

People One Ought to Know. London: Macmillan, 1982; New York, Doubleday, 1982.

Prater Violet. New York: Random House, 1945.

Ramakrishna and his Disciples. New York: Simon and Schuster, 1965.

Sally Bowles. London: Hogarth Press, 1937.

A Single Man. New York: Simon and Schuster, 1964.

The Wishing Tree. San Francisco: Harper and Row, 1987.

The World in the Evening. New York: Random House, 1954.

BOOKS AS COAUTHOR

Isherwood, Christopher, and W. H. Auden. *The Ascent of F6.* New York: Random House, 1937.

———. *The Dog beneath the Skin.* London: Faber and Faber, 1935; New York: Random House, 1935.

———. *Journey to a War.* New York: Random House, 1939.

———. *On the Frontier.* New York: Random House, 1939.

Isherwood, Christopher, and Edward Upward. *The Mortmere Stories.* London: Enitharmon Press, 1994.

BOOKS AS EDITOR

Isherwood, Christopher, ed. *Great English Short Stories.* New York: Dell, 1957.

———. *Vedanta for Modern Man.* New York: Harper, 1951.

———. *Vedanta for the Western World.* New York: Marcel Rodd, 1945.

Books as Translator

Isherwood, Christopher, trans. *The Intimate Journals of Charles Baudelaire.* Hollywood: Marcel Rodd, 1947.

Isherwood, Christopher, and Swami Prabhavananda, trans. *How to Know God: The Yogi Aphorisms of Patanjali.* New York: Harper, 1953.

———. *Shankara's Crest Jewel of Discrimination.* Hollywood, Vedanta Press, 1947.

———. *The Song of God: Bhagavad-Gita.* Hollywood, Marcel Rodd, 1944.

Vesey, Desmond, and Christopher Isherwood, trans. A *Threepenny Novel* (Bertolt Brecht's *A Penny for the Poor*). Fiction translated by Desmond Vesey, with verses translated by Christopher Isherwood. New York: Grove Press, 1956.

Other Sources

Aiken, Conrad. *Collected Novels of Conrad Aiken.* New York: Holt, Rinehart & Winston, 1964.

———. *Selected Poems.* London: Scribner, 1930.

Auden. W. H. *Another Time.* New York: Random House, 1940.

———. *A Certain World: A Commonplace Anthology.* New York: Viking, 1972.

———. *Collected Poems.* Edited by Edward Mendelson. New York: Random House, 1976.

———. *Collected Shorter Poems.* New York; Random House, 1966

———. *The Dance of Death.* New York: Random House, 1934.

———. "The Dyer's Hand." In *The Anchor Review.* New York: Doubleday, 1957.

———. *The Dyer's Hand.* New York: Random House, 1962.

———. *The English Auden.* Edited by Edward Mendelson. New York: Random House, 1977.

———. *Forewords and Afterwords.* Edited by Edward Mendelson. New York: Random House, 1973.

———. "The Group Movement and the Middle Class." In *Oxford and the Groups,* edited by R. H. S. Crossman. London: Blackwell-Oxford, 1934.

———. "Interview with W. H. Auden." *Antaeus* 13–14 (spring 1972): 136–72.

———. *The Orators.* London: Faber and Faber, 1932

———. *The Orators.* London: Faber and Faber, 1966.

———. *Poems.* London: Faber and Faber, 1930; New York: Random House, 1934.

———. *The Prolific and the Devourer.* Hopewell, N.J.: Ecco Press, 1993.

———. "Review of *Open House.*" *Saturday Review of Literature,* 30 April 1931.

———. *Secondary Worlds.* New York: Random House, 1968.

———. *Spain.* London: Faber and Faber, 1937

———. "Squares and Oblongs." In *Poets at Work,* by Rudolf Arnheim et al. New York: Harcourt, Brace, 1948.

Cather, Willa. *Death Comes for the Archbishop.* New York: Alfred A. Knopf, 1927.

Crossman, Richard, ed. *The God That Failed.* New York: Harper and Brothers, 1949.

Day Lewis, C. *The Buried Day.* London: Chatto and Windus, 1960

————. *Collected Poems and a Hope for Poetry.* New York: Random House, 1935.

Ellman, Richard, and Robert O'Clair, eds. *The Norton Anthology of Modern Poetry.*. New York: Norton, 1988.

Finney, Brian. *Christopher Isherwood: A Critical Biography.* London: Oxford University Press, 1976.

Gehman, Geoff. *Down but Not Quite Out in Hollow-Weird: A Documentary in Letters of Eric Knight.* Lanham, Md.: Scarecrow Press, 1998.

Gide, André. *Return From the U.S.S.R.* New York: Alfred A. Knopf, 1937.

Halpern, Daniel. "A Conversation with Christopher Isherwood." *Antaeus* 13–14 (spring/summer 1974): 366–88.

Hamovitch, Mitzi, ed. *The Hound and Horn Letters.* Athens: Georgia University Press, 1982.

Heard, Gerald. *The Emergence of Man.* London: Jonathan Cape, 1931.

Heilbrun, Carolyn. "Christopher Isherwood: An Interview." *Twentieth Century Literature* 22 (October 1976): 253–64.

————. "An Interview with Gavin Lambert." *Twentieth Century Literature* 22 (October 1976): 332–43.

Huxley, Aldous. *The Burning Wheel.* London: Blackwell, 1916.

————. *The Genius and the Goddess.* New York: Harper and Brothers, 1955.

————. *The Human Situation.* New York: Harper and Row, 1977.

————. *Island.* New York: Harper and Row, 1962.

————. *Limbo.* London: Chatto and Windus, 1920.

————. *Music at Night.* London: Chatto and Windus, 1931.

————. *On the Margin.* London: Chatto and Windus, 1923

————. *The Perennial Philosophy.* New York: Harper and Brothers, 1945.

————. *Point Counterpoint.* London: Chatto and Windus, 1928.

————. *Texts and Pretexts.* London: Chatto and Windus, 1931.

———— *Vulgarity in Literature.* London: Chatto and Windus, 1931.

Hynes, Samuel. *The Auden Generation,* Princeton: Princeton University Press, 1976.

Izzo, David Garrett. *Aldous Huxley and W. H. Auden: On Language.* West Cornwall, Conn.: Locust Hill Press, 1998.

————. "The Student and the Master: A Pupil Recollects W. H. Auden." *Carolina Quarterly* 48 (summer 1996): 29–38.

Jameson, Storm. *Journey from the North: Autobiography of Storm Jameson.* New York: Harper and Row, 1969.

Kierkegaard, Søren. *The Living Thoughts of Kierkegaard.* Edited by W. H. Auden. Bloomington, Ind.: Midland Press, 1963.

Lao Tzu. *The Way of Life.* Translated by Witter Bynner. New York: John Day, 1944.

Lehmann, John. *The Whispering Gallery.* London: Longmans, 1955.

Levin, Harry. *The Power of Blackness.* New York: Vintage, 1958.

Needham, Joseph. *Time the Refreshing River.* London: Unwin, 1943.

Orwell, George. Introduction to *The Complete Short Stories of Raffles,* by E. W. Hornung. New York: St. Martin's Press, 1984.

Page, Norman. *Auden and Isherwood: The Berlin Years.* New York: St. Martin's Press, 1998.

Piazza, Paul. *Christopher Isherwood: Myth and Anti-Myth.* New York: Columbia University Press, 1978.

Roberts, Michael. *New Signatures: Poems by Several Hands.* London: Hogarth Press, 1932.

Schwerdt, Lisa. *Isherwood's Fiction.* London: Macmillan, 1989.

Scobie, W. I. "The Art of Fiction: Christopher Isherwood." In *Writers at Work: The Paris Review Interviews,* edited by George Plimpton. New York: Viking, 1974.

Smith, Elton Edward. *The Angry Young Men of the Thirties.* Carbondale, Ill.: Southern Illinois University Press, 1975.

Spender, Stephen. *The Destructive Element.* London: Jonathan Cape, 1935.

———. *Journals.* Franklin, Pa.: Franklin Press, 1985.

———. *Letters to Christopher.* Edited by Lee Bartlett. Santa Barbara: Black Sparrow Press, 1980.

———. *Poems.* New York: Random House, 1934.

———. *Poems of Dedication.* New York: Random House, 1947.

———. "Review: *Portraits,* by Desmond MacCarthy," *Criterion* 11 (April 1932): 554–57.

———. *The Thirties and After.* New York: Random House, 1978.

———. *World within World.* London: Hamish Hamilton, 1951; New York: Harcourt Brace, 1951.

Summers, Claude J. *Christopher Isherwood.* New York: Ungar, 1980.

Turner, Arlin. *Nathaniel Hawthorne: A Biography.* New York: Oxford University Press, 1980.

Upward, Edward. *Christopher Isherwood: Notes on Remembrance of a Friendship,* London: Enitharmon Press, 1996.

Wescott, Glenway. *Continual Lessons: The Journals of Glenway Wescott.* New York: Farrar, Straus, Giroux, 1990.

Wilde, Alan. *Christopher Isherwood.* New York: Twayne, 1971.

Wilder, Thornton. *The Eighth Day.* New York: Harper, 1967.

Wilson, Colin. "An Integrity Born of Hope: Notes on Christopher Isherwood." *Twentieth Century Literature* 22 (October 1976): 312–32.

INDEX